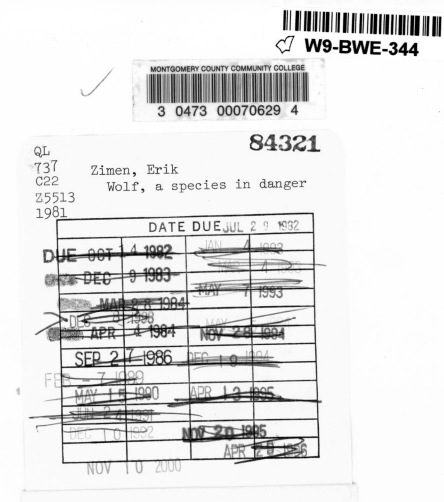

THE WOLF

THE WOLF

A Species in Danger

ERIK ZIMEN

*Translated from the German
by Eric Mosbacher*

DELACORTE PRESS/NEW YORK

Published by
DELACORTE PRESS
1 Dag Hammarskjold Plaza
New York, N.Y. 10017

This work was first published in the German language by Meyster Verlag GmbH, Munich, Germany, as DER WOLF: MYTHOS UND VERHALTEN (© Meyster Verlag GmbH, Wien, Munchen, 1978).

Jacket photographs by Peter Thomann, Hans-Jörg Anders, and Erik Zimen. Plate 1 by Peter Thomann; Plate 15 by Hartmut Jungius; the rest by Erik Zimen. Line illustrations by Prill Barrett.

Manufactured in the United States of America
First printing

LIBRARY OF CONGRESS CATALOGING IN PUBLICATION DATA

Zimen, Erik, 1941–
  The wolf, a species in danger.

  Translation of Der Wolf, Mythos und Verhalten.
  Bibliography: p.
  Includes index.
  1. Wolves. I. Title.
QL737.C22Z5513 1981 599.74'442   80-20962
ISBN 0-440-09619-7

84321

Acknowledgments

The selfish gene and evolutionary stable strategies may govern the behavior of wolves, but they do not seem to have guided the humans who helped me in the course of my work with wolves or on this book. The gratitude we feel for altruistic behavior toward us presumably belongs to the field of cultural evolution, and a cultural ritualization bids us express this gratitude from time to time.

In the first place I must thank my two teachers, Wolf Herre and Konrad Lorenz, to whom I am indebted for more than material facilities for my work. Both, each in his own way, are obsessed with biology, and to come within their sphere of influence and not be infected by their enthusiasm one would have to be a stone, emotionally and intellectually. I am indebted to them for part of my own enthusiasm for the subject as well as a taste for controversy and lively discussion. Being great teachers, they never suppressed a pupil's rebellion—in fact I think they were sometimes actually delighted by it. The same applies to my relationship with Paul Leyhausen. Accustomed though he is to those sensitive creatures, cats—watching him observe cats is a revelation—he also took pleasure in those not always exactly sensitive creatures, wolves, and has been very helpful to me particularly in recent years.

Many friends and colleagues helped me in the daily observation of wolves, carrying out experiments with them and looking after them. Hans-Peter Dorn, for instance, sat with me in the enclosure through several warm summer nights and some long cold winter ones in order to establish the rhythm of the wolves' activity (only once did I find him asleep when I relieved him). Michael Mauscherning, Hermann Ellenberg, and

Jasper Jaspersen looked after the animals during my absence and helped in many separation experiments as well as in searching for escaped wolves on a number of occasions. Michael Bohr, Gabi Kippmann, Gudrun Mühlhofer, and Charley Gallenberger looked after and observed the wolves in the Bavarian Forest.

For my work at Kiel I received a grant for three years from the German Academic Exchange Service (DAAD), and I had a grant from the Max Planck Society for four years for my work in the Bavarian Forest. The state forest administrations in Schleswig-Holstein and Bavaria put land and enclosures for the wolves at my disposal. My thanks are due in particular to the administration of the so-called National Park of the Bavarian Forest, whose cooperation was excellent—at any rate in the early years when we still hoped that a real national park might be established in Germany. Cooperation with Hermann Puchinger and Leopold Grönzinger, experts on enclosures and feeding wolves, was friendly to the end, and they are thanked accordingly.

The Abruzzi project was backed by the International Union for the Conservation of Nature and Natural Resources (IUCN) and the World Wildlife Fund (WWF). The cooperation of Hartmut Jungius and Arturo Osio ensured that our work was harmonious and free of complications. The cooperation of Luigi Boitani was especially helpful to me. We complemented each other, I believe, and I very much hope that one day we may be able to work together again on a conservation project. The findings resulting from the Abruzzi project quoted in the book are his "intellectual property" too. The continued exchange of ideas with Dave Mech, whose observations of wolves living in freedom first put my own observations of captive wolves in the correct (ecological) light, was similarly helpful.

Discussions with many other colleagues also helped me to develop a large number of the findings and conclusions presented in this book. Listing all their names here would be tedious. I am especially indebted to Hartmut Pruscha, who succeeded in systematizing an enormous amount of data with the aid of a computer. I must also mention the cooperation of Conny Schröder-Lipp and Andreas Hopf in the shaping of this book. Prill Barrett was responsible for the drawings, which I think excellent.

Finally, I had active family support. My mother-in-law, Friedl Thiel, worked tirelessly for years summarizing and arranging the daily notes. She also typed several versions of the manuscript. My parents, Eva and Karl-Erik Zimen, read through the manuscript very critically and eliminated a number of linguistic errors and improved many of my phrases. And finally, in spite of occasional protests, my wife, Dagmar, has lived and worked with me and the wolves through all these years.

Dedicated to
Wolf Herre and Konrad Lorenz

Contents

Introduction

On January 28, 1976, men clearing snow in the wolf enclosure in the Bavarian National Park caused the animals to panic.[1] They jumped up at the fence, tore a hole in the thin wire at the top, and nine young wolves, four females and five males, escaped before anyone noticed. A hunt for the exceedingly shy creatures began at once, accompanied by huge headlines in the press—"Hungry Wolves Escape in Siberian Cold" was an example. A female was shot by an employee of the National Park in the immediate neighborhood of the enclosure on the very first day. The other wolves scattered in the big forests that line the border between Bavaria and Bohemia. A second wolf was shot the next day at Buchenau, about thirteen miles north of the enclosure. The marksman was a forester employed privately by the president of the Bavarian Senate. The wolf was said to have attacked his geese. In 1971 the same man had shot the first lynx to be reintroduced into the Bavarian Forest, that time on the pretext that it had attacked his dog.

This killing of a young wolf caused a wave of indignation among some people. A protest movement was founded, posters were printed, the wolf's right to life was proclaimed, and prominent scientists made appeals on its behalf. The Bavarian nature conservation society and the World Wildlife Fund (WWF) in Switzerland offered to pay compensation in the event of losses of livestock, private individuals gave guarantees, and the Czechs announced that no wolves would be shot by sportsmen or frontier patrols on their side of the

1

border. There were court cases at Regensburg and Munich, and the Bavarian Minister of the Interior, who had issued an order to shoot to sportsmen, frontier guards, and forestry and police officials only after the first wolf had been shot, eventually had to revoke it. A big battle seemed to have been won.

But slowly the opposition re-formed. The wolves quickly learned to hunt roe, and soon newspaper reports multiplied about alleged havoc done to game. Long stories were printed about the harmfulness of wolves, in the Carpathians, for instance, where they allegedly exterminated all wildlife, and extracts from old church records that described attacks by wolves in earlier centuries were reprinted; and, though the escaped animals were certainly confined to the forest area along the frontier, wolves were soon sighted throughout Bavaria. People claimed to have seen them from cars driving along the Munich–Nuremberg autobahn. Self-appointed experts identified footprints in the snow as being those of wolves, whereupon the police issued warnings to the local population. Finally the *Bildzeitung* said that wolves had been heard howling at the gates of Munich. How they succeeded in crossing the Danube was never mentioned.

The only people who were really affected—that is, the inhabitants of the Bavarian Forest—at first reacted in more relaxed fashion, even though occasional pedestrians were given "the fright of their lives" by stray Alsatians or sudden noises in the undergrowth. Many parents of children who had to go to school through the forest alone expressed concern; and, in fact, of the seven surviving wolves, a female, generally followed at a distance by a male, appeared with increasing frequency in the neighborhood of human dwellings. Twice she trotted past a group of children waiting for their morning school bus. Meanwhile the other wolves were leading a very secluded life on both sides of the border. The increasingly tame she-wolf, however, seemed to have given up hunting, and looked for food in the villages around the National Park, where she was sometimes fed by wolf lovers.

All attempts to catch her failed. On a Sunday at the end of March she came across a group of children playing at the edge of the forest. They stood quite still, and she sniffed at them. But when a boy of four suddenly ran away she jumped at him from behind, and he fell. She held him by the seat of his trousers, whereupon an

2

older boy lifted the little chap to his feet. But the she-wolf went on pulling at the seat of his trousers, and a brief tug-of-war developed. Not till a third boy hit the wolf on the head with a stick did she let go and trot back into the forest, followed at a distance by her male companion.

The damage to the small boy was limited to a hole in his trousers and a scratch on his bottom, but the police took him to the hospital, where he was inoculated against rabies. The next day's headline was: "Small Boy Lacerated by National Park Wolf." Though the unfortunate she-wolf was shot the same evening by a National Park employee, the demand that the threat from these monstrous wild beasts be finally eliminated became irresistible. The Ministry of the Interior ordered a squad of mobile police into the area, the Agriculture Ministry sent professional hunters, and local sportsmen joined in. Television teams arrived in helicopters, and reports from the "wolf front" in the other media were comprehensive. The police were given visual instruction about how to recognize wolves, and the hunt, organized with General Staff thoroughness under the leadership of the National Park office, was on. "Strategic points" were guarded day and night, roadblocks were put up, different areas of forest or farmland were surrounded and systematically combed. Many dogs were shot; school buses were held up at roadblocks and the children sometimes poured out of them and broke through the police cordon on the way home. The chaos was complete, but no wolves were sighted. The local administrative council called for army reinforcements and started negotiating with Czech officials for a joint major operation, but the Czechs declined to cooperate. Only when fresh snow fell after the hunt had been on for a week did National Park marksmen succeed in tracking down the tame she-wolf's male companion and killing it. By this time the other wolves were miles away.

What sort of animal is the wolf that it should rouse such emotions in human beings and set free such energies directed at its destruction? For thousands of years it has been hunted down in almost unparalleled fashion, and it still crops up as a ferocious beast, the very symbol and embodiment of evil, in countless fairy tales, sagas, and proverbs, and in recent times also in films, novels, and travel stories. There is hardly a Russian winter-night's tale that does not include the howling of wolves, and hardly a story from the forests of Canada or Alaska without an attack by a wolf followed by its inevitable killing by the hero.

The Laplanders of Scandinavia equate the wolf with the devil, while North American Indians talk of it as their brother. In Western mythology the wolf is not always wholly evil, but is also a symbol of motherliness, love, and self-sacrifice, as in the legend of Romulus and Remus and the founding of Rome. There are Indian legends about so-called "wolf children," allegedly reared by a she-wolf. In Jack London's fiction the wolf is presented as the very opposite of pernicious human beings, as a symbol of nature, the all-embracing northern wilds. Finally, in the Third Reich the wolf was made to serve as a symbol of aggression in the service of the chosen people, incorporating the idea of a group that totally subjected itself to the orders of a strong leader for the alleged benefit of all. It was not by chance that Hitler's headquarters in East Prussia were called the Wolf's Lair, or that U-boat squadrons were called wolf packs. Obviously very different images and ideas of the wolf exist. But in fact knowledge of the wolf is distinctly limited.

The nine wolves that escaped from the enclosure in the National Park in the Bavarian Forest came from the pack with which I work. As a biologist I am concerned with the wolf's behavior and social structure, its ecology, and its influence on its prey and on the environment. At the very outset of my work I realized that if the wolf is regarded from the biological point of view alone, justice will not be served. One is continually confronted with the prejudices and the hate, the admiration, and the fascination that the wolf rouses in men. Thus the reciprocal relations between man and wolf must be superimposed upon biological considerations—that is, if we want to save the last surviving members of the species from extinction.

In the competition between man and wolf the complete annihilation of the weaker party seems inevitable. What was once the most widespread of all mammals is now confined to a small portion of its original territory, and here too its persecution continues. Even in areas where it has long since been exterminated the idea of its "crimes," its alleged bloodthirstiness and dangerousness, survives; and, when it reappears, as in the Bavarian Forest, all these prejudices are quickly revived.

4

In this book I propose to give an account of the wolf as I see it, to describe its behavior, its relations to its conspecifics, and its ecology. I shall take my own work with wolves as my starting-point. This work did not of course develop independent of the many studies by other investigators, particularly those of my North American colleagues, on the ecology of the wolf. I shall mention their most important findings, as well as our joint efforts to protect the last surviving wolves. Here again the relations between man and wolf have a special significance, and it will therefore be important to analyze this relationship in its historical development, a story that is as fascinating as that of the wolves themselves.

Naturally I shall try to paint as true as possible a picture. But who can claim to paint a picture free from error? The acquisition of knowledge, even when carried out with scientific methods, is an ambiguous process, often the result of constructive misinterpretations, sometimes of chance, and always dependent on the inquirer himself as well as on his social and political consciousness and his environmental conditions. So I invite the reader to keep an open mind about what I have to say.

I

In the Beginning Was Anfa

Wolves are born in a den dug out by their mother after a gestation period of sixty-one to sixty-three days; there are about four to seven cubs to a litter. At birth they are blind and deaf. They can move slowly by crawling, with their belly resting on the ground and head dangling this way and that. If the head comes into contact with something warm, they move in that direction. In this way they find their mother and her teats, and in her absence they find their way to one another. They cluster together for warmth, with their heads hidden as much as possible in the middle of the cluster. When the mother returns, things grow lively. Presumably the cubs become aware of her approach by the movement, the tremor of the ground, for not until much later, when they are about two weeks old, do they react to loud and sudden noises.

Anfa was just six days old when I took her from a den in the wolves' enclosure at the zoo at Neumünster, south of Kiel. Previously I had observed the birth and behavior of wolf cubs, puppies, and dog-wolf hybrids at the Institute for the Study of Domestic Animals at Kiel. To be able to follow systematically the ontogenetic development of wolf cubs, it seemed sensible to separate them from their mother at an early stage and rear them artificially.

I crawled head-first into the den while a number of keepers kept the cubs' parents away. The passage led down into the ground for about eighteen inches before straightening and narrowing. After about two yards it was quite narrow. One of the keepers crawled in after me and held my feet. I forced my way through and by the light of my flashlight I saw a round hole with a dark cluster of wolf cubs. There were only three of them. This was disappointing, for I wanted to have four for my work. The zoo would certainly want to keep one for themselves. All three were females. I searched the cave with my flashlight, but there were no more cubs. I could hear the mother running backward and forward and wuffing overhead. The men shouted at her, as a precaution, but she made no sign of defending her den. I took one of the cubs, which were all the same size, in my arm and crawled back, with my feet being pulled from above. Everyone agreed that the mother should be left at least two of her cubs, so that left only one for me. I put her under my jacket and drove home.

My wife named her. I felt that all my wolves should have names beginning with A. Dagmar said that the tiny cub under my jacket was the beginning (*Anfang* in German), so my first wolf should be called Anfa. Names beginning with B were to be reserved for the poodle puppies that were to follow; the first-generation hybrids between poodles and wolves, the puwos I, as we proposed to call them, were to be given names beginning with C, and the second-generation hybrids, the puwos II, were to have names beginning with D.

After completing my course in zoology in Zürich I had begun working on my doctoral thesis under Professor Wolf Herre at the Institute for the Study of Domestic Animals of the University of Kiel. At Zürich I had found two aspects of ethology of special interest: the physiology of behavior, which is concerned with its background in the central nervous and hormonal systems, and the genetics of behavior, which deals with the problems of its inheritance, the traditional question of innate or inherited characteristics. A lecture by Herre at Zürich on his experiments in crossing dogs and wolves gave me the idea of studying the genetics of behavior for my thesis. At his invitation I went to Kiel, where he immediately took me into the institute zoo. We went into an enclosure where a black creature, a female puwo I, I was told, jumped up at us excitedly. The professor, crawling on all fours, disappeared down a dark hole, and I crawled in behind him. There was a smell of urine, food, and dog. In the half light I could make out my future supervisor with a small swarm of puppies crawling all over him. He picked up one of them and handed it to me. "There's your work," he said.

Herre and his colleagues at the institute had come to the firm conclusion on the basis of a large number of skull measurements and examinations of the size and structure of the brain, blood factors, and number of types of chromosomes that all dogs, whether Pekinese, bulldogs, or Alsatians, were descended solely from the wolf[1] and not, as has often been assumed, from the wolf and the jackal. The best evidence for believing the wolf to be the sole ancestor of all dogs was provided in 1927 by Professor Klatt, of Halle,[2] who in his time was Herre's supervisor. He noticed that the size of the brain of domestic animals was on an average about 30 percent less than that of their wild ancestors. Dogs have such a diminished brain in comparison with the wolf. (That does not mean that dogs are "stupider" than wolves. The reduction lies above all in parts of the brain that deal with sense impressions.) Now, the jackal's brain is smaller than the dog's. If the jackal had played any part in the dog's ancestry, this would be the only case in which enlargement of the brain followed domestication, and that is very unlikely.

Experimental crossings of dogs with jackals at Kiel and with another close relative of the wolf, the North American coyote, at institutions in the United States and Canada[3] have shown that all three are capable of interbreeding, of producing viable offspring themselves capable of reproduction. We cannot exclude the possibility that somewhere—say in the Near East or in the neighborhood of an Indian village on the American prairies—jackals or coyotes may have mated with dogs, and that these half-dogs may again have mated with other village dogs, so that jackal and coyote gene material may be present in our domestic dogs. But further crossings with dogs must certainly have soon eliminated these genes; and, even if such crossings were more frequent than we assume today, this would not amount to a domestication of the jackal or the coyote.

By domestication I mean "a process of genetic change in an originally wild population of animals and plants when these have been kept genetically isolated from the wild form for many generations in favorable breeding conditions for the use of man."[4] Thus the taming of a single wild animal—such as we undertook with Anfa, for instance—does not amount to domestication. Many generations of training are required for this. The domesticated wolf is the dog.

9

If the wolf is the ancestor of all dogs, a comparison between the wolf and the dog should be well suited to throw light on changes in behavior brought about in the course of domestication. A great deal of work had been done at Kiel on the changes brought about by domestication in the brain, internal organs, skeleton, and hair structure, but changes in behavior had not been taken into account, and this was now to be my task. By comparing the products of first- and second-generation interbreeding between wolves and poodles, I hoped to be able to reach conclusions about the inheritance of individual characteristics.

Herre chose the poodle for his interbreeding experiments because he is a poodle lover and a poodle breeder. Long before I arrived in Kiel at the end of 1966 he had put two standard poodles into an enclosure with a one-year-old she-wolf of South European origin. The she-wolf soon bit one of the two males to death, but she mated with the other, and she produced a litter of five to seven puwos every spring that followed. The choice of the poodle for this research turned out to have been a good one. Among the important breeds of dog there is hardly one that looks more unlike the wolf; and this made the puwos correspondingly interesting in appearance. They had their mother's long, straight, coarse hair, but the black coloring was their father's; their erect ears were their mother's, but the length of the ears was the father's. The appearance of the second-generation animals was even more interesting. Three puwo I breeding pairs were kept at the institute and, as the females inherited the dogs' twice-yearly heat periods, a large number of puwos II were soon born. In complete accordance with Mendelian theory, a wholesale splitting up of individual characteristics now took place. There were light-colored, woolly-haired animals with slack ears, and black-to-gray-haired animals with erect ears, as well as quite different mixed forms with reddish coloring and one erect and one drooping ear. Obviously a multitude of different external characteristics were freely combined. The same applied to the internal organs, the skeleton, and the brain, which were examined when the animals were killed at the age of one year.

How would such differences manifest themselves in the behavior of living animals? Professor Herre at first believed that the puwos II that were closest to the wolf in appearance were the more timid animals, while those that looked most like poodles were tame and

trusting. But if there were a free combination of individual characteristics, this could not be the case. I wanted to clear up the question. To avoid exposing myself to the objection that the differences
observed between four groups of animals (wolves, poodles, puwos
I, and puwos II) might be the result of different experiences in the
first months of life with entirely different mothers, I decided to rear
them all under identical conditions, which involved taking them
away from their mothers and feeding them artificially. Should differences in behavior then appear, these, I believed, would to a large
extent be genetically conditioned, that is, anchored in the genes.

The institution zoo was not suitable for such investigations. Too
many different animals were running about, and there was a great
deal of disturbance by human beings. I wanted to get away from
these restricting enclosures, but where was I to go? The state forest
administration of Schleswig-Holstein came to the rescue. A forester's house had just been vacated in the Rickling forest area, and
my wife and I moved there in the spring of 1967. We made one big
and three small enclosures and waited for the birth of our various
cubs and puppies. But for the time being all we had was little Anfa.

Bringing Up Anfa

With her big round head, small ears, and short legs, Anfa was irresistible. Writing exactly ten years later, with our six-week-old son
lying close to me on my desk and looking at me with his big eyes, I
must confess that my feelings toward Anfa were not essentially different from those I now feel toward my child. Adult reactions to infants is obviously highly undifferentiated, and the feelings of affection and solicitude that are released are not confined to the young of
our own species. To replace the warmth of the nest that she had
lost, I carried Anfa about with me constantly. She could not manage a bottle, but another method of feeding had been developed at
the institute. So I bought myself a rubber tube equipped with a
valve and a big 50-milliliter syringe. The tube was lowered into
Anfa's stomach through her mouth, and she was then pumped full
of milk with the aid of the syringe. This method certainly failed to
harmonize with my paternal feelings, but it was rational and relatively safe in comparison with the bottle. Whenever I tried to bottle-

11

feed Anfa, the fluid kept going down the wrong way. I feared she might die of pneumonia as a result of the presence of foreign material in her lungs.

She was born unusually early in the year, on March 31, 1967, so that for nine weeks, until other cubs arrived, she was alone with us. We made a box for her in the living room. When I did not have her with me, an electric heating pad served to maintain the necessary body temperature. To meet her need to suck I tried various babies' pacifiers but she would have none of them. So I put a finger in her mouth, and she sucked at it for hours. When she was twelve days old tiny slits appeared in the skin on the right and left sides of her face, and both eyes opened two days later. Meanwhile she had grown very skillful at clambering out of the box by raising herself with her forepaws while planting her hindpaws firmly against the side. She was very lively and could hardly be restrained. Our living room was unceremoniously turned into a playroom for her benefit. Her first teeth broke through, and anything not actually made of steel was chewed into little pieces: the leg of a chair, the cover of the sofa, and above all my notes. At first she would defecate and urinate only after a belly massage, but when she was ten days old she defecated of her own accord for the first time, standing on small, wobbly legs. When she was a fortnight old she did this as far away from her box as possible. Obviously she already knew her way around the room. If I put her down outside it, however, she started to "cry" loudly. She was in a phase of very rapid development, and I could hardly keep pace with her in my notes on newly observed behavior patterns.

When I drove to the institute at Kiel I put her under my jacket and carried her about as a kangaroo does its young. Generally she slept the whole time, but when she was seventeen days old she once put her head outside my jacket and howled. It was a ringing but melodious sound and lasted for about twenty seconds. Then she crawled back into my jacket, curled up, and went to sleep again. I remembered this incident years later—when my son smiled at me for the first time—the first social contact.

When she was twenty-four days old I offered her minced meat for the first time. She swallowed it, and after that she was given bigger and bigger portions every day. But with more solid food in her diet there was a corresponding increase in the amount of her feces and, what was worse, they became more foul-smelling. In spite of the trouble I took wiping up urine and feces immediately, removing torn articles of clothing, and putting overturned boxes, chairs, and books back in their place, Dagmar's protests multiplied, and finally I had to give in. Anfa was banished from the house, at first only during the daytime. Only a few days before she had shown great fear in the strange surroundings, but now—and this was another leap forward in development—she dashed about the garden, examined every corner, played with sticks, bit at flowers, and finally curled up on the grass next to me and went to sleep. Not till years later did I have a chance to observe how wolf cubs growing up in a state of nature leave their dens for the first time at the age of three weeks and begin making bigger and bigger reconnaissance trips all around. At six weeks they stay outside for quite long periods and sometimes sleep in the open, huddling close together.

In this respect Anfa's development was perfectly normal. At first she returned to her box in the house at night. As her consumption of solid food increased she no longer needed milk at two-hour intervals all day and all night. She grew more and more independent, and sought close contact with me only when she went to sleep. She followed close behind me outside the garden, but undertook longer reconnaissance expeditions only in my company.

First Walk

When she was eight weeks old she followed me across the big field to the forest about four hundred yards away for the first time. In the open country she behaved very anxiously and whimpered gently, but in the forest she seemed transformed. She dashed about in the dense undergrowth, and I had great difficulty in not losing sight of her. Once she suddenly stopped, as if rooted to the spot, gazing into the trees. I went on, but she stayed behind. She went on gazing anxiously ahead, with slightly bent hindlegs and raised head and pointed ears. She wuffed, took a few steps forward, but turned and ran back again. I could see no reason for this alarm and could not imagine what was worrying her, so I walked on again, and Anfa, still cautiously on guard, came creeping behind me on bent legs. Eventually I discovered what was bothering her. About fifty yards

13

ahead of us there was an old-fashioned plow. Under the yellow grass and with its brown, rusty color, it was hard to spot as not a natural part of the forest. Even its shape had adapted itself to the undergrowth, for it looked like the root system of a dead tree that had fallen and rotted. Though I had often gone this way I had never noticed it before. But Anfa, who could hardly see over the top of the grass, had spotted it from a distance and reacted as if it were a highly dangerous object. How was that possible? This was the first time in her life that she had been in a forest. How could she tell it was an alien object made by the hand of man?

We went on and reached a small clearing with a high platform that could be reached by a wooden ladder. As we passed it Anfa suddenly dashed off into the trees on the left. Again I wondered how she knew that the ladder and the high platform up in the old fir trees were not natural and why she was afraid of them. Slowly I led her to the wooden ladder. She cautiously sniffed it and then ran on untroubled, and again I was full of new questions.

In the days and weeks that followed Anfa grew more and more independent outside the house and garden. The area she covered around our house grew larger and larger, but when she was alone she always stayed close to the house. On longer expeditions she would follow only Dagmar and me, and she hardly ever went more than thirty yards away from us. If she lost us she whimpered, first gently, but then more and more loudly, and sometimes the whimper developed into a howl. As soon as she discovered where we were she came dashing toward us, with her legs bent. When she was close to us the back part of her body would almost touch the ground, and quite frequently she urinated. She wagged her tail, rolled on her back, jumped up at us, and if we bent down she tried to lick our faces or hands. All this was very expressive. In the house or the garden she greeted strangers who moved slowly and cautiously in the same way, but in open country or in the forest she panicked if she saw a strange human being and took refuge in the nearest dense undergrowth. And she still showed great respect for man-made objects. She circled an abandoned trailer in the field until she got windward of it and then approached it cautiously.

Anfa's fear of strangers gave us our first experience of a quite different aspect of wolf reality, that is, the relationship between wolf

14

and man. On May 25, when Anfa was just eight weeks old and was about the size of a miniature poodle, I wrote in my diary:

> In the morning I spent a long time with Anfa in the garden. She followed me everywhere and whimpered a great deal. I went to the village for a short time, and when I got back she had gone. Dagmar said she had run after the car, but lost me on the road in front opposite the forester's lodge. The forester saw her and wanted to bring her back, but she ran away, whereupon the forester asked a woodman to catch her, but she was too quick for him and ran away into the forest. Dagmar and I went out and started calling. Anfa appeared immediately, wagged her tail excitedly, whimpered, saw the woodman, and dashed back into the wood. Only when he went away did she come out and follow us closely back to the forester's lodge.

The whole incident lasted for perhaps twenty minutes. It was clear to us that the time was coming when we would have to keep her in the enclosure, but we did not suspect what the consequences of the episode would be. The next day a journalist appeared. He had heard the story in the village—the woodman had obviously been talking about the incident—and wanted to have a look at the little wolf for himself. Anfa jumped up at him, tugged at the ends of his shoelaces and licked his hands, and he took photographs of her and of Dagmar giving her the bottle. He said he would write a short article for the local press and perhaps also for a newspaper in Hamburg.

We thought no more of the matter until a few days later, when we were shown a copy of the *Bildzeitung*. There was a big headline saying: "Holstein Village in Fear of Wolf. News Spreads Like Wildfire That Wolf Has Escaped." The text described mothers hurriedly bringing their carriages into the house, while their menfolk combed woods and fields with guns at the ready "to destroy the evil Siberian monster." Right at the end of the article the startled reader discovered that things were not quite as bad as that, as the wolf was only a little one and still slept in a basket and "Mum" still fed it from a bottle.

Angrily I telephoned the journalist, who was ready for me and read me the story he had actually sent to the *Bildzeitung* in Hamburg. This story was completely unobjectionable; he had accurately described what he had seen and heard and he also mentioned that

Anfa had run away for a short time because the corpulent forester had frightened her. The story had obviously been rewritten in the Hamburg newspaper office in the well-tried manner, exploiting all the old prejudices. The last sentence made us all laugh: "Incidentally, anyone who has a young wolf at home should send it to Zimen, who is still looking for some."

We had been working with a young wolf for barely two months, and already the relationship between man and wolf stood out as the central problem. This question was to occupy me a great deal in the ten years that followed.

Wolves are born in a den where they are at first looked after by their mother. At birth they are blind, deaf, and very dependent. The opening of their eyes at the age of barely two weeks introduces a phase of very rapid development, in the course of which so-called socialization with other individuals takes place. Normally a wolf cub grows up with other wolf cubs and makes the acquaintance of other members of the pack, and so socialization takes place with individuals of its own species. It learns what other wolves look like and smell like and how they behave. But if at an early stage man takes over the role of mother, siblings, and other members of the pack, the cub's social behavior toward human beings is what it would otherwise be toward its conspecifics. It looks to man for food and protection, and behaves exactly as if the human being it knows were a wolf, a member of its pack. Also, unless fear predominates, it greets strangers as if they were wolves. Thus the wolf generalizes its knowledge of the person who looks after it to the rest of mankind.

Presumably men brought up young wolves like this 10,000 or 15,000 years ago and habituated them to human beings, and the dog developed from these domesticated wolves. This is certainly a very important aspect of the relationship between man and wolf. A further phenomenon in this connection is the enormous shyness and cautiousness of the young wolf in the face of everything that is not natural but is the work of man, and this in spite of its socialization and continual confrontation with human handiwork. For thousands of years men and wolves lived in the same territories, and throughout this period the wolf has been hunted down by man. This may have led to great innate cautiousness in regard to man and all man-made objects as well as to a genetically laid-down iden-

16

tification of what is not a product of nature but rather is man's handiwork and is thus dangerous.

Finally, the *Bildzeitung* report of Anfa's first running away was not only an example of manipulation of news but also a demonstration of conventional prejudices about the wolf. Apart from the fact that the wolf was said to have originated in (red) Siberia, the article reiterated the commonly held notion that the wolf is *a priori* dangerous—an evil monster that must be destroyed.

2
Wolf and Dog

Out of this evil monster, the wolf, there developed man's favorite domestic animal, the dog. To clarify what was said about domestication in the last chapter, let me mention some of the differences in behavior between wolves and dogs. Dogs live in an entirely different environment from their wild ancestor, and in the course of their 10,000- to 15,000-year history, changing factors in the process of natural selection as well as artificial selective breeding have resulted in the adaptation of dog behavior to the new conditions. Some examples of flight and socialization behavior (the social "imprinting") of cubs and puppies and of the hunting and social behavior of older wolves and dogs will show how this adaptation took place.

New Arrivals

In May, when we had just got Anfa through the phase of feeding and nursing, reinforcements arrived from Kiel: three standard poodles, four puwos I, and four puwos II. All were just ten days old and their eyes were not yet open. Like Anfa, we fed them in our living room. But we still needed more wolf cubs. After my acquisition of a single cub from Neumünster, we had asked a number of zoos whether they were expecting the birth of any young European wolves and, if so, whether they had any to spare. But most European zoos have wolves from North America or hybrids of unknown origin. Thus the situation gradually grew precarious. What was I to do without wolves?

Then one day a stranger called and said he had read in the newspaper that I was looking for young wolves, and he had one. We were speechless. Was it possible that the idiotic report in the *Bildzeitung* had done us some good after all? The man was a breeder of Alsatians and wanted to introduce a wolf to "improve the breed," as he put it. He had bought from a dealer a young female to cross with his male Alsatians. The dealer had also given him the female's brother, and, as he had no use for it, he had brought it along to us.

The young wolf and its sister were in a small box, and they were filthy. The dealer had said they were of Siberian origin, but he didn't know where or when they were born. I judged them to be about five or six weeks old. Both were very timid. They immediately crept into a corner under the bed, and each tried to hide its head under the other's body. We picked them up, but they remained motionless, completely rigid with fear. They seemed to have had nothing to eat for days, as their bellies appeared empty, but they did not touch the food we offered them, even when we went outside and looked at them through the window. They remained lying stiffly on the floor, just as we left them. This small pile of misery was certainly no advertisement for the animal-dealing trade. I hesitated a long time in deciding whether to keep the male. Unlike the other animals, he had not been reared under controlled conditions, so I could not use him for my work, and I didn't know what else to do with him. But since at this point I had only one wolf, we kept him, and called him Alek.

A few days after we were given this timid creature, good news arrived. Cubs had been born to Finnish wolves in the Rotterdam zoo. They were already three weeks old. We drove there immediately. There were seven cubs altogether, of whom I chose three, two males and a female.

Flight and Socialization

The Rotterdam cubs—Andra (Swedish for "second"), Anselm, and Grosskopf ("Big Head"—the size of his head caused us to forget our intentions about names), showed the elements of flight behavior whenever we tried to feed them, and in spite of all our efforts they grew no tamer. On the contrary, they grew more timid with every day that passed, and it became harder and harder to catch them to feed them. They showed none of the social behavior toward us that Anfa had so intensively demonstrated at the same age. Precocious flight tendencies obviously prevented socialization to human beings. The fact that, unlike Anfa, these cubs did not grow up alone with human beings was certainly partly responsible for this. Presumably even more important was the fact that Anfa, who was two months older and correspondingly bigger, acted as a kind of substitute mother to them, while human beings increasingly triggered off the reaction of flight in them. They followed Anfa about as she had followed me, rolled on their backs in front of her, whimpered, jumped up at her and licked her face; and Anfa, though she was only three months old, sometimes behaved exactly like an adult wolf in relation to them. When they whimpered she went to them, lay down with them, licked their bellies and coats, and sometimes brought them food. When they begged vigorously she actually regurgitated food for them several times, thus demonstrating a behavior pattern normally observed only among one-year-old wolves when young cubs in the pack solicit it. Thus the maternal role she was called on to play caused her to display patterns of behavior that in the course of natural development appear only much later. Perhaps this unnatural development contributed to her disturbed behavior, which later caused us a great deal of concern.

The size of the object of socialization, in this case Anfa, seemed to be important. This corresponds to the situation of cubs that grow up in freedom who have to attach themselves to big, adult members of the pack. Sometimes I thought I detected attempts to establish friendly contact with me on the part of the three new cubs. At a distance of two or three yards they would suddenly start wagging their tails, bending their legs, laying their ears down and back, and they would make a few skipping movements in my direction. But then they seemed to take fright, for they turned and fled.

Their attitude seemed to be governed by two opposite trends: flight from human beings on the one hand and a simultaneous tendency toward socialization with a bigger creature who was a dispenser of warmth and food. In Anfa's case the tendency to flight was overcome by timely habituation. The older male cub we had been given showed not the slightest tendency toward socialization. For him the time when it was still possible to establish bonds with human beings had to a large extent passed. He remained extremely timid. He gobbled his food, and at the age of six months he swallowed a stone and died a few days later of an intestinal stoppage.

Observation of wolves reared differently shows that the phase of natural socialization is limited to a brief period in the first few weeks of life. Experiments in the Chicago zoo certainly show that in special conditions wolves of any age can socialize with human beings. Adult wolves were isolated from their conspecifics for long periods. A human being sat for many hours every day in the enclosure until the animals overcame their great initial shyness and made the first attempts to establish contact. Various drugs helped to accelerate this otherwise very lengthy process.[1]

Of course, such conditions do not correspond with those in which wolf cubs are normally reared. With them the process of learning social identification and the recognition of conspecifics takes place in early infancy and can later be changed only with difficulty. As the development of flight behavior appears very early in the course of ontogenetic development, socialization with other than conspecifics is normally prevented. Only when the flight reaction to human beings is overcome by early habituation can socialization with them take place.

The three poodle puppies showed a number of marked differences in their socialization behavior. No flight tendencies in relation to human beings were observed in them. Though they were kept with the wolf cubs, they continually tried to establish contact with Dagmar or me and soon demonstrated social behavior both toward us and toward their conspecifics in the manner typical of dogs.

An essential condition for this double imprinting of the dog seems to me to be the slight development of the flight tendency in puppies. Thus puppies reared in normal conditions, by their mother with their siblings, can still develop a strong bond to human beings after the usual separation from the mother at the age of six to ten weeks. Only puppies that have been brought up remote from human beings, by a bitch that has run wild in a wood, for instance,

21

develop great shyness and cautiousness in relation to human beings. Nevertheless, older puppies that are brought into direct contact with human beings for the first time are relatively easy to tame.

In the Abruzzi we found a bitch that had been caught in a wolf trap. Her teats were full of milk, and we did not have to search long before finding two pups about ten weeks old in a drain pipe under a road in the forest. At first they shrank back, but a few hours later they were playing with us like perfectly normal puppies. This would have been unthinkable with wolf cubs of the same age. Only adult dogs that have run wild are no longer so easily socialized to human beings. Socialization can occur only by isolating them from other dogs for a long time and slowly overcoming their flight tendencies by months of cautious approach, a method similar to that adopted in taming wolves in the Chicago zoo.

Thus wolf socialization to other species is possible throughout life, though the period between the fourth and fifteenth week of life, as the Americans Scott and Fuller discovered in the case of dogs, is the most favorable.[2] Because of the wolf's strong flight tendency, the length of the optimum period for its socialization cannot be established by experiments such as those performed by Scott and Fuller. The behavior of Alek, who in spite of all efforts showed not the slightest sign of making contact with us, suggests that this phase is shorter in the wolf than it is in the dog.

An extension of the period of socialization in the dog makes sense if one bears in mind that most puppies are brought up apart from human beings for the first few weeks. Only then are they separated from their conspecifics and taken over by humans. Nevertheless, socialization to the alien species takes place quite smoothly. The experiments of Scott and Fuller showed that puppies separated from their mother and siblings at a very early stage developed excessively strong bonds to human beings and were hardly capable of normal contacts with their conspecifics; conversely, puppies taken over by human beings at the age of three months or later developed only slight bonds to humans.

In this connection observation of the puwos produced interesting results. The behavior of the puwos I, in accordance with expectations, was somewhere between that of the wolf and the poodle, though it was closer to the wolf's in regard to the flight tendency. Nevertheless, they overcame a great deal of their timidity to me,

22

and at the phase of socialization they showed tendencies to attach themselves to me. However, they remained extremely timid with strangers, and even with me they were never as tame and affectionate as Anfa and the poodles were.

But it was the puwos II whose behavior was the most surprising. A fragmentation of behavior was to be expected and it duly appeared, but what could not have been positively predicted was the obviously separate fragmentation of flight and socialization behavior. All four animals were certainly much more timid than the poodles, thus making it seem that the strong flight tendency of the wolf, as of the puwo I, is a dominant hereditary trait secured by many genes. This again shows the great importance of this behavior to the wolf. Thousands of years of natural selection have left only timid, very cautious wolves alive. No type of behavior was of greater importance to them than their flight reaction to human beings. But all four puwo II puppies were not equally shy; two clearly behaved with more trust than the others. In spite of its cautiousness one of the shy ones showed a great deal of affection for me, while one of the two less shy ones barely took notice of me and developed no socialization in relation to human beings. There was a similar if not as strongly marked difference between the second tame pup and the second shy pup. Thus in regard to flight behavior and socialization to human beings, these four animals developed in quite different ways. One female became relatively tame and very affectionate, one male was tame but had no relationship with human beings, a second female was very timid and hardly socialized, and the second male was extremely timid but at the same time extremely affectionate (at any rate to me). After hesitating and looking cautiously in all directions, he would jump up at me just like Anfa, and then he would be almost uncontrollable in his excitement. He was also a very handsome animal, almost black, with erect ears. He looked like a black wolf. Had he not been so terribly shy in every unfamiliar situation, I might have kept him as a house dog. But by the time the rearing period was over, Dagmar had had enough of animals in our living room and definitely rejected the idea.

These observations of developmental behavior show that at least two presumably distinct hereditary factors—flight and socialization behavior—are involved in the formation of social relations, and that at first they develop independently of each other. Only in the course

23

of ontogenetic development do they influence each other, and here early development of flight behavior in the wolf greatly limits the possibilities of socialization. In this connection Niko Tinbergen and his wife have made some interesting observations; they believe that the process of socialization in many so-called autistic children has similarly been prevented by the early development of flight tendencies.[3]

The Ethogram

My original purpose was to study the genetics of various behavior changes, but I soon realized that this task was far too ambitious. In the first place, many more than just four puwos II would have to be studied to cover all the possible combinations of a large number of different behavior patterns. They would also have to be kept in quite a different way, perhaps completely isolated from one another, because, as I was now able to observe, they learned from and strongly influenced one another. But, even if it had been possible, I began to doubt whether it was reasonable to try to tackle such a complex problem before a great deal more was known about the behavior of the two original animals, the wolf and the poodle. In the literature I found that a great deal of work had been done on individual aspects of dog behavior and that a little had been done on wolf behavior. But I was slowly forced to admit that we know very little indeed about the total behavior of our favorite domestic animal, let alone his wild counterpart. So I had to set myself a simpler problem. I decided to send the puwos back to Kiel. A definite task remained: a comparison of wolf and poodle behavior.

Every ethological textbook says that studying the behavior of any species must be preceded by drawing up a catalogue of items of behavior, a so-called ethogram.

That is not such an easy task, as anyone who has set out to observe a species soon discovers. Animal behavior is a continuum; careful and protracted observation is necessary before one learns to detect recurrent uniform items. So in the weeks and months that followed I spent many hours of the day, and sometimes whole nights, in the enclosure simply watching the animals. I tried to note down as accurately as possible all behavior patterns, both of the wolves and of the poodles, that were recognizable and distinct from others. These included such things as ear scratching, drinking, baring the teeth, squatting, and utterances such as growling, whimpering, howling, and so on. At first I simply jotted all these things down indiscriminately in the order in which they occurred, but eventually I fitted them into categories according to their function. Examples of such categories were forms of general movement, comfort behavior, feeding, and social behavior (see Appendix, table 1).

An animal's behavior can be regarded from entirely different aspects. The formal method of description follows the observable course of behavior, that is, the sequence of movements of different limbs, possible utterances, and so on. Behavior can also be examined for its underlying motivation: the mood, the system of drives, the releasing stimuli behind it—in other words, its causation. Alternatively, one can inquire into its function: What are the consequences of the animal's behavior, of what use is it to the animal? Or the ontogenetic development of behavior can be analyzed: What learning processes take place? And finally the phylogenetic development of behavior can be investigated: Comparison can be made with that of related species, and its origin and hereditary transmission can be studied. There are also different levels of observation: formal, physiological-causal, functional, ontogenetic, and phylogenetic. All these things are of course interconnected, for behavior is a unity. But it is useful to the human observer to distinguish among these levels, which have to be tackled by different methods.

The relatively simple formal method enabled me to begin by making a qualitative comparison of the behavior of wolves and poodles. Many of the poodles' behavior patterns were demonstrated in essentially similar form by the wolves. In other patterns changes had taken place, and some behavior patterns of the wolf were no longer to be observed in the poodles at all. Big differences or absences appeared above all in hunting behavior, in the social field, and in utterance, while changes were small or nonexistent in sex, birth, and rearing the young, as well as in the behavior of the young to their mother and to each other, and in comfort behavior.

These last and, to a large extent unchanged, behavior patterns are those that have been relatively uninfluenced by the human environment. Dogs conceive, give birth, rear their young, and scratch themselves behind the ears or lick their wounds themselves, but they get their food from humans, and they are not allowed either to hunt for themselves or to live or hunt in packs. They live with human beings, who communicate with them chiefly acoustically. Many forms of utterance have accordingly changed in the dog. Above all, barking is much more differentiated than it is in the wolf, who uses his simple wuffing almost exclusively as a warning sound. In the dog barking has developed into a very expressive form of communication with man. It can be a warning of danger and can signify aggression or a desire to play, and some dogs bred for hunting actually express by their barking what kind of prey they are after, whether they are just following a scent, whether the prey has already been found, or whether it is at bay or is dead.

Thus the dog has adapted its behavior to new living conditions. Let me illustrate by two examples how this adaptation has taken place.

Hunting and Killing Behavior

The following observations of the hunting behavior of wolves and poodles arose by chance. I used to fetch food for the animals three times a week from a chicken butcher near Rickling, and one day I took home three live young cocks. I wanted to see what behavior patterns these crippled, half-featherless creatures were still capable of.

But I did not get far with that investigation. The young wolves and dogs took a great interest in their new neighbors, who squawked and fluttered about in the temporary chicken yard we rigged up for them. Next morning, when I let Anfa and the poodles out of the enclosure for their daily walk, they started creeping slowly toward the fowl. Then things happened very quickly. Anfa dashed the last yard toward the fence, quickly bit a hole in the thin wire, and jumped at one of the young cocks with her forepaws. She forced it to the ground, quickly bit the creature several times, and then dashed off with her dead prey. Two poodles each seized a young cock and merely held it with their paws, bit it, but obviously did not really know what to do next. Meanwhile Anfa had already begun tearing out the feathers. She started with the belly, tore open the skin, devoured the innards first, and then ate up the rest, from the

26

inside out. All that was left was part of the exterior, down, the wing tips, and the tail feathers. In contrast to this the poodles bit indiscriminately at the dead fowl and pulled out feathers here and there.

This chance observation showed that there had been a notable change in the poodles' behavior in the killing and eating of small prey. They seized it but at first demonstrated no directed killing behavior and did not really know what to do with a dead animal.

On our way back to the forester's lodge a few days later, Anfa ran away for the first time. I noticed it too late, and saw her disappearing among the houses of the village. I ran after her, shouting loudly. In the yard of the first farmer's house I came to, I saw her running away in the direction of a thicket, with a big goose in her mouth, leaving a flock of geese squawking and running about excitedly in her wake. The farmer was standing in the yard and did not seem very perturbed. He calmly mentioned the amount he expected me to pay for the goose, and I promised to give it to him.

I heard children yelling on the other side of the stream, and there was Anfa in the children's playground, surrounded by a host of delighted children. But there was no sign of the goose. Anfa came trotting toward me, with the children trailing behind her. She jumped up at me, tugged at my clothing, and allowed herself to be put on the chain without protest. Then, when we finally got home, the farmer drove up on a tractor. "There's no need to pay," he said, "the goose is alive." What could be the explanation for that? Anfa had carried off the goose in her mouth. "No, no, the goose is alive, it's not even hurt," the farmer said. I had no reason to disbelieve him.

Gradually the poodles' behavior at the chicken hunt became clearer to me. In the wolf's case the killing of prey of that size obviously consists of elements of behavior that are partially independent of one another. First of all there is the slow stalking, followed by the chase, the pounce, and seizure with the teeth, and finally the killing by repeated bites. After this the prey is normally carried in the mouth for some distance before being put down and eaten at some quiet spot. Anfa chased and seized the goose but, presumably because of the many distractions all around her, did not kill it. She merely went on carrying it, more than half a mile, in fact. Then, presumably because she was disturbed again, she dropped the goose, which to her was a very heavy load. Thus in the case of the wolf a

27

whole chain of actions is either carried out or not, depending on events and on how hungry the animal is.

In the case of the poodle, as a result of adaptation to new environmental conditions and also through deliberate breeding in the course of domestication, at least two of the elements in the chain have undergone substantial alteration. It no longer kills with such assurance, and the prey is not so effectively consumed as it is by the wolf. In any case, that was the situation with my young poodles, and later experiments showed similar results. This does not necessarily apply to all poodles, of course, and above all it does not necessarily apply to other breeds of dog that are kept under different conditions and have been bred for different purposes. A pointer, for instance, that discovers its prey stays with raised forefoot at the stalking phase, thus showing its human fellow-member of the pack where the prey is. The greyhound, on the other hand, is bred for the swift pursuit of fleeing prey and the retriever for bringing it back, while many terriers are bred to attack and kill by violent shaking. The poodle, which was formerly used in England in connection with the shooting of aquatic birds, has presumably lost its killing behavior as a result of deliberate breeding—certainly a useful characteristic to the human keeper of a hunting dog, which will thus take back to its master prey that is unconsumed and largely undamaged.

Further important differences in the hunting behavior of wolves and poodles soon emerged in the course of the summer. As she grew older Anfa grew more and more interested in hares, pheasants, and roe in open country and in the forest. At first she chased only rapidly moving creatures. This occasionally led to mistakes. Once, for instance, she saw the roof of a quickly moving car glittering in the sun while the lower part of it was hidden by a hedge. She promptly chased it, and was very shocked when she discovered her error, which she never repeated.

At first she did not recognize other possible prey as such. The cows in the field, for instance, were unimpressed by Anfa as we walked through the middle of the herd, and she made no move to attack any of them. Only eighteen months later, when four other tame wolves accompanied us on our walks and a herd of cows suddenly fled from the pack, did she realize that cows, and later also

28

horses, came into the category of possible prey. The cows' flight behavior seems to have triggered this off.

After this experience neither Anfa nor the four other young wolves could be restrained from "hunting" cattle and horses. These were too big for them, of course, and no cow or horse ever came to any harm. The wolves went for them, but soon learned that horses' hoofs and the horns of cattle were dangerous weapons. But the wolves scattered the herds and that upset the farmers, so I was forced to keep them on the lead when cattle or horses were in the field near the forester's lodge. In the course of time they learned that such animals were too big for them, and their eagerness to hunt them gradually faded away.

These observations show that wolves obviously have to learn what is possible prey and what is not. An important characteristic of prey in this context is rapid movement, which is the first thing that triggers off hunting behavior in young wolves. Success in catching a young hare, for instance, intensifies the keenness with which such prey is pursued. The first attempts of young cubs to catch grasshoppers or mice serve not so much to acquire food as to practice coordinating the motions of capturing prey, and in the process the hunting impulse is reinforced. Wolves learn by trial and error what is not suitable prey for them, as in the case of the automobile hunt, or by repeated failure, as in the case of the cattle and horses.

Observation of poodles showed that keenness for the hunt and knowledge of what was suitable prey developed in the same playful way as it did with wolves, that is, by trial and error with moving objects. But poodles seemed not to lose this playful kind of hunting behavior as they grew older. Long after Anfa had given up trying to catch crows in the field, for instance, adult poodles went on chasing them, as well as pieces of paper flying in the wind. The object seemed to be not so much the catching of the quarry as the chase itself. The same applied to their hunting keenness. Anfa and later the other wolves would pursue a fleeing hare or roe either until they lost the scent or (which was much rarer) until they caught and killed it, while the poodles would sometimes chase a hare and sometimes not. If the hare had too big a start they quickly gave up, preferring to chase each other or even flying leaves.

Flow, my present dog, is quite different. His breed, the large

29

Münsterland pointer, was specially bred for pursuing the birds and beasts of the chase. His passion for the chase might almost be called perverted in comparison with that of the wolf. He is not to be restrained from chasing fleeing hares or roe, and sometimes hunts them to the point of complete exhaustion. For a time we kept rabbits for experimental purposes in the big wolf enclosure in the National Park (a topic to which I shall return later). Flow was fascinated by the rabbits and spent hours gazing at them through the fence. If I left him in the enclosure overnight, I could be sure that, next morning, he would still be standing tensely in the same spot, not losing sight of the rabbits for a moment.

Social Distance

In his writings on the subject, Professor Herre has always insisted that the essential mark of domestication is a big increase in the variability of characteristics, such as size, color, head shape, and so on, among dogs. The same obviously applies to behavior. As a result of adaptation and breeding, a multitude of different variations has arisen out of the relatively uniform behavior of the wolf. This applies not only to hunting behavior in relation to small animals but also, in varying degrees, to all other fields of behavior. The following observation shows how changes can take place in a single field of social behavior (see figure 1). During the first weeks of their lives, both wolf cubs and poodle puppies almost invariably sleep huddled closely together. If the frequency with which they continue to maintain body contact while sleeping is noted, big differences soon appear. At four weeks young wolves begin to sleep apart from one another more frequently, and from four to six months they behave like adult wolves—that is, contact between two sleeping animals is rare and occurs mostly by chance.

Poodles also become more independent as they grow up, but much more slowly. They do not behave like adults in this respect until they are a year old, and even then sleeping close together with body contact is much more common than it is with adult wolves. They also do this in warm weather, so it is not, as one might suspect because of their thinner coat, a matter of heat regulation. The fact is that poodles, even when they are active, keep much more

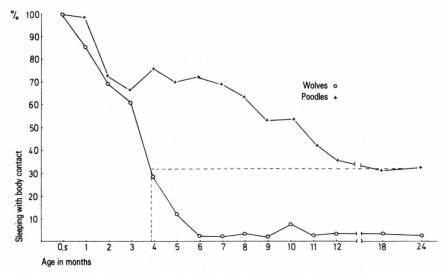

Fig. 1. Decrease in body contact while asleep; wolf cubs and poodle puppies compared.

closely together than adult wolves, who develop great independence in spite of their bond to the pack.

We can consequently recognize two distinct phenomena. In the first place, the rate at which the ontogenetic development of a behavior pattern takes place in the dog is sometimes different from its rate of development in the wolf. In the poodle development of "social distance," as it is called, is retarded in comparison to the wolf. In other fields of behavior—the attainment of sexual maturity, for instance, which the poodle reaches at eight to ten months of age while the wolf normally does so only at twenty-one months—the situation is reversed. Here development has accelerated. Thus in some instances we can talk of retarded behavior patterns in the domesticated dog, while in others there has been an acceleration of ontogenetic development.

Second, the development of a behavior pattern in the dog can come to a stop at a stage corresponding to that of a young wolf. In regard to social distance, for instance, adult poodles behave as young wolves do at about the age of four months. Here we seem to be confronted with a fetalization of behavior.

31

In this context, Konrad Lorenz speaks of neoteny, of a general fetalization of the dog.[4] The observations mentioned above and many others show that, in the dog, we are faced with at least two partially distinct developmental processes: change in the rate of development, and its coming to an end at a stage that is juvenile in comparison with the wild form. However, I believe one cannot speak in general of a fetalization of the dog. Many behavior patterns, particularly those connected with sexual maturity such as aggression, show an acceleration of development, and upon maturation are completely comparable with those of the wolf. There are also great differences between breeds. For instance, so far as social distance when sleeping is concerned, chows develop even more quickly than wolves, from whom they hardly differ when adult. Other breeds occupy intermediate positions between chows and poodles in this respect.

The great variability in the behavior of dogs, as of other domestic animals, can consequently be partly explained by differences in maturation of behavior. There is every grade of transition between the young cub's perpetual seeking of contact and the great independence of the adult wolf. All these stages of transition appear as final stages in different breeds of dog, depending on their degree of fetalization. The same applies to many other behavior patterns. Thus the great variability of canine behavior can be explained by wolf behavior alone without any recourse to other ancestral species.

Most other domestic animals no doubt also derive from a single ancestral wild species. That makes the study of domestication, as well as the comparative study of different processes of ontogenetic development, one of the most interesting and important aspects of biology, not least in regard to our own behavior.

Healthy and Unhealthy Dogs

The behavior of the dog, its varied adaptation to coexistence with human beings, is an important aspect of the relationship between wolf and man. While the wolf has been increasingly hunted down and has accordingly developed an enormous timidity in relation to man, the dog has grown more and more trustful and nowadays lives in close coexistence with him. An essential condition for this devel-

32

opment was certainly the similar social organization of wolf and man, both of whom lived in small, easily manageable family bands. Observation of puwos showed that the timidity of the wolf must be firmly anchored in the genes and is a dominant hereditary trait. Nevertheless, this shyness in relation to man can be overcome both in wolves and in puwos if the young are brought into contact with human beings at an early age and learn to overcome their flight tendencies early in their development. In principle this is the same as in the dog, for we know that if the dog grows up wild in a forest, for instance, instead of in a human environment, it can sometimes be almost as shy as a wild wolf. The only difference is that in the dog, development of flight behavior has been greatly retarded and the phase of possible socialization with human beings substantially prolonged.

Observation of puwos similarly showed that the socialization trend at first develops independent of the flight tendencies, but that, once it has developed, flight behavior can prevent socialization that might otherwise have been possible. Finally, the possible combinations of these genetically distinct development patterns in the puwos II showed the enormous variety that can be attained by crossing different parent animals. The great variety of our domestic dogs arose from different environmental conditions, deliberate crossings, and the rigorous weeding out of undesired characteristics in past centuries. The dog is a specialist that in its own particular sphere can outdo that decathlete, the wolf, from which it sprang. In a dog race, for instance, a wolf—if it were possible to get it to chase a mechanical hare—would put on a bad performance, and as a guard dog, in comparison with an Alsatian or a boxer, for instance, it would not do well at all. But as an all-rounder in its own free environment, it is infinitely superior to the domesticated specialists.

Many of the changes that have taken place can be explained as variations in the speed and extent of processes of ontogenetic maturation. Everything that we can observe in the dog—at any rate in relation to behavior—is already present in the wolf. No single element of dog behavior is known to me that is not also present in the wolf, though some items of behavior—for example, barking—are much more highly differentiated in most breeds of dog, while others—sexual behavior, for instance—have undergone a greatly increased endogenous boost. The latter fits in with a general trend

33

among domestic animals, which are generally oversexed in comparison with their wild counterparts. This is an adaptation to the requirements of man, who regulates the number of his domestic animals and is generally interested in a large number of offspring.

Above all, changes in dog behavior have taken place in areas that have lost their function for the dog, have been subject to slight selective pressure, or are of special importance to man, as is hunting or social behavior. No important changes, however, are to be observed among healthy dogs in areas that have not lost their function in the human environment, as in reproduction or rearing puppies. Only modern breeding methods, governed by commercial considerations and directed solely at appearance, and aided by veterinary medicine, have produced changes in these spheres. Animals that can hardly walk win prizes for their beautiful ears or their silky skin, perhaps, and they are used for further breeding. Creatures that have ceased to be able to give birth properly are delivered by caesarean section, nonviable puppies are reared artificially, and so on. Domestication, as we have seen, generally represents an adaptation to new conditions that is to be valued positively, but these changes are not domestication but real degeneration. It represents a threat to the continued existence of a number of breeds that have a small breeding base.

The degeneration of many breeds of dog is a problem with far-reaching implications, which deserves a book to itself. To go into the question here would take us too far from our subject, the wolf. But whenever I contemplate many of the "achievements" of modern dog breeders, I realize that man is not only vigorously hunting down and if possible exterminating the wild form of the dog—the wolf—but is also undermining the foundations of the life of its domesticated form—the dog—by erroneous breeding.

However, the extinction of the dog is but a remote possibility. There are too many perfectly normal "domesticated wolves" well capable of further adaptation in the world for that. The problem of the wild wolf is far more urgent, and it is to that that we shall now turn our attention.

3
The "Language" of Wolves

How do wolves communicate? Man has his verbal language, which the wolf, like all other animals, lacks. It communicates by direct signals, similar to the "body language" by which humans communicate nonverbally. In this chapter we shall concern ourselves with the signals that wolves give each other, their nature and their meaning. But first let us consider the senses with which the wolf apprehends the world.

The Wolf's Five Senses

Basically, the wolf has the same five senses for gathering information that men have, except that the efficiency of its sense organs differs from ours. Once, for instance, when I took Anfa for a walk in the forest and the wind was coming from behind, she did not spot a roe standing motionless about fifty yards ahead. Only when it moved did she spot the possible prey and chase it, skillfully following each of its sudden changes of direction.

In judging the efficiency of a sense organ the physiologist considers (1) the nature and (2) the strength of the stimulus that causes it to function. The wolf's sensitivity to light and darkness must to a large extent be similar to man's. But wolves (and dogs) are believed not to be able to see colors;[1] they apparently lack the necessary perceptive apparatus. So far as ocular sensitivity in other respects is

35

concerned, in daylight the wolf does not see quite as well as a man with good eyesight. And the resolution ability of the human eye seems to be better; that is, what a man is able to see as a number of separate points is seen by wolf and dog as a single point, like a coarse-grained film. But the wolf's ability to separate a number of stimuli following each other in rapid succession seems to be as good as if not actually better than man's, so that wolves are able to see and follow rapid movements.

In the lower frequencies the wolf's threshold for acoustic perception is similar to that of human beings, while in the higher frequencies dog and wolf are able to hear notes of a frequency of more than 21,000 hertz (the upper limit for the human ear). Thus the wolf is easily able to hear a dog whistle that transmits a high note barely perceptible to the human ear. Nevertheless, all the acoustic signals used by the wolf in intraspecific communication are believed to take place on frequencies that are perceptible to us.

Its olfactory system is far more efficient than man's, however. We do not know exactly how well a wolf can smell, but its ability must be comparable with that of the dog. In the last year of her life the she-wolf we called Mädchen was almost completely blind. Nevertheless, she was able to apprehend men or wolves at a considerable distance, up to about twenty yards if there was no wind, and if she once picked up their scent she could follow it for miles. She was also able to find her way about in strange surroundings, though if an object was suddenly placed in front of her she would crash into it. We humans with our pathetically feeble sense of smell are totally unable to conceive the rich world of olfactory sensation at the disposal of the wolf or dog, in which every blade of grass, every stick, and no doubt also the landscape as a whole, and above all the presence of friend, enemy, and prey, is apprehended chiefly by smell.

Another interesting feature in this connection is that wolves and dogs are not repelled by certain smells, as we are, though our sense of smell is so much weaker. To us putrefying meat, for instance, is nauseating, but they will eat it or wallow in it. This is presumably connected with their adaptation to making use of any food that presents itself. They can digest things that would quite possibly kill civilized human beings, or would at any rate make us ill.

In accordance with their acute olfactory sense their sense of taste is much more developed than that of human beings.

In regard to the wolf's sense of touch, there is little to say, except that its sensitivity to cold, heat, or pain is similar to ours. The muzzle with its tactile hair and presumably also the paws, where hair is either short or nonexistent, are especially sensitive areas.

The Nature of Communication

The difference in performance of our sense organs, in particular our deficient sense of smell, makes it more difficult for the human observer to detect and interpret communication between wolves. By communication I mean an action (a signal) directed by one animal (the transmitter) at another (the receiver) that changes the latter's behavior.

We can of course imagine a form of communication that does not influence the receiver's conduct, but that is something that could not be detected by a human observer. So let us stay with our operational definition, according to which communication is not just the signal alone, but the relationship between the signal and its meaning that expresses itself in the behavior of both animals. Transmitter and receiver are generally animals of the same species. Hunting as an action provoking a corresponding reaction on the part of the quarry is thus not communication in this sense. And the mere existence of an animal that can change the behavior of another animal—as happens in a social group all the time—is not communication, as there is no *aimed* action in this case. By "aimed" action I mean not only action directed at a specific receiver, such as baring the teeth, but also action not directed at a specific receiver to which there may be a reaction later. An example of such action directed to an indefinite receiver is the deposition of scent marks in the form of urine.

Communication between higher animals is completely comparable to nonverbal communication between human beings, which makes use of facial mimicry, body attitude, tactile signals such as stroking, and elementary utterances such as laughing or weeping. Animal communication is similar to this in being specific to the species and universal in it. It is not conceptual, and so does not symbolize objects, characteristics, and above all events, and thus cannot describe events in the past or in the future. Thus, in accordance with the small intellectual capacity of animals, there can be no communication of abstract ideas. Also there is no syntax; the sequence with which signals are transmitted has no relation to their meaning. In human verbal communication "wolf hunts man" means something very different from "man hunts wolf," but such a reversal of meaning by a change in the sequence of signals is impossible in the world of animal communication. An animal is able to communicate only its immediate existing circumstances: "I am here, I am doing this (or that), in this (or that) mood."[2]

A Wolf Pack in Canada

Strange though it may sound, to study the behavior of the wolf in the wild it is first necessary to tame it. For in the wild the wolf is extremely difficult to observe. At first I was unwilling to believe this. In the early summer of 1966 I went to Canada with my friend Christian to look for wolves and observe them in the wild. We had both been to Canada before, chiefly in British Columbia, and so we knew our way about. We started our search in the Chilcotin area in southern British Columbia, where Christian owned some horses. We caught them and rode them for days in the most remote areas but, apart from millions of mosquitoes and black flies, we saw practically no wildlife. All the game in the area seemed to have been wiped out in recent years by sportsmen from Vancouver and the United States. Our Indian friend Eugene told us that nowadays in autumn he had difficulty in finding a moose to shoot for the winter, and he had seen no wolves for a long time.

We gladly consented to be driven away by the mosquitoes and took the Alaska Highway to the north of British Columbia. At Atlin Lake we met a so-called outfitter named Old Henry; he too was an Indian, and he supplied tourists with equipment such as tents, food, horses, aircraft, and so on. As we were short of funds, we took a job with him as guides to shooting parties, and we spent months touring the area, guiding our guests to a moose or a caribou with a still bigger spread of antlers, enabling them to pump these animals full of lead at close range with automatic rifles. It was the most repulsive work I have ever done. Then we were called on to act as guides to a party of bear hunters, who spoke with contempt of shooting mere hoofed animals; to them shooting anything less than a bear was unworthy of real men. But when a bear suddenly appeared they fled like frightened chickens into their mobile super-caravan, and we gave up the job for good.

One evening in late September we were camping above a lake when below us we heard wolves howling, first individually and then in chorus. The howling went on for hours. The whole forest seemed to come to life, and we could hardly await first light to see what was happening. A big pack of wolves was resting on the sandy lakeside. It was an excellent place for them. Behind the beach there was an extensive marshy area. At the top end of the beach there was a broad river, and dense, low-mountain pines restricted the view in our direction.

We had an excellent view of them from our place above the embankment, though they were a long way away. With the aid of our field glasses we were able to count fifteen, of whom four or five were obviously that year's cubs; the cubs played the whole time, and older animals kept joining in. They ran between the bushes into the water, jumped up onto rocks, and defended themselves against playful attacks by their pursuers. Then again they would chase an animal, who would adroitly run in a circle and change roles from pursued to pursuer. It was a moving spectacle and made all the trouble of the previous few months worthwhile.

We soon recognized a certain order in the apparent confusion. A few adult wolves took turns in lying at the upper and lower end of the beach near the river. Some slept while others were drawn into the play. But there was always at least one, sometimes lying on an eminence, keeping watch on the surroundings with raised head.

We spent the whole morning watching the pack from our place on the steep embankment. The nearest wolf was perhaps about four hundred yards away. Chris suddenly wanted to shoot one of them, "to add a wolf to his trophies," for at heart he was still a hunter, but to me the idea of intruding on what was going on in this largely untouched wilderness was inconceivable. The result was a quarrel, in the course of which I assured him that I would immediately start shouting and behaving like a lunatic if he so much as raised his gun. We finally agreed to creep nearer to take photographs. I would have preferred to have stayed where we were and continued observing the wolves, who were now slowly quieting down in the morning sun, but the idea of some good pictures was also appealing. We cautiously went down to the marshland and made our way through the dense wood of mountain pines toward the beach. The wind was favorable, and it was impossible for the wolves to see us through the dense vegetation. We were still perhaps about two hundred yards away when Chris stumbled into a marshy hole and swore quietly. A rapid succession of muffled wuffs followed from the beach. I clambered up one of the bigger pines just in time to see the last few wolves jumping into the river and swimming across. Within seconds the pack had vanished.

On the beach we found many new and old tracks and some old, gnawed white bones; obviously this was not the first time the wolves had been there. Caribou hairs in fresh feces showed what their last meal had consisted of. Where were they now in this huge landscape? We debated whether to continue camping on the slope to await the pack's next visit, but were forced to admit the hopelessness of the idea. The young wolves had looked big enough to be able to follow the pack in its wanderings, and weeks might elapse before they returned.

The first snow had fallen a few days before, so I went back to Europe, obtained some cubs from a zoo, and brought them up with the bottle. Impressive though our only encounter with wolves had been, it was obvious that this was not the way to make a thorough study of wolf behavior. Certainly there are some differences between wolves brought up by human beings in captivity and wolves living in a state of nature, but there must be many behavior patterns that do not change substantially in captivity. No great changes have taken place in the sense organs of captive wolves, nor has there been any change in their methods of communication or the organization of the pack.

Konrad Lorenz later told me that he advised every ethologist setting out to study a species to tame young animals and live on terms of intimacy with them. The quickest way of learning the "language" of a species was to do so as a social partner. He himself has become a master of this method and has been frequently attacked because of it. He has been criticized for being too intuitive in his studies of animal behavior and for not making careful experiments capable of being repeated and verified by others. It is true that there are certain dangers in this "unmethodical" method. As I soon discovered for myself, one soon establishes a bond with the object of one's experiment, and it is easy to see what one wants to see and to overlook things that conflict with one's ideas. On the other hand, it would be good if many "operational" students of animal behavior knew their animals only fractionally as well as Konrad Lorenz knows his.

Fear and Friendliness to Strangers

To Konrad Lorenz the important thing, apart from study of the behavior typical of the species, has always been the individual animal with its definite past and its individual peculiarities. I was never again to get to know a wolf as well as I got to know Anfa. To her, in contrast to the many animals in the enclosure, it was above all human beings who were social partners. When I entered the enclosure she greeted me with the same effusiveness every morning. She came running toward me with bent hind legs and her tail between them wagging excitedly only at the tip. She held her head low, her ears were laid back, and the roots of her ears were pointed downward. Before she reached me she raised her head, jumped up at me, firmly bit my clothing, licked my face if she could, and finished by rolling on her back and whimpering. Later I was able to observe the same behavior in normally brought up cubs, who continually greet adult members of the pack in this way. The latter sniff them, sometimes lick their coat, particularly in the anogenital region and on the belly, let them pull at their coat and climb up and around them, and, in general, are very patient with them. The function of the cubs' effusively friendly behavior seems to be to obtain this tolerance and trigger off the caring behavior of all the members of the pack. Just as our son, who had now reached the age of four months, appealed to us with his big smile at every opportunity and thus mobilized all our feelings of solicitude for him, so does this same behavior by the wolf cubs reinforce the bond between them and the pack and thus ensure the pack's full cooperation in rearing them.

But our son did not only smile at his parents, Anfa did not only greet her human stepparents, and other cubs did not only greet

41

members of the pack whom they knew. If Anfa suddenly came across a strange human being in the forest or in the fields she was very apprehensive. But in the familiar environment at home the enthusiasm with which she greeted strangers could hardly be restrained. Many friends came to Rickling in order to be greeted by a wolf, and whenever this happened I was merely an onlooker as far as Anfa was concerned. On our earliest walks with her Dagmar and I sometimes separated in order to see which of us she would follow, and at that time she always stayed with me. But when she was a few months old she often followed strangers in familiar country. Only when we had gone a very long way indeed would she come running back to me.

At first I was baffled by this temporary preference for other human beings, and I hit on the explanation only years later. As I shall describe, the members of a pack are normally very aggressive to strange wolves. In summer individuals or small groups of wolves sometimes go their own way for a considerable time, and when they return they find strangers in the pack, that is, the newly arrived cubs. The effusively submissive behavior of the latter promptly identifies them as cubs—small, dependent, and nondangerous—and the older animals react accordingly. Thus in most instances we had no difficulty in introducing into an existing pack strange cubs and young wolves up to the age of eight to ten months. Only with older animals did difficulties arise, and it often turned out to be impossible to integrate them.

This aggressiveness to strangers to the pack may explain why strange wolves are given such an effusive welcome by the young. Even at a distance they are identified as cubs, not only by their size but also by their behavior, and a careful olfactory check confirms this first impression. Thus by a kind of pre-emptive act of appeasement the cubs prevent aggression and also trigger off caring behavior directed toward themselves.

As I have mentioned, an infant's smile causes similar reactions in human beings, particularly women, though observations throw doubt on whether this caring behavior is specific to the female sex. Schoolchildren often came to visit us at Rickling. If they were "well behaved" and not too old, an almost stereotyped sequence of events followed. While the girls all rushed to the many puppies and picked them up and cuddled and stroked them with loud expressions of delight, the boys first made for the wolves and, with obvious contempt for the girls, asked questions about their size, strength, dangerousness, and so on. But soon one boy would slip across to the puppies and others would follow, and finally all the children would be among the dogs, all of them, boys and girls alike, trying to stroke the puppies as much as they could.

We must certainly be very cautious in comparing human and animal behavior. Behavior patterns that seem similar may have entirely different functions, while others of entirely different appearance and phylogenetic origin may perform the same function. A further difficulty lies in the fact that many behavior patterns—particularly human patterns such as the one in relation to infants or puppies just described—are overlaid by cultural standards. Nevertheless, comparative observation of human beings and animals can stimulate new ideas, which must then be tested by exact observation or experiment, particularly when species socially organized in such a similar manner as wolf and man are being investigated.

But let us stay with our wolves. We could tell from Anfa's behavior that the way in which she held or moved parts of her body had an informative value for other wolves. Rudolf Schenkel, of Basle, who observed the behavior of wolves in the Basle zoo shortly after World War II, called this form of optical communication with the aid of the body "expressive behavior."[3] With the aid of this body language wolves express their mood and their readiness for action, and this is understood by their fellows. He called the succession of movements carried out by Anfa described above "active submission," and rolling on the back and lying still with splayed legs "passive submission."

Active submission is generally accompanied by an audible whimper, and when the wolf falls on its back and lies still on the ground, the other wolves often sniff its coat and its anogenital region. Quite frequently they will also lick it, and as long as this goes on, the animal will remain lying on its back. Obviously an exchange of information is taking place, not only in the optical but also in the acoustic, olfactory, and tactile fields; perhaps in many cases the sense of taste also comes into it.

Learning the Meaning of Signals

Communication assumes agreement on the meaning of signals between transmitter and receiver. The form of a signal, how it originates and is transmitted—that is, its physical characteristics—and its meaning as understood by the receiver must be carefully distinguished. The form of most behavior patterns that serve the purpose of communication in wolves must be innate. Anfa, for instance, who at first grew up with us alone, with no contact with other wolves or with dogs, bared her teeth, growled, howled, wagged her tail, and moved her ears exactly like any other wolf of the same age. But that did not mean that she necessarily knew the effect of baring the teeth on a possible partner or what it meant if such a partner threatened her in the same way.

Unlike the communicative behavior itself, it seems that the meaning of many signals has first to be learned by cubs. When in the course of time Anfa became a kind of substitute mother herself, she sometimes found the role tiresome. The cubs kept running to her, climbing up on her, pulling her tail, or simply wanting to lie next to her. When this grew too much for her she bared her teeth, growled, snapped at the cubs, or held their muzzles sideways on her

Fig. 2. Positions of the tail and their meaning; from left to right, intimidation, attack, normal attitude, humility, fear.

44

mouth as if to bite them. But the cubs completely ignored these obvious protests, which in fact seemed to make them want contact with her more than ever, and in the end she had no alternative but to go away.

I have noted similar behavior by cubs every summer since then. At first they do not react at all to the threats of adult wolves. The smaller ones may retreat momentarily if the threat comes unexpectedly, but they always start a new "assault" soon afterward. I have often wondered why cubs do not learn more quickly that baring the teeth and snarling represent a threat that may be followed by more aggressive behavior. An adult wolf could hardly afford such failure to react. Presumably the fact that it has no serious consequences is part of the answer. Because adult wolves are extraordinarily careful with their young, the latter learn only slowly that baring the teeth is a preliminary, an announcement of the possibility of more violent reactions. Adult animals obviously refrain from aggressive reactions in relation to cubs.

Thus it is very rare to hear a cub who associates with adult wolves squealing with pain. This occurs much more frequently in cubs' conflicts with each other, particularly when they are two or three months old and the teeth are long enough and the jaw muscles strong enough to deliver painful bites. It seems that it is in play and

in collisions with one another that cubs learn the real meaning of many of the signals that will be so important to them in later life.

Innate Understanding of Signals

Cubs obviously do not have to learn the meaning of some signals, knowledge of which, like the manner of carrying them out, seems to be innate. This fact was demonstrated to me again as I wrote this chapter. Four weeks previously cubs had been born in the big wolf enclosure in the National Park in the Bavarian Forest. I knew the den in which they were born, but in the meantime their mother had taken them to another one. So I searched the enclosure for them with my dog, Flow, who eventually found them in a rocky area closely planted with bushes. The cubs showed no fear of Flow, though this was the first time they had seen him. The mother and the other members of the pack followed us to the cubs. I sat on a projecting rock about thirty yards above and was eventually able to count four cubs.

After a great deal of reciprocal sniffing, whimpering, and running around each other, the pack moved away again. The cubs followed them for a few yards, but then lost the scent and turned back to the entrance to the den. I wanted to see how close to them I could get before they noticed me. I climbed down and sat on a stone about seven yards from the entrance to the den. The cubs looked in my direction, but with their still-dim blue eyes they could obviously not make me out properly. Nevertheless, they were very restless and started at the slightest sound. I assumed they had detected my scent but did not know what it meant. To get a better view of them in the thick scrub I sent Flow on ahead, but this time they ran away. Flow ran after one of them and touched it with his front paw. The cub squealed loudly, and the others immediately fled, each in a different direction. After the peace that had hitherto prevailed they seemed transformed. A squeal by one of them caused a phenomenally swift flight for cubs of that size. One of them hid in a split rock and another dashed straight toward me. I caught it—it was a female. Small as she was, she growled and bit all around her. Only when I held her by the scruff of her neck and picked her up did she fall into a state of rigidity similar to that in which cubs are carried in

46

their mother's mouth. I put her down again, and she dashed off as fast as her little legs would carry her, climbed the slope, and vanished over the rocks.

Meanwhile the other members of the pack had returned, noticed that the cubs had disappeared, and ran about excitedly. The mother ran straight to a slope about two hundred yards away, reappeared with a cub in her mouth, and carried it back to her den. Then she went back to the same slope, and from where I was up on the rock over the den I could see the second cub, followed by its mother and two males, running down the slope. Eventually they caught it about four hundred yards from the den, and again it was the mother who brought it back. On the way back she noticed the third cub. She went on to the den while the two males stayed with it. In the company of the bigger wolves it obviously calmed down. Then it too was carried back to the den by its mother.

Obviously it is not so easy for a she-wolf to keep her young together. But in the present context this is not so important as the renewed demonstration of the extraordinary apprehensiveness of cubs when confronted for the first time with human beings. What interests us here is the cubs' sudden flight when one of them squealed so loudly out of fright rather than pain. Flight behavior as a reaction to this signal presumably does not have to be learned but is innate. I have frequently observed similar behavior on the part of cubs as a reaction to warning sounds made by older wolves. A cub that had to learn that its mother's wuff meant danger would probably have had its last lesson.

What are the various kinds of signals, whether innate or learned, by which wolves communicate? Let us begin with the most difficult.

Olfactory Signals

Smell plays a big part in the recognition by members of a pack of one another. They certainly also recognize each other optically, but in country where vision is restricted or when they are far apart scent becomes increasingly important. This became apparent in our separation experiments, to which I shall return later. We let one wolf run freely while the others went different ways with two groups of different numbers and composition. I wanted to find out which group the free-running wolf would follow. It often took plenty of time to decide. Only after a great deal of running around did it follow one group or the other, but by this time both were well out of sight, and so the choice was often made only on the strength of the scent that was left behind.

Members of a pack obviously recognize one another by direct smell. Hence they engage in anogenital checks much more rarely than we are accustomed to seeing with dogs in the street. Only when a wolf has gone its own way for a long time and then returns to the pack is it smelled intensively. This also applies to strange wolves, whose age and sex is presumably established by this means. In the case of a grown animal no closer check is required. The stranger is recognized as such at a distance and is attacked immediately. I sometimes had considerable difficulties because of this with the older wolves at Rickling. If they saw an adult dog in the area they became greatly excited and pulled crazily at their chains. If they were free, or if they got free, a furious chase ensued in which the dog could save itself only by flight.

Individual recognition by smell presumably has little to do with communication in the sense of the word as defined above, but we do not know whether an aimed signal and a corresponding reaction may sometimes be involved. Also we do not know what may be communicated by the odor of the various glands, for instance, the two anal glands or the precaudal gland at the base of the tail.

We are, however, better informed about the scent-marking behavior of wolves. This is communication delayed in time, to which animals with a good nose are naturally well adapted. Among wolves feces and above all urine play the most important role. Feces are often deposited in noticeable places, say on a stone, by a bush, or on a tree stump. When the feces are fresh the smell is very strong, but even deposits several days old are smelled intensively by other wolves, and sometimes actually dug out from under deep snow.

But marking with urine seems to be more important to the wolf than marking with feces. Wolves, like dogs, can urinate in two different ways. They either urinate directly beneath them, standing with bent legs and producing the urine in larger quantities, the females crouching much lower than the males, who stand nearly erect; or they raise a hind leg—the male sideways and the female more forward—generally squirting only a small quantity of urine sideways against some object. This "squirt urination" is carried out only by sexually mature wolves of high rank in the pack. When they have finished they often move on a few paces and scratch the ground alternately with all four feet, something they rarely do after defecating. Thus they churn up sand, earth, and leaves and leave behind an optical mark in addition to the smell of urine.

My friend Dave Mech, who has been studying the ecology of free-ranging wolves in Minnesota for many years—I shall have a great deal to say about his work later—has made interesting observations on scent marking in conjunction with a colleague, Roger Peters.[4] The different packs in this area hunt in territories ranging in size from thirty to a hundred square miles. These areas are defended against wolves that are strangers to the pack, and so one can speak of territories in the real sense of the word. They remain constant in size for many years and, though each borders on the territories of several neighboring packs, conflicts between packs are relatively rare. Encounters with solitary wolves, generally younger animals that have left an existing pack, are also rare.

Dave investigated the question of how the spatial organization of the wolf populations he was studying was maintained. For years he has been trapping wolves and putting collars with small built-in radio transmitters around their necks before releasing them.[5] Thus with the aid of a receiver and a directional aerial he and his colleagues are able to locate the marked wolves from an aircraft. When snow is on the ground in winter they can follow the wolves' tracks and thus gather information about their behavior, including their marking habits.

They found that the squirt urination of the highest-ranking wolves is much more frequent than ordinary crouching urination or marking with feces. While normal urination and defecation has an excretory function and provides olfactory information only secondarily, squirting with urine is real marking behavior. In particular, prominent bushes, stones, trees, or tufts of grass along traditional routes are marked with a few drops of urine; up to four places per kilometer are marked in this way. Particularly favored for this purpose are places where routes intersect, as well as those previously marked by the same animal. The scent seems to last for nearly a month, because then it is marked again in the same way. As a pack generally visits every area in its territory at least once every three or four weeks, the whole area claimed by it is kept permanently marked in this way. Mech and Peters also found that marking was especially frequent in areas bordering on neighboring territories. Neighboring packs often used the same marking places, and the animals sniffed at these in a particularly excited manner, marked them again, and then vigorously scratched themselves.

Thus it seems that this form of indirect communication by scent not only gives information to individual members of the pack about the whereabouts and movements of their fellows but also contributes to the spatial organization of the wolf population as a whole. The hunting territories of different packs are maintained by this means. Neighboring packs can keep out of each other's way and avoid direct confrontation. Nonterritorial solitary wolves that join up with others and form small groups can also avoid direct confrontation with territory-owning packs, and in the course of their long wanderings may find an unmarked area in which they can remain, rear young, and so form a new territorial pack.

Communication by scent also plays a vital role in the sexual sphere. Throughout the year, but with special frequency before and during the season of heat in winter, the so-called alpha pair, the two highest-ranking wolves in the pack, urinate in succession at the same spot. Sometimes other high-ranking males also take part in these "urination ceremonies." Each intensively sniffs the urine squirted by the others before urinating near it. It is possible that the males discover the state of heat in the female by this means, and urinating together might serve a bonding purpose. As Dave Mech once said, "Wolves that pee together stay together."[6]

Finally, there is a possible method of olfactory communication of which we understand practically nothing. Why do wolves (and dogs also) eat evil-smelling substances such as rotting meat and excrement? Anfa was only a few months old when she wallowed in the stinking remains of a putrefying hare. Afterward she stank accordingly. Human repugnance to the pungent smells of putrefaction is obviously not shared by wolves; on the contrary, they gobble up the stuff, as Anfa did with the remains of the hare. They prefer the remains of wild animals for this purpose. When we fed our wolves on the innards of wild duck, they first rolled in them before eating them, but when they were given the remains of whole bodies of

50

domesticated duck that we sometimes got at the slaughterhouse, they always gobbled them up immediately without rolling in them. Wolves also enjoy wallowing in rotten fruit and feces. It was especially easy to get the untamed wolves that we could not take out of the enclosure to wallow. Almost any unfamiliar object that was thrown into the enclosure—a cigarette packet, a lemon rind, a bit of rag—would be carried about, put down, and then rolled on. Anfa and the other wolves whom I could take out of the enclosure were especially likely to wallow at the beginning of their walks. Then, when we got back again, they were always subjected to intensive sniffing by the other wolves, who sometimes actually tried to rub themselves against the coat of one of the homecomers. The attraction of foul-smelling substances is obviously very great.

To man, with his impoverished sense of smell, this rolling and wallowing is a very strange way of behaving, and we can still only speculate about its function. One suggestion is that the purpose of this "self-scenting" with carrion is to draw the attention of other members of the pack to an available source of food. Another is that it might be a form of camouflage, covering up the wolves' own scent and so enabling them to approach their prey more easily. It has also been suggested that wallowing in carrion has no purpose other than giving pleasure to the individual wolf.[7]

This last theory is unsatisfactory because it is impossible to prove experimentally. So long as no exact observations have been made on wolves living in a state of freedom, and so long as no experiments have been done to test the other theories, it is idle to argue about the function of this type of behavior. Perhaps there may be some justification for all three theories.

Optical Communication

If the purpose of many olfactory signals is still unknown to us, we are rather better informed in regard to optical communication, as one would expect in view of our own capacities in the area. Charles Darwin was an early student of the expression of emotions in men and animals. He used the expressive behavior of the dog to develop his theory of opposites. According to this theory, when men and animals reverse their intentions—for example, from aggression to

51

friendliness—they also reverse all the signals of their expressive behavior. An attacking dog makes itself as big as possible: Its legs are stretched, its back hairs are erect, its ears stand forward, it holds its tail up, and it stares at its opponent with round eyes. In a friendly, submissive dog, all the signals are reversed: It makes itself small and bends its knees, its hair lies flat, it wags its tail, its ears are held down and back. The result is that its face is smooth and its eyes no longer seem so big and staring (see figure 3).[8]

This reversal of the elements of expression can be seen in many animal species as well as in man. But it was no mere chance that Darwin chose the dog as an example. As in the case of the primates (monkeys, apes, and man) body language in the wolf (and thus also in the dog) is especially well developed. Or, rather, to us human beings the optical communication of the wolf seems to be highly developed and many-sided. It is possible that animals with better sight, such as the various species of cat, may need less well-developed signals for communicating and may thus appear to us to be less developed optically. Many cat lovers would certainly support that view, while horse lovers again would point to the facial mimicry of the horse, and so on. Also our visual ability is very dependent on subjective factors such as habits and interests. That again shows how difficult it is to find objective criteria for judging communicative processes, even in the optical field, with which we are most familiar.

For this reason let us limit ourselves to the doglike predators of the *Canidae* family. In spite of all methodological inadequacies, we can say with relative certainty that the expressive behavior of the wolf is especially highly differentiated. But why the wolf?

In normal, undisturbed behavior the wolf's legs are not stiff, the tail hangs down loosely, the face is smooth, the lips are not tense, and the ears move in the direction from which sounds are coming. They can be moved forward, sideways, and backward somewhat independently of each other, so the opening of one ear can be directed backward while that of the other is directed sideways. When the wolf moves its head forward, to smell something or when galloping at full stretch, the ears are normally laid back.

Divergences from this basic attitude appear in social encounters or clashes. The attitude of the body becomes a communicative signal. This naturally depends on the behavior of the other wolf,

Fig. 3. Aggression and active submission in the dog (from Darwin, 1872).

which in turn depends on the behavior of the first wolf. The relationship between two or more animals is determined by a number of factors, of which at least two are constant: the animal's sex and the difference in age between the parties. A third factor, their relative rank, is variable and is a manifestation of the history of their relationship. Apart from the place where the encounter occurs, other factors influencing expressive behavior are above all those that can be summed up under the heading of the animals' motivation or readiness for action: their endogenous drives depending on such things as sexuality, hunger, fatigue, and so on. In the chapters that follow we shall discover what influence these factors have on social relationships between wolves. For the time being we shall consider only the communicative signals and their origin in the various forms of social encounters between two animals.

AGGRESSION AND FEAR

Since Darwin we have been accustomed to explaining the expressive behavior of animals as indicating opposite impulses. In a well-known illustration Lorenz, for instance, explains the facial mimicry of a dog as expressing the interplay between greater or less anger and greater or less fear.[9] An animal that is neither angry nor afraid keeps its ears upright and its mouth shut. With increasing fear the ears are laid farther back, and with increasing anger the mouth is opened and the teeth bared. When both fear and anger are present, the mouth is open and the ears laid back. Fear and anger can thus overlay each other, and both can be very strong simultaneously in certain circumstances (see figure 4).

This interpretation of canine mimicry seems at first sight very convincing, but some observations cause me to doubt its correctness.

Only in two cases have I seen wolves fighting seriously. (Uninhibited attacks directed at the suppression of another member of the pack are also relatively rare.) But in both cases the attack took place without warning and with full violence, and in both all optical and acoustic expressive elements were lacking: There was no facial expression of anger, no baring of teeth, the hair did not stand on end, the tail was not erect, and there was no snarling. On the contrary, the assailant's body attitude corresponded completely to the basic

neutral attitude. The animal's mood was revealed only by the behavior itself, not by any expression. Thus with increasing anger in
the absence of fear there should have been no change in facial
expression in Lorenz's illustration.

Another observation that is inconsistent with Lorenz's theory is
that facial expression—the wide-open mouth, the baring of teeth,
and the laid-back ears, which he believes express maximum anger
and fear—never appeared spontaneously, only reactively, in response to a powerful threat. If the threat ceased, the attacked wolf
ceased to show that expression, and resumed it only in the event of
a renewed attack. It is an expression of maximum readiness for
defense. The animal was certainly afraid, but was simultaneously
also "angry," that is, aggressive.

Interpretations of affective states in animals are certainly to a large
extent speculative, but it would be wrong to abandon them completely, for in some circumstances they approach the truth. But
researchers must always make clear whether they are engaging in
speculation or offering verifiable experimental or observational findings. Thus I now propose to attempt a rather different speculative
interpretation of the expressive behavior of the wolf.

My model is based on the same two impulses: aggressiveness, the
tendency to attack, on the one hand, and a fear of injury that can
increase to the stage of actual flight on the other.

Contrary to Lorenz's description, greater fear increasingly inhibits
the tendency to attack. Hence I leave the top right half of the model
(see figure 5) blank, nonexistent; an overlaying of the two elements
is impossible at any level. Instead, the wolf's expressive behavior
shows the strength of its fear in relation to its aggressiveness. If all
aggressive elements as well as fear are absent, there are many different forms of neutral contact-making in which all the elements of
expression, such as the corner of the mouth, ears, tail, eyes, body
attitude, are normal and movement is loose. With increasing fear as
a consequence of a large difference in rank in relation to the other
party, or in the event of a direct attack by another, the first reaction
is appeasement behavior, beginning with active submission followed
by passive submission if apprehension increases still further. All the
expressive elements show a complete absence of any tendency to attack. If the other wolf's aggressiveness again increases, this now
leads to defense behavior and finally to flight.

55

If one of two wolves is greatly superior in rank and its aggressiveness, in the absence of fear, increases, it will first of all demonstrate its rank in the usual way. Its attitude and movements will still be loose and its back hairs not raised. Its movements will remain loose even if aggressiveness increases further. Its motivation can be discerned only in its behavior, not in any concomitant expressive elements. It will attack without inhibition, showing no other sign of its extreme aggressiveness. If the other wolf stands its ground there will be a real fight, but generally it flees. However, pure aggressiveness without fear is rare.

Most aggressive clashes take place in inhibited form—the animal fears its opponent's reaction to an attack. The assailant advances

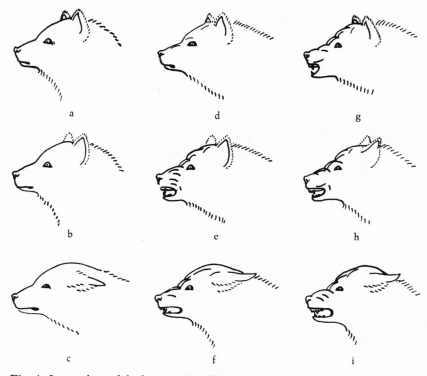

Fig. 4. Lorenz's model of expression. From a to c, increasing fear; from a to g, increasing aggressiveness; i, maximum overlaying of fear and aggression.

with all the elements of expression directed at the other party. If the latter defends itself against the assailant's snaps, the assailant jumps back and keeps its distance. If the difference in strength or rank between the two is slight, the assailant will not try to bite but will use its body weight, pressing against its opponent chiefly with its hindquarters, while the latter repeatedly snaps at the area of the assailant's throat.

The slightly superior party will turn its head away and thus present the most sensitive part of its body to the inferior party. By averting its head, the superior's only dangerous weapon, the inferior's preparedness to defend itself is diminished, and its snapping movements cease. Should the inferior disturb the temporary equilibrium between the assailant's aggressiveness and its fear by further snapping movements and bites, violent reaction on the assailant's part ensues.[10]

There is no other situation in which the extremely delicate balance between aggressiveness and fear in the assailant and fear and readiness for defense in the victim is so plainly demonstrated as in this offering of the throat. Fear prevents the aggressive tendency of the one and the defensive tendency of the other from getting out of hand. Either would immediately lead to an intensification of the clash, with biting and perhaps serious wounding. The inhibition presupposes an accurate assessment of the opponent, a precise understanding of the latter's communicative signals.

If the difference in rank between the two parties is still further reduced, we observe so-called intimidation behavior. This may be carried out by one party only, the one superior in rank, or two wolves of almost equal rank may try it on each other. The raised back hairs, the strongly inhibited movements, and the averted eyes are all plain signs of fear coupled with aggression. This again generally prevents serious fighting from developing.

A special form of inhibited aggression is the threat behavior of baring the teeth. This is a ritualized inhibited bite and is always a warning. If the other party reacts appropriately by increasing its distance or at any rate by not reducing it, generally no attack will follow. But if it fails to react appropriately the consequence, depending on the relative rank of the parties, will be the forms of aggressive clash previously described. Only the most extreme forms—serious fighting and flight—are not preceded by any threats.

57

Fig. 5. Strength of fear in
relation to tendency to
attack. From bottom left
to bottom right,
increasing tendency to
attack. (Neutral making of
contact, demonstration of
rank, fighting in earnest
with no expressive
elements.) From bottom
left to top left, increasing
fear. (Active submission,
passive submission, flight).
Right, intimidation
behavior, presenting the
throat, intensive defense
against snapping attack.

In threat behavior an increasingly aggressive or defensive trend is expressed by the extent to which the bridge of the nose is wrinkled and the teeth are bared. The extent to which the mouth is open also indicates how great the readiness to bite is. Shortly before the animal actually bites the mouth is opened wide. If the other party still does not react as expected, biting will indeed take place at this point.

The fear that inhibits the tendency to attack is expressed by the length of the corner of the mouth and the position of the ears. The longer the corner of the mouth and the farther the ears are drawn down and back, the greater is the fear. Withdrawing the roots of the ears makes the skin of the face smooth, and this, combined with the "flickering" look in the eyes, contributes to the anxious expression of the face, which is very hard to see. If there is less fear and more aggressiveness, the ears are held erect and forward. The structures of the facial skin now appear; in particular, the black spots under the eyes and the eyes' fixed gaze make them look quite different from how they look when threatening is accompanied by fear.

It is interesting to note that when there is an intensive defense threat the corner of the mouth becomes shorter again; this expresses a high degree of readiness to bite. Only the eyes and the position of the ears now betray how frightened the wolf really is.

There are many transitions between the various elements of expression. Sometimes combinations occur that are actually comic. Several times I have observed a low-ranking wolf defending a piece of food looking as if it were brave in front and frightened behind; in front it threatened with short lips and ears held forward, but its hind legs were bent and its tail was between its legs.

THE BITING INHIBITION

Few aggressive confrontations between wolves lead to serious fighting. Fear seems to play an especially important part in this. It generally prevents serious biting, for if biting occurs the other wolf responds in the same way. In the hard conditions in which wolves live any wound is a threat to life, and a system that prevents such wounds therefore appears extremely sensible.

A great deal has been written about the so-called biting inhibition among wolves. Lorenz assumes that (1) it is innate; (2) it is triggered

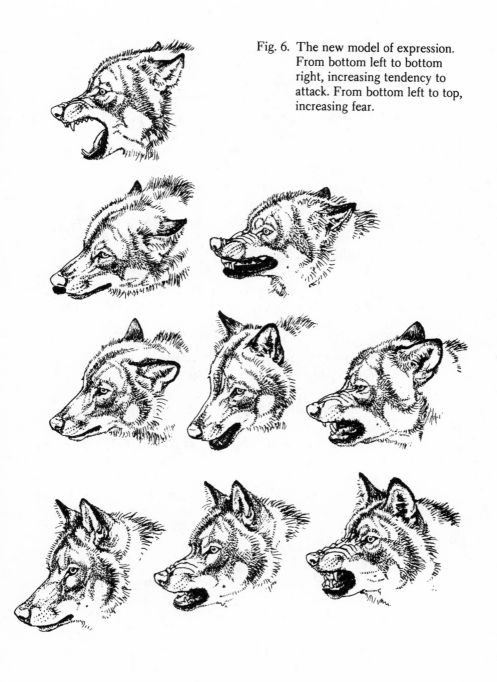

Fig. 6. The new model of expression. From bottom left to bottom right, increasing tendency to attack. From bottom left to top, increasing fear.

off when inferiority is acknowledged by submissive behavior; and (3) it assists in the preservation of the species by preventing the wounding or death of the defeated party. [11]

Once again it was observations of Anfa that caused my first doubts about these existing ideas. Rough play with the other young cubs at first resulted in a great deal of squealing. Anfa's playful bites were obviously too hard, and the young cubs reacted with squeals and bit back angrily and hard. But these attacks did not worry the relatively big Anfa; she went on playing, and as a result the play became very aggressive. My first impression was that her behavior was disturbed and she did not understand what was happening. Only when she was five months old and the other cubs barely four did play become more peaceful.

I still knew too little to understand this development of aggressiveness among the cubs and thought it was connected to Anfa's special situation. But observation of later litters in the next few years resulted in a similar picture. In the first few months of life the frequency with which aggressive behavior patterns appeared among cubs, particularly at play, was always very high, only to decline rapidly later. The frequency increased again with cubs over the age of one. [12]

The high frequency of aggressive behavior among cubs seems to me to depend not on a high endogenously conditioned aggressivity but on the lack of a biting inhibition as well as on the ignorance of the meaning of many communicative signals. It is only at play that cubs discover the meaning of these signals and also learn that biting too hard leads to being bitten, which hurts. Thus the biting inhibition seems to be a mechanism acquired by a learning process and depending on a fear of pain that to a large extent prevents members of a pack from harming one another.

However, as frequently occurs in the analysis of the behavior of more highly developed animals, this explanation of the biting inhibition is not sufficient by itself. Why, for instance, are adult wolves so cautious in handling cubs? It cannot be because of fear of being bitten. Here innate inhibiting mechanisms seem to be at work, just as they seem to be at work in the case of the signals that are vital to survival. These benefit wolves when they display submissive behavior, acting just like cubs and delivering themselves apparently helplessly to the mercy of their superiors and thus exploiting the latter's

Fig. 7. Play behavior. From top
to bottom, play face,
playful threat to attack,
invitation to play, chasing
play with pursuer and
pursued, biting play.

inhibition against biting cubs. This way of appeasing an aggressor with the aid of infantile signals is very common in the animal kingdom. We shall see later, however, that appeasing behavior among wolves is effective only when the situation is *a priori* not so aggressive that serious biting is about to take place. The submissive wolf obviously knows that it is not in danger of being seriously bitten. Otherwise it would keep its distance or, if that was not possible, would vigorously defend itself. Thus the biting inhibition is not primarily triggered off by submissive behavior, as Lorenz assumes, but depends on the aggressor's experience and is connected with its fear of being bitten if its biting were to result in vigorous defensive behavior on the part of the victim.

This biting inhibition does not serve an abstract common aim such as preservation of the species, but merely the individual interests of the animal that refrains from biting, who by doing so avoids the risk of being bitten itself and refrains from endangering its own or closely related progeny. I observed uninhibited biting and the killing of conspecifics only when vital interests were at stake, as in struggles for the alpha position in the pack, in driving rivals out of it, or in clashes with wolves that were alien to it. I shall go into the questions of group and individual (or genetic) selection that are important in this connection in chapter 7.

SIGNALING FRIENDLY FEELINGS

Wolves can also express friendliness. As in submissive behavior, in doing so they avoid all signals indicating aggressiveness; their whole bodies are loose and they wag their tails. Tail wagging is above all a sign of excitement. Small cubs wag their tails vigorously when suckling, and later they do so excitedly when begging adult wolves for food. They jump up at the bigger animals and try to lick the corners of their mouths. This often results in the bigger wolf dropping food it has in its mouth or regurgitating food from its belly. The whole behavior pattern greatly resembles that of active submission, though in begging for food the licking motions are directed exclusively at the big wolf's mouth and the expressive elements of submission, such as the position of the ears and the tail, are not so marked.

Active submission presumably originated from begging for food.[13] However, that does not mean that it develops in the course of ontogenetic maturation out of begging behavior, as an individual learning process, so to speak, such as is the case of the biting inhibition, for instance. One simple observation shows that that cannot be the case. With all my cubs I saw the beginnings of both active and passive submission long before they ate much solid food and so begged adult wolves for it. What we have here is a phylogenetic process, a ritualization, as we ethologists call it. By this we mean a change in a behavior pattern for the sake of its signaling effect. Sometimes these behavior patterns arise from the group of functions in which the signal is used; thus the intention to bite, for instance, comes to signal the threat. The behavior pattern of active submission, however, comes from a group of functions entirely different from that of the acquisition of food. A signal has also developed out of the cub's excited tail wagging when soliciting food. This always indicates that the wolf is in a state of increased excitation. In intimidation behavior, for instance, the tail generally moves slowly and very stiffly, while in friendly greeting it moves loosely this way and that. Thus the way in which a wolf moves its tail shows whether it is in an aggressive or friendly mood.

But its fellows do not conclude from a wolf's tail movements alone what state of mind it is in. Rather, they communicate by a combination of many expressive elements, such as those of the ears, facial mimicry, and body and tail attitude. An animal's mood cannot be inferred from the position of the ears alone, for instance, for, apart from their expressive function, the ears are used to locate sounds, so they are never held in the same position for more than a few brief moments. The message conveyed by a wolf's whole body must be taken into account, as well as any utterances it may make. Also every member of a pack knows all the other members as well as its relations to them, so that it will know from experience what another wolf is trying to convey.

PLAY BEHAVIOR

This situation-governed recognition of signals can plainly be seen in the last of the social fields that remains to be dealt with, that of play behavior.

There are basically three types of aggression that a member of a wolf pack can carry out against another member. The first we have already met—I call it simply the attack. Without showing any preliminary sign of aggression, the assailant makes a lightning dash at another wolf and bites it unless it escapes by flight. The second type, which I shall call the "chase away" to distinguish it from attack, is directed at an animal of lower rank, and in this case the aggression is inhibited. When chase away runs its full course, the following occurs: the aggressor fixes its eyes on the victim from a distance. Then it creeps slowly toward it, suddenly breaking into a charge at full speed, making especially high leaps in the final phase. This results in a practically simultaneous landing on all four legs, making a slight muffled sound. If the victim has not already noticed what is happening, it notices it now, and generally it flees. The aggressor seems more concerned with driving the other wolf away than catching it. The third form of aggression is the "play" attack. This challenge to play, however, is not distinguishable from the chase-away charge. The slow creep-up and the galloping, leaping charge make it look exactly like the latter, except that just before reaching the other animal the assailant may demonstrate its playful intentions by swinging its head or zigzag leaping, for instance. Instead of running away, the other animal stands its ground, and soon vigorous play takes place.

In the last two cases the assailant's purpose cannot be discerned from its body attitude or from any sound it makes, as, apart from the soft landing, no sound is made in either. But, as has been frequently pointed out, the relationship between aggressor and victim based on a shared past makes the former's intentions perfectly clear.

This way of transmitting messages independent of any signals certainly plays an important part in communication between both higher animals and men. It enables many signals to be reduced to a minimum without losing their intelligibility. Often only the slightest hint of aggression from a distance is sufficient to dissuade a low-ranking wolf from its purpose, and time and energy do not have to be wasted on a full-scale charge. Such reduction of signals can of course involve dangers; a slow change in the usual behavior of another animal may possibly pass unnoticed. Thus it is clear that in spite of all habituation some patterns of behavior peculiar to wolves are always carried out in unmistakable fashion. These are above all behavior patterns of submission, protest, and demonstration of rank, which in the last resort help to avoid violent conflict and the danger of being wounded.

Returning to play, it is characterized above all by what are apparently superfluous and sudden movements, such as swinging the head and body, zigzag leaping, and advancing in little jumps. These playful elements appear chiefly at the outset, when an animal challenges another to play. One form of this we have already met. In another a wolf will lie down in front of another with its forelegs apart and the front part of its body nearly on the ground. The tail and sometimes the whole hindquarters as well as the head are moved jerkily, and the eyes are big and round and are fixed briefly on the other animal. It will then either suddenly run away, thus challenging the other animal to chase it, or it will run at the other, whereupon biting play develops.

Different roles can be detected in play. In the chase there are the pursuer and the pursued. The pursuer shows some of the expressive elements of aggression, and the pursued puts its tail between its legs and lays its ears back as if it were really fleeing. But, in contrast to what it would do if fleeing in earnest, it may run in a circle and thus become the pursuer itself. Or it may suddenly stand its ground, whereupon biting play ensues. But the pursuer may itself start running away and, with its tail between its legs, be pursued.

This alternation between attack and defense also occurs in other games, and here too expressive elements such as the opening of the mouth are copied from the corresponding nonplayful behavior. But when the mouth is opened in play the teeth are not bared and no threatening sounds are made, so there is never any doubt about the animal's playful intentions.

This applies only to completely unaggressive play among adult wolves, among whom there is an easy transition from playful to aggressive behavior. Playful expressive elements can serve to camouflage intentions that are really aggressive. Men are not the only ones who can bluff. But more of that later.

Let us return for a moment to the question we asked at the outset, which is, why is expressive behavior so highly developed in the wolf in comparison to its closest relatives, the jackal, the coyote, or even the fox. These animals threaten, for instance, in very stereotyped fashion by merely opening the mouth—just as the wolf does when making its final defensive threat—independent of the relative rank of the opponent or any other relationships of strength. Devra Kleimann, who studied many different kinds of *Canidae* in the London zoo, attributes the highly developed expressive behavior of the wolf to its ecological situation in relation to food. While most canids, such as the jackal and the fox, generally hunt smaller prey, which they kill alone, the wolf chiefly lives on prey that, being bigger than itself, it can kill only with the aid of its fellows. In adapting to this the wolf has developed a tendency to exist in bigger groupings, while most other canids are either solitary or live in small family groups. The necessarily more complex processes of decision in a bigger pack have led to a differentiation of communicative signals in the wolf, particularly in the field of optical communication.[14]

Acoustic Communication

We can distinguish about six different basic sounds made by the wolf. These are whimpering, wuffing, snarling, squealing, and howling, as well as others made not with the vocal cords and the buccal cavity but with the aid of other parts of the body. The emission of sounds is either combined with optical and olfactory signals at close quarters or is used to communicate information at a distance. Within the individual types of utterance there are many gradations and individual variations, and there are many transitions and mixed sounds. As in the case of the optical expressive elements, most sounds convey no precise message in themselves but acquire their full significance only in combination with the whole behavior of the wolf in a definite situation.

Whimpering is a very variable form of utterance. It is generally on a light, clear note expressing restlessness, dissatisfaction, or mild excitement, but it can also be used to solicit, in the sexual sphere, for instance. Cubs whimper when they are cold, hungry, or lonely, and older wolves do so to lure them from the den or when they bring them food. In the big enclosure in the Bavarian Forest I was often able to attract young cubs by whimpering. They came toward me, thinking that their mother was coming back, and only realized their mistake at the last moment and ran away again. This trick worked only during the first weeks after they were able to walk. After that they seemed to be able to distinguish their mother's whimpering and that of other wolves from mine. By that time they were also able to recognize a stranger by his scent, which made them more cautious.

Older wolves whimper in many social situations; it is by far their most common form of utterance. Above all, younger and lower-ranking wolves whimper on individual encounters with older animals of higher rank, and they also whimper excitedly at the group ceremonies so typical of the species. Wolves whimper in connection with all forms of soliciting, for example, when they want to get another wolf to get up. In the preheat period the female whimpers to solicit the male. When the period of heat is at its height the situation is reversed, and the male whimpers to solicit the female.

A monosyllabic wuff is a warning sound. It draws the attention of the pack to a possible danger and leads to flight by the cubs or by the whole pack, depending on the situation. In a situation that is not so tense, the wuff is often preceded by a sound made by jerky expiration through the nostrils. If the situation is tenser wuffing can develop into a polysyllabic incipient bark. This is an indication of the greatest excitement. An approaching enemy is barked at from a distance by the older members of the pack while the cubs and younger wolves make for a place of safety. Presumably it serves as a diversionary maneuver and warning of the approach of an enemy, such as a bear or a human being, and perhaps also of strange wolves. Especially aggressive fighting in the pack sometimes leads to excited barking by wolves not directly involved. In comparison with the barking of dogs, this sound is not differentiated and is much rarer.

Snarling underlines the optical threat of baring the teeth and is thus used to threaten. A wolf will snarl in protest against excessively importunate cubs; a superior in rank will snarl at impermissible behavior by an inferior; an inferior will snarl in protest against attempts at oppression by a superior; animals that are eating will snarl when others approach, and so forth. In cases of lesser intensity wolves will sometimes snarl without even a slight baring of the teeth; only rarely will the opposite occur and teeth be bared without a sound being uttered. But with increasing excitement the two signals invariably appear together, and the more the teeth are bared and the mouth opened, the louder is the snarl.

As the defensive urge increases sounds mingle with the threatening growl that may ultimately develop into a squeal. This is a shrill expression of fear, pain, and terror. A wolf being bullied by a superior or by a number of wolves but not actually being bitten (in which case it would try only to defend itself or to flee) will squeal loudly. Squealing is much commoner among cubs than among adult wolves and is frequent in their early, still very rough, play together. A cub will also squeal at the sudden appearance of danger; the other cubs respond by immediate flight, as previously described, and the adults immediately direct their attention to them.

In connection with this passive defense of squealing is another threatening sound that comes under the heading of those not produced by the vocal cords—chattering of the teeth. A cornered wolf will make a kind of snapping movement in the air, bringing the teeth of the upper and lower jaws sharply into contact, producing a muffled sound that is often repeated several times. This expresses extreme readiness for self-defense and serves as a strong deterrent against further attacks.

Another sound not made with the vocal cords that has a signaling effect is that of the landing of all four feet in the charge. Finally, there are sounds arising from certain activities that cannot be said to have any signaling function but nevertheless arouse the attention of other wolves. These occur in eating, for instance, in tearing flesh or breaking bones and also in regurgitating food. In particular, they draw the cubs' attention to possible sources of food. The cubs run in the direction of the sound and try to get some of the food for themselves.

THE HOWL

The most characteristic sound made by the wolf is the howl, a long-drawn, melodious U-sound produced by expiration through the mouth, which is slightly opened with the lips drawn forward. A howling wolf will generally hold its head up and lay back its ears.

A howling bout will often last for up to twenty seconds. After a short breather another bout may follow, so that the howling may go on for several minutes altogether. Sometimes individual wolves go on howling for hours. In that case the pauses between howls are generally rather longer.

70

Individual wolves in a pack often have a very characteristic howl of their own. I have never found it very difficult to distinguish the howls of my various wolves, and the animals can of course do so. This is made clear by notes recording the sequence in which the wolves of a pack join in the chorus. To a wolf the howling of another wolf is a powerful stimulus to follow suit. Consequently an initial howl by one animal will often quickly lead to a chorus by the whole pack. But this does not invariably happen. The initial howl of an animal of low rank, for instance, is a less effective trigger than that of a superior animal. Thus wolves are obviously able not only to distinguish individual howling but also to connect it with a definite animal. They are also able to distinguish the howling of strange wolves (or dogs) from those known to them.

The howling of cubs and young wolves is generally on a rather higher note than that of adults. They initiate it less often, but respond very quickly to the howling of adults. Anfa's spontaneous howl at the age of seventeen days previously described shows that howling is of great importance to cubs also.

There has been much speculation about the function of howling, but we are only slowly acquiring data enabling us to form an objective opinion. According to the present state of knowledge, howling serves a number of purposes. Theberge and Falls, in conjunction with the studies of Doug Pimlott and his colleagues in Algonquin Park, Ontario, found that when the wolves of a captive pack were separated they howled much more frequently than when kept together.[15] When we went for walks at Rickling with Anfa and other tame wolves, those left behind howled regularly when we moved away from the forester's lodge. Later experiments in Bavaria showed that it was chiefly high-ranking wolves that were left behind that howled, particularly when their partners, that is, other high-ranking wolves, or cubs were taken from the enclosure. And when a high-ranking or the top-ranking wolf came with us, the pack that was left behind howled more often than when a low-ranking wolf was taken.

These experiments also showed the extent to which I myself was integrated into the pack, at any rate for a time. At Rickling we lived next to the enclosure, while in the Bavarian Forest the big enclosure was about three miles from our house. For several years I had two Norwegian horses that I used to ride over to the wolves' enclosure in the forest every day. When I set off for home in the evening after finishing my day's work, the wolves almost invariably howled when I reached a small eminence a few hundred yards from my observation hut and the enclosure. From there I was able to hear the concert very well. If it failed to occur, I needed only to howl briefly myself to get an immediate response.

These observations and experiments show that when wolves are separated they try to maintain or reestablish contact with other members of the pack by howling. The question that arises is whether howling indicates more than the howler's own whereabouts, combined with a request for information about the whereabouts of other members of the pack. Theberge and Falls found that wolves howled differently, depending on whether they began of their own accord or were responding to the howling of others. They concluded that perhaps more information was passed than the mere whereabouts and number of wolves in the group.

This seems to me not unlikely. But I do not believe that differentiated information, about the direction in which the pack is moving, for instance, or its employment at the moment or its success in the hunt, is transmitted by howling. When wolves hunt, for instance, they do so in complete silence. Simpler information—about the mood of the howling wolf, for example—might be conveyed, however.

Nowadays howling can be used to locate and actually count wolves in an area. The first researchers to do this were Doug Pimlott and his colleagues in Algonquin Park.[16] During the summer they howled regularly at definite places in the area they were investigating. As cubs in particular were especially ready to respond, believing that it meant their elders were coming back with food, they were able to establish exactly where the cubs were at the time. They also established their probable numbers and, as older wolves often answered as well, they were able to estimate the minimum number of adults in the pack. They discovered not only where cubs were being reared, but also the extent of the pack territory as well as the territories of neighboring packs. This enabled them to estimate the total wolf population in the area, as well as the success of the various packs in rearing their young, which in turn enabled conclu-

72

sions to be drawn about the age structure and birth rate of the total wolf population. As they continued their observations through several summers, this relatively simple method, together with other direct observations, gave them a very good picture of the ecology of the wolf population. So successful was the technique that in the evenings so-called "howling excursions" were arranged in which many visitors to the park took part, thus certainly contributing to demolishing conventional ideas about the wickedness of the wolf.

Dave Mech adopted this method farther south in Minnesota to supplement his work with radio transmitters. He also took another step. He raised the question of whether howling might have a territorial function similar to that of marking with urine. Perhaps howling conveyed information, not only to members of the pack, but also to outsiders and neighboring packs, thus contributing to the spatial organization of the total wolf population.

Like Pimlott and his colleagues before him, Dave began by using howling to discover the whereabouts of the cubs, the so-called rendezvous places. When cubs give up using dens when they are eight to twelve weeks old, they are taken by the older wolves to a remote place, generally protected by thick undergrowth, where they spend the weeks and months that follow. Here adult members of the pack also keep returning after their hunting expeditions, which they undertake in pairs or in small groups, or sometimes alone.

Dave invited me to accompany him on his work. We went to an already known rendezvous, an old clearing in the forest that had become thickly overgrown again, where, upon howling, we were immediately answered by about five cubs and an older animal. I climbed a tree to get a better view, and kept howling in my "European wolf dialect" while the cubs responded in "American." The howling of American wolves is in fact different from that of their European counterparts. I maintained that the howling of European wolves was more protracted and melodious, while that of the American wolves, perhaps because of stronger emphasis on the initial syllables, seemed rather louder. So far as the melodiousness of the howling was concerned, Dave and his colleagues naturally did not agree with me.

So I sat in the tree and howled, while the others recorded the howling of the cubs on tape. The cubs, attracted by my howling, drew nearer and nearer, and eventually five of them—skinny little fellows about four months old—were sitting under my tree, and we went on howling at each other.

In the course of their work the Americans recorded the frequency of response of adult wolves in relation to their distance from their rendezvous and the boundaries of their territory. It turned out that they were particularly apt to respond in border areas. This suggests that howling—like bird songs or the howling concerts of many kinds of monkey—may represent an acoustic demarcation of territory.[17]

In our walks with Anfa at Rickling she sometimes went off on her own. No amount of calling helped in such circumstances, but I soon discovered that howling worked wonders. Anfa would come running back excitedly, and she would jump up at me, wag her tail, and finally raise her head and howl too.

Later I observed similar behavior among pack wolves many hundreds of times. After the long midday rest a wolf would slowly get up, stretch, yawn, and disappear into the undergrowth, sniffing at the ground. A second wolf would look at him, stand up, stretch, yawn, and lie down again. A third would blink in the sunshine while another gnawed at a bone, but most of the wolves lying within an area of about fifty yards would still be asleep. Suddenly the wolf who had disappeared into the undergrowth would begin howling, first quietly and then more loudly, standing on a stone some distance from the pack. The other wolves would quickly get up, stretch, wag their tails, and run toward one another. The younger animals would try to lick older ones in the face, crowd around them, jump up at one another, fall on their backs, and whimper, all very excitedly. The whole pack would form a huddle in which every animal came into direct body contact with every other. Another wolf would raise its head and start howling, others would join in, and soon the whole pack would be howling. In some cases the howl would at first be more of a whine—a not-exactly-pleasing mixture between whimpering and howling, in which the mouth is not as rounded as in a proper howl but is opened wider. It was above all the younger and lower-ranking animals that whined while moving restlessly around one another. But then they would stop, raise their heads, and join in the howling chorus.

Adolph Murie, who was the first to make a systematic study of wolves in a state of freedom—he worked in the Mount McKinley

National Park in Alaska in the early forties—called this pack ceremony the "friendly get-together."[18] His wolves did not always howl
on these occasions, and it was the same with my pack, but generally
howling formed part of it.

What is the function of this friendly get-together accompanied by
howling in chorus? Murie observed it chiefly before the evening
departure for the hunt. In my pack it often also occurred in the
early hours of the evening and early in the morning, as a prelude to
the evening or morning phase of activity, as the case might be. All
suppressed wolves, or animals that had been expelled from or had
left the pack, did not take part.

This restriction to "insiders" suggests that the ceremony reinforces
the cohesion of the pack. The wolves confirm their friendly, cooperative feeling for one another, so to speak. The timing also suggests
that it serves the purpose of synchronizing and coordinating the
phase of activity that follows. The wolves that have just awoken
from sleep are quickly put into a mood that facilitates a joint en-
terprise.

At Rickling I took notes of all the howling choruses for a whole
year. It turned out that in winter wolves howl much more often
than in summer (see figure 17). As a pack keeps more closely
together in winter than in summer—similar observations have been
made of wolves in a state of freedom—this is consistent with the integrating function attributed to the howl. But there is also another
consideration. For several years in the Bavarian Forest I kept a record of which wolf initiated howling (see appendix, table 2). In summer
it was nearly always a member of the pack, while in winter—and
above all in the season of heat from January to March—it was very
noticeably wolves not integrated into the pack that began howling
spontaneously. When these loners howled they always did so a long
way away from the pack, and they directed their howling not at the
pack, but out of the enclosure. This kind of howl is known among
wolves in a state of nature. The Americans sometimes call it "the
loneliness cry," which is certainly not a bad description. It would
seem that the lone wolf is seeking company in this way, looking for
another wolf in the same situation. Lone wolves accordingly do not
react aggressively to strange wolves or strangers to the pack, but are
exceedingly friendly and try to make contact as quickly as possible.

Thus, besides being a means of communication within the pack over large distances and serving an integrating function when the pack howls in chorus, as well as serving to mark off the pack's territory from that of other packs, howling seems to play a part in the formation of new packs. Lone wolves can use it to make contact with one another; they can meet, run together, perhaps mate, and, if they find an unoccupied territory, successfully bring up their cubs.

Tactile Communication

We have already come across many kinds of body contact that have a signaling function—snapping, biting, face licking, or pressing against another animal with the whole body. All these are elements of complex communicative behavior patterns. The two most frequent social behavior patterns are coat and muzzle contacts. Apart from possible olfactory exchanges of information that may take place in these contacts, tactile signals may also be involved. In the course of my walks with a number of free-running wolves, one day I counted the number of such swift direct contacts and was surprised at how frequent they were. On an average there was a direct muzzle-to-muzzle or muzzle-to-coat contact six times per hour per wolf. Once more it was chiefly the leading wolves, the superior adults as well as the cubs, that made contact with one another (see tables 7 and 12). This indicates that this constant reciprocal contact furthers the cohesion of the pack.

Information is also transmitted by means of coat licking. The mother wolf licks her cubs dry after birth, and in the next few weeks she gives preference to the anogenital region and the belly. This massage causes the cubs to urinate and defecate. The products are swallowed by the mother (no doubt to keep the den clean). Later all the members of the pack take part in looking after the cubs. Again it is the region of the belly to which preference is given. The cubs lie motionless on their backs to be licked. Adult wolves also lick each other's coats. In the season of heat the male licks the female's genital region and often also her back hairs before mounting her. Open wounds are licked by other members of the pack. Many interesting observations were made in this connection. It is often males close to each other in the ranking order that lick each other's wounds, some-

76

times for hours on end, and this is frequently done by the wolf that inflicted the wound. I noted that aggressive clashes between wolves were more frequent during the season of heat, and these resulted in minor wounds. But away from the females the males became more peaceable again and licked each other's wounds. Apart from its hygienic function, this behavior pattern seems also to be a signal of appeasement. It would seem to imply that "in spite of all our conflicts of interest we remain friends."

4

The Ranking Order

Behavior in the pack is governed by the wolves' experiences with each other and is manifested in the ranking order. In this chapter I shall therefore deal with the development of hierarchical structures in the pack. These become intelligible when we consider the relations among the cubs of a litter in the course of their development, how they come to terms with older members of the pack at the juvenile stage, and finally how they behave toward each other as adult animals.

A New Litter

Wolves do not reach sexual maturity until the age of two, so no new arrivals were to be expected of Anfa and the others in the spring of 1968. So again I sought cubs to rear myself. This time I was luckier than the year before. I was able to take over all five cubs born to wolves from Finland in Hagenbeck's zoo. I fetched them from Hamburg when they were thirteen days old and looked after them in the house, just as I had done with the older cubs. Once more I wanted to follow their development closely and, as I did not want to keep them perpetually in an enclosure, they would have to be tamed so that it would be possible to take them out on a lead.

I succeeded in this, though the cubs were reared together and Anfa was involved. To Anfa they were her "young," and she soon

78

became an almost complete substitute mother to them. The only thing she could not give them was milk, so we fed them, like the previous year's cubs, with the aid of a syringe and a rubber tube. They became completely tame. This was presumably due to the intensive care my wife and I took of them and our perpetual presence, and also to the fact that Anfa was so tame and showed no fear of us. They learned from this that there was no need to be afraid of us, but they never established such a strong bond to us as Anfa did. Throughout their lives they sought social partners among other wolves, and their attitude to human beings was rather reserved. They always showed great fear of big or noisy persons or those who went about with any kind of implement or tool, particularly if they wore working clothes.

Conditions in our living room soon became chaotic again, and Dagmar reacted accordingly, so I tried putting the cubs in the enclosure with the other wolves during the daytime. However, this did not work. The rather small and by now low-ranking male Anselm reacted very aggressively to their presence. So long as I was in the enclosure he kept his distance or ran away when the cubs approached him effusively. But as soon as I left the enclosure he went for them and bit them hard. They squealed, I shouted at him, and he let them go. This sequence was repeated several times, with the result that I had to keep the cubs out of the enclosure. Grosskopf and Andra, however, were very friendly and solicitous toward the cubs.

I observed similar behavior by low-ranking young wolves toward cubs in later years, though they were never so aggressive as Anselm was. He actually tried to bite them through the fence, so I was forced to strengthen the fence between the wolf enclosure and the part of the garden where I kept the cubs. In spite of this one of them managed to stick his muzzle through in an attempt to make contact with the big wolves, and Anselm bit it so hard that it was broken in several places. We had no alternative but to destroy the little wolf.

Another cub made the same mistake, but withdrew in time to lose only a little bit of his nose. After that we called him Näschen ("Little Nose"). A third cub, Wölfchen, was also bitten by Anselm and lost several teeth; and Mädchen, the only female in the litter, had one of her toes bitten off.

The cubs could not be kept in the house forever, so Anselm had to go. In trying to catch him I made one of the biggest mistakes I have ever made in my work with wolves. We had nothing with which to catch animals in the enclosure, so I had to drug Anselm in order to get at him. We did not yet have a tranquilizer gun at the institute, so the only thing I could do was to give him something with his food. The Kiel veterinarian who worked at the institute knew of no oral drug suitable for dogs (in fact there are no satisfactory drugs for dogs and wolves that can be mixed with their food or water). He therefore suggested two ten-milligram tablets of Valium, which I concealed in a piece of meat. I threw to each of the other three wolves in the enclosure a dead chicken and gave the prepared meat to Anselm, who swallowed it immediately.

I waited an hour, then two, then three, but Anselm was as fresh and cheerful as ever. So I threw him another piece of meat, containing another two Valium tablets, and when Anselm showed no signs of tiring I repeated the process three hours later. By this time it was late afternoon. When I next went to the enclosure he seemed rather sluggish when he got up, but there was still no hope of catching him. I ran after him, but he was much too quick for me. Damn it, I said to myself, six tablets must be having some effect, so I went on with the chase. After about ten minutes he slowly weakened, and in the end I caught him. He allowed himself to be carried to our Volkswagen, helpless and breathing heavily. Dagmar drove, and I stayed with him in case he revived. But he never got up again. He died three days later at Kiel of the consequences of a circulatory collapse.

Cubs and Ranking Order

As happens with all cubs, there were frequent violent squabbles in the first weeks and months among Alexander, Wölfchen, Mädchen, and Näschen. Growling and biting took place even at play, and sometimes small fights broke out about food. These fights were not always between two cubs; two or even three would sometimes attack the fourth. Nevertheless, a few minutes later they might all be huddled together, sleeping peacefully, and by the time the next squabble broke out three new friends might have formed an alliance. No lasting enmities or permanent relations of strength that decided battles in advance could be deduced from these frays. Also sex played no part. Mädchen had to look after herself just as her brothers did, sometimes aggressively, sometimes by appeasingly falling on her back. No permanent attitude could be deduced from the current expressive behavior of two cubs engaged in combat. Their expression always reflected the relations of strength existing at that moment, and in a new situation a few minutes later it could be totally different.

All this is in complete contrast to the aggressive behavior of older wolves. Cubs in their clashes seem to be concerned only with momentary conflicts of interest and not with any question of status. They make no attempt at long-term suppression of their siblings and so—apart of course from satisfying their immediate needs—they have no expansionary tendency aimed at extending their own freedom of action at the expense of others.

I concluded from these observations that there was generally no ranking order among wolf cubs, and in the years that followed I have had no reason to revise this view. It conflicts, however, with other authors' observations both of wolf cubs and of puppies.

Scott and Fuller tested the rank relationships between siblings of a litter of various breeds of dog with the aid of a bone.[1] This was placed between two puppies in a small arena in which they had previously played, and their behavior was observed for ten minutes. It was very rare for siblings to gnaw the bone together. Sometimes they alternated in possession of it, but more frequently fighting broke out, and in some cases one puppy grabbed the bone and did not surrender it for the next ten minutes. A puppy that retained possession of the bone for at least eight minutes was described as dominant. At the end of the period the bone was taken away and given to the other puppy. If the first puppy immediately seized it again it was described as completely dominant; otherwise it was described as incompletely dominant.

At the age of six weeks no dominant relationships developed among the puppies of all the five breeds studied. But at eleven weeks one puppy was completely dominant over the other in nearly 50 percent of all cases. There was little change in this respect until the age of one year, though bigger differences among the breeds became discernible. In the aggressive breeds, fox terriers, basenjies, and shelties, the authors found completely dominant relationships

Fig. 8. Expressive behavior in the wolf. In the background a female is eating in the normal attitude. The ranking order of the three males in the foreground is evident from the attitude of tail, head, and body.

in nearly 50 percent of all cases, while among the more peaceful beagles and cocker spaniels the average was well below 50 percent.

A ranking order in regard to feeding established itself at an early stage among the poodle puppies at Rickling, and it survived until they were adult. Are we to conclude that puppies differ from wolf cubs, which develop no dominant relationships at that stage? I think not. What Scott and Fuller found in their experiment and I observed with poodles was merely dominant relationships in regard to feeding. They found a feeding and not a social ranking order. In order to understand the difference, I must explain what I mean by dominance and ranking order.

A relationship of rank or dominance between two animals depends on each animal's estimate of the strength of the other in relation to its own in a definite situation. Thus it does not necessarily correspond to their real relations of strength and does not necessarily have to be established by direct confrontation. Dominance is revealed in (and thus can be measured by), among other things, the area of individual freedom that an animal has in relation to others.

This area of freedom can manifest itself in access to definite objects such as food or sexual partners, or in freedom of movement in purely social encounters. The greater the difference between the areas of freedom possessed by any two animals, the greater is their difference in rank.

We shall see later that complete dominance, as in the relations between young cubs and adult wolves, for instance, is exceptional. In the great majority of other relationships between two animals the area of freedom of each is restricted to a greater or lesser extent by the other. In many higher developed species, and thus to a special degree in the case of wolves, self-confidence, inhibition, and fear in relations with conspecifics are manifested in body attitude and movement. The relationship in rank between two animals can be recognized by their expressive behavior. We saw in the last chapter that a higher-rank wolf holds its head and tail higher, while the inferior bends its legs and if it feels great insecurity holds its tail between its legs.

The equilibrium between one animal's area of freedom and another's is not very stable, but is subject to frequent shifts as a result of the expansionary tendency of both. But some states of equilibrium are more stable than others. Stable relationships are above all object-related; for the sake of access to a particular object the parties are concerned to maintain or expand their area of freedom, but not to diminish that of others. This applies to competition for food. A cub is interested in filling its belly but, provided it gets enough food for itself, is not interested in keeping another cub away from it.

Relationships in the purely social sphere that do not arise directly out of conflict in connection with access to an object are different in kind. In these the individual's tendency to expand his area of freedom is accompanied by a tendency to try to restrict that of the other party. These relationships are fluid. Obviously the situation so far as the animals' interests are concerned is different here, and we shall in fact discover that to many wolves it is advantageous to suppress others. We shall also see that relations between two wolves can also depend on their relations to a third. Thus the ranking order of all the wolves in a pack is more than the sum of all the relationships between two animals. But first let us return to our subject, cubs and puppies.

According to our definition of rank relationships, an estimate of the assumed strength of an adversary depends on the situation. So Scott and Fuller did not investigate the social ranking order of their puppies, but their feeding ranking order. Cross-connections certainly exist between different ranking orders, as many observations of wolves have shown, but they are not necessarily uniform. There is nothing whatever to prevent a wolf that is inferior to his fellows in social matters from enjoying precedence over them at feeding and maintaining this precedence for considerable periods. Thus Scott and Fuller's findings are comparable only with observations of the feeding ranking order of wolf cubs.

I therefore tried to carry out similar experiments with a bone at Rickling. Unfortunately they failed, as any change from the usual feeding situation had a very disturbing effect on the cubs, and different ones on different cubs. While Alexander hardly minded being carried about and put in the small "arena," Wölfchen invariably crept into a corner, though in normal feeding conditions he had no difficulty in holding his own against his siblings. The experiments were thus discontinued.

But comparison between wolf cubs and poodle puppies fed in comparable conditions showed that the puppies developed a feeding ranking order more quickly than the cubs. I attribute this to two factors. In the first place, differences in body size among puppies were much greater than among cubs, who at first were all roughly the same size. Also female cubs were the same size as the male cubs for the first few months, while among the puppies there were much bigger differences between the sexes. These differences may have existed among the puppies used in Scott and Fuller's experiment. Big differences in body size and strength naturally favor the stabilization of dominant relationships.

In the second place, it is possible that in the course of domestication many elements of social behavior are suppressed in favor of patterns that serve the interests of the individual. The poodle is dependent for its survival not on the survival of other poodles but only on its human keeper, while the wolf is much more dependent on the welfare of the fellow-members of its pack, with whom it must jointly hunt for food. So when food is ample wolves generally eat side by side without conflict, while among poodles the order in which individual animals ate was strictly laid down. First came the highest-ranking male, followed by the second-highest, followed in turn by the highest-ranking female; the smallest puppy came last of all. This arrangement was disturbed only by the very youngest puppies, who enjoyed relative freedom for a short time.

Does domestication lead to selfishness, then? Only apparently, it seems. In the last resort evolution is *always* concerned only with the survival and propagation of the individual's genes. For this purpose the wolf has to come to terms with the members of the pack on whom it, or the survival of its genes, depends. But from the point of view of the poodle's genes, those of other poodles are a matter of indifference, so to speak. Basically they are merely troublesome competitors, and the animals behave accordingly.

So far, so good. But Mike Fox, a pupil of Scott and Fuller, states in his comprehensive book on the behavior of different canids that young wolves establish a social ranking order among themselves. He even claims to be able to predict a wolf's future rank on the basis of physiological data when it is still a young cub.[2]

I hope to be able to show in this and the next chapter that a wolf's eventual rank depends on many different factors and to a considerable extent not least on chance. Presumably some animals have an impulse to climb high in the ranking order that is stronger than that of other, more peaceable, animals. But the extent to which these differences are innate, are based on experience as cubs, or are governed purely by the situation is a question that cannot yet be decided.

But how did Fox's ranking order come about? I can explain it only by the absence of adult wolves. Like Anfa, who also grew up in the absence of older conspecifics, such animals develop much more quickly in many ways. Animals growing up normally are always subject to older animals in the pack, and this presumably has a vital influence on their behavior toward their siblings. They remain cub-like for a longer time and behave accordingly, while cubs that grow up alone have to adopt adult roles at an earlier stage and behave accordingly.

Outings with the Pack

My long walks around the forester's lodge with Anfa and the four cubs were most enjoyable. To the cubs Anfa and I were something in the nature of pack leaders, so as long as I had Anfa under control I was to some extent able to take the cubs where I wanted. Only when they chased a hare or started wildly chasing each other did they sometimes vanish from sight. Here howling helped. But I had to keep Anfa on the lead; otherwise she would dash off with the four cubs behind her. Five free-running wolves would soon have gotten me into a great deal of trouble. Or, instead of Anfa, I could put one of the cubs on the lead. Anfa was always concerned to keep the cubs together, and with one of them on the lead she kept coming back. Also, under usual circumstances single cubs never went off on their own—there had to be at least two of them. They went off on their own only when there was danger or when we got back to the forester's lodge.

Then there was pandemonium. When we crossed the fields toward the house the cubs followed more and more reluctantly. Just before reaching the fence they dashed off in different directions, with me behind them. There was nothing for it but to carry each cub separately into the enclosure, or take it in on the lead. As they bit furiously through any kind of string or leather, I procured some thin steel chains that they could not destroy. Very soon they were much faster than I was, but there was a way of catching them in spite of that. When I chased them I shouted loudly and threw the chains after them, sometimes actually hitting them, whereupon they stopped and waited submissively, lying on their backs.

That, I think, was the only "order" I was ever able to instill in them. All attempts to teach them to "come here," "sit," and so forth, completely failed. But at least my shouting and chasing and their frightened reaction prevented them from running away during all those years.

Throughout the summer these excursions led to no real difficulties. Occasionally pedestrians or unsuspecting mushroom hunters were rather startled, of course, but not more so than the wolves were by them. And in the course of time local sportsmen grew slightly worried. They claimed, for instance, that deer would not cross a wolf trail and that their freedom of movement would thus be severely restricted. After the first snowfall in late autumn I was able to convince them that that was not so. One evening I walked all five wolves on a chain around the whole wood. The next morning we counted the deer and roe tracks that crossed the broad trail of the wolf pack. No fewer tracks were visible than when there was no wolf trail.

Most of the area in which I walked the wolves belonged to the Rickling municipal shoot. I knew the farmers who used it and got on well with them. I think they took pleasure in the wolves too. Only one tenant farmer from Kiel objected.

From his point of view, perhaps he was not completely wrong. In the late autumn the young wolves—they now looked almost fully grown—became more and more independent, and they began running off alone, leaving Anfa and me as well as the other cubs. As long as we kept going in the same direction they stayed together, but when we stopped, or were on our way back to the forester's lodge, their tendency to go off on their own greatly increased. Sometimes I had to spend hours looking for them. When I had enough of that I put all four, or sometimes only two of them, on a long chain and let them go. It wouldn't be long before one of them wanted to go around one side of a tree while the other wanted to go around the other side.

That was not a satisfactory solution, of course. Meanwhile after a long, peaceful summer the cubs were becoming distinctly more short-tempered. By now each had its own individual distance, which meant that another wolf could approach it closely only with friendly or playful intentions; otherwise there would be an immediate aggressive protest.

By "individual distance" ethologists mean the distance between two animals that must be preserved in normal social situations. Among wolves this distance is very small; and, as the social situations in which it may be infringed upon are very frequent, it is also difficult to observe. It is best seen when the animals are asleep. Cubs generally sleep in close contact with one another, while adults seldom lie less than about a yard apart. When wolves are running in the pack it is evident that direct body contact is avoided. If a wolf closely approaches another, its expressive behavior signals a peaceful, or at any rate a nonaggressive, mood. Brief muzzle-to-muzzle

87

contact may take place, for instance, or the muzzle may briefly touch another wolf's coat, but then they part again. Longer contacts are preceded by clear play or submission signals. Aggressive infringement of an animal's individual distance invariably leads to some form of defensive reaction.

Thus aggressive clashes sometimes arose when wolves got entangled in the undergrowth or by a tree. But Dagmar had an idea. If the wolves now had to be taken out on a chain, why should they not be harnessed to a sledge, thus reversing the traditional idea of wolves attacking sledges? I was skeptical, but a saddler at Rickling thought it a wonderful idea and agreed to make the necessary harness. When it was ready of course it had to be tried out.

At first the wolves resented the leather straps around their breast and belly, and tried to slip out of them or bite through them or shake them off. With the first set that was made, which was rather too big, they succeeded. Gradually they grew accustomed to the second set, which was smaller. But putting it on was a complicated business, as it involved not exactly peacefully restricting each wolf's individual distance and freedom of movement. They protested loudly, snarled and bit about them, but not hard. Any tendency in that direction was met immediately by a firm slap from me, with the result that the biting inhibition observed in my other dealings with them was maintained. Also I tried to carry out the whole thing in a relatively playful way. In spite of that there was always a tremendous hubbub until they were all harnessed.

The first attempts to harness them one behind the other to the sledge were also chaotic. I practiced first with Anfa, who very willingly allowed herself to be attached to the draft chains and actually pulled the sledge by herself. But the younger wolves at first resisted frantically. They entangled themselves in the chains and went for each other, obviously holding each other responsible for this restriction of their liberty, and soon the shambles was complete. Then I lengthened the chains so that the wolves were not so close together. I attached Anfa to the draft chains and tied her to a tree, and tied the other end of the chains to a tree, so that they were well stretched. I then attached the four young wolves to them one at a time. I put the pugnacious Näschen behind Anfa, with Mädchen behind him, so that he was separated from his brothers. Next came Wölfchen, with Alexander last of all. Alexander was always the quietest and also the laziest of them, so he acted as a kind of brake-man. Thus the two parallel draft chains running along the outside of the wolves were kept taut and the wolves were separated from each other. Finally the sledge was hitched on behind Alexander. Dagmar took her place on it, and thus served as an additional brake. I led Anfa out of the garden and into the fields, with four unruly wolves pulling the sledge behind me.

The winter of 1968–1969 was unusually cold, and the snow lay for a long time. We practiced nearly every day and eventually reached a stage at which for a few moments it really looked as if proper sledging were taking place. The wolves pulled the sledge with Dagmar as a passenger, and I walked alongside, encouraging them, and we actually had the impression that the wolves were en-joying themselves. But then one or another of them would decide that it had had enough and would lie down, or Anfa would choose a di-rection that inevitably created problems, such as up or down a steep embankment or into the wood.

But the biggest shambles took place on a cold, stormy day in Feb-ruary. We were resting on a track through the wood. The snow was driving across the fields, but we were sheltered behind some fir trees. The wolves were lying peacefully side by side in the snow when a robin landed on Näschen's back. Näschen looked around and the bird flew off, but it settled again right in front of him in the snow. In this cold weather it obviously sought the warming proxim-ity of the wolves. Näschen slowly rose to his feet and made as if to sniff at the bird, which flew off again and settled on Anfa, where-upon Anfa too stood up. The bird flew off again and settled first in the middle of the wolves, then on the back of one or another of them. At first they were quite calm, but they were curious about this crea-ture that kept flying around. They climbed over one another and jumped up when it flew off and tried to sniff at it when it settled near them. As the chains grew more and more tangled, the wolves grew more and more aggressive. Näschen went for Wölfchen, Alex-ander went for Mädchen, and Anfa went for all of them.

It is characteristic of such frays that the wolves do not bite really hard, but they make all the more noise for that. The robin had long since vanished, snow kept dropping from the trees, and the chaos was complete. I did not much like the idea of plunging into the midst of that seething bedlam of angry wolves, but I managed to get hold of part of the draft chain and tie it to a tree. As a result I was slowly able to pull one wolf out by its tail and free it. Then one by one I managed to pull out the others and free them too, until only Näschen, who was still wildly biting about him, was left. I threw my coat over him and forced him to the ground with the weight of my body, and freed him too. Meanwhile Dagmar ran after the freed wolves in the deep snow and put them on the lead, and so we eventually had them all under control again. But that day it was we who dragged the sledge home through the snowstorm.

The wolves, who were now nearly a year old, had grown quite large. The three males weighed nearly 90 pounds; Mädchen, who was by now noticeably smaller than they, was more than 65 pounds. With the beginning of winter they showed a distinct increase in aggressiveness. Some clashes between Alexander and Näschen seemed not just to serve the purpose of maintaining their own area of freedom in a particular situation, but to be preliminary skirmishes in a struggle for the number-two position in the pack behind Grosskopf. In these clashes Alexander was always the challenger; he strutted provocatively past Näschen, holding his head and tail high. Näschen replied by threatening, and Alexander threatened back. Squabbles between the two over food and sometimes starting in play developed into noisy though still harmless biting frays, similar to those that broke out when they were harnessed to the sledge. To a large extent Wölfchen kept out of these squabbles.

In February and March 1969, when Anfa and Andra were two years old and Mädchen just one, the two older females were in heat, but Grosskopf, the only adult male in the pack, was totally uninterested. In later years two-year-old males showed sexual behavior and actually fathered cubs, though sexual behavior appeared in full force only among males aged three or more. But no reaction was discernible in Grosskopf. This may have been connected with the incest barrier that is to be observed among wolves; I shall deal with it later.

Though there was no real season of heat that winter, very interesting behavior developed among the three females.

Female Battles for Rank

At the end of the summer of 1968, when Anfa and Andra were eighteen months and Mädchen six months old, Anfa was obviously socially superior to the other two females. Social ranking order among them was the result of the difference in age. Aggressive clashes were rare and, if they took place at all, were innocuous. The three played with each other a great deal.

With the coming of autumn the two older females grew more and more aggressive to each other. Andra displayed a distinctly expansionary trend in relation to Anfa's dominant position. This first appeared in play, for which reason I did not notice it properly for a time. When Anfa suddenly squealed loudly and threatened Andra, and sometimes snapped at her, I was merely surprised. Andra would then jump away and walk around Anfa with her tail up. This was quite unusual behavior, and I slowly realized that Andra was biting Anfa at play rather harder than usual.

Andra's aggressiveness, first camouflaged by play behavior, assumed more and more manifest forms, and she ended by making it quite obvious—and not only at play—that she no longer accepted Anfa's dominant position. In January and February neither of the two older females was superior to the other. Andra kept strutting around Anfa demonstrating intimidation behavior, but Anfa did not surrender her position. The situation between the two became extremely tense, and no more play behavior was to be observed. Andra also became increasingly aggressive to Mädchen and repressed her by direct attacks, demonstrations, and threats, with the result that Mädchen ended by being severely inhibited in her social activity and hardly played at all, even with her brothers. She still showed distinct submission behavior toward Anfa, but simply kept out of Andra's way.

In March Anfa and Andra were in heat, and Mädchen also had slight vaginal bleeding. Andra's perpetual threatening and intimidating had by now given her a position of slight dominance, though to my knowledge there had been no serious fighting between her and Anfa. She tried to repress all forms of social activity on the part of the other two females. The other two kept apart, no longer played, and were obviously restricted in their freedom of movement. Whenever they tried to make contact with each other or with one of the males, Andra immediately intervened and tried to stop them. Anfa protested loudly against this oppressive behavior, but Mädchen ran away with her tail between her legs. The situation between the three females was extremely tense, but the males ignored it. When we took Anfa and Mädchen, with the latter's three brothers, out of the enclosure for their daily walk, the two females played a great deal with each other and with the three males, but when we put them back in the enclosure the performance between Andra and Anfa started all over again.

Then in May for some reason or other Andra's aggressiveness declined. This was discernible chiefly from the renewal of play activity between Anfa and Mädchen; when Andra now took it into her head to protest against the social activity of the other two, Anfa's protests were distinctly more vigorous. It was interesting to note that the increasing social freedom of the two oppressed females was associated with an increase in aggressive clashes. This was the first sign of the fact that stable rank relationships, however structured, prevent aggressive behavior, while any change in these relationships is accompanied by an escalation in aggressive clashes.

The instability of these relationships lasted into June, but was restricted to the two older females. Mädchen had meanwhile regained her social freedom to a large extent, no longer put her tail between her legs, and played again quite often. Then, on June 29, 1969, the relationship between the three she-wolves suddenly changed. In the morning all three animals played together a great deal in the rain, and this time it was Anfa who kept making playful attacks on Andra. The big battle took place in the afternoon.

I quote from my diary for that day:

4:30 P.M. Put pail with food outside garden enclosure. Wolves very excited, minor biting frays, snarling, spitting, etc.

4:35. Feed poodles in garden enclosure. Aggressiveness among wolves very great.

4:40. Sudden big battle between Anfa and Andra, Anfa the aggressor. Mädchen suddenly joined in against Andra. Uninhibited biting followed by violent head-shaking, also full use made of body weight. This was fighting in earnest. Furious attacks of the other two gave them the upper hand, and Andra retreated defensively into a corner of the enclosure. Other two went on attacking. Total committal. Tried to part them, but impossible. The males stood around the females, but interfered only marginally by occasionally snapping at a passing female. Poodles barked like mad. Took food into the enclosure, which diverted the males. But the three females were not to be parted. Much blood flowing. Andra hardly defending herself.

4:50. At last I managed to part them. I tied Anfa to the fence. She showed no aggressiveness toward me or the other animals. On the contrary, she wagged her tail, licked my face, etc. Then she saw Andra at the back of the enclosure, and her back hair and tail rose again. She managed to free herself and dashed at Andra. But Andra now defended herself more vigorously in her corner. She snarled loudly and directed powerful snapping movements at Anfa, accompanied by chattering of the teeth. Anfa succeeded several times in breaking through her defense and using her body to pin her down and bite her flanks and hindquarters. Mädchen helped her. It's a mystery to me how the she-wolves managed always to bite the right leg and right throat in the confusion.

5:30. The casualty list: Andra has wounds all over her body—her back, sides, and legs are full of wounds. Anfa has deep wounds on the head, tail, and throat. Her left foreleg is lame and her left upper lip is badly swollen. Mädchen has slighter wounds on her head and muzzle. Anfa and Mädchen spent a long time displaying intimidation behavior. Their back hairs stood up. Andra remained in her extreme defensive attitude.

During the next few days Andra was attacked again and again by the other two females. They would confront her from different directions, and when she made defensive advances against one, the other would attack her from the rear and bite her hard. She would then go for this new assailant while the other again attacked her in the rear, and so it went on. The result was that the whole hind part of her body became an open wound. But as she vigorously defended herself totally uninhibited fighting was not resumed. Males occasionally joined in these attacks on her, but in a more playful manner. The result was that Andra became the pack's scapegoat, totally without social rights. She kept away from all the other wolves in the pack, but knew perfectly well which animals were dangerous to her and which were not. Thus she allowed the males to approach quite close before she bared her teeth or advanced on them making snapping movements, but she threatened Anfa and Mädchen

93

vigorously from a distance. Only Grosskopf, her brother, kept out of the whole business.

With this change in the ranking order the behavior of Anfa and Mädchen suddenly altered. Anfa again became the great initiator of play in the pack and, though she was hampered for a long time by her wounds, she was very wild and relaxed at play. Mädchen also joined in very vigorously and, just as the two older females had done, she began to show the first expansionary tendencies directed against Anfa at play. She sometimes bit rather harder, and play between the two females became more and more aggressive.

Extract from my diary for July 12:

> During afternoon walk Mädchen several times made unexpected attacks on Anfa. Anfa protested vigorously, but Mädchen merely jumped away and attacked again from behind. Only when I put Mädchen on the chain and let Anfa run free did the aggressiveness stop.
>
> 8:35 P.M. Situation between Anfa and Mädchen explosive the whole evening. I watched from window. Mädchen suddenly ran at Anfa and this time fixed her teeth in the hair at the back of her neck and shook. Anfa vigorously defended herself, and uninhibited fight ensued. I ran into the enclosure shouting, but fight already over. Both badly wounded. Sand in enclosure red with blood. Both lay down, staring at each other, and licked their wounds.
>
> July 13, 6:30 A.M. Slept in the enclosure and saw no more fighting between Mädchen and Anfa. At first light Mädchen again began circling Anfa, but still kept her distance. Anfa protested loudly, but obviously had strong inhibitions about attacking Mädchen. Mädchen had her tail up and walked with springy step while Anfa moved around in a bowed attitude with her tail tending to be between her legs. Neither took any more notice of Andra.

In the next few days the situation between Anfa and Mädchen was very fluid. Neither played; each was concerned solely with keeping an eye on the other, circling around her, threatening and intimidating. Anfa in particular was hampered in her movements by her leg wounds.

Extract from my diary of August 21:

5:30 P.M. Mädchen as usual directed intimidation behavior at Anfa. Anfa attacked and directed powerful snapping movements at Mädchen's throat. Mädchen averted her head, and for quite a time the two stood side by side, threatening loudly. Anfa again snapped at Mädchen's throat; Mädchen then leaped up and turned her head toward Anfa. A serious battle suddenly developed again. Andra appeared from behind and joined Anfa's attack on Mädchen. The fight lasted for about ten minutes and was completely silent, as usual. Mädchen defended herself vigorously, but could not hold off the violent attacks of the two others and fled in a defensive attitude. Anfa chased her, now with her tail up and with springy step. Her back hairs and the hairs on the back of her neck were standing up. Mädchen defended herself in a corner.

In the days and weeks that followed, Anfa, now restored to her position as alpha female, kept making vigorous repressive attacks on Mädchen and occasional less vigorous ones on Andra. Mädchen was again at the bottom of the ranking order. On August 22, the day after the loss of her alpha position, Mädchen tried a single-handed attack on Andra, but was at once driven into a corner by Anfa. Andra gradually became socially freer and occasionally took part in play. She showed intensive submissive behavior toward Anfa, who left her more or less in peace.

After this long phase of struggle for rank the situation among the females in the pack gradually quieted down. Repression similar to that which took place in the winter did not recur. When the ranking order was finally settled and generally accepted, aggressive clashes grew rarer and peace returned to the pack.

Anfa's and Andra's increasing aggressiveness in the autumn of 1968 was connected with their attainment of sexual maturity and reached a temporary peak at the season of heat in late winter. Mädchen's attempt to attain the alpha position was made at a younger age, however. Presumably she was encouraged to make her attempt by the aggressiveness between the two older females; she took advantage of Anfa's weakness after her fight with Andra and succeeded in attaining the top position, though only briefly. It is interesting to note that at the age of one year, that is, before attaining sexual maturity, she was aware of the sex of the other wolves in the pack and was also obviously fully aware of her own.

95

Attacks on Human Beings

Among the untamed wolves the increase in aggressiveness that accompanied the attainment of sexual maturity led only to intraspecific clashes. Andra and Grosskopf were no more aggressive to or less shy of human beings than they were before. But with wolves that were socialized in relation to human beings and thus regarded them as social partners, the situation was different—and this, unfortunately, was very unpleasant and also dangerous. Once more it was Anfa, the animal with the closest relations with human beings, who stood out in this respect.

I first noticed the slow change in her attitude in the summer of 1968, when she was just over a year old. An elderly, slightly built and rather short gentleman, a pensioner from Rickling, often used to come to see us. Sometimes he spent hours outside the enclosure watching the wolves. For a long time Anfa greeted him effusively, as she did everyone else, but then one day I saw her direct a furious attack at the man on the other side of the wire fence; she jumped at it and locked her teeth on it. Her behavior was so unusual that I thought he must have annoyed her in some way, perhaps thrown stones at her or hit her with a stick, but this suspicion turned out to be completely unjustified.

The second victim of Anfa's aggressiveness was our good friend Jasper, a Rickling doctor, who looked after the animals whenever Dagmar and I went away for a few days. Anfa was his great favorite, and the friendship seemed to be mutual. But one day in the winter of 1969 when he was taking food into the enclosure, as he had often done before, Anfa came running excitedly toward him and greeted him in her usual effusive manner. She kept running toward him, wagging her tail, with bent legs and her ears laid back, jumping up at him and licking him in the face, then running away and starting all over again, but then suddenly, without any warning, she bit him. It was not a hard bite, it was really only a snap, but it was directed at a very sensitive spot, the penis. That was the end of a friendship.

Not long afterward another friend, Peter, a photographer for *Stern* magazine, had a similar experience. We had been out for a long walk with the wolves, who fully accepted him. He had been able to approach them, take them on the lead, play with them, and again it was of course Anfa that was the favorite. We returned to the forester's lodge in the late afternoon and took the wolves into the enclosure. Peter took a few more photos, and we left the enclosure. Then, without my noticing it, he went back into the enclosure alone. All I heard was a suppressed cry. Anfa had dashed at him and, again without the slightest warning, had snapped at him, as in Jasper's case, not very hard, but at the same part of the body.

Peter was quite pale, but a little while later was able to laugh at the incident. His colleagues at Hamburg also laughed a great deal, and nowadays, when I meet a journalist or photographer from *Stern*, they still talk about Peter and the wolf. The fact that his wife became pregnant a year later was described as a miracle.

Well, it was not really a laughing matter, even though no one suffered anything more serious than a fright. Anfa developed increasing aggression against some people while she went on greeting others with her usual effusive friendliness. It was chiefly smaller, slightly built, quiet, elderly men whom she attacked in this way, at first generally only against the fence inside the enclosure. After this no one except me went into the enclosure for her. Outside it she continued to be as peaceable as usual until one day she attacked again. This time the victim was Arndt, a friend and colleague from the institute.

Several of us had wanted to take the wolves for a walk. Anfa had already made a furious attack on Arndt behind the fence, and so I took her on the chain and tied her to a tree outside the enclosure while I let the other four animals out. Suddenly she struggled free, dashed at Arndt, and bit him in the leg. Arndt stood still, as if frozen, and made no sound. I hurried to his assistance and was able to open Anfa's mouth and release him. The wound was not serious; there were only two small, deep toothmarks that hardly bled. We took Arndt to a doctor immediately, who gave him a tetanus injection. The wound did not have to be sewn or even bandaged. We seemed to have gotten off relatively lightly again.

We thought so until Arndt developed a high fever three days later. He took a taxi to the university hospital and mentioned casually at the reception desk that a few days earlier he had been bitten by a wolf. The result was general consternation. The head of the hospital took him into his office and got in touch with Professor Herre, the head of our department, who in turn telephoned me and told me furiously that Arndt was in a serious condition and it was necessary to consider the worst.

This was a blow, and I was shattered. But Dagmar was the first to point out that there was something about all this that was not quite right. We drove over to see Jasper, who, as I mentioned, was a doctor at Rickling. He too thought the story inexplicable and telephoned Kiel, where a colleague of his student days was senior registrar at the university hospital. He had examined Arndt himself and thought that his high temperature probably had nothing whatever to do with the bite. His chief, however, had spoken of a possible incompatibility reaction. He did not know what was meant by this, but nevertheless the excitement was still very great.

Three days later Arndt was released from hospital; he had had tonsilitis; there had been much ado about relatively little. If Arndt had mentioned that he had been bitten by a dog, nobody at the hospital would have connected it with his fever. But a wolf! Again this irrationality. It was a lesson to us all. But it was obvious to me that Anfa could no longer be allowed to run free.

After two and a half years my work with the wolves and poodles came to an end. I had begun evaluating the results in the summer of 1969, and the first pages of my thesis had been written. We found it hard to give up Rickling and our life with the wolves. But as the forest administration needed our house for a new forester we had to go, and the freedom of the wolves came to an end.

We left in the autumn of 1969. First the three older wolves and later the four younger ones too were sent to the institute zoo at Kiel (this time the untamed wolves were immobilized with the aid of a tranquilizer gun). The new enclosures were very small, so we separated the animals. Anfa and Grosskopf were put in one enclosure, and Alexander, Näschen, Wölfchen, and Mädchen in another. Andra was destined henceforward to "produce" puwos and was put in an enclosure with a male poodle. I was able to give away most of the other puwos. I no longer remember how many I was able to save from dissection in the institute in this way. I was told again and again how pleased the owners of these strange, woolly, long-tailed standard poodles were.

When all the enclosures were empty Dagmar and I went to Sylt, where I spent several months writing my thesis undisturbed. During this period we were able to observe the beginnings of a very interesting change in the ranking order of the males, which I shall now describe.

Male Struggles for Supremacy

So long as Grosskopf was in the pack he was the unquestioned alpha male. There was no discernible difference in rank among Alexander, Näschen, and Wölfchen. Grosskopf played with all three and did not attempt any kind of repression. Only to Alexander, the strongest of the three brothers, did he sometimes demonstrate his superiority by mild intimidation behavior, jumping at him and pressing him down with his body. This was presumably connected with the fact that Alexander did not accept Grosskopf's alpha position as fully as Wölfchen and Näschen did, but manifested a slight upward expansionary trend, again particularly at play. But on the whole the male ranking order was stable until they were parted.

When Grosskopf was removed from the pack at the end of October, aggressive clashes between the three younger males immediately increased, as if they had suddenly shaken off an inhibition. They threatened and directed intimidation behavior at each other, and sometimes there were biting frays. But respect for the other fellow was still so great that really hard biting was not observed. Näschen was by far the most aggressive, but was not able to secure the alpha position. The aggressiveness slowly subsided again.

When they were moved to Kiel in December 1969 the clashes continued. As before, Näschen was the more active and aggressive, but his attacks on Alexander gradually ceased and he attacked Wölfchen only. Alexander also concentrated his attacks chiefly on Näschen; he grew stronger and stronger, and on January 23 there was a battle royal. Wölfchen immediately joined in on Alexander's side. All three demonstrated biting and shaking, and they bit silently and uninhibitedly but, though the fighting was in earnest, it was not nearly as ferocious as it had been between the females. After a few minutes Näschen was beaten. He was not badly wounded and was able to fight off further attacks, but he had lost the alpha position that had never been securely his. The new alpha male was Alexander.

In the period that followed the male social ranking order was very stable. Aggressive clashes were rare and harmless, but Alexander grew more and more aggressive toward me. I used to drive to Kiel from Sylt once a week to have a look at the animals and clean out the enclosures. At first I did not notice the change in Alexander, but one day when I entered the enclosure he suddenly jumped up at me and put both paws on my shoulders. He was so big that he looked down at me, baring his teeth. Whenever I moved he snarled more loudly, his big white teeth came alarmingly closer, and I did not feel at all comfortable. I tried to calm him, and spoke to him gently, saying: "Alexander, Alexander, be quiet, be quiet," but it made no difference. He stayed there and went on snarling. Meanwhile my institute colleagues had noticed what was happening and gathered at the windows to watch. I did not know how to extricate myself honorably from the situation, so I went on talking to Alexander. Whenever I made the slightest movement he snarled more loudly and bared his teeth more threateningly. Probably he was just as frightened as I was. Any sudden or incautious movement might have made him attack, and I would have been no match for him. So I had no alternative but to stick it out and go on talking to him. Gradually the growling grew more gentle and his face friendlier. I went on talking, and at last—probably to the disappointment of some of my colleagues, who would have liked to have seen more action—he removed his paws from my shoulders and walked away, snarling, to the nearest bush, where he lifted a leg and urinated. To avoid completely losing face, I did the same. Then I strutted proudly around the enclosure, walked slowly to the door, and left.

When I went to Kiel again a week later I cautiously took a shovel with me into the enclosure, and this time Alexander seemed to have greater respect for me. On each of my visits after our move to Sylt I had taken the wolves for walks on a lead in the university grounds, but with Alexander this was no longer possible. He still let me put him on the chain and take him out of the enclosure, outside which his aggressiveness toward me ceased to a large extent, but he was so excited, insisting on urinating on every tree and scratching at the ground threateningly with his back hairs standing on end, that taking him out ceased to be a pleasure. He also threatened strangers, and when a dog appeared it was hard to hold him on the chain. Therefore I preferred to leave him in the enclosure.

A few weeks later a critical situation arose with another wolf, Anfa. On my first visits from Sylt she still greeted me effusively and would not leave me. But on a visit in February I noticed even before entering the enclosure that her attitude toward me had changed in some way. She wagged her tail and whimpered excitedly, but at the same time she gently bit the fence, so I thought it would be better to put her in the neighboring stable while I cleaned out the enclosure. I lured her into it and shut the door to the enclosure from the outside. I watched her in the stable through a small square hatch about six feet up. She recognized me and put her forelegs up against the door and growled gently. I went out and walked down a passage and entered the enclosure from an outside door. I had just begun cleaning it when loud noises broke out in the stable. Damn it, I said to myself, the hatch must be open, and perhaps she's trying to get out. I dashed back—and Anfa came charging at me. She leaped at me with full fury. I managed to get hold of her by both sides of the throat and lift her so that her feet were off the ground, and I carried her—where I got the strength from I don't know—to the door of the enclosure. I kicked it open and threw her inside. She twisted and turned while still in the air and hardly had she landed when she leaped at me again. I was able to slam the door just in time and she jumped against the grill. She was crazed with excitement and she bit the fence wire so furiously that her teeth bled.

I was glad to be outside. After that her aggressiveness toward me never subsided, and I never again went into her enclosure. Six months later she and Grosskopf were sent to the Neumünster zoo, where Dagmar and I went to see them several times. On one occasion nearly two years had passed since our last visit, but Anfa recognized us immediately. She made a furious attack on me on the other side of the fence, then rushed toward Dagmar in friendly, submissive fashion, then turned and dashed furiously toward me again, then again turned toward Dagmar and was the most peaceful wolf imaginable; and all this within seconds. I have never seen such swift and total reversal of the expressive structures in any other wolf.

Why did Anfa begin suddenly to "hate" me after such a long and affectionate friendship? Alexander's aggression toward me was un-

101

derstandable. As the new alpha male he was concerned to assert his position of dominance in relation to me too. But in Anfa's case, I believe, the causes lie elsewhere. Her behavior could be described only as neurotic. Perhaps the whole thing was connected with the history of her cubhood. She was reared by human beings, with whom she established powerful bonds, and then had to spend most of her life parted from her favorite social partners.

To anticipate misunderstandings, neither Anfa's nor Alexander's was typical wolf behavior. Both were tamed animals that behaved toward human beings as they would toward wolves, and that behavior includes aggression. To wolves who grow up in freedom human beings are enemies and not social partners.

I could tell many stories of experiences that others have had with tame wolves. Nearly all resemble those we had with Anfa and Alexander. Cubs, when tamed, were exceptionally friendly at first and gave their keepers a great deal of pleasure, though they were always timid with strangers and therefore difficult to keep. But difficulties always arose when they reached sexual maturity; at that time they became aggressive and dangerous. So anyone who is toying with the idea of rearing a wolf as a pet is forewarned.

But let us return to the clashes among our male wolves. The social ranking order established in the winter, with Alexander in the first position and Näschen and Wölfchen joint second, did not remain stable for long. Wölfchen's "long march upward" began in February. Though he had played only a subsidiary role in earlier clashes, he started slowly growing aggressive, first toward Näschen. Their clashes grew more frequent and vigorous. On March 23 there was a short, violent fight between them that Wölfchen lost. Alexander was shut up in the stable at the time and could not intervene. Näschen enjoyed a slight superiority over Wölfchen for a few days, but Alexander's support of Wölfchen soon changed this. Wölfchen fought his way up at first only against his closest rival, Näschen, and ended by being clearly superior to him, and Alexander's position remained unchallenged throughout the summer.

Then Wölfchen began to show the first signs of an expansionary trend against Alexander, as usual at first only at play. But aggressive clashes quickly increased in frequency and intensity, while friendly, playful behavior grew rarer. The initiative mostly came from Wölfchen, who permanently kept close to Alexander and attacked him at every opportunity with his tail down and bent legs. Alexander confined himself almost exclusively to intimidation behavior and did not attack Wölfchen directly.

The decisive battle took place on October 1. Unfortunately I did not see it, but the animal keeper, Herr Zobel, a good observer, reported that Wölfchen made a sudden vigorous attack on Alexander from the rear, fixed his teeth in him, and shook violently. Näschen joined in against Wölfchen but was rather marginally involved. The battle lasted for about fifteen minutes and seems to have been very hard fought. Herr Zobel failed to part the animals, though he used a powerful jet of water from a hose of which the wolves were generally afraid. In the course of the battle Alexander was severely wounded in several parts of the body. He withdrew to the stable, where he had to go on defending himself for several hours.

In my experience that was the only serious fight in which a single animal succeeded in asserting itself against two opponents. Näschen's intervention was presumably not very vigorous.

In the next few days Wölfchen, now the new alpha male, tried to attack the wounded Alexander in the stable. Alexander remained there and was not seen again in the enclosure until three weeks later.

Relations between Wölfchen and Näschen were also marked by frequent aggressive clashes. Again it was the inferior, that is, Näschen, who played the more active role. He approached Wölfchen, snarling loudly and baring his teeth, but Wölfchen generally merely averted his head in the intimidation attitude and thus frustrated his attacks. But if Näschen was inattentive for a moment Wölfchen would vigorously attack him from the rear and, to judge from Näschen's yelps and violent reactions, bite him very hard.

Wölfchen seemed to succeed in confirming his alpha position by these "underhanded" attacks. In the later part of the autumn the relationship between the three males was stable to a large extent. As Wölfchen's attacks declined in vigor the two subdominant males reacted with submission behavior instead of flight or protest. Soon all three were playing together again.

Interestingly enough, there was no difference in rank between Näschen and Alexander. After losing his supremacy Alexander did not become the general scapegoat, which is the usual fate of deposed alpha animals. On the contrary, Näschen seemed very concerned with his wounds. He licked them and often lay beside him in the stable. If Wölfchen tried to attack him there Näschen promptly went to his assistance and attacked Wölfchen in protest. The relationship between the two lower-rank males was just like that among the three brothers when Grosskopf was still the alpha animal: There was little aggressiveness, individual distance was small, and there was a great deal of play and friendly behavior.

The changes in Wölfchen's and Alexander's behavior when the struggle for power was over were interesting. Immediately after the fight Wölfchen strutted around the enclosure in the attitude of an alpha animal, and outside it he also behaved exactly as Alexander had done previously. He kept his tail up and urinated at every corner, and on the chain he was very restless and kept whimpering. Inside the enclosure he showed the first signs of intimidation behavior toward me, first in play, later as soon as I walked in.

From the day on which he lost his alpha position the previously so aggressive Alexander was the "nicest" wolf imaginable. He walked quietly on the chain and submissively greeted every stranger with an effusiveness generally to be observed only in young wolves.

First Model of the Social Ranking Order

So far we have been able to observe only how the social ranking order develops among young animals, and this in a pack whose numbers have not been increased by the birth of its own cubs. All the same, we are now in a position to distinguish some essential facts about the system.

Among wolves there are rank relationships connected with objects, such as food, for instance, and others not directly connected to any object but arising out of social life. Clashes for the purpose of bringing about changes in social rank take place only between wolves of the same sex. Thus there are two separate ranking orders in the pack, one male and the other female. Younger wolves are aware of the sex of other members of the pack and of their own by the age of one at the latest.

These clashes, particularly when the more keenly contested positions among the older wolves are at stake, are not just a "private affair" between two animals; other members of the pack, especially those of the same sex, take part with greater or lesser vigor. Thus every change in rank between two animals, whether the inferior shows an expansionary trend upward or the superior exercises pressure downward with greater or lesser intensity, leads to an increase in aggressive behavior, not only between those two animals, but also between other members of the pack. Stable rank relations seem to have a curbing effect on the frequency of aggressive behavior.

Social relations between animals of the same sex are presumably also dependent on internal hormonal factors, for in winter, particularly in the mating period, the top animal seems to have an increased tendency to repress inferiors. This was especially evident among the females.

5

Development
of the Ranking Order

After I finished my thesis at Kiel in the autumn of 1970 the question arose of how to continue the work. Many questions about the social behavior of wolves were still unanswered, and because of my friendly relationship with Professor Herre I would have been very happy to have remained at the institute at Kiel. On the other hand, I had an offer from Konrad Lorenz and Paul Leyhausen to continue the work at the Max Planck Institute at Seewiesen. However, because of the many ducks and geese at Seewiesen an enclosure could not be built there. But the Bavarian state forest administration offered to build a big new enclosure for studying wolves near Waldhäuser in the newly established National Park in the Bavarian Forest.

That decided the question, for it meant a unique opportunity to observe wolves, if not in complete freedom, in much greater freedom than in the small enclosures at Rickling. In this chapter I shall describe how a new pack was developed, starting with the four wolves from Kiel, how wolves were integrated into the pack while others were expelled from it or left it voluntarily, and how the two ranking orders all the way up to the top slowly changed. From these observations a general model of the social ranking order of wolves will emerge. But before coming to that there were some interesting marginal events.

In the Bavarian Forest

In February 1971 we hired a truck and loaded it with our few sticks of furniture as well as four boxes with a wolf in each. The wolves were Alexander, Näschen, Wölfchen, and Mädchen. Our animal keeper at Kiel did a good job of making the boxes—particularly in the case of Näschen, who immediately tried furiously to smash his from the inside. But it survived until we got to Waldhäuser, our new home in the National Park in the Bavarian Forest.

Waldhäuser is a high-lying island of cleared forest on the slopes of the mountains between Bavaria and Czechoslovakia. It lay on the celebrated Guldene Steig, an old salt and trade route into Bohemia by way of Passau and Grafenau, and it was the last place at which oxen and horses could be changed before the long climb and the crossing of the Bohemian Forest. Nowadays villagers work chiefly at forestry and the tourist trade. We moved into an empty house belonging to the frontier police around which the national park administration had already built a temporary enclosure for the wolves. It was snowing on our arrival and did not stop for the next few days. The wolves cautiously took possession of their new territory—the feeling of the bottomless quantities of snow into which their feet sank was new to them, and they mistrusted it.

During the previous winter at Kiel none of the three males had taken any interest in Mädchen when she was in heat, but this winter, a few days after our arrival at Waldhäuser, Alexander and Näschen, and eventually Wölfchen too, tried to mount her. Mädchen rejected their advances, but when we met a dog outside the enclosure at the beginning of April she stopped when it mounted her. We managed to separate them just in time. The incest ban seemed to be entirely on the female side, but more about that later. For the time being I was faced with the fact that in the spring of 1971 once more no cubs were to be expected.

So again I had to look elsewhere. We obtained a healthy cub from the Innsbruck zoo that we called Psenner, after the head of the zoo. As usual, he was bottle-fed. No cubs of assured Eurasian origin were born in any of the zoos known to me that spring. As we urgently needed more cubs for our work, I was delighted when Professor Herre offered me six four- and six-week-old cubs born in

107

freedom in Afghanistan that he had just received from Kabul. One of them, a male, was only about half the size of his siblings. He reacted with vigorous defensive threats to any approach, whether by us or by adult wolves or even by the other cubs, opening his mouth in completely stereotyped fashion, just like a jackal. The defense mimicry varying in accordance with the intensity of the threat that is so typical of wolves was completely lacking. His retarded physical development and his constant fear seemed to reduce his behavior to the most elementary—an interesting case of phylogenetic retardation. He soon died of general debility in spite of all our efforts.

The other cubs, of whom Näschen in particular took great care, developed well. They were all named after places in the neighborhood. We called the three older ones St. Oswald, Schönbrunn, and Finsterau and the two younger ones Rachel and Lusen. (The interested reader can look up these and other wolves in table 3 in the appendix.)

A new fifteen-acre enclosure for the wolves was built during the summer. In its center was an elevated platform reached by a path from which visitors to the National Park could watch the wolves. This platform turned out to be invaluable for my work, because from it nearly the whole of the enclosure could be surveyed with field glasses. I spent many thousands of hours watching the wolves from that vantage point in the morning and the evening. I generally limited myself to those times, because during the daytime the platform was often crowded with visitors, and the early morning and the evening are the wolves' most active periods.

In August 1971, when the enclosure was finished, we celebrated the event by giving a party for friends and acquaintances, as well as all the men who had taken part in the construction. We set the wolves free in their new home, and I think many of the guests were surprised at not being eaten alive immediately. While the wolves explored their new territory we sat around a blazing fire, the beer flowed, woodmen sang to the accompaniment of a concertina or discussed ranking orders among wolves and men. Every now and then a wolf or two trotted past, and children, no longer so anxiously watched by their mamas, ran after them. It was a very good party, I think.

Runaway Wolf

A few days later Näschen ran away. After our move to the Bavarian Forest I took the wolves out into the National Park practically every day, and so it was on September 1, 1971. After a long climb I stopped for a rest in a clearing and tied the older wolves to a tree but left little Psenner free and, as Näschen always looked after him, I let him run about freely too. The two played together while I picked bilberries. After a time we went on, and I noticed too late that Näschen was missing. I hurried back but could find no trace of him and got no answer to my calling or to my and the cubs' joint howling.

Uneasily I went back to the enclosure with the other wolves, where I waited all night, but Näschen failed to appear. I spent days looking for him in the area in which he had disappeared, and discovered that a forester had seen him from a platform in the evening not far from where he had run away. Some tracks enabled me to reconstruct his first hours of freedom. He had apparently disturbed a deer and chased it. After losing it he had wandered about for a time and then come slowly back in the direction of the enclosure. I went back to the enclosure, but too late. Some tourists told me that a wolf had trotted past them, but they had no idea where he was now. So it went on in the days that followed. When I was searching for him in the country he was near the enclosure, and when I waited near the enclosure he was seen near the village down below.

He was used to human beings, but in spite of that and in the course of a very few days he grew shyer and shyer, and was seen more and more rarely. Some woodmen who knew him from their work on the enclosure told me they had seen him three days after his disappearance; he had emerged from the wood about 150 yards below where they were working. They had stood quite still, but he had spotted them and promptly disappeared into the undergrowth in a crouching attitude.

Näschen's disappearance could not be kept from the press, of course. Soon after our move to the Bavarian Forest the *Bild am Sonntag* had published a spine-chilling story about "the village that was living in terror of wolves," meaning Waldhäuser. I had the impression that it was the handiwork of the same man in Hamburg

109

who had sensationalized the story of the cub Anfa four years earlier. But this time, instead of mothers hurriedly taking their carriages indoors, it was anxious farmers driving their cattle into their stalls. And, as on the previous occasion, the journalist who had called on us in Waldhäuser swore he had written an entirely different story. So I feared the worst. The inhabitants of the Bavarian Forest were by no means hostile to the wolves; on the contrary, in fact. But if the tourist trade suffered as a result of sensational stories in the press, the mood might quickly change.

So I told the journalist how harmless Näschen was and why, assured him that the local population was actively helping in the search, and finally appealed to him not to make sensational exaggerations. The consequences were surprising. This time the usual wolf stereotype was turned on its head. The Munich *Bild*, for instance, published a heartrending story about poor little Näschen wandering forlorn and hungry in the forest, unable to find its way home, while its master frantically searched for it, helped by all the good people of the neighborhood. Reports in other newspapers were similar in tone, though they did not go quite so far as that.

No doubt as a consequence of this general goodwill, the rural district administrative office at nearby Grafenau issued an order that the animal must not be shot. But when Näschen failed to return after three weeks all frontier police stations, customs and forestry service officers, and tenants were instructed by the administrative officer to shoot it at sight. His pretext was that he had shot six wolves in Russia and knew how dangerous they were.

The consequence was a storm of protest. Näschen became the symbol of all misunderstood and persecuted creatures. Expressions of support for me in what was considered to be my just struggle poured in from everywhere. Nevertheless, I appreciated the administrative officer's point of view. If anything had happened, he would have been held partly responsible. I knew that Näschen was harmless, but how was he to know that? All the same, I was very glad when many sportsmen telephoned and assured me they would not shoot. The head of one police station told me that of course he had to pass on the order to his men, but he had authorized them to shoot only with their rifles, which they were not allowed to take on patrol.

In this atmosphere of universal goodwill Näschen was soon sighted all over Bavaria, and right up into north Germany. A doctor's wife wrote from the Eifel that she was sure it was in her area, and another woman telephoned from Upper Bavaria to say that it howled every night outside her window. When I asked her how she knew it was a wolf's howl she replied: "It sounds so dreadful." What else could it have been? Holiday-makers at Waldhäuser daily reported "quite positive" sightings, and a whole busload had seen a wolf chasing chickens in a farmyard. A talk with the driver revealed that an animal, probably a fox or a dog, had run across a field in the direction of a wood, causing a lot of pigeons to take to the air.

Even some sportsmen allowed themselves to be deceived. Five weeks after Näschen's disappearance a game tenant telephoned from his village in the neighborhood to tell me that one of his men, who had seen wolves in the Carpathians, had seen the wolf several times with 100 percent certainty, the last time only a few minutes previously.

It struck me as rather strange that Näschen, who had hitherto apparently remained in the dense forest that ran along the crest of the mountain range that marked the border, should suddenly have moved into an inhabited area, and in particular into open country such as that around this village. Nevertheless, I went there immediately. In the marketplace I met the game tenant, who was as skeptical as I was, a number of villagers, and some excited sportsmen. We spent a long time searching unsuccessfully. I was just about to leave when a message arrived; this time the wolf had been seen by peasants in a field. Several carloads of us hurried to the spot. The peasants called us over and pointed in the direction of a small hill. We hurried up it, and then heard excited cries of "The wolf, the wolf" from below. So we hurried down again and surrounded a thicket into which the wolf was said to have disappeared. I slowly made my way into it and drove out a small, shaggy dog that had run away from somewhere and now made off, trembling with fear, with its tail between its legs.

I relate all this, not to pour ridicule on all these good people, but to show how easy it is to make mistakes in an unfamiliar environment, which is what nature is to most of us. Such mistakes occur when reality is overlaid by one's expectations. If a wolf is said to be

111

in the neighborhood, a noise, a shadow, a dog, or a fox that in normal circumstances everyone would immediately recognize as such is promptly and with total certainty transformed into a wolf.

In other situations in which such highly charged expectations were absent it was the other way about, and wolves were not recognized as such, as, for instance, on an occasion when I took them on a chain through the pedestrian zone in the center of Kiel. Children are not so easily deceived by generally received ideas. We had an excellent example of this once in the Neumünster zoo, where we took the one-year-old Anfa to see her parents. While we were standing in front of the wolf enclosure in which Anfa's parents were kept, a girl of about ten pointed out to her mother that the animal on the lead was a wolf too. The woman replied indignantly that it was an Alsatian. "No," the little girl said, "it's a wolf, I can see it's a wolf." There were a lot of people around the enclosure, and the woman felt ashamed of her stupid daughter, who kept insisting that it was a wolf, and she dragged her away. I told her the girl was perfectly right; it really was a wolf. She turned and looked at me wide-eyed and with flushing cheeks, and the girl was delighted. Then the woman took her away, and the other onlookers made off pretty quickly too. But children quickly gathered around, and all of them wanted to stroke Anfa, who incidentally took not the slightest interest in her parents.

However, in spite of everything there were some reports of sightings in the Bavarian Forest that seemed reliable; these came chiefly from foresters and woodmen. They indicated that Näschen must have extended his wanderings farther and farther in the frontier area, though he came back more and more often to the neighborhood of the enclosure. But because of his great shyness he was rarely seen, and he was not caught in any of the traps that were set for him. Then these trips became rarer and rarer. For a time he stayed in the Arber and Osser area, about twenty miles to the northwest of the enclosure. I found feces there that must have been his. They showed that he had been living chiefly on the guts of deer and roe that were shot at that time of year, and perhaps on some roe that he had killed himself. The feces invariably contained many bilberries and in some cases the stones of fruit and remains of insects. Snow was late that winter, and so tracking him was impossible.

Then on January 10 our neighbor, who knew the wolves well, reported he had seen Näschen crossing the road not far from the enclosure. I went there immediately, but as there was still no snow on the ground I could find no trace of him. So I took Alexander and Mädchen on the lead and searched the area with them. They stopped at a number of places, spent a long time sniffing, and then kept pulling excitedly in the direction of the enclosure. As we had just come from there I dragged them in the opposite direction. By evening we had found no trace of him and went back. Right outside the entrance to the enclosure Näschen came toward us, and he wagged his tail and jumped up at us just as if he had not been away for four months and ten days.

There was rabies in our neighborhood, and as a precaution I took him to Waldhäuser first. He was in excellent condition, but his first feces in captivity consisted only of dried leaves, grass, and pine needles. He was obviously very hungry and ate huge quantities of meat.

Incorporating the Cubs

Meanwhile the cubs had turned into young wolves. A slight difference in rank based on difference in age was observable in some of them, but this did not manifest itself in any persistent, aggressive quarreling. What interested me in this connection was their behavior toward the adult animals, and I made some interesting observations in this respect.

Spontaneous submission behavior toward their elders is typical of cubs. For the first few weeks this behavior was directed impartially at all adults alike, but at four months the cubs clearly differentiated between the 1.1 ♂ Wölfchen[1] and the 1.2 ♂ Alexander (see figure 9). (Näschen had run away at this time.) Submission behavior directed at Wölfchen became more and more frequent while toward Alexander it became increasingly rare, so they were obviously aware of differences in rank between adult animals. At this stage the 1.1 ♂ played the key role to all the cubs, independent of their sex.

With the coming of winter there was a distinct increase in aggressiveness, as there was every year. Aggressiveness was also directed at me. After some great excitement in the pack in the middle of January, I was suddenly violently attacked by the two 1.1 animals,

Mädchen and Wölfchen. I managed to grab a thick stick and defend myself with it, turning in a circle. Both wolves' back and neck hairs were erect. They kept trying to leap at me from behind while avoiding blows from the stick in front. My hair stood up too, but slowly fear gave way to rising anger and my blows were better aimed. The young wolves kept up their attack, but at a bigger distance from one another. Mädchen received a hard blow on the head and collapsed unconscious, and Wölfchen went on attacking alone, but now kept a bigger distance. In the end a hard blow landed on his head too, and he reeled but did not collapse. I was able to retreat to the safety of the platform. After a few minutes Mädchen got up again, while Wölfchen kept trying to jump up to the platform. Their aggressiveness toward me continued through the winter, but they evidently regarded me as dangerous. As I had a similar respect for them, we kept our distance from one another.

In the pack the pressure of the two 1.1 wolves similarly increased, and a separation of the sexes now became evident. Mädchen grew more and more aggressive toward Schönbrunn, the biggest female among the young wolves, and Schönbrunn ended by having to keep away from the pack altogether. If she approached it Mädchen drove her away immediately. To save Näschen from being alone at Waldhäuser I took Schönbrunn from the enclosure and put her with him. At first the two took no notice of each other and behaved like strangers, but gradually they made contact, with Schönbrunn showing inhibited submission behavior. In the light of the obvious recognition of each other by the older wolves this was an interesting observation, since it again demonstrated the importance to cubs and young wolves of being recognized as such by adult wolves who return to the pack, thus avoiding the risk of being attacked as strangers to it.

After Schönbrunn's departure Mädchen's repressive activity was directed at the next female, Finsterau, who was now the top female young wolf. This had a stimulating effect on the two lower-rank females, Lusen and Rachel, who soon became superior to Finsterau without any fighting, to the best of my knowledge. This was a way of bringing about a change in rank that was to be observed often later. Thus the relationship of subdominant wolves to each other is partly governed by their relationship to the number-one animal.

Presumably as a consequence of the increasing repression of

young wolves of the same sex, the latter showed an increasing tendency to subject themselves to the 1.1 wolf of that sex. As is evident from figure 9, a distinct difference developed in behavior toward the 1.1 ♂ and the 1.1 ♀ respectively. While the 1.1 ♂ was the important figure to all the cubs and young wolves at the universally friendly pack ceremonies, it was chiefly the female young wolves that subjected themselves to the 1.1 ♀. Thus cubs not only discover the difference in rank between older animals at an early stage, they also discover those animals' sex as well as their own through the behavior of the older animal toward them.

Clashes between young animals of the same sex increased as they were gradually integrated into the adult ranking order. I have already described how Finsterau temporarily lost her position among the young females. Psenner, who enjoyed a slight superiority in rank among the young males because of his greater age, lost his position in a different way, that is, at play. The young wolves grew more and more aggressive at play as they grew older. Joint attacks on one of their fellows developed at the age of about eighteen months. Everybody's turn to be the victim of these attacks came in the end, and then each had to defend himself very vigorously indeed. For a time Psenner was the favorite victim, with the consequence that he lost his rank in other social encounters to his contemporary Oswald. The young wolves went so far as to try the same thing on Alexander (1.2 ♂), who in the course of the winter had grown more and more aloof, went his own way, howled a great deal on his own, and at most still made contact only with young wolves. He was subjected to increasingly aggressive attacks, and ended by reacting more vigorously and making his position in the hierarchy perfectly plain again. At all events, attacks on him, including playful attacks, ceased.

More New Arrivals

In a state of freedom most members of a pack are born into it. Even though the cubs that were added to our pack every spring were apparently accepted just as if they were its own, in order to study the social behavior of a pack in conditions as close to the natural as possible it was necessary that cubs should be born to it. But no new

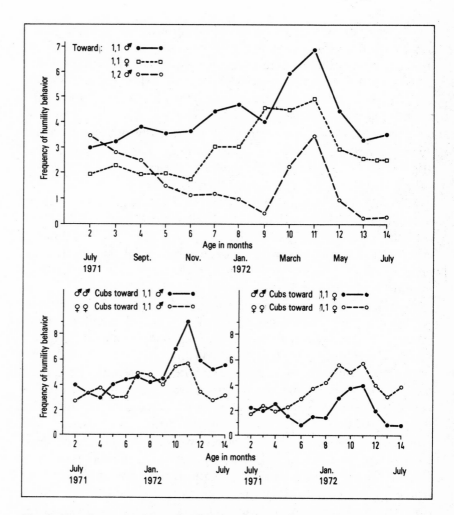

Fig. 9. Development of humility behavior of five cubs to three adult members of the pack.

cubs were to be expected that year (1972) either. Mädchen had again rejected all advances by her brothers during the mating season, so I had to search for cubs for a fourth time. This time I acquired a male and three females a fortnight old from the zoo at Olomouc in Czechoslovakia. The parents had been caught wild in the Carpathians.

At Waldhäuser the new arrivals were promptly adopted by Näschen and Schönbrunn. I bottle-fed them for a few weeks, but otherwise mostly left them alone. After their gradual weaning from the bottle they grew shyer and shyer and ended by no longer allowing themselves to be caught.

All the same I was able to take them out of the enclosure with Näschen for experimental purposes and let them run about freely in the fields. They kept close to Näschen, and as long as I kept my eye on him I had them under control. Then one day in July, when they were ten weeks old, Näschen suddenly ran away, with the cubs behind him. They soon lost him from sight and started running about helplessly. When I tried to catch them they hid in a clearing among the pine trees, where searching for them was hopeless.

Was there to be a repeat performance of Näschen's disappearance, this time accompanied by four cubs? Fortunately, nothing of the sort happened. Näschen came back a few hours later and took an active part in looking for the cubs, no doubt motivated by his assumed paternal role. He found the male in the same clearing, and the reunion was the occasion for effusive rejoicing. But there was no trace of the females. We searched the whole neighborhood up to a mile and a half from our house, but in vain.

Late that evening I heard whimpering down at the enclosure. Two of the cubs were waiting at the entrance and dashed inside as soon as I opened the door. I heard the wolves running about excitedly for a long time in the dark enclosure beneath our window. Schönbrunn, who had been left alone, had howled for hours, and this presumably helped the cubs to find their way back. But now that she had three of them back she evidently considered it sufficient and stopped howling. So how was the fourth to find her way back? Surprisingly, she managed it; she suddenly turned up the next evening. She was very hungry, but her protracted submission behavior to Näschen and Schönbrunn hardly allowed her to eat. The

117

other cubs subjected her to a great deal of sniffing and then to a pretty thorough playful beating-up.

A few days after these remarkable feats of orientation one of the cubs died. The weather was unusually hot for Waldhäuser, and the cubs played a great deal. When I came back after a few minutes' absence, the biggest cub was lying on the ground, lifeless but still warm. I tried artificial respiration. I had had a similar experience with a young female poodle at Rickling and had revived it with cardiac massage and artificial respiration, but this time my efforts were in vain; the little wolf was dead. The post-mortem showed nothing unusual. I assume that rapid growth at that age represents a strain on the heart and the circulatory system and that sudden excessive strain had led to heart failure.

The other three cubs were given names from their country of origin: Olomouc, Tatra, and Brno. I shall have a great deal more to say about Olomouc later, but at this stage he was still a cub, and no one could suspect that for many years he would be the dominant male in the pack. But first let us consider the rise of his future partner, Finsterau, which was also very instructive.

FINSTERAU'S RISE TO EMINENCE

In the course of the summer there was little change in the pack. Wölfchen and Mädchen, the two 1.1 wolves, were still closely associated. Alexander began by successfully defending his 1.2 position, but remained rather aloof. Among the young wolves there were changes of rank several times a month. The young animal who was dominant for the time being behaved to his contemporaries exactly as the real 1.1 wolf did to all the members of the pack. He kept his tail up and was active and self-confident until he lost his position again. Clashes were still harmless. A change of rank was frequently the result of play or came about indirectly through changes in the position of two other young wolves, which again influenced relations to and among the other three members of that age group. No clear distinction could be made between the ranking order of the two sexes, and everything was still very peaceful.

When we put Näschen, Schönbrunn, and the three cubs from Waldhäuser into the big enclosure, the situation suddenly changed. The cubs were accepted immediately, and soon Wölfchen and in particular Psenner began caring for them. But Rachel and Lusen, who were the lowest-ranking wolves at the time, reacted to them rather aggressively. During the first weeks they kept nipping them, running at them, and knocking them over or frightening them by feint attacks. All this was done playfully, but to judge from the squealing of the cubs it was not meant only playfully. This slight aggressiveness toward new cubs on the part of young wolves of lower rank was observed again and again in the years that followed, and seems to me to be a phenomenon analogous to the jealousy of young children. What its function is, apart perhaps from handing on to others the aggression that the animal has suffered itself, I do not know.

The first meeting between Wölfchen and Näschen after a separation of nearly a year was dramatic. They circled each other, threatening and using intimidation behavior, and a fight seemed imminent. But first Näschen had to vigorously defend himself against the young wolves, particularly the number-one male, who did not recognize him and attacked him as if he were a stranger. He defended himself forcefully and made plain his claim to membership in the pack.

He was fully integrated again, though perhaps the attacks made him rather more cautious. At all events he did not again challenge Wölfchen's 1.1 position, but shared the 1.2 position with Alexander. But it was a long time before a real bond was established between him and the young wolves; Finsterau in particular was very reserved toward him for some time.

The most violent clashes after the two packs were brought together took place, as so frequently happens, between the females. On their first meeting Schönbrunn displayed unmistakable submission behavior to Mädchen, who circled her with straight legs and her tail up and her back hair standing up. If Mädchen came closer than about three yards Schönbrunn immediately retreated and demonstrated her friendly, submissive feelings from a distance; Mädchen followed her in the intimidating attitude. But Schönbrunn slowly became aggressive too. She went to a bush, raised a leg and urinated, and afterward scratched excitedly—a behavior pattern to which only the top female is entitled. Mädchen did the same, and they then circled each other exactly like two dogs in the street.

119

I did not see the beginning of the fight, which started suddenly in thick scrub. The other cubs came running up, and soon fighting was going on all over the place, but only between Schönbrunn and Mädchen was it in earnest. The shrubs bent beneath the weight of their bodies. The two females fought in silence; nothing was to be heard but the rustling of the leaves and the nasty sound of cracking bones. The animals soon parted again. Mädchen was badly wounded in the face and was covered with blood, but she had held her ground.

For the next few weeks the two wounded females kept out of each other's way. Schönbrunn looked after "her" cubs and Mädchen nursed her wounds. But Finsterau—Schönbrunn's sister, who had now been 2.1 ♀ again for a long time—became more and more active and showed the first signs of an expansionary tendency at the expense of Mädchen, no doubt as a consequence of diminishing pressure from above. She began by giving up submission behavior toward Mädchen. This aroused Mädchen's aggressiveness, and thus relations between the two became increasingly tense. Soon Finsterau actually attacked Mädchen from the rear, skillfully exploiting her rival's weaknesses. During this period she kept submissively soliciting Wölfchen, Mädchen's year-long partner. Mädchen too suddenly started showing submission behavior toward Wölfchen. In the process of losing her 1.1 position she subjected herself to her uninvolved partner. All this was very exciting, though I was getting more and more worried about Mädchen's severe wounds.

The expected decisive battle took place in the late autumn. Mädchen had to fight not only Finsterau but also the two subdominant young wolves Rachel and Lusen, who—apparently in memory of their earlier suppression by her—now joined in the attack on her. Unfortunately I did not see the fight, but soon afterward found Mädchen in the enclosure, severely wounded. While I was carrying her out of the enclosure the three extraordinarily excited females, behaving as if they were actually crazy, went for her again. If I had not removed her from the enclosure they would certainly have killed her.

During the summer we had built a small enclosure next to the big one, and I put Mädchen into it. After a few days' rest—she was in a bad way but she was tough—I tried to put her back with the pack, but Finsterau, backed by all the other young wolves, including the males, made an uninhibited attack on her, so I quickly put her back in a place of safety. She had obviously lost her status for good. It might be called the nose-dive effect, after the loss of her alpha position.

Male Struggles for Dominance

There were many other struggles for dominance that autumn. After Mädchen's downfall and removal from the enclosure, twelve wolves remained in it. That meant a total of sixty-six different relationships, the development of all of which cannot be described here. But I shall give a brief account of one change of rank among the males since it illustrates the difference between male and female aggression among wolves.

After his return at the end of August Näschen shared the 1.2 position with Alexander. Two months later I noticed the beginnings of aggressiveness between these two subdominant males. Näschen threatened when Alexander went by, approached him stiffly with his tail up, rested his head on Alexander's back and remained like that for nearly half a minute before jumping up and resting his forelegs on Alexander's body. Alexander stood there as if this were no concern of his, took a few steps forward, and then went away as if nothing had happened. Näschen went to the nearest bush, raised his leg, urinated, and then excitedly scratched the ground.

Such incidents were repeated frequently in the days and weeks that followed. Näschen threatened, used intimidation behavior, and urinated, while Alexander seemed to ignore the whole thing and did not go out of Näschen's way. Näschen grew more and more aggressive, followed Alexander threateningly, reacted to each of his changes of movement with a noisy baring of the teeth, got in his way, used intimidation behavior, jumped up on him, and so on.

In the long run Alexander could not ignore this constant provocation, and he began protesting and threatening back. At the beginning of November he attacked for the first time, making snapping movements at the throat that Näschen presented, and this developed into a noisy wrestling match. Then something very interesting happened. The two young males, Psenner and Oswald, joined in

121

and began aggressively snapping at Alexander too. They retreated when Alexander made for them aggressively, only to advance on him again when he had to turn his attention to Näschen.

He could not stand up indefinitely to these joint attacks, and at the end of November I saw him for the first time displaying active submission to Näschen, whereupon Näschen's aggressiveness toward him ceased. He was able to resist the expansionary tendency of the two "little alphas" toward him, especially as these two began to have difficulties with each other, but he kept away from the pack more and more and almost completely gave up playing with the young wolves and the cubs that had now grown up. Though for the time being they showed no aggressiveness toward him, they showed no submission either. He had apparently left the pack half voluntarily.

Expulsion from the Pack

The two struggles for rank I have just described illustrate some essential differences between males and females. Among females attacks were aggressive from the outset, with no biting inhibition, preliminary threatening, intimidation behavior, or other demonstration of strength. All the females were involved, and the loser went on being attacked uninhibitedly and would have been killed if I had not taken her away. Among the males (though in this case it was only the second position in the ranking order that was at stake) clashes were much less aggressive. Threats, intimidation behavior, and protests dominated the scene. There was hardly any hard biting, and consequently there were no serious wounds. Also fighting was limited to animals next to each other in the ranking order, and the loser suffered no nose-dive effect. Both losers, Mädchen and Alexander, left the pack and, while the female was compelled to do so, the male seemed to do so to a large extent voluntarily.

Though decisions had now been reached in both big ranking orders, peace did not return to the pack; Finsterau, the new 1.1 ♀, saw to that. After her defeat of Mädchen she turned her attention to Schönbrunn, on whom she made surprise attacks, backed by the two other females, and soon Schönbrunn had to keep away from the pack. Soon afterward it was the turn of the next female, Rachel.

After a brief phase of inhibited aggression, such as threatening and using intimidation behavior, Finsterau began making furious attacks on her, sometimes supported by the fourth female, Lusen, and in January 1973 Rachel had to leave the pack too. Lusen was still tolerated. She sometimes joined Finsterau in attacking Schönbrunn, who fled at once. But if Schönbrunn and Lusen met alone in the enclosure, Schönbrunn showed that she was obviously superior to Lusen and chased her away. Thus the relationship between these two depended on the social environment.

At the beginning of the season of heat in February Lusen, the last of the three subdominant females, was driven out, so that Finsterau was the only sexually mature female left in the pack. She had begun with the highest-ranking female and finished with the lowest. It was interesting to note that in her first battle she had the support of all her three contemporaries and in subsequent ones the support of all those that remained. Afterward each expelled female was threatened by her again and again. These females never resorted to joint defense and showed no sign of making social contact either with each other or with other members of the pack. Each lived in isolation. Among wolves there is obviously no solidarity among the weak and the oppressed.

Male Adolescent Behavior

In her attacks on expelled females during the winter Finsterau enjoyed the increasing support of the young wolves Olomouc, Tatra, and Brno, who gladly joined in when occasion arose to chase an animal away or attack it when it was cornered. But they did not join in attacks on Schönbrunn, their former stepmother, which indicates that personal links play an important part in social life in addition to relationship, age, sex, and rank.

These three animals showed increased signs of "little alpha" behavior in the "rowdy adolescent" group. I had previously made an interesting experiment in this respect. When the new enclosure next to the big one was finished I noted the order in which wolves entered it when the gate between the two was opened. At first the new situation made them uneasy. But after a few minutes Wölfchen, the 1.1 ♂, hesitantly entered the new enclosure (as a cub and young wolf he had always been the most nervous) and he was followed by Mädchen, who was still 1.1 ♀. Next came not Alexander, the third adult wolf, but the two "little alphas," Oswald and Finsterau. I saw Alexander and the other young wolves enter the new enclosure only several days later.

I made similar experiments in later years, and always with the same results. In coping with new situations, or on special occasions such as attacks on strangers to the pack, it was always the two 1.1 wolves and one or two subdominant males accompanied by the highest-ranking young animals who took the lead. Sometimes it was actually comic to watch these juveniles accompanying the alpha pair with their tails up and back hair erect, trying to raise a leg while urinating, scratching, and then going back to playing together again. As they were to a large extent tolerated by the grown-up animals, they were able to develop into ringleaders among the "rowdy adolescents."

The inferior young wolves showed no submission behavior toward their young superiors. Positions were not fought for as vigorously as they were by adults, and were not nearly so stable. Changes of position among animals of middle or low rank were accordingly much more frequent than they were among those at the top of the ranking order (see appendix, table 4). The relative strength of the young wolves Psenner and Oswald changed several times in the course of the autumn, but as winter approached they became increasingly intolerant of each other, which again was first observable in the pack. And then something happened that resembled what had happened a few months earlier in the struggle between Näschen and Alexander. The new young male, Olomouc, who was only eight months old but by now was nearly as big as Psenner and Oswald, who were a year older, began to direct intimidation behavior at both. They were so preoccupied with each other that at first they ignored him. He grew increasingly self-confident, and ended by remaining in an intimidatory attitude in front of Psenner and Oswald when he met either of them alone. They protested loudly at this provocation, but the appearance on the scene of their rival distracted their attention.

This developed into a ritual. Without Olomouc's contributing much to the situation, the stalemate between his two older rivals enabled him to creep up unnoticed to the fourth position in the male ranking order. Psenner and Oswald in no way subjected themselves to him, that is, they showed no submission behavior toward him, but let him pass by with his tail up higher and his legs straighter, and ended by avoiding him when they met.

Dynamics and Structure of the Social Ranking Order

We have now gathered enough information to enable us to complete the model of the social ranking order begun in the last chapter, so at this point I shall interrupt my account of developments in the pack and summarize some of the principles that govern the development of social rank relationships and deduce from them the structure of the ranking order (see figure 10).

Two wolves A and B may be equal in rank, or A may be domi-

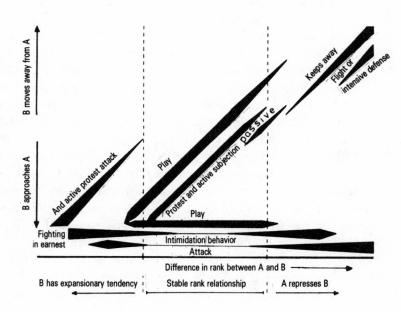

Fig. 10. Behavior of two wolves depending on the nature of their rank relationship.

nant over B. In the latter event three types of relationship are discernible, the behavior being the more pronounced the higher the disputed position is.

1. The relationship may be stable. In that event it is marked by frequent and friendly contacts and by play behavior; acts of aggression, if they occur, are situation-governed and innocuous. B shows spontaneous submission toward A as well as reactive submission in response to mild threats by the latter, whose superior rank is generally demonstrated only by its holding its tail slightly higher.

2. The relationship may be characterized by attempts at repression by the superior. These generally make their first appearance at play. If B cannot defend itself against them in the early stages, the play becomes more and more aggressive. A eventually uses intimidation behavior against B, leaps at it, pins it to the ground threateningly with its paws or its whole body. B at first reacts with passive submission, which increasingly develops into defensive behavior. The first attacks take place, after which B keeps its distance. If B does not succeed in escaping by flight, biting, generally directed at its hindquarters, takes place in earnest, and A is not infrequently aided by other animals. They surround B, who turns to face the attacks of each of its assailants and defends itself by snapping and baring the teeth. When this takes place in its most aggressive form B is defeated by uninhibited attacks, now directed chiefly at its head, throat, and back, with hard biting and shaking. B takes flight whenever A approaches, and if A catches up to it, defends itself by vigorous biting. B has become a scapegoat and generally leaves the pack.

3. The situation may be characterized by a struggle for rank. An expansionary trend against A on B's part can manifest itself inhibitedly or uninhibitedly. The former is by far the more frequent mode of expression and first appears in occasional more vigorous biting at play. If A does not defend itself sufficiently decisively against these initial acts of aggression, relations between the two become increasingly tense; threatening and intimidating behavior develop, and finally there is serious fighting. Both contestants may be helped by one or more members of the pack, either by occasional snapping or by uninhibited intervention.

A new relationship in rank comes about when one of the parties loses a serious battle, that is, if it takes flight or is able to resort only to self-defense. At this stage submission behavior is of no more use; the winner generally continues its uninhibited attacks.

Whether the loser remains in the pack depends on the behavior of its fellows. If these attack it, it has obviously lost its former dominance and becomes a scapegoat (the nose-dive effect). This last is chiefly observed among females, who are thus forced to leave the pack.

If the loser remains in the neighborhood of the pack, the situation slowly returns to normal. When friendly, relaxed social activities take place in the pack, it approaches the winner and shows incipient submission behavior from a distance. If this is tolerated, the first attempts to establish contact, often in a playful attitude, soon follow. In this way the relationship between two enemies gradually becomes friendly and tolerant again.

When B's expansionary trend against A assumes the rare uninhibited form, the preparatory phases are omitted. B begins by biting A's hindquarters hard and immediately jumping away again. These attacks gradually become more violent, and finally the battle-royal takes place. I have seen the campaign take this form only twice, and in both cases the combatants were female.

WHO FIGHTS WHOM?

In the first place, we have seen that both repressive attacks and battles for rank among adult wolves take place only between animals of the same sex. This separation of the sexes is less marked among young wolves. During their first autumn their competition for rank is innocuous, and only during the winter do the first expansionary trends become discernible, generally directed against their seniors by a year, among whom there are already a superior male and a superior female who behave toward other juveniles as the two alpha animals do toward the whole pack. Incorporation of young animals into the adult ranking order takes place during the second half of their second year and lasts into the third. Finally, aggressive behavior among cubs is not linked with sex. Aggression is only of brief duration, is about food, for instance, and does not lead to lasting rank relationships.

Second, we know that the object of a repressive attack is always

127

an animal of lower rank, while a struggle for rank is always begun by an animal of lower rank against its immediate superior. The higher the position at stake the more vigorously is the campaign conducted. Changes of rank in the lower part of the ranking order are accordingly much more frequent than in the higher part. In both repressive attacks and battles for rank the aggressor may be supported by other members of the pack. The latter are often younger animals, and sometimes of the other sex. Support for the aggressor is generally more vigorous the closer the attacked wolf and the aggressors' supporters are in the ranking order. In a few instances the attacked wolf may also receive support, for example, if there is competition for rank independent of the immediate clash between the aggressor and those who come to the attacked animal's aid. Also parents defend their cubs against attacks by other members of the pack. But normally an attacked wolf fights alone.

Such are the dynamic principles that govern the structure of the social ranking order. It must be borne in mind that a ranking order in a group of animals as perceived by a human observer can only be a great oversimplification. In a group of twelve wolves such as I observed in the Bavarian Forest, each wolf has relationships with eleven other animals, all of which are influenced by the total of fifty-five interrelationships between all the other wolves. These relationships can be very diverse, and it is obvious that applying the terms "position in the ranking order" and "difference in rank" to all of them represents a considerable oversimplification (see figure 11).

Thus the important structural characteristics of the social ranking order of wolves are the following:

There are two social ranking orders in the pack, one male and the other female. The top position in each is generally held by an older wolf. To a large extent every ranking order is structured according to age.

Among superior wolves differences in rank are great. They are less marked among those of lower rank, and among cubs they are nonexistent.

When there is very strong pressure from above, differences of rank between animals of lower rank are wiped out. This is observable among females in particular.

There is a social ranking order in miniature among contemporary subgroups in the pack, except among the cubs.

128

Fig. 11. Social rank in the wolf pack. Top, the two senior animals (1.1 ♂ and 1.1 ♀, with whom the 1.2 ♂ is often associated). Below, some young subdominants (1.3 ♂ and 1.2 ♀). Some juveniles behave like "little alphas." At the bottom of the ranking order come the cubs.

There is no ranking order between adult wolves of different sexes if they are at the same level in the male or female ranking order. But when there are substantial differences in age or in position there is a corresponding ranking order between males and females, though this never leads to a struggle for rank.

6

Sexuality, Mating, and Cub Rearing

What benefit does the pack derive from the social ranking order? The dominance exercised by some members of the pack over others seems to be by far the most important element in their relationship. So far we have discovered how and among which animals such relationships arise, but not why they arise. What advantage does the pack as a whole derive from the development of definite relationships of strength, and of what use is high rank to a wolf and what disadvantage does he suffer if he remains of low rank? We shall see that the advantage of an individual is not necessarily an advantage to the whole pack, and vice versa.

Before we can answer these questions we need to know more about the influence of the ranking order on wolf behavior. We know a good deal about rank-related behavior patterns, particularly those that bring them about and cause them to manifest themselves. But what influence does the ranking order have on sexuality in the pack, on mating, and on the role of its individual members in cub rearing? These are fields of behavior that are of vital importance both to the pack as a whole and to each of its members.

Remember the situation of the most important members of the pack shortly before the mating season in January and February 1973. Of the four females that had reached maturity, only Finsterau remained; the other three had been driven out. Any attempt by them to approach the pack was prevented by Finsterau's violent attacks. Wölfchen was still supreme in the 1.1 ♂ position and hardly concerned himself with the clashes of his inferiors.

131

Sexuality and Mating

After the middle of February all four sexually mature females exhibited vaginal bleeding. Months before this Finsterau kept pressing against Wölfchen and whimpering, rolling on her back in front of him, and pulling his coat. Now she became positively importunate, but the more importunate she became the more he withdrew. The dominant male showed not the slightest sexual interest in her. Psenner, soon followed by Näschen, made up for this by becoming all the more solicitous. Finsterau let Psenner carry on without taking much notice of him, but at first vigorously warded off Näschen's approaches. Relations between them had been tense ever since Näschen's return, but Näschen refused to be discouraged. He repressed Psenner and followed Finsterau about everywhere, licking her coat and finally her genitals, which Finsterau tolerated. He hardly slept, ate little, and his attention was completely concentrated on Finsterau. Before the season of heat she had been very active in soliciting Wölfchen and sometimes the other males too, but now she became more and more inactive. She spent a long time wandering around the enclosure and frequently urinated on bushes and tree stumps. She was closely followed by Näschen with the other males behind him, and the two younger females, Tatra and Brno, brought up the rear. They all congregated around Finsterau, who was now obviously the most important animal and governed the activity of the others, deciding the pace and direction in which they should go. Even Wölfchen sometimes joined this pack and slept near it, and continued to be greeted with friendly submission. But he had now obviously surrendered his principal role in the pack to the alpha female.

The animals that had been expelled kept away from the pack, and each went its own way. The vaginal bleeding of the females quickly ceased without a male having tried to cover any of them.

All the males in the pack, including the young Olomouc, took a great interest in the places in the snow where Finsterau urinated. They sniffed them, bit into them, and then raised their heads, continuing their chewing movements. For a few seconds their eyes were directed into the void in characteristic fashion. Everyone who has kept a male dog knows this behavior pattern and its meaning, which is that the male has smelled the urine of a bitch, or in this case a she-wolf, in heat.

Näschen kept almost perpetual skin contact with Finsterau. At the end of February Finsterau for the first time stopped, though only briefly, when Näschen tried to mount her. A few days later things progressed to a point at which she presented herself by approaching Näschen sideways and then in front of him, with her tail turned to one side. Näschen mounted her and, after a number of vigorous thrusts of the pelvis the two "locked" in the fashion typical of canids (the penis swells in the female's vagina and cannot then be removed). Finsterau fell on her back, squealing loudly, and bit about her, but Näschen remained standing there quite calmly, and eventually Finsterau got up again. They remained coupled together for the next fifteen minutes, with their heads pointing in different directions. The other wolves were at first extremely interested, but were kept at a distance by Näschen's very obvious threat behavior. They lay next to the copulating couple and did not get up until the latter parted. Näschen and Finsterau briefly licked their own genitals, and then Finsterau dashed excitedly at Näschen, jumped up at him, whimpered, and rolled on her back in front of him exactly like a wolf showing friendly submission. The others also began running about, and they all ran around one another in friendly, excited fashion.

During the next ten days mating was repeated two or three times in each twenty-four hours, and then Näschen's interest obviously faded. But Finsterau went on presenting, to Psenner and Olomouc also. Both tried to mount her without being prevented by Näschen, but I saw no more copulation. Soon Finsterau's soliciting ceased too. The season of heat was over.

Wölfchen resumed his position as the dominant member of the pack and, as before, Näschen adapted himself to that. But something new and unexpected happened. Näschen's and Finsterau's attitude to each other had previously been completely negative, and they had been brought together only by sex during the mating season, but henceforth they were inseparable. The bond was mutual. When Finsterau disappeared Näschen looked for her, just as Finsterau looked for him when he went off on his own. They rested with a distinctly smaller distance between each other, and the frequency of neutral or friendly contacts increased enormously.

Mating had obviously led to a social bond. As Näschen and Wölf-chen also kept closely together, these three animals now formed the inner circle of the pack around which the other members revolved.

In the course of the next few months there was a noticeable relaxation in Finsterau's repression of the expelled females. Schönbrunn soon gained enough courage to return to the pack, but the other two, Rachel and Lusen, still had to keep away, as they were invariably attacked by the young wolves. But Finsterau developed an attitude of sovereign tolerance similar to that of Wölfchen.

The Birth

Finsterau showed no outward sign of pregnancy until a few days before her cubs were born. She was as mobile and ran as swiftly as ever. The only change was in her behavior. She dug small holes at several places in the enclosure, preferably in the sandy soil immediately under a tree stump. Generally she stopped when she got to the roots. But by the middle of April she had dug herself a splendid den a long way away from the visitors' platform with its perpetual disturbances. The nature of the soil also made the choice a good one. The sand was easy to dig in, and the roof of the den was protected by the wide-spreading roots of an old pine tree which assured it against collapse. By now she had shed the hair between her swollen mammaries.

On the morning of April 29 I saw her running about as usual. She was still not very fat, but her mammaries were now plainly visible. When I returned in the afternoon she was nowhere to be seen. Näschen was lying right outside the entrance to the den, and the other members of the pack were sleeping not far away. When they became active again in the evening they showed great interest in the den.

An extract from my diary for that day:

> 7:10 P.M. After a great deal of friendly running around one another and around Wölfchen, all the wolves went to the den. Näschen got up and threatened loudly. The younger wolves played relaxedly, and Wölfchen joined in. Schönbrunn, Rachel, and Lusen tried to approach the den. Only Alexander was not to be seen. Näschen threat-

ened everyone, including Wölfchen, who approached the den, and did not respond to invitations to play. Whenever the sound of whimpering came from the den some of the animals would stop and turn their head and then go on playing relaxedly around the den. Of Finsterau there was no sign.

I went to the den four days later. Finsterau dashed out and was very aggressive. She threatened me, with her back hairs erect, stamped on the ground with both forefeet, but kept her distance, so I was able to creep into the den and count the cubs—three males and a female.

I quickly crawled out again, but the experience had obviously been too much for the mother. She dashed into the hole, came out again holding a cub in her mouth, ran unhesitatingly to a stony area about three hundred yards away, and then came back straight away for the next cub. Before giving birth she had obviously prepared a second den to which she now took her cubs after the disturbance. After putting the last of them into the new den, she returned to the old one for a fifth time, disappeared inside, and then emerged again. Evidently wolves are not very good at counting.

In later years I observed this preparation of two dens not too far away from each other over and over again. An obvious disturbance was not always necessary to persuade a mother to move her young to an alternative site. Every year she moved her cubs to a new den at latest after a fortnight. I noted several times that she buried food near the new den, and then I could nearly always be sure that she was going to move her cubs very soon. Still more dens were made as the cubs grew older. In the five years that followed the wolves in the two enclosures used nine different dens. Two were under big stones, four were under the roots of old or cut-down pine trees, one was in sandy soil at the edge of a small beechwood, and one was under a long trough we had put in the enclosure as a refuge for rabbits. None of the dens was in dense woodland. All were at light places near or actually at the edge of the wood, and always a long way away from the visitors' platform or other places where there was a good deal of disturbance, for example, at the entrance through which a Jeep came in three times a week with food. The entrances to the dens measured about twenty by twenty square inches. They

135

led to a passage into the earth, and when the ground was sloping were always made from below against the slope. The passage grew narrower and after about a yard continued horizontally for between three and ten feet and ended in a round chamber that was the real den.

Finsterau, who gave birth to four more litters, continued every year to use the den under the rocks to which she took her first cubs so quickly, but she made at least one new den every year. Tatra, who bore cubs in the big enclosure in the spring of 1977, also built two very fine dens beforehand, but bore her cubs in the den dug by Finsterau under the big rocks during the first year.

Only the pregnant mother digs the den, but the cubs help to extend it. In the spring of 1974 Finsterau took her six-week-old cubs to a new den under a fine old tree trunk. After they had spent about three weeks there I thought I heard one of the cubs, whose hindlegs were rather weak, whimpering. I waited for a couple of days, by which time the other cubs had again been moved to another den, but I still thought I could hear the whimpering of a cub inside the den. Several of us dug the den out, but we found nothing, even when we took a big mechanical excavator into the enclosure to expose the last part of it. The cub had already left, and a few days later we saw it playing with the others, but we were very surprised at what we found—a positively foxlike labyrinth of passages and chambers covering an area of about sixty square yards. Many of these passages were so narrow that only the cubs could have used them—so it was only they who could have dug them. There were cross-connections between several of the resting places and also between the three principal tunnels and exits. Some of the smaller passages also led into the open. It was a real "cub house," and it was a pity that we had to destroy it in our search.

When the four cubs born in the early summer of 1973 were three weeks old, they emerged from the den for the first time. The excitement among the other wolves was great, but Finsterau and Näschen prevented contacts from getting too effusive. The two scapegoats, Rachel and Lusen, acquired the privilege of associating with the cubs, playing with them, licking them, and bringing them food. Finsterau was in any case very tolerant by now. Only Alexander and Psenner, who by this time had also been expelled from the pack, apparently took no interest in the cubs and remained aloof.

Cub Rearing

Differences soon appeared among members of the pack in their behavior toward the cubs. At first it was of course the mother who took special care of them. But when she stopped suckling them after about ten weeks—toward the end she did this standing up outside the den—she ceased to be particularly outstanding in caring for them in comparison with other females. Lusen and Brno in particular kept bringing them bigger and bigger quantities of food, and so did Finsterau's brother Oswald and the young Olomouc (see figure 12). Others remained in the cubs' vicinity but took little part in bringing them food; this applied to Wölfchen and Näschen, who developed into "watchdogs" (see figure 13). If they heard one of the cubs squealing, they hurried along immediately. One day when a customs official (who patrolled the nearby frontier) approached the enclosure from the forest they did not take flight, as they usually did, but sprang at the fence to attack the stranger.

Apart from this watchdog role, Wölfchen and Näschen did not take much notice of the cubs. If the cubs approached them they allowed them to crawl over them and pull their coat and tail, but after a few minutes the adults went and lay down somewhere else. Direct contact with the cubs was more the business of the younger wolves, who licked their coats or played with them long and often.

I noted a similar division of labor in later years also. In the first few days after the cubs were born it was chiefly the father who brought food to the mother, who never left her cubs for longer than a few minutes. When the cubs began to eat solid food, it was still chiefly the mother and a few younger wolves who brought it to them, though other members of the pack also did so. And, while the father and one or two superior males kept watch for hours in the neighborhood of the den, it was the younger animals, the one- or two-year-olds, and the females in particular, who concentrated on making direct contact with the cubs. Even when the pack went roaming over long distances in the enclosure in the morning and evening, these animals often stayed behind with the cubs.

When the cubs were three months old they no longer slept in the den and did not flee to it when danger threatened. They now lived in a very inaccessible area where there was dense undergrowth,

137

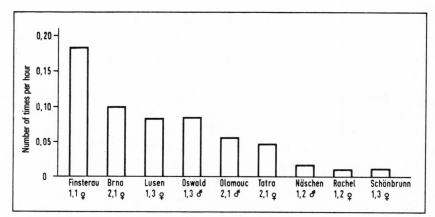

Fig. 12. The frequency with which members of the pack brought the cubs food. The 1.1 ♂ Wölfchen and the two males, Alexander and Psenner, no longer in the pack, were not observed to do this.

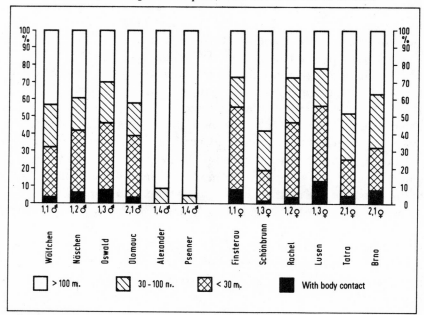

Fig. 13. Distance from the cubs kept by different wolves in the period between August 4 and 14, 1973. This was observed for a total of 1,984 minutes (100 percent = 1,984).
It was evident that at this period the pack spends most of its time with the cubs. Apart from Finsterau, the mother, the two subdominant females, Rachel and Lusen, as well as Finsterau's brother, Oswald, spent most time with the cubs. (Observations on which Figs. 12 and 13 are based were made by Michael Boer.)

fallen trunks, and big boulders. From there they made longer and longer expeditions together, always accompanied by at least one juvenile watchdog. When they returned, wild games developed in which all the members of the pack sometimes joined. Food for the cubs was always brought there at every feeding time. This was always a very peaceful time in the pack.

But peace did not last for long. Toward the end of that summer clashes broke out again, and once more aggressiveness first affected the lower in rank. Psenner had already been expelled, and now it was Oswald's turn to be attacked, first by Näschen and soon afterward also by the "rowdy adolescent" brigade. But he always managed to convert aggressiveness against himself into play. The way he responded to every threat and every attack by play behavior and so succeeded in avoiding the worst was positively phenomenal. Rachel and Lusen were not so clever. No doubt in memory of past times, they fled when Finsterau made a first attack on them, and this triggered off aggressive behavior by other members of the pack, who chased them, causing them to run even faster with so many at their heels. This in turn stimulated their pursuers to further attack. Thus a single attack initiated by Finsterau and taken up by the others was sufficient to drive both of them out of the pack, one after the other.

In the autumn of 1973 Näschen grew more and more aggressive toward the 1.1 ♂ Wölfchen. At the same time Olomouc, who used to display the most effusive submission behavior toward the two top males, now directed it only at Wölfchen and grew more and more rebellious to Näschen. Näschen occasionally protested when Olomouc did not get out of his way, for instance, but he was so preoccupied with Wölfchen—that is, with his own upward expansionary trend—that he did not correctly assess this expansionary trend on the part of his junior. The clash between Näschen and Wölfchen took its usual course, and the expected battle-royal took place at the beginning of December. They separated after only a few minutes with honor intact. But more fighting took place in the days that followed, and Wölfchen ended by obviously keeping his distance from Näschen and the pack. Näschen had won, if not by a knockout, at least on points.

Olomouc took no part in these battles, but changed his behavior toward Wölfchen when the latter's dominance over Näschen ended. Instead of submission he showed him intimidation behavior, but

Wölfchen did not react. Thus Olomouc reached second place among the males without fighting for it. He showed no humility behavior in relation to the new 1.1 ♂ Näschen, but for the time being merely kept out of his way.

The mating season began in February. As in the previous year, Näschen was tireless in his pursuit of Finsterau. Olomouc as well as Wölfchen, who had never shown any interest in sex when he was 1.1 ♂, also took an interest in Finsterau. So she now had a retinue of three adult males and their three ten-month-old sons. First came Näschen, who warded off all attempts by the other males to make contact with her. The two "locked" for the first time on January 31. Olomouc and Wölfchen were very excited by this, as they were on the following occasions on which it occurred, and for the first time I saw extensive "homosexual" behavior between adult males. Generally it was Wölfchen who mounted Olomouc.

During the next thirteen days Näschen and Finsterau copulated several times daily. To Näschen, who never left Finsterau's side and kept having to keep the other males away from her, this must have been a great strain, and in the end it must have been too much for him, for in the middle of February I suddenly saw Olomouc copulating with Finsterau without Näschen doing anything to stop it; he merely stood there with a hanging head. Afterward Olomouc walked past Näschen with springy stride and his tail up. He had very skillfully exploited Näschen's physical weakness and now took over not only the 1.1 position but the female also. When Näschen tried to mount Finsterau again the next day Olomouc jumped at him and Näschen fell on his back. Never again did I see such a noncombative ascent to the position of alpha animal.

During the three days that followed Olomouc and Finsterau copulated several more times, but then Finsterau's period of heat came to an end. There were five other sexually mature females in the enclosure, all of whom showed vaginal bleeding. Two of them, Rachel and Lusen, remained completely apart, and none of the males took any interest in them. Tatra and Brno, now barely two years old, were still tolerated in the pack by Finsterau, but had no suitors and showed no soliciting behavior. But Schönbrunn, who had continually solicited Wölfchen in the autumn, seemed to be getting somewhere when the mating season arrived, for Wölfchen's interest slowly shifted from Finsterau to her. However, whenever he tried to mount her, Finsterau, Näschen, and Olomouc dashed up and separated them by vigorous attacks. Thus the two animals never had enough time for the protracted foreplay that has to precede copulation. At all events I saw none, and it was only Finsterau who gave birth two months later, to seven cubs. Also after the end of the mating season no bond developed between Wölfchen and Schönbrunn as had developed the year before between Näschen and Finsterau and this year between Finsterau and Olomouc. The leading trio now consisted of Olomouc, Finsterau, and Näschen. The former 1.1 ♂ Wölfchen increasingly went his own way unaccompanied by Schönbrunn. Repeated copulation is obviously required if a bond is to arise out of sexual activity.

Reduction of the Pack

After the birth of seven cubs there were twenty-three wolves in the enclosure. Because of the many expulsions the size of the pack had remained roughly constant, but the expelled wolves had to be fed too, and feeding twenty-three of them was too much for the administration of the National Park. Also there were now too many wolves in the enclosure for me to observe. (Five hundred and six different individual relationships multiplied by 48 possible ways of behavior gives 24,288 possible combinations.)[1] In addition, aggression in the enclosure had increased. That summer none of the females expelled during the winter were allowed access to the cubs as had happened the year before, and there was continual squabbling between the males too.

So some of the animals had to be disposed of. But how? Enough wolves were born in German zoos. There were plenty of private individuals who were willing to buy a wolf. In the course of the year I had had about a hundred inquiries, all of which I had to decline. Either the cubs were not tame and would have had to live a sad life in an excessively small enclosure, or the owner would succeed in taming them, which would be much worse, because then difficulties would be actually programmed into the situation. That year a tame wolf had bitten a small boy to death in north Germany. The animal broke out of its box and ran around for three days without attempting to chase any of the many roe in the neighborhood and

141

ended by attacking a boy of eleven, whom he killed by biting him in the throat.

The same thing happens several times every year with dogs. Most dogs are peaceful or are so well looked after that nothing happens. But dogs trained to attack, whom their handlers can no longer control, are a real danger. Here we are concerned, not with dogs, but with wolves socialized to human beings, and it is this that makes them neurotic. They become unpredictable and dangerous. Anfa, after close coexistence with her first social partner, a human being, had to live in an enclosure, and it was surely that that led to her increasingly disturbed behavior. The wolf is a wild animal and should be left where it belongs, in freedom. It should be kept in captivity only in exceptional circumstances and under responsible control. Unfortunately, the conditions in which wolves are kept in many zoos do not fulfill their minimum requirements. The enclosure, sometimes only a cage, is much too small, the distance from visitors is too small, and the unfortunate animals, who often have only a concrete floor to pad about on, dash backward and forward along the fence in perpetual flight. Behavior stereotypes then develop that are possibly dangerous and certainly please no one, not even visitors to the zoo. Given my choice, I would prohibit the keeping of animals in this way, and that does not only apply to wolves.

So what were we to do with our surplus animals? I was thinking of shooting some of the expelled wolves and some of the cubs, when I had an inquiry from a state zoo in the Eifel. They had just made a big wolf enclosure and wanted some suitable animals. This was an immense relief to me, and I sent them seven animals—two cubs, one of the juveniles born the year before, and four of the expelled wolves, Schönbrunn, Oswald, Rachel, and Lusen. Then I put three other expelled animals (Alexander, Wölfchen, and Psenner) with Mädchen in the neighboring small enclosure. I also put a six-month-old cub named Türk with them, whom tourists had brought back from Turkey.

The three adults in the small enclosure realized only slowly that their time of repression was over, and a long and turbulent period of changes in rank followed. Every week there was a new situation to observe, and I could not keep pace in my note-taking. Things got to such a pitch that all three adults eliminated one another, and the top position devolved for a time upon Türk, who was under one

142

year of age and did not properly understand what was happening. Although he treated the whole thing as a kind of game, it was clearly not a game. One of the three older males was continually to be seen running around wounded. Wölfchen had pieces bitten off his ear and his tail, and after that he no longer looked handsome. All this showed that aggressiveness in the pack depends partly on its composition. In a pack that develops naturally by rearing its own cubs there is less conflict than in a group forced by man to stay together.

In the big enclosure the frequency as well as the intensity of aggressive clashes declined sharply for a time after the big exodus. But in the autumn of 1974 Finsterau, supported by her three remaining cubs of the previous year, attacked Tatra, who was now two and a half years old, and ended by driving her from the pack; and a few weeks later she did the same to Brno. So during the mating season there was again only one sexually mature female in the pack, Finsterau.

This time something especially interesting happened. Ever since the autumn Finsterau had as usual been pressing more frequently against her two escorts, Olomouc and Näschen, lying down in front of them or pulling at their coats. With the arrival of the season of heat this soliciting behavior greatly escalated, and the first to react was Näschen. During the first few days he copulated with Finsterau as Olomouc, the 1.1 ♂, stood by. Two of Finsterau's now barely two-year-old sons also copulated with their mother. Olomouc only gradually became sexually motivated, and he then took charge for a week. After that he weakened, and the other males were again able to try their luck. To Finsterau this was obviously a matter of indifference; she mated with anyone who solicited her energetically. Thus it looks as if the selection of a partner for the 1.1 ♀ is to a large extent settled among the males, the 1.1 ♂ normally playing a key role.

Three cubs were born in the spring. As the period of gestation is from sixty-one to sixty-three days, it was easy to establish the date on which fertilization took place, and according to this the father was the 1.1 ♂ Olomouc. No cubs were born in the small enclosure, where the males showed no interest whatever in Mädchen during the mating season, though it was evident from the behavior of my dog, Flow, that she was in heat. As has often been noted before,

143

more than just an olfactory signal seems to be required to trigger off sexual behavior among male wolves.

The rest of the story of the pack can be told quickly. When nine wolves broke out of the big enclosure shortly before the mating season in January 1976, it is interesting to note that all the wolves in the enclosure did not take advantage of the opportunity to escape. The leading trio, Olomouc, Näschen, and Finsterau, remained, as did Tatra, who had been living on her own for years. But Brno as well as all Finsterau's cubs—that is, the three males of the first litter who were now three years old and the two males and three females of the previous year's litter—escaped.

In order to build a trap in the small enclosure in case the wolves returned, we had to put the two packs together in the big enclosure. The result was fierce fighting. As the newly introduced pack from the small enclosure outnumbered the few nonescapees, they soon gained control. They left Tatra in peace, but Olomouc, Näschen, and Finsterau were forced back into a small rocky area around the visitors' platform. Here the three of them were relatively safe, but at the front uninhibited fighting kept breaking out, and Mädchen and Näschen received wounds that they died from not long afterward. Mädchen had never completely recovered from the effects of her big battle with Finsterau five years before. She was too stiff and too slow, and soon became Finsterau's helpless victim. I took her from the enclosure, but she died a few days later. Näschen had grown fat and indolent. I don't know why he ate so much. He allowed no one, even the 1.1 Olomouc, to approach the food, and after each feed his fat belly hardly allowed him to move. He was continually attacked by the newcomers, and, interestingly enough, Finsterau was among the assailants. Thus she took part in the downfall of the partner with whom she had once had such a close relationship. Later I observed similar behavior in the case of two other couples. Evidently there is no such thing among wolves as marriage "till death do us part."

After I took him from the enclosure Näschen died of wounds that did not look particularly serious. In earlier years he would have survived them easily, but those days were past. As his first escape had given him a certain celebrity, the press reported his death with headlines such as "Furious Wolf Tears Rivals to Pieces," and when I protested they made it "Näschen Dies of Love." All the same, it was a pity that he died. Apart from Anfa, he was the wolf with whom I had had the closest relationship. But of course such things do not count in scientific work.

Soon after the escape, which to Finsterau meant the loss of her "bodyguard," Tatra started regaining her freedom. The new pack in the enclosure kept Finsterau in check, while Tatra was accepted into it. Not a week passed before she began moving about the enclosure with complete freedom and forced her old tormentor, Finsterau, back into the rocks. There were a few serious fights between the two, which the rather bigger Tatra always won. Thus she had been kept subordinate for years by a rival who was her inferior in strength, a fact that shows that assumed and not real strength is the decisive factor in rank relationships between wolves.

The mating season set in while all these battles were in progress. Finsterau, the mother of several litters, did not subject herself to Tatra, but stayed with Olomouc. Psenner, who was also attacked by the others, joined them, and so they formed their own small pack. Both males copulated with Finsterau. As Tatra did the same with Alexander, who again became 1.1 ♂ in the big pack, we had hopes of soon getting more cubs after all the losses, but none was born. Obviously the great aggressiveness and perpetual excitement that prevailed during the mating season either prevented fertilization or caused miscarriage. So I separated the two packs again as soon as it became clear that the small enclosure and the trap in it would not be needed. In the next year, 1977, both females had cubs, Finsterau seven and Tatra four. So there was an end to the shortage of young wolves.

7
Function of
the Ranking Order

The traditional view of the function of hierarchical structures is that they contribute "to avoiding continual friction and neutralizing aggression"[1] and are therefore advantageous to the group. But is that really the case? A hierarchical structure is a characteristic of the group and not of an individual. Can group characteristics have an evolutionary function if selection takes place in the individual or his genes?

I will not delve into the central question in the debate on present-day evolutionary theory, which is whether there is really such a thing as group selection. The interested reader is referred to the admirable summaries of the matter by R. Dawkins and by W. Wickler and U. Seibt.[2] Here we shall deal with it only to the extent that wolves are concerned.

If it is really advantageous to the wolf pack that there should be as little friction as possible—as is to be assumed is the case in the joint tasks of hunting or cub rearing—would it not be much better to live in a completely egalitarian group in which there were no differences in rank? Doesn't the existence of such differences actually encourage aggression? And wolves do not live in groups in which there is no aggression; so aggression and hierarchical structure must be advantageous, if not to the group, then to individual wolves. We shall come closer to an answer to these questions if we take another look at the seasonal rhythm of social behavior and of aggressiveness in particular.

146

Seasonal Variation in Aggressiveness

As can be seen in figure 14, a distinct increase in the frequency of general social behavior patterns takes place during the winter months and then declines again during the summer. In figure 15 we see that there is also a cyclical rhythm in aggressive behavior. But in comparison with the seasonal course of nonaggressive behavior patterns, such as howling in chorus, squirt urination, or neutral contacts (see figures 15–17), the increase in aggressive behavior in autumn generally takes place rather late, but very suddenly, and it is also late in fading away in the spring. We also see that there is a distinct drop in aggressive clashes during the mating season in midwinter. Finally, figure 18 shows that the increase in aggressive behavior is disproportionate, that is, is much more marked than the increase in general activities in winter. A similarly endogenously governed stimulus obviously affects all behavior patterns in winter, the course of most of the changes following the sexual cycle. But aggressiveness is evidently subject to additional influences.

The delay in the increase and decline of aggressive behavior can perhaps be explained as follows. In the summer the pack is busy with the cubs, and the endogenous factor in aggressiveness is small. Underlying it presumably are hormonal factors about which we know nothing. (In many other species a connection has been demonstrated between aggressive behavior and the male sex hormone testosterone.) In autumn aggressiveness increases, but firmly established rank relationships dating from the summer prevent this at first from actually manifesting itself in increased aggressive behavior. Relations between many members of the pack become tenser only gradually. Cubs show the first beginnings of competition for rank, juveniles show an upward expansionary trend, and older animals make the first repressive moves against those below them. Eventually fighting breaks out, and the first changes in rank follow. Changed rank relations among individuals have an influence on many other relationships, and the social ranking order becomes increasingly unstable from the bottom up. Finally, clashes arise between the older wolves with their much more firmly established rank relations, and this is accompanied by a big increase in aggressive behavior.

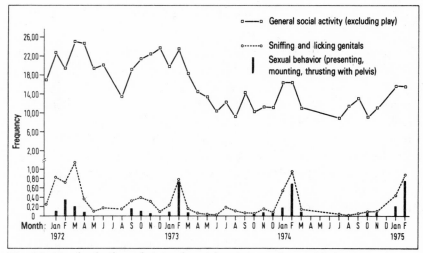

Fig. 14. Yearly rhythm of general social activity and sexual behavior.

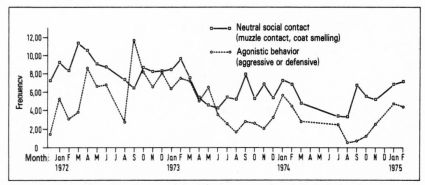

Fig. 15. Annual cycle of neutral social contact and agonistic behavior.

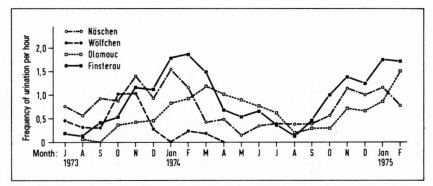

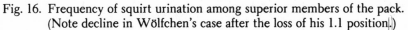

Fig. 16. Frequency of squirt urination among superior members of the pack. (Note decline in Wölfchen's case after the loss of his 1.1 position.)

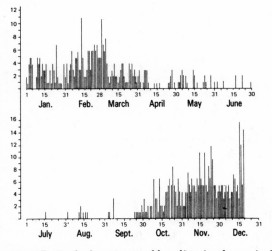

Fig. 17. Daily frequency of howling in chorus in 1969.

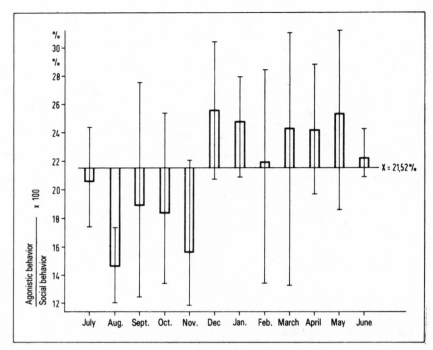

Fig. 18. Relationship between agonistic behavior and general social behavior (excluding play behavior). In the long term 21.52 percent of all social contacts were aggressive in nature. The columns give the average divergence from this and the thin lines, the greatest divergences.

As a result of these clashes a new ranking order is gradually established, a new equilibrium that again leads to a decline in aggressive behavior. The mating season sets in and takes its course with many minor, localized conflicts, but generally without major battles. When it is over there is a sharp decrease in the endogenous factor behind aggressiveness. This was very evident every year, particularly in the behavior of the 1.1 ♀, who was to a large extent responsible for the great aggressiveness before the mating season but was always distinctly more friendly after it. The repression of subdominant females diminishes as a result, and the males are quieter too. Consequently there is another change in relationships, because the previously established equilibrium becomes unstable again as a result of the reduction in pressure from above. More fighting and

150

more changes of rank ensue, and by the beginning of summer a new order has been established and aggressive behavior again diminishes.

Aggressive behavior, according to this theory, has both endogenous and social causes. In the autumn a solidly established social order prevents for a time the increased endogenous impulse from actually manifesting itself in aggressive behavior; in spring the reduced endogenous impetus is responsible for another increase in aggressive behavior. The influence of the ranking order manifests itself both in the delayed increase and the delayed decline in aggressive behavior. Aggressiveness is therefore neither simply a consequence of spontaneously increased endogenous impulse nor exclusively a socially governed reactive phenomenon. Rather, it arises as the individual comes to terms with his social environment in a very finely tuned system of both impelling and inhibiting mechanisms.

Aggression is helpful to the individual in competing with his conspecifics. But uninhibited aggression by every individual would disrupt the social organization of the pack. The hierarchical organization makes it possible for relatively stable conditions to exist temporarily at any rate, since by a kind of negative feedback it curbs aggressiveness. This is advantageous to the pack as well as to each of its members, for it prevents fatal wounds and makes possible the carrying out of vital common tasks.

Thus there must be an optimal equilibrium between the interests of the individual and those of the pack, which in the last resort are also its own. But what are the interests of the individual? What is the use of higher rank? Is it always a disadvantage to be of low rank? To be able to answer these questions we must take another quick look at what actually happens in the pack.

Constancy of Pack Size

In spite of yearly accessions, the size of the pack after an initial growth phase remained relatively constant (see figure 19). I did not remove from the enclosure a single member of the pack, but only animals that had been expelled or had left it voluntarily; and once I removed three cubs; also a large part of the pack escaped, as I have

151

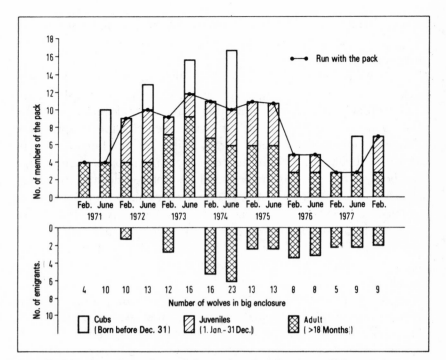

Fig. 19. Number of members of the pack and of "emigrants" from it in February and June 1971 to 1978. Note that the pack does not exceed a definite size.

mentioned. Thus the size of the pack was to a large extent regulated by the wolves themselves. The upper limit in this enclosure seemed to be about eleven adult and juvenile animals, apart from the cubs.

It is interesting to note that, according to Dave Mech, wolves in Minnesota leave existing packs chiefly in autumn and spring.[3] To a large extent this coincides with experience in our pack (see table 3) and corresponds to the periods of increased social unrest to which I referred. The times when new rank relationships are established are presumably also the times when both enforced and voluntary departures from the pack take place.

Who left the pack, and why? With the exception of the first year, when the juvenile age group was missing, the leavers were always adult wolves, who could be divided into two categories. Either they were former alpha animals who had lost their position or they were animals who had just reached adulthood. Figure 20 shows that the number of those born each year who remained in the pack grew smaller every year. Only one or two animals of each age group remained in the pack as adults. This age-conditioned reduction of pack size makes it possible to construct a general model of the wolf pack. Its nucleus is a pair of 1.1 animals, who may be joined by one or more adults, generally males. These animals are usually either children or twins of one of the two 1.1 animals, but they can be completely unrelated, as is shown by observations of wolves in a state of freedom.[4] This small group of adults is supplemented by the surviving young animals born in that and the previous years. Looked at in this way, the social organization of wolves differs from that of other canids who live alone or in small groups only in the fact that the cubs stay with their parents for a longer time. But that does not apply always and everywhere; it is not true, for instance, of the wolves in the Abruzzi. There, as a result of the early departure of young animals, the packs are very small and their social structure is more like that of the fox. This is connected with the adaptation of

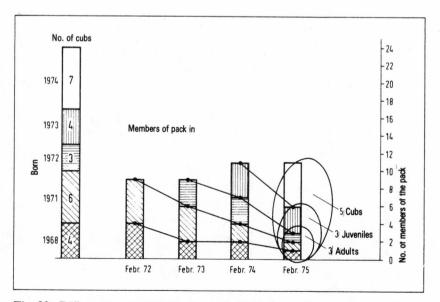

Fig. 20. Different generations in the pack. With increasing age fewer and fewer animals remain.

153

the size of the pack to the special ecological conditions existing there, which shall be discussed later.

Differences are also to be observed among wolves that have left the pack. The females generally seem to have been forced to do so; either they have lost their high rank by defeat in battle or they are young, sexually mature animals who have been driven out by the alpha female. With the males the situation is rather different. The former 1.1 ♂ Wölfchen left the pack voluntarily rather than as a result of compulsion. Similarly, some of the younger inferior males left voluntarily, while others, such as Oswald, tried to remain in the pack in spite of violent attacks and finally left only under the greatest pressure.

Why do some young animals manage to remain in the pack and advance to the top position while others leave it? Two typical examples are Finsterau and Olomouc. Both grew up in an existing pack, and in both cases their attainment of sexual maturity coincided with upheavals among the superior adults in which they themselves were not at first involved, but which they were able to exploit to their advantage, advancing immediately to the highest ranks in the pack.

If these processes that I observed are also characteristic of other packs, the following picture emerges. Many animals of the rising generation remain in the pack until they attain sexual maturity. If stable relations exist among the small group of older superior wolves, these younger animals sooner or later leave the pack and go their own way. Only if upheavals take place in the superior group, whether as a result of death or loss of position through defeat in the struggle for rank, can young animals advance into that group and remain in the pack. The "little alphas" among the young animals are in an especially favorable starting position for this.

High rank has a number of consequences. It increases the chances of the young remaining in the pack, even if a large amount of luck is required for this. Among the older animals it increases the likelihood of being able to take part directly in reproduction, to have cubs themselves. In the words of the modern evolutionary biologist, high rank increases personal fitness and the probability of transmitting one's genetic material to the next generation.

The "Selfish" Gene

But if only two animals at a time produce cubs and thus reproduce their genes in the next generation, why do juveniles help the reproducing couple (who are generally their parents) to rear the cubs who are their younger siblings? Why do some sexually mature animals remain in the pack without having cubs of their own, and why do they take such an active part in rearing other animals' cubs? Is not their fitness (their chance of reproduction) diminished by this? This question is vital to our understanding of the ultimate causes of pack formation among wolves. Let us consider what happens to animals that leave the pack.

In the enclosure they lived to a large extent in isolation without producing cubs. In a state of freedom they would be able to leave the area, perhaps find a partner and an unoccupied territory and rear young themselves. That is presumably how a pack usually begins. But for those who leave the pack the prospects are poor. We still lack accurate data on the subject from territories with different kinds of game, but we can assume that in areas with a high-density wolf population and territorially established packs it must be difficult for newly formed couples or small groups to find and maintain a territory of their own big enough to ensure the rearing of cubs. In territories where the game is big it is extremely difficult for small packs to kill enough, and above all to do so regularly enough, which also means that the chances of rearing cubs successfully are poor, as observations on Isle Royale have shown.[5]

But the increased expectation of life of an animal that remains with a territorially established pack does not explain why so many members of a pack besides the parents should share with such apparent altruism in the rearing of the cubs.

This brings us to the modern evolutionary idea of kin selection and the theory of inclusive fitness proposed by Hamilton and others, which is gradually being accepted. In this context fitness of course always refers exclusively to reproduction, the probability of producing and rearing offspring that in turn will produce offspring of its own, and so on.

Obviously, it is in the interests of every member of the pack, particularly the older animals who have been integrated into it for a long time, that the young should be reared successfully to preserve the pack as an effective hunting unit to the general benefit. If an animal is unable to rear cubs of its own, it makes sense that if the goal is reproductive success, it should take part in the rearing of related cubs, with which it has genes in common. Discounting incest, 50 percent of the genes of parents, children, and siblings are on the average identical, while the figure for uncles and nephews is 25 percent and for cousins, 12.5 percent. The "inclusive fitness" of an animal is measured by its individual contribution to the reproduction of its genes plus the contribution it makes to the reproduction of the same genes through related animals. The more closely related two animals are, the higher the proportion of their identical gene material, the more "worthwhile" it is for one of them to renounce possibly unsuccessful reproduction in favor of the successful rearing of the young of the other. The probability of its genes being transmitted to the next generation is thereby increased.

It should not be assumed that wolves—or human beings, for that matter, to whom the theory of inclusive fitness must also apply if it is correct—understand exactly what it is that the successful propagation of their genes increases. On the contrary, such genetically sound results develop through natural selection, because the bearers of the less "selfish" gene grow relatively fewer and fewer.

The theory of inclusive fitness or the "selfish" gene not only explains why some adult wolves remain in a pack in which only one litter a year is produced, but it also explains why one wolf remains subordinate to another for years—as Näschen was to Wölfchen (his brother) and later to Olomouc (his stepson), or as young wolves are to older ones. It also throws new light on the inexplicably violent aggression of an alpha female against her slowly weakening partner of many years' standing, such as Finsterau's attacks on Näschen (which incidentally refute the myth of the permanent fidelity of wolves to their mates). There is only a very distant relationship between the reproductive partners in a pack. To rear cubs successfully, a strong partner is invaluable, and a partner weakened by old age or wounds must be driven out in the interests of "fitness," or reproductive success. The theory also explains the phenomenon of friendship among the wolves of a pack because of population genetics. (Oswald, for instance, who was Finsterau's twin brother, took an especially big part in the rearing of Finsterau's cubs.) But, as was men-

156

tioned earlier, more investigation is needed into the causes of friendship and enmity in the pack. In general, it seems to me that we are only at the beginning of the functional analysis of social behavior.

Our model of the individual wolf's prospects for survival and reproduction if it remains with or leaves the pack and whether it accurately reflects what happens in the pack and the wolf population has yet to be tested by observation of wolves in freedom. According to my observation of packs in captivity, a wolf's rank in the hierarchical structure of his age and sex group plays a vital part in his fitness. As long as the cubs enjoy the general goodwill of their elders, they have no need of any ranking order. Access to food is maintained by localized clashes. Only when a vacancy occurs in the highly restricted adult group does the superior animal in the rising generation enjoy an advantage. Finally, the highest rank is advantageous to adult males; to females it is a *sine qua non* for reproduction.

From that point of view a wolf should always be trying to improve its position in the pack. But we have seen that many animals do not do this, and we now understand that this is in the interests of their inclusive fitness. This applies above all to older subdominant animals. To younger ones, however, a high position is essential if they are to remain in the pack, and they should therefore have a greater interest in climbing up the ranking order. In fact, clashes of rank are much more frequent among these animals than among their seniors. But in the interests of the effective functioning of the pack as a whole in securing food and rearing cubs, it is clear that these conflicts should be suppressed as often as possible, and the hierarchical structure of the pack makes a vital contribution to doing just that. Thus a delicately balanced equilibrium prevails between the interests of the individual and the social community of which he is a part that preserves the efficiency of the whole in spite of individual upward pressure.

8

Formation, Maintenance, and Leadership of the Pack

By "role behavior" ethologists mean typical behavior patterns of individual animals within a group that influence the behavior of other members. We have already come across some roles, such as the behavior of the mother and of young wolves toward cubs, the "watchdog" role of older males, and the principal, activity-directing role of the 1.1 ♂. The conventional idea is of course that there is always a leader of the pack to whom all the other members are subordinate. We shall now consider more closely the role behavior of individual members of the pack, the individual interests manifested by this behavior, and the contribution it makes to the efficient functioning of the pack. The first question that arises is how the pack is held together, and how decisions are reached such as when and where to sleep, when to move on, what game to hunt, and so on. Does the leader of the pack decide, or are decisions arrived at in a more complicated fashion? But first we must consider the bonds between individuals in the pack.

Assessing the Bonds

Whether there is a special social bonding drive or whether bonding comes about as a result of other impulses such as sex, protectiveness, or aggression is a controversial question among ethologists. I therefore propose to use the term "bond" not causally but opera-

158

tionally, defining it as the tendency of two or more animals to remain together or rejoin each other after a separation. Its strength can be assessed by the distance the animals keep from one another. (An alternative is to assess it by the speed of return after spatial separation.)

Theoretical considerations suggested the following questions: [1]

To what extent was the bond among members of our pack dependent on age, sex, and rank? What was the influence of the environment (open country, for instance, in comparison with woodland, or familiar surroundings in comparison to unfamiliar surroundings)? What was the influence of seasonal changes? And what was the effect of the size and composition of the group?

MEASURING DISTANCES

Distances of members of a pack from one another were recorded on different days and at different times of the year, both in the enclosure and on walks with tame, free-running wolves. Also separation experiments were made with tame wolves on these outings. The animals' distance from one another could, of course, only be estimated, but this could be done with sufficient accuracy after some practice. Experiments with students showed that after big initial mistakes good results could very quickly be obtained, most easily in estimating distances from where the observer was standing. As a suggestion for your next walk, try the following. First measure a distance accurately, preferably choosing a slope. Then practice walking this distance, both up hill and down, taking strides exactly one yard in length. The stride you have practiced is then used to check your estimates. This can be great fun.

Some difficulties arise, however. Two animals may, for instance, each have a bond to the same place and may be close to one another only for that reason. Here is an experience that illustrates this kind of problem.

After the loss of her 1.1 position Mädchen was in a bad way. Her wounds did not heal well and her winter coat grew badly, no doubt as a consequence of the fighting and the stress connected with her loss of rank. She suffered from the cold, so I took her to Waldhäuser and put her in the enclosure next to our house. She still suf-

159

fered from the cold, so I made a comfortable bed for her in the cellar—a layer of hay with a blanket over it and an infrared lamp for warmth. But still she wasn't happy. She spent hours scratching at the cellar door in order to get out, presumably wanting company.

My mother-in-law took pity on her and suggested we should take her into the house. I was doubtful about this, but allowed myself to be persuaded—on the condition that she should be allowed to sleep only on the floor. But she soon discovered that the sofa in the living room was softer and more comfortable. Her stubbornness was exceeded only by my tenacity; I kept throwing her off the sofa. My mother-in-law was less consistent in the matter, however, and when I wasn't there Mädchen would soon be on the sofa again, with my mother-in-law sitting beside her. It is hardly necessary to add that after that Mädchen's bond to my mother-in-law was far closer than her bond to me.

One day Mädchen discovered there was a place even more comfortable than the sofa, namely my mother-in-law's soft featherbed. During the day I put her in the enclosure. It was spring, it was warm, and the snow was melting rapidly. During the evening a small avalanche of snow from the roof crashed into the wolf enclosure. Later, when I went out to bring in Mädchen for the night, there was no sign of her. Had she been buried by the avalanche? A party of students had just arrived, and I put them to work immediately. Like rescuers after a real avalanche in the Alps, we plunged long sticks into every square inch of snow, but there was no sign of her. Then we dug deep holes everywhere in the heavy, wet snow, but there was still no sign of her. At about midnight we gave up and went back into the house, exhausted, where we found Mädchen snoring on the big feather-filled pillow on my mother-in-law's bed. She must have climbed up the big heap of snow to the open window and got in that way. The doors were open, and so she soon found the softest and warmest place in the house, which was that bed. She did not allow herself to be disturbed by our laughter. She looked up briefly and dozed off again, and it was only to the accompaniment of vigorous protests that she was later removed from the bed.

After this that bed was the object of all her aspirations. She developed an extraordinary ability for finding her way to it, and we often had to concede defeat. Now, suppose we had had two wolves with a

160

similar bond to such a place. If the usual method of measuring the social bond between them had been applied, it would have shown a very powerful one indeed. Though a warm featherbed would not necessarily be the favored spot of normal wolves, this experience clearly shows that wolves can develop a bond to a place that could lead to animals being frequently seen together without meaning that the bond between them was necessarily correspondingly strong. However, in a species as mobile as the wolf, which is constantly on the move, the danger of such a mistake must be relatively small. A real bond to their den and its surroundings is observable only among young cubs.

Certain bonds to places existed, however, among the wolves in the enclosure. They slept by choice in the higher part of it, as far as possible away from the visitors' platform, in places from which it was possible to keep an eye on the surroundings. Also the expelled and persecuted wolves kept to the rocks around the platform. Here they were safer from attack, because the pack wolves avoided that area, where they were distracted by the proximity of human beings and consequently attacked with less determination. For the same reason some of the expelled wolves kept relatively close together without having any particular social contact with one another.

Mistakes can also result from the by no means unusual circumstance of two animals both having a strong bond to a third. As a result the two may often be seen together without it meaning that there is necessarily a strong bond between them. If the third animal disappeared, each would probably go its own way. Finally, the fact of two wolves keeping closely together does not necessarily imply the existence of a strong two-way bond between them; it may mean that only one of them seeks the proximity of the other. Thus to establish the real situation the rest of the animals' behavior toward each other, and above all the frequency of their social contacts, must be taken into account.

INFLUENCE OF AGE

We now come to the observations and the findings resulting from them. (In addition to the diagrams on the pages that follow, the interested reader will find further details in the appendix.) As I was concerned with reciprocal relationships, I had to note both the spatial behavior of older wolves to the growing cubs as well as the cubs' behavior toward their seniors. We already knew a great deal about the mother's bond to her cubs and that of other members of the pack to them. During the first few days after the cubs were born, the mother spent her time almost exclusively with them, and only gradually did she begin going farther away from them for longer periods. When they were about three weeks old she often did not go back into the den to sleep but slept outside it, and went to the cubs only to suckle them. The adult and juvenile members of the pack showed a great interest in the newborn cubs' den, and in the months that followed the place where the cubs lived was the center of the pack (see figure 13).

This bond to the cubs and their dwelling place suddenly weakened when they were four months old, that is, at the end of August and the beginning of September. By this time they were quite big and independent and could often be a real nuisance to their elders. Then in late autumn the older wolves again tended more and more to be observed sleeping near the cubs. But now the bond seemed to a large extent to come from the cubs' side. They followed the pack around the enclosure and slept where their elders did. The relationship between wolves and cubs had developed into one among members of the pack.

Thus in early autumn the adult and juvenile wolves changed their behavior toward the cubs. But how did the cubs behave? At first they kept closely together and, as is shown by the findings from Rickling (see figure 21), they hardly ever moved away from the older animals if they could help it. Until late autumn there was no difficulty in taking out all the animals and letting them run freely, as no cub ever moved more than about a hundred yards away. Only at about the age of ten months, during their first winter, did they begin to become increasingly independent. The situation is no different with wolves in freedom. The cubs leave the area where they were reared in early autumn and follow the pack on longer and longer roamings. Then in their first winter they tend to go their own way, and a few leave the pack for good.

Observations show that an endogenously governed process of maturation underlies both the breaking away of the older wolves from the cubs and of the cubs from one another and from their elders. The development of independence among the cubs takes place

162

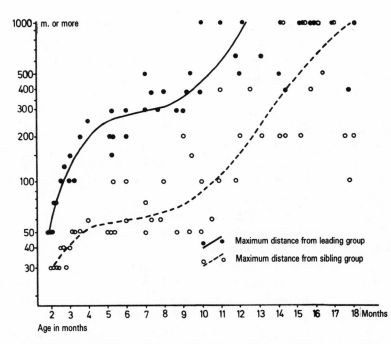

Fig. 21. Maximum distance of four cubs from leading group (Anfa and the author), as well as maximum distance single cubs kept from sibling group. The cubs obviously kept more closely together.

later than the breaking away of their elders from them. This is certainly advantageous, as it means that they stay with the pack during the critical period of their first wanderings. Only at the age of ten to twelve months are they able to begin to fend for themselves. Meanwhile the older animals stop bringing them food. They hunt for themselves or take their share of the prey hunted and killed by the pack.

There is another interesting point in connection with this process by which young wolves become independent. It struck me at Rickling that when the young wolves were alone they always stayed close to us, but were much more likely to move away when there were two of them or more.

To test the strength of this sibling bond I made the following experiment later in the Bavarian Forest. During the summer I took

Ho and Tschi, two cubs born that year, out of the enclosure together with Alexander and Wölfchen. Two students who had reared Ho and Tschi accompanied us, as well as my dog, Flow, to whom Ho and Tschi were very attached. After we had walked a short distance for purposes of habituation, we let one of the two cubs free and split up into two different groups (see table 15). The cub ran restlessly backward and forward between the two groups and went on trying for as long as possible to keep contact with us all. When this was no longer possible, in almost every case he chose the group that included his twin, even when this group was much smaller than the other.

Figure 21 shows that this close bond between cubs diminishes only at ten to twelve months. Up to six months it is even stronger than the bond to other members of the pack. The explanation was perhaps to be found in another experiment. I wanted to find out whether the older animals would notice whether a cub was missing, and so in the summer of 1974, when there were seven cubs in the enclosure, I tried removing one, two, or three cubs at a time. My attempts caused the greatest excitement, influencing the behavior of all the animals in the enclosure for hours. Consequently it was only on the few occasions when I succeeded in removing cubs without being spotted that I obtained any useful findings, but these sufficed to show that, at least in the case of the mother, anxiety and search behavior were closely correlated with the number of missing cubs. In two cases out of three she showed no discernible reaction if one cub was missing, but two and above all three missing cubs triggered off intensive search behavior.[2] Schönbrunn had reacted in the same way in the spring of 1973.

When a cub goes out into the world it is clearly important that it do so in the company of its siblings. The older wolves' bond may be to the cubs as a whole and not to each individual cub. Hence the absence of several cubs is noticed much more quickly than that of a single cub. It is more important for the cubs to stay together than it is to individually follow older animals with whom they might quickly lose contact. As long as they remain in the group the adults pay attention to them, but on their own they are left to their own devices, which can be difficult when one is small. Observations of wolves in freedom show that cub mortality is especially high in early autumn.[3]

INFLUENCE OF RANK AND SEX

As far as spatial organization in the pack is concerned, figure 22 shows that it is usually superior adults who were to be found in close proximity to other animals. The 1.1 ♀ and a group of superior males who were joined by juveniles and cubs moved, rested, and slept together with special frequency. The pack kept even closer together in winter, particularly in the mating season, while in summer the individual animals tended to be encountered alone or in smaller groups.[4] These findings are in complete agreement with our previous knowledge of the pack and also in essential agreement with conditions in packs living in natural conditions.

Closer analysis of spatial behavior in the pack showed some surprising differences among individual animals (see appendix, table 6). The higher an animal's rank, the more frequently was it to be seen in the company of others. This was in accordance with our expectations—as was the fact that the two superior males (Olomouc

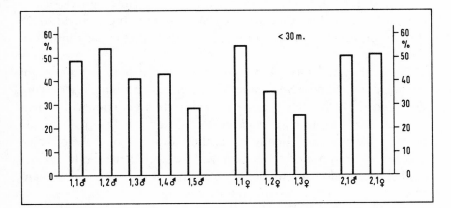

Fig. 22. Percentage of occasions on which wolves of different status were observed less than 30 meters away from other wolves in the enclosure. Total number of observations, 22,199, was made between December 1972 and July 1973. Note that the two superior males, the superior female, and the juveniles were most often in the company of other animals, while the inferior adults increasingly went their own way.

165

and Näschen), the superior female (Finsterau), and the superior juvenile (Gelbauge) kept closely together. But while the three adults were to be seen together with equal frequency, the superior juvenile associated almost exclusively with the 1.1 ♂ Olomouc. Thus there were firm reciprocal bonds among the three adults, while the superior juvenile's bond was chiefly to the 1.1 ♂. The cubs helped the two inferior juveniles integrate. The cubs frequently associated with the 1.1 ♂ and the two juveniles associated with the cubs, with the result that both groups frequently ran with the pack.

Similar findings resulted from experiments with free-running wolves in the Bavarian Forest. After our move to Waldhäuser I took the tame wolves for long walks every day. At the time Wölfchen was the undisputed 1.1 ♂, Mädchen the 1.1 ♀, Näschen the 1.2 ♂, and Alexander the 1.3 ♂. After we had walked for a while I recorded the distance between them at two-minute intervals. The first thing that struck me was that in comparison with Rickling, the animals kept much more closely together. Why? I think it was connected to their changed status. At Rickling they had been cubs and later subdominant juveniles, while now they were adults of high rank. It was they whom the younger wolves followed in the enclosure, and this was also evident when they were running free. It was obvious, as it had been in the enclosure, that the hierarchical structure of the pack was a vital influence on the way the pack moves in the country.

It was above all the 1.1 ♂ Wölfchen with whom the others kept seeking contact and who kept making contact with others (see figure 23). The 1.1 ♀ Mädchen came second in the frequency with which she ran close to another wolf, while Alexander, the male of the lowest rank, was most frequently farthest away. Also, if the distance between the animals is noted, it will be seen that Wölfchen occupied a central position. Both Mädchen and the two subdominant males kept a smaller distance away from him, while the bond between Mädchen and Näschen (and even more obviously, that between Mädchen and Alexander) was more indirect and came about by way of their bond to Wölfchen.

These findings were confirmed by two other experiments. On September 1, the day on which Näschen ran away and thus brought this experiment to a premature end, instead of recording distances I noted the frequency with which the wolves made contact with one

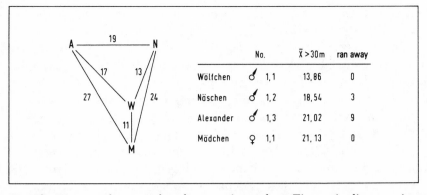

		No.	X̄ > 30 m	ran away
Wölfchen	♂	1,1	13,86	0
Näschen	♂	1,2	18,54	3
Alexander	♂	1,3	21,02	9
Mädchen	♀	1,1	21,13	0

Fig. 23. Distances between four free-running wolves. Figures in diagram give percentage of occasions on which individual animals were observed to be running more than 30 meters away from each other.

another while running (see appendix, table 7). The initiative for this came by far the most often from Wölfchen, and he was also most frequently at the receiving end of this rapid contact making. The two subdominant males also made contact with each other relatively frequently, but rarely with Mädchen.

In the second experiment I either allowed the four adults to run free one at a time while the others stayed on the lead with me, or I allowed all of them to run free except one, who stayed with me. Comparison of the data so obtained showed that all four wolves made contact much more often with the big group that was with me than with the small one; and again it was Wölfchen who made such contacts with the greatest frequency. Sometimes he ran for minutes on end next to the wolves on the chain and never went far away.

ALEXANDER'S ITCH FOR FREEDOM

These outings in the National Park were a rich source of information on individual bonding behavior and its influence on the cohesion of the pack. Wölfchen, for instance, was always very restless when the two subdominant males went off together. He went after them and quickly reestablished contact. But then Mädchen would be missing, whereupon Wölfchen would overtake the two males and make play movements in their direction obviously intended to induce them to follow him. I often noticed that a wolf would induce another to change direction and follow him by challenging him to play. When Alexander or Näschen went off on his own Wölfchen was less worried, and in particular he took the least interest in Alexander, the lowest in rank.

Perhaps I am only imagining it in retrospect because it fits in with my ideas, but Alexander seemed to run away on these outings much more often than the others; he did so nine times altogether, in comparison with Näschen's three (though one of his escapades lasted for a very long time) and Wölfchen's and Mädchen's none. That indicated not only that Alexander had a stronger trend to independence than the others, but also that Wölfchen was more willing to let him go than Näschen or Mädchen.

When Alexander left the pack there was never any difficulty in finding him. He always left the forest and went down to where there were villages, dogs, rubbish heaps, and children's playgrounds. If any of my wolves was real material for domestication—in the form in which it must have taken place 10,000 or 15,000 years ago—it was the friendly, unterrifying, and titbit-loving Alexander. The local people soon got to know him and, after their initial mistrust, stopped being afraid of him. So I was not in the least worried on one occasion when Alexander disappeared yet again on an outing up into the mountains with Professor Grzimek and the other wolves. Grzimek looked worried, however, for as the head of a zoo he had had many negative experiences as a result of popular reaction to the escape of zoo animals. When we got back to Waldhäuser after a long forced march it was the zoo director in him that must have dictated his answer to a little girl who obviously recognized him and asked him whether we were looking for a wolf. "No," he said, "not a wolf, just a little one that's not at all dangerous and certainly wouldn't—" "But it *is* a big one," the little girl interrupted, indicating with her hand how big she considered Alexander to be, and that was really quite big. "It's just been down to the playground, and we've been playing with it."

There is indeed a children's playground just below Waldhäuser, and I hurried toward it, but I did not have to go very far, because Alexander came bounding across the fields toward me. As soon as he saw me he naturally tried to make off again, but as usual I succeeded in intimidating him by shouting and swinging the chain, to

168

which I eventually attached him. The little girl's father—the family was on holiday in the neighborhood—later told me that Alexander had sniffed at a number of children in the playground and had then tried to play with a dachshund. Some children had wanted to stroke him, whereupon he had disappeared again in the direction of the village.

It really must have been wolves like Alexander who were the ancestors of our dogs. But he also demonstrated better than any other wolf how dependent individual behavior is on social status. He was not always so friendly. A year previously, when he was the 1.1 ♂, he had attacked me, and many years later, when he was again the alpha male, he resisted all attempts to remove him from the enclosure. At that time he was the central figure in the pack, was consequently always mindful of contact with its members, and from behind the fence made furious attacks on strange dogs as well as people whom he had previously greeted effusively. This went on until he again lost his alpha position and left the pack, whereupon he again became good-natured and always sought contact. I do not think there could be a better demonstration of the influence of social rank on wolf behavior.

INFLUENCE OF THE ENVIRONMENT

As the data gathered on these excursions show, environmental factors and age influence the spatial behavior of the pack. First I evaluated the material according to familiarity with the country (see appendix, table 8). I assumed that wolves would stay more closely together in unfamiliar territory, and this was confirmed. But even more marked differences appeared in regard to the structure of the country. In dense forest in which visibility was restricted, the wolves kept more closely together than on forest roads and tracks that afforded long views.

This was not really surprising. Contact in the pack is obviously maintained partly by sight. Another observation that at first surprised me more was the way in which wolves kept closely together on a steep ascent. At first it did not occur to me to note the angle of inclination, but I was soon struck by the way the animals kept together when climbing, and after that I always noted the angle of inclination. The results showed that my intuition was correct,

169

which was not really so surprising, since wolves too must find that a long climb tires them. In those circumstances, just like human beings, they do not make any unnecessary spurts or detours and do not indulge in play, but plod steadily uphill and in closer proximity to one another.

It also struck me that wolves dislike leaving a route or changing a direction. For a long time I simply followed the wolves on our outings; it was they who decided the direction. But that would not always do. The German-Czech frontier, marked only by a forest track, runs along the crest of the mountains, and overstepping it might perhaps have had unpleasurable consequences for the wolves, but it certainly would have had unpleasurable consequences for me. Also there were inhabited areas below the National Park that I did not want to enter with the free-running wolves. So several times a day I had to decide which way to go and change direction accordingly, and I always had difficulty in getting the wolves to come with me. Generally I had to put one or two of them on the chain and use sheer muscle power to impose the new direction on them all.

INFLUENCE OF THE SIZE OF THE GROUP

This difficulty in getting the wolves to change course raises the question of pack leadership. But before we deal with it we must look at the influence of the size of the group on the spatial behavior of the individual animal. I wanted to carry out some experiments concerning the matter in the Bavarian Forest, but Näschen frustrated my plans by running away. However, I had previously made some experiments at Rickling, which I shall briefly describe.

I made them in the summer of 1968, when Alexander and his siblings were eighteen months old. I had taken them out with Anfa almost every day since they were cubs, and it was always Anfa, whom I kept on a chain, and I who decided where to go. We were the leading group, so to speak, whom the four young wolves followed. I wanted to find out how strong was the influence of this leading group on the decision-making process of each of the young wolves. For this purpose I put three of them on the chain and only one, the animal being tested, was allowed to run free. I changed the test animal each time, and the experiment itself, in intention at any rate, was very simple. With the aid of Dagmar and later of several colleagues from the institute, all of them well known to the wolves, we formed two groups that parted after walking together for several minutes and went their separate ways at an angle of about ninety degrees. In the first series of experiments I took another juvenile in addition to Anfa, who always stayed with me, and Dagmar took the other two. Thus the two groups were of equal size. In the next series Dagmar took all three juveniles, while I took only Anfa. After that a friend joined the group consisting of Dagmar and her three cubs, then two more friends, so that there were always at least three human beings, and usually more. Thus the group that separated from the "traditional" leading group (Anfa and me) grew bigger and bigger.

As Näschen at this time would have left the pack completely if he had had the chance, we could not use him for this experiment. But in spite of these difficulties and frequent searches for runaway wolves, the results (see appendix, table 9) were interesting. When two groups of the same size separated, all three of the wolves tested invariably went with the leading group, that is, with Anfa, me, and another young wolf. The choice was made at an early stage, and practically no attempts were made to search for the other group. When the split was four (Dagmar and three young wolves) to two (Anfa and me) the test animals still preferred the leading group, though not invariably. As the size of the other group was further increased, the test animals chose it more and more often, and they ended by actually preferring it. But it was often difficult to make sure which group the test animal was following, as it spent a long time running backward and forward between them. Sometimes we had to walk on for as much as half an hour until either a definite choice was made or the experiment had to be broken off.

Generally this was a relief, for Anfa could be made to separate from the others only by a choke chain and persistent forceful tugging. She objected to any separation far more vigorously than the young wolves on the chain, and she objected even more violently the bigger the departing group was. As soon as I relaxed my hold she immediately tried to rejoin the other group. This agreed completely with Wölfchen's behavior when he was the alpha animal a few years later in the Bavarian Forest. In no other animal is the affinity to the group so marked as it is in the alpha animal.

I also did some experiments in which one group stayed where it

171

was after a rest while the other went on. These showed that the group that went on exercised a powerful attraction on free-running wolves (see appendix, table 10).

Cohesion and Leadership of the Pack

These experiments showed that some animals contribute more than others to the composition of the pack, and they do so in two ways. In the first place, they exercise a strong attraction on other members of the pack, and, second, they actively seek contact themselves. A wolf that is attractive to the members of the pack is itself strongly attracted by them.[5]

With cubs the situation is different. During their first few weeks of life, their attractiveness to their elders is obviously greater than their own bond to them. When they are about five months old, this state of affairs seems to be reversed. The cubs lose some of their attractiveness to their elders but are strongly attracted to them. This helps the pack to become mobile again in early autumn. It makes it easier for the older animals to move on, and the cubs are better able to follow the pack on its travels.

But let us return to the fact that some wolves contribute more than others to the cohesion of the pack. If there are strong bonds between A and B and A and C, it does not necessarily follow that there is also a strong bond between B and C, though they will often be seen together because they both have a bond to A. In the pack it is the superior adults to whom strong bonds exist, and this applies to a special extent to the 1.1 ♂; this explains his predominant role in assuring the cohesion of the pack. There can also be strong bonds among other animals, among cubs and those members of the pack that take special care of them. Such bondings between a few animals must in the last resort be of vital importance to larger packs in particular.

The strongest and most stable bonds occur in the small group of superior adults, between the 1.1 couple and perhaps another male that has a strong bond either to the 1.1 ♂ or the 1.1 ♀. As this group keeps closely together, it has great attractiveness for other wolves, depending not only on the "quality" of its members but also on their number. My separation experiments showed plainly that the

172

size of a group has a vital influence on the behavior of other members of the pack. This gives the superior adults an additional attractiveness that their inferiors lack. The inferiors have less interest in perpetual contact and do not form rigidly defined subgroups. It is not surprising that they are the first to try to leave the pack of their own accord and the last to be prevented by others from doing so.

In this context we must also consider the question of the leadership of the pack. No member decides alone when an activity is to begin or end, or which way or at what speed the pack is to move, or exercises sole power of command in any of the other activities that are vital to the cohesion of the pack. The autocratic leading wolf does not exist. Nevertheless, there are animals that have a stronger influence than others on the choice made by the pack, just as there are those who effect its composition. They are not necessarily the same animals. We have seen that a high degree of attractiveness is exercised by adult and above all by superior wolves on younger ones; by superiors on other superiors; by cubs on their parents, other superior adults, and juveniles; by big groups on small groups or on individuals; by active or departing animals and groups on remaining ones; by animals and groups that stick to a route that has been set out upon.

But all "attractive" animals do not have to be leaders of the pack; cubs, for instance, are certainly not leaders. Also wolves that get up and go do not necessarily decide whether the whole pack follows. The "initiator" does not have to be the "decider." But who decides? Observations of free-living wolves on Isle Royale in Lake Superior on the border between the United States and Canada, where the ecology of the wolf has been studied for many years, have shown that in 70 percent of all cases it is one of the two alpha animals that runs at the head of the pack. Rolf Peterson, who has recently been in charge of studies there, concluded that the leadership of the pack comes to a large extent from the alpha animals.[6] In principle that is certainly correct, though my experiments have shown that things are not always quite so simple.

It seems rather that all the members of the pack contribute to the decision making, though not to the same extent. It is a qualified democracy. The older a member is and the higher his rank, the more weight he has, though he never has enough to outweigh all the others. The 1.1 ♂ cannot have his way against the will of the majority, nor can the 1.1 ♀ even in the mating season when she seems to exercise unrestricted control over the activity of the pack. Several times I have observed how a 1.1 ♀ in heat—usually followed by a cluster of males—stopped at once when for some reason (generally a quarrel) they ceased to follow her. Also I have often had the impression that the 1.1 ♂, who has such a strong influence on events in the pack outside the mating season, is himself very strongly influenced by others. The process of decision making in the pack is much more complex than one would expect from traditional ideas on the subject. Observations and experiments have revealed some of the trends involved, but I believe there is still a great deal to be learned in this respect.

9

The Adaptive Value of Strategies of Social Behavior

Wolves display big differences in their social behavior, just as they do in the spatial organization and the cohesion of the pack. We have found out a great deal about this, but we do not know the reason for many of these differences. What interest does the 1.1 ♂, for instance, have in the cohesion of the pack for him to take so much trouble to preserve it, and why is it that the 1.2 ♂ is so aggressive and the subdominants so dispirited? What is the function, the adaptive value, of the various behavior patterns, roles, and social strategies that are displayed?

In order to tackle the question I drew up a so-called "sociogram" for the pack, showing who did what, when, and with whom. Nearly every day for several years I recorded every discernible social interaction in the pack (first on tape and then in a daily report). Altogether forty-eight different social behavior patterns, such as coat sniffing, threatening, attacking, playing, and so on, were noted.

The reports showed how often animal A displayed behavior pattern X toward animal B during the period of observation on day Y. All this information was summarized monthly. Independent of such quantitative data, a qualitative record was kept of the expressive behavior of the animals in their interaction with one another, and this was used to establish the social ranking order in the pack every month. This made it possible to deduce wolf behavior in relation not only to age and sex but also to rank. The vast mass of data that was accumulated in this way could be evaluated only with the aid of

175

a computer, and in this I was greatly helped by Helmuth Pruscha, mathematician at the Max Planck Institute of Psychiatry at Munich.

I was able to obtain a behavior matrix for each of the recorded behavior patterns, and examples of such matrices are reproduced in the appendix. I shall not discuss them all here, but shall confine myself to a selection of especially characteristic ones. They provide a basis for recognizing different behavior strategies and make it possible to answer the question of why a wolf behaves as it does.

Social Contacts

Apart from play behavior, no social behavior pattern is so frequent as simply making contact (see appendix, tables 11 and 12). Coat sniffing, for that is what muzzle–coat contact is about, took place between animals of different ages and sexes and also between different ranks. The coats of cubs were sniffed with special frequency, while inferior adults, as was to be expected, made few social contacts. Muzzle-to-muzzle contact occurred chiefly between pack members of equal status, that is between superior adults, and was very intensely practiced between juveniles and, interestingly enough, between juveniles and inferior adults. Similarly European human adults, independent of age and status, nearly always shake hands on meeting, while stricter rules apply to addressing each other in the familiar second-person singular. But muzzle contact among wolves does not completely correspond to the latter, since adults did not display this form of behavior to cubs. When two wolves of such very different status engage in muzzle contact, the inferior generally shows inhibited forms of active submission, whereupon the superior generally averts its head. Both forms of social contact are presumably a constant assurance and reciprocal confirmation of a peaceful, nonaggressive atmosphere between members of the pack.

Submission Behavior

Jostling is a behavior pattern that appears chiefly in connection with active submission. Members of the pack gather around the senior animals, press against them, jump up at them, lick them in the

176

face, and so on. Had I not noticed a small detail, I might have added jostling to the active submission complex. But there was one animal in the pack that displayed this form of behavior with special frequency, namely the 1.1 ♀. This seemed to bring it within the field of sexual stimulation and will therefore be dealt with later.

The formal differences between active and passive submission were discussed earlier (chapter 4). By far the largest number of all the incidents of active submission observed—about 40 percent— were directed to the 1.1 ♂. To a lesser extent they were also directed toward the 1.2. ♂ and the 1.1 ♀. As was to be expected, this behavior was displayed, not only by cubs, but more frequently by juveniles, by males toward the 1.1 ♂, and by females both toward the 1.1 ♂ and the 1.1 ♀. Also the 1.2 ♂ submitted with surprising frequency to the 1.1 ♂ (see appendix, table 13).

Active submission was always displayed from below to above in the ranking order, both when the difference in rank was big and when it was small but stable. Wolves in middle positions with their less-stable relationships rarely showed submissive behavior to one another. This points to the conclusion that active submission is a kind of precautionary act of appeasement that helps to stabilize rank relations and thus prevents the development of aggression.

Passive submission, unlike active submission, was much more frequently directed toward the 1.2 ♂ than the 1.1 ♂. This accords with his great aggressiveness, to which those at whom it is directed frequently respond by rolling on their back. Passive submission tends to be a direct form of appeasing aggression. It helps to prevent an increase in aggressiveness that has already been displayed.

Agonistic Behavior

We discovered the essential facts about aggressive and defensive (that is, agonistic) behavior in connection with the social ranking order, and noted, for instance, the slow increase in aggressiveness in the course of the ontogenetic development of the cubs. Against whom is this aggressiveness among juvenile and adult members of the pack directed? Let us first look at the influence of sex on aggressive behavior. I divided aggressive behavior into four levels of intensity, and found that with increasing intensity aggressiveness was

177

directed against members of the same sex.[1] This accords with the division of the pack into two ranking orders, male and female. Threatening, as an aggressive behavior pattern of low intensity, can take place among all animals, to an extent independent of sex and rank, but more aggressive behavior patterns are increasingly an outcome of rank-related clashes.

First of all, let us take a closer look at threatening (see appendix, table 14). In the first place, it was very frequent; 26 percent of all aggressive behavior patterns were limited to threats, and it was a striking fact that no wolf in the pack threatened nearly so frequently as the 1.2 ♂. On the whole he vented his displeasure almost as much upward at the 1.1 ♂ as downward at the 1.3 ♂; and the juvenile males also received their share. The 1.1 ♂ threatened much more rarely; his displeasure was also directed downward at the 1.2 ♂ and the juvenile males. As these animals were together a great deal, this high frequency of threat behavior might at first be considered to be an outcome of conflict inevitably arising from close coexistence. But it was noticeable that the 1.1 ♀ and the juvenile females who were closely associated with this group were more rarely the targets of this masculine displeasure. Also the 1.1 ♀ often threatened juveniles of the same sex, as well as superior and juvenile males. This happened chiefly before and during the season of heat as a reaction to the only too importunate behavior of her escort.

Closer analysis of the behavior of the animals concerned *before* the threat takes place (see appendix, table 15) shows that not only defensive threatening but also offensive threatening is, in the great majority of cases, a reaction to some unaggressive form of annoyance, such as an infringement of individual distance, whether the offender has simply come too close or has disturbed the offended party while asleep or has been too importunate in submission behavior. One might conclude from this that threats are bound to follow all annoyances of this kind but, as I have said, in the great majority of cases it is immediate inferiors, or in the case of juveniles, potential rivals, that provoked threat reactions. This shows that even in comparatively unaggressive everyday situations there is a perpetual testing of rank relations or other traditional rights, such as access to food or to the sexual partner. Threat behavior is an expression of these mini-conflicts.

Biting frays sometimes develop out of these threats. The two adversaries go for each other, snarling furiously and with wide-open mouths, and often stand on their hind legs and rest their forepaws on each other, so that a kind of wrestling bout develops (see figure 24). It is characteristic of these frays, however, that the biting is only simulated and that both animals act in the same way; neither can withdraw, avert its head, or bite any harder. Thus this form of behavior can take place only between wolves of equal or nearly equal rank, and consequently I observed it almost exclusively among juveniles and cubs. When there were two animals in the 1.2 ♂ position for a time (Näschen and Alexander in the autumn of 1972), such frays were very frequent between them. These frays took place between animals that had a basically friendly relationship, but, in contrast to threat behavior, the animals had to be of the same rank. An increase in biting frays between two animals is not infrequently a prelude to more vigorous competition for rank.

Before the stage of serious fighting starts, this takes the form of intimidation behavior, as we know. The beginning of either an expansionary or a repressive trend can manifest itself by an increase in intimidation behavior. Thus the 1.1 ♂ displayed this form of behavior

Fig. 24. Biting and wrestling fray and muzzle seizure.

179

(see appendix, table 16) chiefly against the 1.2 ♂, who in turn directed it at subdominant and juvenile males (subdominant males direct it at each other); the 1.1 ♀ directed it at subdominant and juvenile females; juveniles, now plainly separated according to sex, directed it at each other and occasionally also at subdominant adults. In other words, it occurred wherever conflict for rank might arise. Thus, like the aggressive behavior we have already discussed, intimidation behavior takes place chiefly between animals of neighboring rank, but differs from it in that it is a manifestation of a substantial existing struggle for rank.

The following behavior patterns differ from such clashes between animals of neighboring rank. First of all, there is the very common cornering or encirclement of a victim in which many members of a pack may take part. Once more the 1.2 ♂ was prominent in this respect; he frequently led attacks on lower-rank males. Juveniles, rowdy adolescent, both male and female, immediately joined in, as well as older inferior males if the victim was one of their number, and even cubs joined in too.

The victim would be continually attacked by animals advancing one at a time from the ring of its persecutors, and again, in addition to the 1.2 ♂, it was above all the juveniles who did not shrink from taking part in an attack on one of their number. The cubs, however, were often content with merely taking their place in the ring.

Yet the juveniles were obviously afraid of taking part in the snapping that developed. They were present at every attack, and sometimes advanced on the victim, but refrained from direct body contact, while the 1.2 ♂ and the 1.1 ♀ snapped when they advanced.

Though the cubs and juveniles did not enter fully into the fray, they affected the outcome, for their aiding and abetting enabled the real aggressor—and again this was often the 1.1 ♀—to get close enough to inflict damaging bites (see appendix, table 11). The victims in these cases were inferior females, who had hardly appeared in this connection previously.

The difference between dominant males and the 1.1 ♀ in the repression of inferiors is also evident in two other behavior patterns, the chase away and the pursuit. In the chase away the animal walks or runs behind another without necessarily trying to catch it; the object is merely to drive it away. In the pursuit it tries to catch the rapidly fleeing victim to attack it in earnest if it can. While the males—and here again the 1.2 ♂ was prominent—above all engaged in the chase away, it was the 1.1 ♀ who pursued her rivals and so expelled them from the pack.

All that needs to be said about defensive behavior is that it faithfully reflects aggression; the more violent the attack, the more violent the defense. This was particularly evident in the reaction to driving away and the chase. While subdominant males merely kept away from the dominant males that drove them off, subdominant females fled from the 1.1 ♀ that pursued them.

In addition to agonistic behavior in the pack there are also two other forms of aggression that must be considered: that directed at wolves returning to the pack and that directed at wolves that are complete strangers to it. At Rickling it struck me that when I put young wolves back in the enclosure after an outing, they were always "beaten up" by the older wolves that had been left behind. The superior animals approached them threateningly and jumped at them, and they immediately flung themselves to the ground, squealing loudly. Later in the Bavarian Forest the same thing happened when inferior animals returned to the enclosure, whether they were cubs, juveniles, or adults. Only the top wolves were given an effusively friendly welcome.

The reaction to strange animals was much more aggressive. I have already referred to this, and mentioned in particular how cubs that at first are so friendly to strangers gradually begin to react aggressively to them, just like their elders, their aggressiveness being ultimately very dependent on their position in the pack. I carried out some experiments in the matter in the winter of 1972–1973. On forty-eight occasions I took a total of ten dogs of different breeds and sizes with me to the enclosure and noted the reaction of members of the pack on the other side of the fence. On almost every occasion the superior wolves reacted frantically, threatening, jumping at the fence, urinating, and scratching. If they had been able to, they would have gone straight into the attack. On a few occasions, when I took dachshunds with me, they seemed more surprised than aggressive. The juveniles, now aged between twenty and twenty-two months, also reacted aggressively, while the older inferior adults, some of whom were much older, either took no notice or tried to smell the strange dog through the fence without showing

Fig. 25. Cornering a "scapegoat" and chasing away an inferior.

Howling with the wolves.

1

2

3

4

The house at Rickling, with enclosure for wolves and poodles.
Artificial feeding. A rubber tube is let down into the cub's stomach
 a milk preparation especially prepared for puppies is slowly
nped into it. This method proved very successful.
The four-week-old Anfa eagerly accepts raw meat.
To upset traditional ideas, we attached our wolves to a sleigh.
 2. Various ways of threatening. While the jackals (8), here we see
 black-backed jackals *(Canis mesolelas)* in the Serengeti, threaten
very stereotyped fashion, merely opening their mouths wide, wolves
play a highly differentiated threat mimicry, depending on how fright-
d they are. Näschen (7) threatens very self-confidently, while
lfchen (12), Braunauge (11), and Brno (9), a female expelled from
 pack in winter, express increasing fear. Also the two females (10)
not dare make an all-out attack on each other. Finsterau (top left),
r the escape of her young in the winter of 1977, is obviously more
rehensive than Tatra (right), the new alpha female from whom the
ression proceeds. Note among other things the attitude of the ears
well as the variation in the retraction of the corners of the mouth.
 dog (6), Flow, has a differentiated threat mimicry similar to that
the wolf—further evidence of the dog's sole descent from the wolf.

6

7

8

9

10

11   12

13. Psenner, Finsterau, and Olomouc form their own small pack after the 1976 escape.
14. Alexander and Mädchen, aged six months, show distinct respect for a cow.
15. Prey of the size of a deer can satisfy several wolves without much squabbling.

14

15

16

17   18

18. A serious, silent, and uninhibited fight for the alpha position between Wölfchen (left) and chen (right) develops out of intimidation display.

The inhibition on biting works in spite of my considerable "aggression" toward Näschen, whom I pinning to the ground.

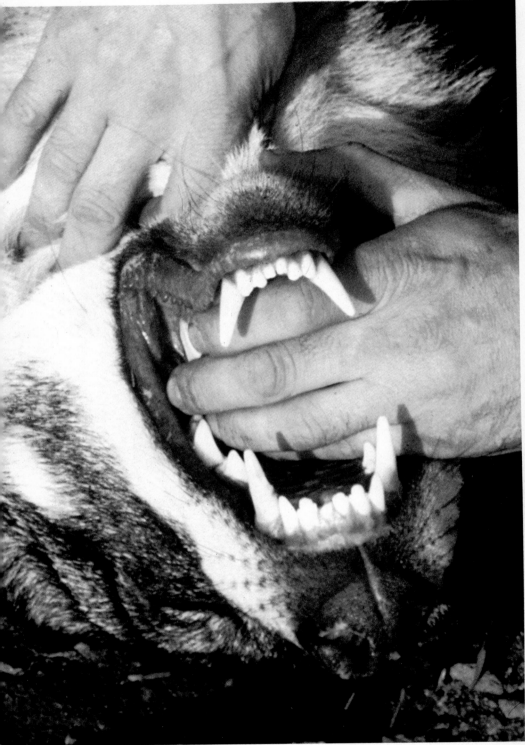

20

21

22

23

–27. Scenes from the 1975 mating season. A subdominant male (Braunauge) tries to cover the alpha ~~male~~ (Finsterau). A subdominant male (Braunauge) tries to mount the alpha female (Finsterau). The ~~pha~~ male (Olomouc) appears, threatens, and leaps at the younger animal when the latter fails to react ~~the~~ threat, and then "beats him up." Finsterau appears indifferent, but shuts her eyes when things get ~~ough~~ (22). She tolerates a simultaneous attempt by two males to mount her at the beginning of the ~~riod~~ of heat (27). Previously she was more active, continually seeking contact with the alpha male ~~omouc~~ without giving up her close bond to Näschen (24). During the mating season other members of ~~e~~ pack keep especially close together (26).

24

25

26

27

28

29

30

31

8. All the members of the pack take an interest in the cubs. Here one of Finsterau's cubs is trying to ackle, while one of the previous year's cubs (Braunauge) looks on.
9. Cub aged five weeks.
0–31. Gelbauge, now one year old, tries to "rescue" a cub from me by carrying it away.
2. Lusen, a female long excluded from the pack.
3. Finsterau, the alpha female.
4. Ho, son of Finsterau and Olomouc and alpha male since autumn 1976, was shot in the enclosure by der of the National Park authorities without my knowledge and for no discernible reason.

35

36

A wolf, still under the influence of the anesthetic (note his undirected gaze). He is fitted with a metric collar with built-in radio transmitter.

Large amounts of strychnine and other deadly poisons were used to combat predators in Italy every ter. Here one of our radio-marked wolves, a young male, has eaten poisoned bait and died. The use of son has since been forbidden in Italy.

Dave Mech with directional aerial and receiver (in the satchel).

Dave Mech, Luigi Boitani, and I with the first wolf we caught. Six months later this wolf was shot and nded in the Abruzzi National Park. He apparently died days or even weeks later.

A foal killed by wolves near Pescasseroli. Note that the mare is hobbled.

40

41

40–42. Three ideas of the wolf. The "naive" is closest to reality. Wolves wait outside the village for the last lights to go out before entering it to look for food. In the "Roman" version, the Capitoline she-wolf is a symbol of motherliness (floor mosaic in Siena Cathedral). This is one of the few favorable representations of the wolf, though the many stories of children reared by wolves, whether from Rome or from India, certainly cannot be true. The she-wolf's lactation period of at most twelve weeks makes the rearing of human children impossible. Finally, the "traditional" view is that the wolf is a dangerous beast and enemy of mankind (picture by F. Vater, woodman in the Bavarian Forest).

any sign of aggression. When I took one of them from the enclosure it actually tried to play with the generally very intimidated dog (see figure 26).

It also struck me that aggression toward strangers was especially great in the enclosure or its immediate neighborhood. When I took members of the pack for walks in Waldhäuser and the surroundings after the move to the Bavarian Forest, they did not at first react aggressively to the village dogs. That happened only after they had "established" themselves in the area, so to speak. The few overconfident dogs that jumped down into the enclosure from the visitors' platform did not survive for very long. Several times I found the bodies of dogs bitten and torn to pieces in the enclosure, and once I saw the beginning of an attack on a dog but managed to rescue it.

Also I have the impression—though again I have no figures to prove it—that aggressiveness can vary with the size of the pack. When we had two packs in separate enclosures, the dominant wolves of the small pack (some had been dominant in the big one) were much less aggressive to strange dogs. Alexander, who was 1.1

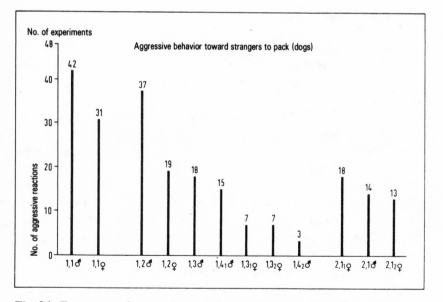

Fig. 26. Frequency of aggressive reactions to dogs brought to the enclosure by members of the pack of different status.

♂ first in the small pack and then, after the big escape, became 1.1 ♂ for a time in the big one, became really aggressive only in the latter. But I have no figures to prove this; my impression has still to be tested.

Play Behavior

An international conference of ethologists was held at Bielefeld at the end of August 1977. For students of behavior from all over the world this biennial event is a great treat. Many of us spend long periods alone in remote places, and intensive contact with friends and colleagues and new ideas is particularly stimulating. The subject of one of the many round-table discussions was play behavior. Anne Rasa, the leader of the discussion, who has spent many years studying the behavior of the mongoose, wrote out on the blackboard some of the chief characteristics of play.[2] These were as follows:

1. The normal sequence of events in a course of action is broken up (in contrast to serious behavior, individual acts in a behavior sequence appear in infinitely variable combinations).

2. Repetition (individual behavior patterns are repeated over and over again) is present.

3. There is a change of role (in social games roles such as those of assailant and defender keep changing).

4. The field is relaxed (play occurs only when no impulses from other fields of function such as hunting, hunger, flight, fatigue, are present).

5. It is end-inhibited (when hunting is played at, the final act, the kill, does not occur).

6. There is an absence of reference to serious things (play is for play's sake, not for any other purpose).

In the discussion that followed the question was raised whether play, which has so far been observed only among mammals and some birds (the raven) is a single phenomenon or not. There was also a long discussion on whether play should be defined by its form, its function, or its motivation. These approaches were continually confused, and it was even argued that consideration should be given to complex forms of human play, such as piano playing, for instance, or the activity we were engaged in at that moment. But eventually, as was appropriate for ethologists, we agreed on a provi-

Fig. 27. Invitation to play used as a diversionary maneuver by an attacked wolf.

sional formal definition of animal play, and we then noted that the most essential characteristic, a loose, relaxed, exuberant way of moving, was missing from Anne Rasa's enumeration, which was amended accordingly.

It struck me that some forms of play among wolves lacked all the characteristics described (with the exception of the seventh one that had just been added). I quoted instances of play being used as a tactical move in social clashes, as a diversionary maneuver to escape aggression, or as a trick to get at another individual's food. In this "simulated play" the movements were also relaxed and exuberant, but the other characteristics enumerated were lacking, in particular the relaxed field and the absence of relationship to serious matters. This kind of play was thoroughly serious.

My only purpose was to show that only the last characteristic, that of relaxed muscle tone, was always applicable, while other characteristics might be but were not necessarily present.

A colleague pointed out that in accordance with modern theories of genetic selection, a modification of play on these lines was to be expected. The possible costs (expenditure of energy, danger of being wounded, social consequences) resulting from the securing of an objective (for example, a bone) by simulated play would be less than those involved when an animal follows the traditional course of engaging in an aggressive clash. Wolves would obviously behave in accordance with this expectation, and presumably similar behavior would be found in many other socially highly developed animals.

The idea was that the fitness of an animal that discovered these new tactics would be increased, and that simulated play, once it had been discovered, would rapidly spread. Play among older wolves is in fact never entirely devoid of some serious reference. It is used frequently in social conflicts, rank relations, sexual soliciting, initiatives in leadership, and the distribution of available resources (such as food or sleeping places). The reason why conflicts are not carried out only playfully is that all older wolves are well able to use the method and are able to see through any "tricks" that might be tried on them. I have observed that older wolves are able to distract only younger ones from a piece of meat, for instance, by inviting it to play in order to grab it for themselves. Older wolves would presumably realize at once what the game was and would not be taken in. Also younger wolves are taken in only if they are not very hungry. If they are devouring food hungrily it would not occur to any of their companions to try the trick on them, as they have learned that it would be useless. Using play behavior for tactical purposes requires a correct assessment of the situation, and for that experience is necessary.

Thus the function of play seems to change in the course of the wolf's ontogenetic development. Among cubs play serves to help the animal practice complex forms of movement; solitary play is frequent at that stage. But soon play takes place almost exclusively in the group, and in the course of it social patterns of reaction are learned, such, for instance, as the fact that hard biting results in aggressive reaction by the wolf who has been bitten. Thus the biting inhibition develops, and play behavior quickly becomes more peaceful (see figure 28). Only with the increasing aggressiveness of older cubs and juveniles, particularly among the females, who in general are the more aggressive, does play become more aggressive again. At this stage play has already acquired a new function; it has become a strategy for carrying out social conflicts.

According to this theory of its function, social play should chiefly be indulged in by wolves close to one another in rank, and this indeed turned out to be the case (see appendix, table 17). The sovereign 1.1 ♂ played most rarely and the 1.1 ♀ came next. The inferior adults played noticeably often in comparison. They actually stood out in the pack because of their frequent submission behavior toward the superior adults and the physical attitude they displayed in doing so, in particular their perpetually playful, "childish" behavior. They seemed to be retarded as a result of the social pressure to which they were subjected, condemned to remain at a stage of infantile behavior. But play is infantile only in appearance. In reality it is completely serious. What is at stake, as far as the subdominant animals are concerned, is whether they remain in the pack—and that can be a matter of life or death.

The juveniles played with one another even more frequently than with the inferior adults, and in this there was an obvious development from the cub stage, when play was independent of sex, to play with partners of the same sex.

Analysis of play behavior shows that it is used as a tactical method of solving social conflicts, both to appease the aggressiveness of superiors or of attacking groups or to camouflage aggression in the case of expansionary trends directed against superiors by younger or inferior animals. Thus it forms a kind of buffer between friendly and aggressive behavior. It prevents minor conflicts from being carried out in earnest and thus delays the outbreak of damaging aggression; it therefore performs a vital function in helping to preserve the cohesion of the group.

Sexual Behavior

We have already noted one important fact about the sexual life of wolves. Only one female a year had cubs in our pack, though there were a number of sexually mature females in the enclosure for

187

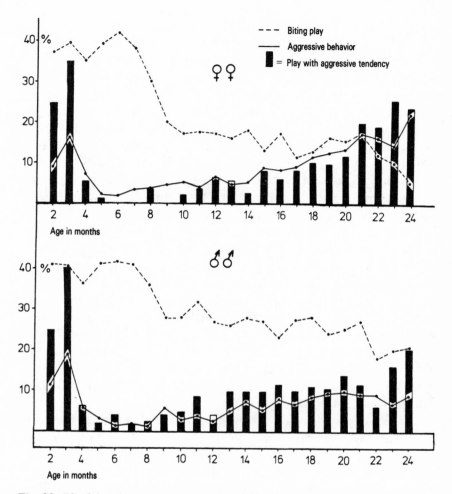

Fig. 28. Playful and aggressive behavior as well as tendency to aggression in play behavior among young wolves.

many years in succession. If every sexually mature female had had cubs every year from 1967 to 1977, there would have been twenty-two litters altogether. In fact there were five, with a total of 25 cubs, or an average of 5 cubs a litter. So if we assume 5 cubs as the average for the unborn litters, only 25 out of 110 (or 23 percent) of possible births in fact took place.

The question of course arises whether this small number of births is characteristic of all wolf packs, or perhaps only of packs in captivity, or of our pack only. Well, in the Frankfurt zoo and others several she-wolves have been pregnant simultaneously. But those are exceptions, for an explanation of which these zoo animals will have to be observed carefully for a period. At Brookfield zoo in Chicago, for instance, only the 1.1 ♀ had cubs for several years running. When she died the three subdominant females failed for a time to settle their ranking order and all three promptly had cubs. The next year the issue had been settled in favor of one of them, and again only one litter was born.[3] In the East Berlin zoo two females had cubs for several years in succession, but the cubs of the inferior female always died, whereupon she helped to rear the cubs of the superior female.[4]

The causes of low reproduction rates seem to be many and diverse. Before dealing with the question let us take a look at the conditions that prevail in freedom. The available data yield an equally diverse picture. In one summer in the Mount McKinley National Park in Alaska, Murie, who was the first to observe wolves, found a pack with two leading females who had obviously borne their cubs in separate dens but afterward joined forces and reared all the cubs together, helped by the males. The relationship between the two females was not known, but Murie assumed that one of them was younger and was perhaps the daughter of the alpha female.[5]

Isolated observations such as that are not very conclusive, and better results are obtained from the examination of the sexual tract of a large number of killed animals. Of eighty-nine females, including both adult and two-year-olds, shot in various parts of Alaska in March and April of each year from 1959 to 1966, all except ten had been pregnant;[6] that is, 89 percent. Thus, if these figures are representative of conditions in wide areas of Alaska at the time of the investigation, nearly all sexually mature females there had cubs. But

189

of seventeen adult females killed at Algonquin Park in Ontario, Canada, only ten (or 59 percent) had given birth to cubs during the previous spring.[7] These figures were supported by observations from other areas in North America. Dave Mech reports that many of the females with radio transmitters do not give birth. On the big island of Isle Royale most of the females seem not to have cubs. At all events, at the beginning of winter only a small proportion of the wolves observed from his aircraft were identified as cubs. This observation is a difficult thing to do, and there is a big margin of error. But Rolf Peterson, who now works on Isle Royale, is sure that the proportion of cubs is relatively small. That is attributable either to a high death rate among young cubs or to a low birth rate. Rolf assumes the latter, chiefly because he has often observed how the 1.1 ♀ prevents the mating of subdominant females.[8]

How are we to explain the high birth rate in Alaska and the relatively low one farther to the east? Is the behavior of wolves in Alaska different from that of the timber wolves in the east? Probably not. It seems to me that it is the human influence that is decisive here. In Alaska wolves are still vigorously hunted down, while in the three areas in the east referred to above they are protected. Thus the death rate of adult wolves in Alaska was very high, about 50 percent, while it is about 10 percent on Isle Royale. Consequently there is a bigger proportion of cubs in Alaska (44 to 60 percent) in comparison to 31 percent in Algonquin Park and presumably a still lower percentage on Isle Royale.

Additionally, in the areas in Alaska where they are hunted the packs are relatively small. This is obviously connected with the low density of the wolf population resulting from the high hunting pressure. In 1953, when shooting wolves was prohibited in one area (Game Management Unit No. 13), the original population, estimated at twelve wolves, increased to from 350 to 400 by 1965. At the same time the size of the packs observed substantially increased. In the winter of 1960–1961 not a single pack consisting of more than seven animals was observed, while five years later 56 percent of all the packs sighted consisted of more than seven animals. High hunting pressure leads to low density of population and small packs. In light of our knowledge of the social structure of the wolf pack, we must assume that only one sexually mature female generally lives in such small packs with a high proportion of cubs. Thus practically every sexually mature female in the population produces cubs.

In areas where hunting by human beings is forbidden, the packs are bigger and the average age is higher. Also many older animals live on their own in small, nonterritorial groups. The percentage of reproducing females is consequently smaller.

That high reproduction rates do not occur everywhere in Alaska is shown by Gordon Haber's findings in the Mount McKinley area, in which wolves are also protected.[9] As is fitting for a modern American student of wildlife, he observes wolves from the air— something that his great predecessor Murie, who often used dog-drawn sleighs, would never have even dreamed of. By this method Gordon, who has become an enthusiastic partisan of the wolves of Alaska, has in the course of his many years' work accumulated a mass of data that will one day be included in a book of several volumes. In the meantime, we must take his word for it that by no means do all female wolves give birth. In the Abruzzi in Italy, with which we shall deal later, the reproduction rate is also low—very low indeed if the few data I gathered are representative; four females fitted with radio transmitters who could have produced six litters during the period of observation produced only one. In this case the causes lie neither in high-density population nor in big packs, but in the fact that the nonreproductive females found no males.[10]

It seems that the reproduction rate, or the percentage of reproductive females in a wolf population, depends partly on the density of the population. The percentage is low when the density is high, increases with diminishing density, and is then drastically reduced when the density is very low.

The percentage of cubs in a population makes it possible to estimate the extent of human influence on wolves. Pimlott made calculations and came to the conclusion that a percentage of from fifteen to thirty shows that no or minimal hunting pressure exists, while a percentage of fifty or more indicates that the wolves are being vigorously hunted. Only very intensive hunting indeed—such as existed until recently in the Abruzzi, where the wolves were on the brink of extermination—again leads to a low proportion of cubs, because at that stage a critical density has been reached at which the few surviving sexually mature wolves often cannot find a mate.

191

Dave Mech has made an interesting observation in this connection. In a high-density population in north Minnesota, fifty-two cubs out of seventy-seven, or 66 percent, were male. In two other areas in Minnesota where wolves were vigorously hunted (with low density as a consequence) only four of fifteen captured wolves, or 27 percent, were male.[11] These figures are not comprehensive enough to exclude the possibility of chance, but they point to the possibility that in saturated populations an excess of males might be partly the result of an unequal ratio between the sexes at birth. That might contribute to regulation of the population.

What about populations, except density, decides whether a female will be covered, produce cubs, and rear them successfully? According to my experience with the pack in the Bavarian Forest, there seem to be four factors that may prevent or put obstacles in the way of a female mating during the period of heat.

1. A barrier against incest between twins. There was no copulation between the 1.1 ♀ Mädchen and any of her three brothers between 1970 and 1972. The 1.1 ♂ Wölfchen took little interest in her, and Näschen and Alexander were very active but were rejected by her. Oswald, the brother of the new 1.1 ♀ Finsterau, also took no interest in his sister when she was in heat. During the period of heat in February 1974 he was the only one of the four sexually mature males in the pack who made no attempt to cover her. I know of matings between siblings that have taken place in some zoos, so the few observations in our pack do not establish a general rule but merely indicate a tendency to avoid sex with a twin if possible.

The extent to which an incest barrier may exist between mother and son or father and daughter cannot be decided by observations of our pack. Finsterau rejected advances by her sons, but she did the same to other inferior males, so this cannot be conclusively attributed to the close relationship. (My subjective feeling for wolf behavior tells me that I should not be surprised if an alpha female rejected her sons just as she rejected her twin brother. Thus the same principle would apply—if possible, avoid sex with a son.)

2. The aggressiveness of the 1.1 ♀. In some cases Finsterau (and later Tatra) prevented copulation by subdominant females by a direct attack. Much more frequently, however, the repressed females did not even try to solicit a male. They all had vaginal bleeding, and my dog, Flow, showed unmistakable reactions, but the

192

male wolves did not. Why they were content simply to trail along behind the 1.1 ♀ in the great majority of cases I do not know. The synchronization of sexual activity seems to be a highly differentiated affair among wolves, and I await with great curiosity the findings of Dave Mech and his colleagues in Minnesota, who are now studying seasonal hormonal developments among wolves in captivity. Whatever their findings may be, this type of frigidity as a consequence of social stress seems to be a frequent cause of failure to mate.

3. Severe wounds. After the loss of her 1.1 ♀ position and the wounds she suffered, Mädchen did not go into heat during the 1973 season and showed few signs of it in the years that followed. In any event, the males in the small enclosure were not stimulated in any way. (That oversexed product of domestication, Flow, was susceptible to the stimulus. But because all the bitches at Waldhäuser, not merely the she-wolves, were in heat in late winter and were kept away from him, he went after anything that season that showed the slightest sign of canid femininity.) Wounds, like social repression, seem to produce a stress syndrome among wolves that prevents the full development of heat with all the behavioral and olfactory signals that go with it.

4. Low age. Females are normally sexually mature at twenty-two months. Dave Mech reports the bearing of cubs by a one-year-old female, but that is certainly an exception. The twenty-two-month-old females—with the exception of the 1.1 ♀ Finsterau—showed no sexually tinged behavior before or during the period of heat, though they obviously had vaginal bleeding and were not at all repressed by the 1.1 she-wolf. In no instance did the males show any sexual interest in them. Here too there seemed to be a socially conditioned frigidity that prevented young subdominant females from reproducing.

Apart from these factors noted among captive wolves, there must certainly be other causes of failure to mate among animals living in freedom. I have already noted one of them from the Abruzzi—the female in heat is on her own and cannot find a mate. The state of the food supply may be another; severe undernourishment may prevent the animal from going into heat. But nonfertilization and miscarriage are probably more important in this connection.

We know from Alaska that not all mature eggs are fertilized and that fetuses can die in utero. [12] We do not know the exact causes of this, but we can assume that food shortages, wounds, and stress may play a part. Neither Finsterau nor Tatra had cubs in the spring of 1976, though both had copulated several times. Perpetual fighting and chasing were certainly responsible for this.

Cub Mortality

The mortality of cubs after birth, particularly during the first few weeks and then in the course of the first autumn and winter,[13] by far exceeds the mortality *in utero*.

Some cubs die at birth, but we do not know what the death rate is at this stage, because they are born in a den to which we have no access. Also cubs that are stillborn or die soon after birth are generally eaten by the mother, as we were able to observe at Kiel, where cubs were born in a kennel open to inspection.

Expectant mothers did not always use the kennel, however. Once when I was on Sunday duty at the institute a puwo I female produced her pups outside in the open. The temperature was several degrees below freezing point and the tiny puppies lay helpless on the hard-frozen sand. When I picked them up to put them inside I thought one of them was dead; it was quite cold and stiff. As it was Sunday, I took it into the institute and put it in a refrigerator to await dissection. During the afternoon I happened to pass by and—incredibly enough—the sound of whimpering came from the refrigerator. The cub had thawed and was crawling about inside. So I took it down to its mother, who was soon suckling it. It survived, and thus provided evidence of the hardiness of newborn wolf cubs and puppies.

Of course no wolf cub can survive protracted cold and hunger. For the first few weeks cubs are totally dependent on their mother, and if she is forced to go out hunting and spends too much time at it and is unsuccessful, many cubs will die. Only rough estimates on this matter are available about wolves in freedom. Pimlott, for instance, reckons on a cub mortality rate of up to 75 percent in the course of the summer and autumn. Dave Mech discovered that the weight of cubs in autumn plays an important part in their chances of surviving the first winter. In a trapping operation in autumn he weighed and measured a total of seventy-three cubs before earmarking them, fitting them with radio transmitters, and releasing them. This enabled him to keep track of many of them. It turned out that cubs that were underweight (that is, that weighed less than 75 percent of what they should have weighed according to a "standard weight curve" previously established among wolves in captivity) had little chance to survive.[14]

Finally, observations on Isle Royale showed that cubs' chances of survival depend to a large extent on the size of the pack. Bigger packs were generally more successful in keeping their cubs alive until the following winter, while solitary couples or small groups either had no cubs or soon lost them. Obviously they were unable to provide enough food for them.[15]

Mating

In autumn the 1.1 ♀ in our pack became increasingly aggressive to other females, simultaneously she displayed increasingly friendly behavior (such as jumping up at, jostling, and active and passive submission) toward one or more superior males. Later this assumed an obvious sexual coloring, for instance when she stood sideways over the male and rested her paws on him, mounted him from behind, thrust at him with her pelvis, and finally presented. Also squirt urination now became much more frequent, the initiative shortly before and during the period of heat coming almost exclusively from the alpha female. The places where she urinated were sniffed by most of the males, but only a few—such as one or both of the two superior males and perhaps also the superior juvenile—squirted urine at the same spot. These same animals were the only ones that had the privilege of sniffing her genitals. Attempts to do so by others were warded off either by the female herself or by one of the superior males. The behavior and also the olfactory change in the 1.1 ♀ seemed to stimulate the production of sperm by the males as well as their sexual motivation. They then assumed, to a large extent, the sexual initiative during the season of heat.

Before the period of heat the 1.1 ♀ directed her soliciting behavior chiefly at the 1.1 ♂ and her last year's partner, who were not always the same animal. Either for the whole of the period, which lasts for two or three weeks, or for a few days only, one of these two

195

males would keep the other males away and would be the only one to copulate with her. Generally it was the 1.1 ♂ who, at any rate in the period of maximum heat (that is, roughly, the ten days in the middle of the period when the 1.1 ♀ shows the maximum receptivity), drove the other males away, copulated with her, and fathered the young. The 1.1 ♀ certainly showed preferences; above all she warded off her twin brothers, as well as inferior males and her sons. But which of the superior males copulated with her seemed to be a matter they decided among themselves.

Some observations of free wolves—particularly those by Gordon Haber in Alaska—corroborate the observations in our pack that the 1.2 ♂ can be the principal partner. Why the 1.1 ♂ is not sexually active in these cases we do not know. Dave Mech's hormonal studies may throw some light on this. The number-two male was never observed to copulate with the 1.1 ♀ on Isle Royale, but in contrast, a close bond between him and the alpha couple was observed more frequently.

Gordon Haber also observed copulation of the 1.1 ♀ with several males during the period of heat. According to our observations, this was actually the rule; the other males had their chance chiefly at the beginning and end of the period—that is, at a time when fertilization was improbable. Working backward from the date of the cubs' birth, it always turned out that the father was the partner of the 1.1 ♀ during the period of maximum heat.

Individual Interests and Behavior Strategy

The genetically programmed behavior patterns of wolves are obviously highly differentiated. A large number of different "behavior strategies" are available to enable the behavior of the individual to adapt to different social conditions, that is, to maximize its overall fitness. The different ways of social behavior come into play in the pack according to the situation of its individual members, which can be quite different, depending on sex, age, and rank. The same applies to adaptation to ecological conditions. Let us look at these behavior strategies from the point of view of the interests of the individual member of the pack. In order to understand an animal's interests, we must understand its behavior. If we can then coordinate what we know about this behavior with the facts of selection and evolution, we can fit this observed behavior into a wider context.

I must emphasize that when ethologists talk about animals' "interests," they do not mean that the animals have a conscious idea of what these interests are. The situation is rather that the wolf's behavior has adapted itself by natural selection to the conditions in which the pack lives. Genetic standards of behavior result in male behavior differing from female behavior in many respects, in the behavior of an older wolf differing from that of a younger one, that of a superior wolf from an inferior, and so on. There are, of course, individual peculiarities of behavior independent of status, but these do not arise in this context. Instead, let us consider behavior in terms of sex, age, and rank with respect to the different interests of individual members of the pack depending on their status.

THE ALPHA FEMALE

Young cubs need a great deal of food. At five or six months they have to be big enough to take part in the roamings of the pack. It must therefore be in the interests of a sexually mature female that as many wolves as possible should help to feed and rear her cubs. It must also be in her interests to prevent other females from having cubs that will compete with hers.

We already know the strategies by which the female copes with this situation. By her aggressive behavior she drives other sexually mature females from the pack, and if this fails she sees to it that they do not mate. If this too fails, she prevents the cubs from being born, or if they are born, from being reared. When the period of heat is over her aggression diminishes, and the expelled females can sometimes be reintegrated into the pack and help in the rearing of her cubs. If the pack is very big it seems that she continues to prevent the reintegration of expelled females, for which there is no need in such cases.

In addition to friendly behavior during the autumn and winter, actual sexual contact seems to play a highly important part in bonding a male to the 1.1 ♀. It is certainly helpful to her reproductive success that her partner should be a superior and experienced wolf. Hence her preference for the 1.1 ♂. But matings with other males also occur. This is certainly not the rule, but it occurs more

197

frequently than was previously supposed. (Belief in the allegedly firm bond between two wolves has often assumed moral dimensions.) The advantage of these matings to the 1.1 ♀ is obvious. It binds a number of superior males to her and her cubs. All these males behave like the real father—that is, as if the survival of their genes, which may be up to 50 percent identical with their own, were at stake.

Is this guile on the part of the alpha female? We know from Maynard Smith's calculations with a mathematical model of the evolution of social behavior that "lying" and "deception" have only a limited duration because, as he says, they cannot be an "evolutionary stable strategy."[16] It is true that the "deceiver" at first enjoys a reproductive advantage; his genes are spread in the population. But animals capable of discovering the deception practiced on them would have an even greater selective advantage, with the result that the "deception" would soon become useless or actually disadvantageous.

This development can certainly take a long time. An excellent example is the cuckoo. The young cuckoo is reared by stepparents while its real parents withdraw to southern, warmer climes that are richer in food. The almost complete similarity of the color of the cuckoo's egg to those of its stepparents shows that the exploited animals were, in the past, easily able to discover the "deception." Only rigorous selective pressure causing eggs with poorly imitated color to be discovered and removed could have led to this high degree of adaptation. The deceptive technique was discovered, but instead of being abandoned by the cuckoo was improved upon. Why don't the exploited species improve their capacity to detect the better-adapted cuckoo's egg? Its size, for instance, should make this possible.

Presumably the answer lies in the rarity of the cuckoo's egg. As it is responsible for only a small proportion of deaths among the young of the exploited parents, the selective pressure is not great enough. That may also explain why there are not more cuckoos. When I was a boy I always wondered why the cuckoo, which is by no means short of food, is not much more common than it is. If it were more common and laid its eggs in many nests of other species, these others would have a much greater interest in discovering the "deception," and a much more rigorous selective pressure would set in to the cuckoo's disadvantage. An evolutionary stable strategy between the cuckoo and the population of stepparents permits only moderate exploitation.

The situation in regard to the "deceived" male in the wolf pack seems to me to be similar. Whether the "deception" is revealed or not is not a matter of great consequence, for generally he is a close relative of the father. From the point of view of general fitness (reproductive success of all genes identical with his own), it is actually an advantage that he should take an active part in taking care of the cubs with whom he probably shared some identical genes. If he is the father's brother the proportion is 25 percent as against the father's 50 percent. If he is the son of the reproducing couple the cubs are his siblings, with whom he shares 50 percent of the same genes, just as if they were his own offspring. Even if he is totally unrelated, successful rearing of the cubs is to his long-term advantage. They can be expected one day to join with him in the hunt and help to meet his food needs. Packs that have no cubs soon reach a critical size at which they can no longer kill enough game or successfully defend their territory. Such a pack quickly goes under, very likely before the outsider attains the alpha position and is able to reproduce. It must therefore be to his interest that the cubs should prosper, even if they are unrelated to him. Thus the "deceived" male has little interest in revealing the "deception," and the promiscuity of the female can be regarded as an evolutionary stable strategy.

THE ALPHA MALE

It must also be in the interests of all the other members of the pack that the cubs should be reared successfully and that peaceful coexistence should prevail, enabling the pack to enjoy the greatest possible success in the hunt. Inasmuch as the reproduction of their genes is concerned, this is of special interest to the two alpha animals. Certainly the interests of the 1.1 ♀ are somewhat divided, as she needs a peaceful atmosphere for the rearing of her cubs but has to be extremely aggressive at times because of her exclusive claim to maternity. The same applies to most other members of the pack, who benefit from a friendly atmosphere but can sometimes take advantage of quarrels to improve their position in the ranking order. Only the 1.1 ♂ has no interest in this. So, apart from the cubs, no wolf is more interested in a friendly, cooperative atmosphere than he.

No animal in the pack is more concerned with the maintenance of a friendly atmosphere and the cohesion of the pack than the 1.1 ♂. He makes the vital decisions. He is·the experienced initiator, the watchdog and protector against external dangers, the friendly and tolerant center of the pack. I have never seen him in the role of conciliator or mediator. Why not? Perhaps he does act in that capacity and I was not sufficiently observant. Perhaps he uses very subtle signals. A special investigation would certainly be well worthwhile. But perhaps this role is superfluous in captivity, in which smooth and frictionless functioning of the pack is less important. Nevertheless, it seems to me that the 1.1 ♂ contributes a great deal to friendliness in the pack. He is the initiator and center of the many friendly get-together ceremonies that take place, particularly during the aggressive winter months. These, like the many individual friendly and submissive encounters with him that take place in the pack, certainly contribute to the reduction of aggressiveness and tension.

The 1.1 ♂ is particularly aggressive to strangers to the pack. These are generally unrelated to him, and represent a danger because of possible attacks or competition for food. Recruiting a strange animal could be an advantage only to a very small pack. My few observations of the dependence of aggressiveness to strangers on the size of the pack correspond with these theoretical expectations.

But what of the situation in which a strange male turns up and assumes the alpha position in a small pack consisting of a female and her young? He is not the father of the young animals and is presumably unrelated to them. One would expect such an alpha male to try to keep some of the young animals in the pack in the interests of the successful rearing of his own cubs, or to try to drive them away in the interests of food distribution as well as to better his own cubs' subsequent chances of remaining in the pack.

While I was correcting the proofs of this book, I was involuntarily given an opportunity of testing this prediction. During the 1978 mating season the two top-ranking males in the big pack (Ho and Tschi), as well as some others, were shot by order of the National Park administration without my knowledge and for reasons inexplicable to me. The alpha female (Tatra) was left alone in the enclo-

200

sure with her four cubs of the previous year. A strange male (Olomouc) from the small enclosure was put in with her, and they mated within a few days. (They were twins, but had been separated for two years. The speed with which the female was willing to mate after the loss of her previous partner was consistent with previous observations.) The two adults and four young wolves soon formed a pack but, in contrast with previous observations, that spring I noted a high degree of aggressiveness toward the young wolves on the part of the new alpha male. Olomouc, who had been so friendly to his own cubs, continually attacked these strange juveniles and, when his own cubs were born, drove a young male from the pack.

This young male then lived completely apart—the youngest outcast I have ever seen. The remaining young wolves showed great respect to Olomouc.

His behavior seems to fit in with the expectation that an alternative behavioral strategy is available to the alpha male. If he does not get to the top in his own pack but joins a small pack in which the female already has young, he treats the latter indifferently or aggressively in the interest of the new cubs fathered by him. Further observations are of course necessary to substantiate this assumption (or disprove it). Dave Mech has observed wolves that left the pack as early as in their first winter.[17] A state of affairs such as I have described may have prevailed in their case. Young "dispersers" may come chiefly from small, newly constituted packs.

This increased aggression on the part of the new alpha male is reminiscent of the behavior strategy of lions. A pride of lions normally consists of a number of closely related lionesses and their cubs as well as a few adult lions (generally two) who come from other prides. These take over the pride only for two or three years, after which they are driven out again by a new group of strange lions. Bertram[18] has observed that after strange lions have taken over their pride, they regularly kill the young animals fathered by their predecessors. This behavior is totally inexplicable by the traditional idea of behavior as adaptation for the purpose of preservation of the species, and Bertram explains it as a process of genetic selection, a behavioral strategy in the interests of the fitness of the new lions. Because lion cubs develop slowly, the females have to look after them for a long time and so cannot give birth to more cubs for twenty or thirty months at the earliest. But if they lose their cubs at an early stage they soon go into heat again and are thus available as reproductive partners for the new males, who in their relatively brief period of dominance would perhaps not otherwise have offspring of their own. (These observations by Bertram have had a prominent place in the debate on the new theory of genetic selection and are discussed at length both by Dawkins[19] and by Wickler and Seibt.[20])

THE 1.2 MALE

The number-two male in the ranking order is just as aggressive to strangers to the pack as the 1.1 ♂ but is much less friendly to members of it. In our pack this may perhaps have been due to the "personality" of Näschen, who occupied the position for years. But this increased aggression agrees with what one would expect of individual strategies in the pack. Its members behave with great friendliness and submissiveness to the 1.1 ♂, and they obey him. But the upward expansionary tendencies of the young males, their attempts to secure a permanent position in the pack, are to a large extent directed at the 1.2 ♂. He has to defend his position against pressure from below and at the same time preserve his chances of eventually succeeding the 1.1 ♂. He is the aggressive pivot around which the males revolve, and at the same time he is one of the decision makers. There is a close bond between him and the 1.1 ♂, and sometimes also between him and the 1.1 ♀. He helps in the rearing of the cubs and brings them food but, like the 1.1 ♂, often leaves direct contact with them to others and concentrates more on their protection.

THE SUBDOMINANTS

The subdominants are generally younger animals. As departure from the pack normally means a diminished expectation of life (at any rate in areas where the animals on which they prey are large), it must be in the interests of subdominants to stay in it. On the other hand, their chances of having cubs and successfully rearing them are relatively poor. But this again is partially compensated for by the fact that the cubs born in the pack are probably their full or half siblings, with whom they share 50 or at least 25 percent identical genes.

Their chances of remaining in the pack are partly dependent on their rank, that is, on the number of animals superior to them and the general need of the pack. If this is friendly, their chances of remaining in it are better. There is, however, a certain conflict. On the one hand, they must aspire to attaining as high a rank as possible, which generally cannot be achieved without conflict; on the other, aggression is undesirable. Their bond to the pack also involves conflict. If they remain closely associated with it, they are generally assured of food and are not exposed to aggression on returning after absences. But their prospects of breaking away in a favorable situation, finding a partner, and producing offspring themselves in the future are small.

An optimal behavioral strategy must take all this into account (as it of course does, for I have drawn my conclusions about it from the animals' actual behavior). Among themselves they try to attain the highest rank possible, but without totally unlimited aggression. Violent aggressive clashes lead immediately to an extension of conflict, which is not in their interests. Instead they try to disarm aggression from above by intense humility behavior, and clashes with one another as well as with the 1.2 ♂ are often conducted playfully. Also, without breaking with the pack, they go off on their own or in small groups for hours, days, or even longer. This tendency increases the lower they are in rank, in other words, the more improbable it is that they will ever reach the number-one position and be able to reproduce. It is true that when they leave the pack their chances of reproduction are relatively small, but presumably the chances are still better than if they remain with it. They are friendly to strange wolves and actually seek contact with them, which is possible only away from the pack. The fact that departures from the pack by inferior males tend to be voluntary while departure by females tend to be involuntary is presumably due to the more aggressive clashes involved in establishing female ranking order.

THE JUVENILES

Early separation from the pack is even more dangerous to young animals, because of their inexperience. Apart from occasional acts of self-assertion, they must remain closely integrated into the pack, from which they have a great deal to learn. This applies not only to

203

hunting but also to cub rearing, which they experience for the first time. The likelihood that the cubs are their siblings is much greater than it is in the case of the older subdominants. So they generally take a very active part in looking after the cubs. As they are treated with great tolerance by the older wolves, they do not have to worry very much about staying in the pack, and thus are able to exploit every opportunity of improving their starting position in relation to the later issue of whether or not they will remain in the pack. Their best way of doing this is to join in attacks started by others on young adults higher up the ranking order. Apart from the 1.1 ♀, these "adolescent rowdies" are the most pugnacious members of the pack. As a result, vacancies at the top are often filled by them.

THE CUBS

Finally, the cubs have no problem staying in the pack. Unlike the juveniles, it is in their interest that there be as many members of the pack as possible to bring them food and protect them against danger. Their extreme friendliness and "infantile" displays are directed primarily at all the members of the pack—and in particular at those who return to it after longer periods of absence, who are strangers to them. This behavior saves them from aggression and triggers solicitude from the older wolves. Only when they are bigger and more independent do they direct their demonstrations of infantile harmlessness and dependence mainly at the animals that are still the most important to them, their parents, who are also the highest-ranking members of the pack.

Stability of the Pack and Incest

The relatively great stability of pair bonding between the reproducing wolves, the recruiting of new reproducers from the existing pack, and the great aversion to strangers to the pack lead eventually to incest within the pack. The increase in recombinations of similar genotypes leads to a decline in genetic differences in the pack and to an increase in the differences between different packs. Selective pressure on different recessive combinations of genes makes possible the rapid development of new adaptive genotypes. The wolf's high

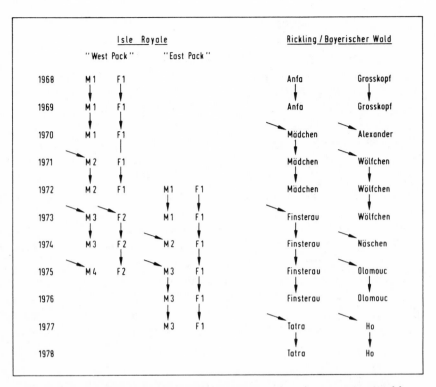

Fig. 29. Length of time for which alpha position in pack was maintained by different males (M) and females (F) in two free-living packs on Isle Royale and in captive packs. Observations made during mating season in February.

degree of adaptability must certainly be the result of accelerated evolutionary processes within the stable pack. On the other hand, the accumulation of recessive characteristics within closely related groups also involves dangers. Eventually this raises the question of the duration of the life of the pack as the exclusive unit of reproduction. How long does a pack of two not closely related animals last before being brought to an end by the death or dispersal of its members or until the admission of strange animals?

That is a question we cannot yet answer. On Isle Royale, where noncaptive wolves have been studied since 1959—longer than anywhere else—it has not been possible to mark the animals, so when

205

the annual winter observations take place it has been possible to recognize only a few animals from the previous year. One pack was observed to break up after the loss of the alpha male. Observation of our own pack suggests that a change in one of the two alpha positions leads to a period of great unrest and restructuring, in the course of which the pack may break up. Even though complete disruption is not a necessary consequence, it is certainly a period of maximum upheaval, marked by the breakaway of whole groups or the accession of strange animals. Hence the length of the time during which the alpha animals retain their position is an indication of the duration of stable conditions. We observed interesting possible differences between males and females. In our pack Finsterau was the undisputed 1.1 ♀ for five and a half years, while among the males Wölfchen lasted only for three years and Olomouc for two. As disturbances from outside could not be avoided, these figures are by no means conclusive, but figures from Isle Royale (see figure 29) show a similar picture. It was not possible to establish how or when the changes in rank took place there or what were the concomitant circumstances. All that was attempted every winter was to identify the alpha animals in the two packs on the island, and it turned out that changes were more frequent among the males than among the females. Also no former alpha animals were seen again in the pack.[21] As in our pack, loss of the alpha position involved, if not death, at least departure from the pack.

The few data available from Isle Royale do not of course exclude chance, but as they show a trend similar to that in our pack we can grant them a certain amount of weight. Thus it seems that a change in one of the two top positions takes place at relatively brief intervals, and a reproducing couple does not stay together for more than a few years. As a period of increased instability is involved, it is to be assumed that the life of a pack—or at any rate the period of its total exclusivity—is limited, and that incestuous conditions generally do not last for many generations. These observations seem to corroborate my own theory that a wolf pack in which the alpha male plays such an outstanding and predominant role is in reality a matriarchy. It is the alpha female, the mother of the cubs, that is the principal figure governing the life of the pack, gathering round her for a longer or shorter period one or more adult males that father, procure food, and protect her offspring.

206

IO

Ecology of the Wolf

Why do wolves live in packs? This form of social organization must be an adaptation to their environment, to ecological conditions. Hence in the absence of knowledge of the ecology of free-living populations, any analysis of animal behavior is necessarily incomplete. The converse is also true; knowledge of wolf behavior is essential to the study of their ecology. The border zone between ethology and ecology has hitherto been called either etho-ecology or eco-ethology, depending on the student's starting point. Nowadays it also goes by the name of sociobiology. But in practice there is still a distinct division of labor resulting from traditional attitudes and methods of study.

So far we have dealt with wolf behavior on the basis of my work with captive animals. Ecological studies of free-living wolf populations have been carried out chiefly by American colleagues. A list of their most important publications will be found in the appendix, and a new and comprehensive account of their findings in book form is, I believe, planned by Dave Mech. I shall now introduce to the reader some of my American colleagues and their working methods and shall summarize their most important findings, and in the next chapter I shall go into the question that interests us both, that of the regulation of pack size that leads to the regulation of the wolf population.

Treetop Wolf Hunt

I met Dave Mech for the first time in 1973 after the international ethological conference at Washington, D.C. He picked me up at the airport at Minneapolis, and on the same day we went with his wife and four children to the area where he works in north Minnesota. We started discussing the questions that interested us on the way. How does a wolf pack optimize its size? What influence does its spatial organization and corresponding behavior have on the regulation of the wolf population? Like many open-air ecologists, Dave was skeptical about ethologists who, as he put it, "tried to explain the world" on the basis of the few observations of and experiments with captive animals. It turned out that our findings were in agreement to a large extent, and an animated and stimulating discussion quickly developed. It was not superior young wolves that left the pack because of their competition with the alpha animal, as had often been claimed, but inferior animals; and leadership of the pack was "democratic" rather than "authoritarian." The aggressiveness of the alpha female, the food supply, and bonding—these and many other questions that seemed so unimportant in isolation were highly important for understanding how the population was regulated. It was not until late that night that we reached the experimental station where Dave's colleagues were awaiting us. I was given a room in the big, handsome wooden house, while Dave and his family were put up in a tent. I was amazed. It was explained to me that the families of government officials (Dave is employed by one of the top nature conservation offices) were not allowed to stay in the house, so his wife and children were plagued by flies outside while I slept in a bed under a mosquito net as a guest of the American government.

The next day I accompanied him on one of his usual inspection flights. He had fixed two aerials to the wings of his Cessna 182 so that he was able to take his bearings at an angle of 90 degrees downward to the longitudinal axis. Then off we went. As we flew over a vast, almost unpopulated area of forests and lakes he explained his techniques to me. Wolves were trapped nearly all the year round and fitted with radio transmitters, each of which transmitted on a different wavelength, making it possible to identify each animal. At that time he had nine wolves and a lynx under control in this way. A switch on the receiving set in the aircraft made it possible to change from the left to the right aerial or vice versa. Soon we heard our first signal, from a male, the alpha animal in his pack. By switching between the two aerials Dave knew which way to go and signaled to the pilot accordingly. If the signal on the left was louder than it was on the right, it meant we must bear left, and so on. The signal grew louder, and then suddenly faded; we had overrun the wolf. The pilot put the aircraft down into a steep curve and a search just over the treetops began. The circles grew smaller and smaller until we spotted four wolves sleeping close together on a sunny rock just above the level of the trees. This was our marked male's pack. The animals were not in the least perturbed by the aircraft and did not even look up. Obviously they were totally used to it. I was so fascinated that I completely forgot that the continuous circling should have made me feel ill.

Then we searched for other wolves. At first we followed a she-wolf who that morning had penetrated unusually deep into neighboring territory. In earlier years Dave had never observed such behavior, which was now becoming more and more frequent, and he explained it as due to the dwindling deer population in the area. The big clearings that had been made in the forest ten and twenty years earlier had provided the deer with excellent grazing, but the clearings were gradually growing over again, with a resulting slow decline in the numbers of deer, followed after a short interval by a decline in the wolf population.

At first the packs grew smaller, as a result both of increased cub mortality and departures. At the same time there was an increase in incursions into the territories of neighboring packs. The intruders generally soon returned to their own territory without a confrontation with the "owners." Dave had only twice observed encounters between two packs; on one occasion a wolf was killed and on another one was wounded.

It took us a long time to track down the female intruder. We spent at least twenty minutes flying over the forest in closer and closer circles, but failed to find her. When we had given up and were flying on, we suddenly spotted her immediately beneath us, swimming the wide river that formed the boundary of her own territory. Presumably the noise of the aircraft while she was in foreign territory had made her uneasy and she was now on her way back to safety.

Why do wolves not try to expand their territory at the expense of neighboring packs when food runs short instead of only occasionally intruding into alien territory and otherwise remaining in their own territory with a smaller pack? We discussed the question while searching for the next wolf, a young male. The most plausible explanation seemed to us to be the danger of being wounded in trying to drive a neighboring pack away. Even a slight wound at the beginning of winter could have fatal consequences. From the point of view of the wolf's strategy for survival, respecting the existing territorial organization to a large extent, if possible making more rational use of the available food supply and, if necessary, forcing other animals to leave the pack and the territory, seemed preferable to expending energy and risking one's life in a "war for living space." It seemed to us that changes in the spatial organization of a wolf population would take place only in the event of drastic long-term changes in the food supply and its distribution.

At this point I cannot resist making a comparison between men and animals. With wolves as with other animal species (excepting some kinds of insects, where quite different reproductive and kinship conditions prevail), there is nothing comparable to the phenomenon known to mankind as war, conflict carried out with lethal weapons between suprafamily units such as nations, tribes, states, or classes. Attempts to explain the phenomenon of human warfare with the aid of ethological models of aggression are therefore doomed to failure. Animal aggression and human warfare as a struggle for resources such as land, food, or power (rank) may have ultimately comparable causes, but comparison of the motivation of the individual involved in the conflict reveals fundamental differences. Animals act basically selfishly because of the selective advantage of the "selfish" gene. Even apparently unselfish behavior ultimately serves their collective fitness and is therefore basically selfish. Truly altruistic, self-sacrificing behavior in the interests of suprafamily organizational units exists only in man. The causes for this lie in the cultural rather than the biological sphere. How a cultural development such as self-sacrificing behavior, which sometimes conflicts with biological evolution, came about—with all its positive and negative consequences for us—is one of the most interesting problems of human history. To the biologist the question of how men can be persuaded to kill other men—for whatever reasons—at the risk of being killed themselves remains completely open. [1]

But to return to our wolves. The last wolf for which we searched was a two- or three-year-old male who had left his pack and had been wandering in a southwesterly direction for weeks. We ended by finding him a long way outside a closely forested area in a wood near a big human settlement. To judge by the regularity of the signals, which show marked variations in strength when the animal was moving (because of the changing direction of the transmitting aerial) he was sleeping somewhere in the scrub, so we failed to spot him. In the course of his wanderings he must have crossed roads, railways, and even a highway several times. Dave was not exactly pleased at this, because in densely populated areas wolves are bound to come into conflict with human interests. A dead dog or a sheep torn to pieces would encourage the enemies of the wolf and call into question the measures to protect it that had been enacted in Minnesota despite strong opposition.

Dave had to take his family home the next day, because of school. I stayed a few days longer, accompanied his colleagues on their daily work and sat in a tree and lured four young cubs out of their hiding place by howling, and finally went back to Europe.

WOLVES ON ISLE ROYALE

Two years later I went to Minnesota again, this time with my friend Luigi Boitani, my Italian colleague on the Abruzzi project. As on the previous trip, Dave began by taking us to look for wolves from the air, and then he took us to Isle Royale, where he did his first work with wolves. Isle Royale is an island of 210 square miles in Lake Superior, just fifteen miles from the Canadian coast. At the beginning of the century moose had settled there, and wolves crossed to the island for the first time by way of an ice bridge in 1949. In 1959 Dave, under the leadership of D. Allen, began one of the longest continuous investigations of the development of predator-prey relationships that has ever been conducted in the history of ecology. It is now being continued by Rolf Peterson and the objective is the same—to establish the quantitative relationships ex-

211

isting on the island among the vegetation, the only big herbivore, the moose, and the only predator of the moose, the wolf.[2]

I had read a great deal about the work being done on the island, and had actually written about it and mentioned it in lectures. When I saw the enormous effect the moose has on the vegetation, which in no way compares to the damage done by game in the National Park in the Bavarian Forest (where there are no wolves, but too many deer and roe), I was astonished. In the Bavarian Forest the foresters complain of the damage done by game, but feed the animals in winter and then shoot them to "save" the forest from further devastation. On Isle Royale events are left to run their course, without human interference. Even attempts to put out the forest fires that occur naturally have been abandoned, because their importance in the natural development of the ecological system has been recognized.

However, this natural development looked quite different from what I had expected. Rolf and his colleagues call it a "moose-spruce-savannah." The moose had stripped the island bare of everything they liked, and in many places only the spruce—which, as in Europe, is the last tree on the ungulate menu—had survived. As a result of fires new grazing areas continually developed, with the result that the feared collapse of the moose population had not set in. Nowhere else was it so clear to me that big herbivores, like the moose, are limited in number not by the wolf but primarily by the supply of vegetation. This also means that it is not the wolf that governs the size of the moose population, but the moose that governs that of the wolf population. This is a topic to which I shall return.

IN ALGONQUIN PARK

From Isle Royale we flew on to Toronto, where we met Doug Pimlott, chairman of the wolf group of the International Union for the Conservation of Nature and Natural Resources (IUCN), whom we already knew from the visit he paid us in the Abruzzi. He had just returned from the Arctic, where he was investigating the ecological consequences of drilling for oil in the Arctic Ocean. Hitherto we had only read the enormously expensive propaganda of the oil companies in the matter, and he talked to us about the possibly catastrophic consequences of an oil carpet under the ice sheet. Un-

212

fortunately he could not accompany us to Algonquin Park. So, while Luigi visited friends in New York, I went there alone and spent some days in the area accompanied by one of Doug's colleagues. As far as big herbivores and the wolf are concerned, the ecosystem is similar to that in north Minnesota and on Isle Royale, but the ecological connections between the individual links in the food chains are quite different. It was very clear to me here that every complex ecosystem has very special characteristics. Any attempt inductively to draw up universally valid principles can lead only to very crude models indeed. What follows should be read in light of this.

Competition for Prey

After Näschen's escape I found the remains of insects in his feces. In the Abruzzi we saw wolves eating spaghetti with tomato sauce or dead animals on refuse heaps, and wolves in the Canadian Artcic are reported to have fed for quite a long time on lemmings.[3] The wolf seems to be almost omnivorous, and yet it has survived only in areas in which there is an adequate supply of bigger animals, from beavers, roe, or sheep on up. All investigations carried out so far have shown that in the long run animals of that size provide by far the largest proportion of its diet and that rodents or domestic refuse can be only a supplement or can only satisfy it in the short term. Calculation of its dietary needs show why small animals cannot be sufficient.

It has been calculated that a wild wolf consumes from 2.5 to 10 kilograms a day.[4] Wolves in captivity can be kept healthy on 1 kilogram (2.2 pounds) a day, though inferior dietetic components such as heavy bones, skin, contents of the stomach, and so on, are not counted. Also most animals in captivity are less mobile, and a warm sleeping place is often at their disposal. Thus a free wolf has greater needs. If we put a wolf's minimum needs at about 2.5 kilograms daily, it would have to catch about one hundred rodents a day to remain alive, which would be possible only in exceptional circumstances, such as a mass multiplication of lemmings. In most cases the energy expended in catching them would greatly exceed that derived from eating them, and this would lead to early death. If a wolf succeeded for a time in living by this means, it could not compete in the long run with the fox, which is much better adapted to hunting of that kind. Not only does the fox need much less food, it is also a much more skillful hunter of rodents. To get domestic refuse the wolf has to compete with the fox, the dog, and the cat, which can approach this source of food, generally to be found near human settlements, with much less danger to their lives.

In hunting medium-sized prey, ranging from the rabbit and the hare to the roe, the wolf has to compete in many areas with the fox and also with another predator, the lynx. According to a study carried out in the Carpathians in Czechoslovakia, the lynx mostly kills roe while the wolf kills deer.[5] The lynx prefers prey of the size of rabbits and hares in America too, while the wolf chiefly hunts ungulates. The coyote, the bear, and the wolverine similarly display feeding habits distinct from those of the wolf. In the evolution of terrestrial predators a certain amount of specialization took place, in which the wolf developed into a predator of the ungulates in the mountain, forest, and tundra areas of the northern hemisphere. In large parts of this territory he is almost without competition. Only in areas with a high density of game, such as western North America with its favorable biotopes for big herbivores, does he have to face competition from the puma (see table A). The puma has a more specialized hunting technique and therefore needs a greater density of prey. In the highly productive primeval forest areas of south and west Asia, specialized species such as the tiger, the leopard, and the hyena occur that—like the puma in the extreme west of America—have driven out the wolf. Thus the number of species that hunt ungulates depends to a large extent on the biomass of the prey at their disposal, and this again depends on the primary production exploitable by ungulates—that is, grasses, shrubs, and low trees. This becomes plain when we consider the number of species of bigger predators on the East African savannah with its enormous density of game.

The wolf is basically a hunter of bigger animals that occur in relatively low density. But it also uses all other opportunities of procuring food that present themselves, as long as its security is not threatened and the energy balance of the hunt is positive. The young wolf has to learn when hunting is worthwhile. Dave reports that a wolf pack observed by him very quickly broke off the hunt when it

Habitat	Ungulate Species	Density (per sq. km.)	Weight (kg.)	Biomass (kg. per sq. km.)	Predator(s)
Tundra Favorable biotope Northern Canada	Caribou	0.75	100	75	Wolf
Coniferous Forest Algonquin Park Ontario	White-tailed deer	4	70	280	Wolf
Isle Royale	Moose	1	350	350	Wolf
Mountains Rocky Mountains National Park	Bighorn sheep, Wapiti, Moose, Deer, Caribou, Rocky Mountain goat	14	140	1960	Wolf (Puma)
Chaparral Average in California	Black-tailed deer	12	70	840	Puma (Wolf)
Favorable Habitat	Black-tailed deer	38	70	2660	
Savannah Albert Park Congo	11 species	35	350	11,500	Lion, Leopard, Cheetah, Hyena, Cape hunting dog

Table A. Habitat and density of ungulate populations and their predators.

realized that the quarry was too fast for it or a moose at bay was too dangerous to attack.[6] Gordon Haber told me it was the same at Mount McKinley: young wolves that had broken away from a big pack sometimes kept a moose surrounded for days until they finally realized that there were not enough of them to tackle it.[7] As we know, when my tame wolves were cubs and juveniles they chased animals they had no chance of catching. They learned quickly that they had no hope of catching crows in the field, and it took a little longer for them to stop chasing hares that had a big start; and it took them a very long time indeed to realize that they were no match for the cows and horses at Rickling.

DAILY HUNTING ROUTINE

How does the wolf adapt itself to hunting big game in areas where food is relatively scarce? Hunting and living in groups presumably developed simultaneously with the hunting of such game. Then there is their perpetual mobility; they are able to kill only a small proportion of a small number of animals that are generally scattered over a wide area, so they have to travel big distances daily to find them. In their roamings they trot at about four to five miles an hour. If necessary they can keep this up for a long time; for instance, reports from Finland state they have covered 125 miles in twenty-four hours on hard snow.[8] Normally the distances covered are much less than that, as they do a great deal of sleeping, playing, or eating in between. One winter Dave followed a pack on Isle Royale for thirty-one days, in the course of which they covered a distance of 279 miles, or an average of nine miles a day. But for twenty-two days they stayed near an animal they had killed and moved only in its immediate vicinity, so they actually covered 279 miles in nine days, or an average of thirty-one miles a day. As they kept up an average speed of about five miles an hour, they were on the move for about 20 or 30 percent of the day. They spent the rest of the time sleeping, playing, in other social interactions, or in hunting unsuccessfully. Only when they were successful again did they stay with their kill for several days, generally until it was completely consumed.

Thus for all their hard work wolves have to manage without food on many days. When they have made a kill they can devour enormous quantities of food at once. There is a report of a wolf that ate nearly 20 pounds at a single meal.[9] To judge by my experience with captive wolves, this does not strike me as unusually high. Also food is digested in a very few hours, so that wolves are soon able to eat again. This is the only possible explanation of the fact that a wolf pack can cause a 900-pound moose to disappear completely, apart from some skin and bone, in two days. A wolf can eat up to 44 pounds in twenty-four hours, but can also go without food for a very long time. Dave believes that wolves can easily continue their normal wanderings for a fortnight without eating.

The way the day is divided up among roaming, hunting, eating, social contact making, and sleeping of course depends on the season, the nature of the country, the availability of prey, and so on. In the Abruzzi, for example, wolves behave quite differently, as we shall see. They also behave differently in the Canadian Arctic, where they follow the herds of migrating caribou, or in Finland, where they are vigorously hunted by men. But common to all wolves is their ability to go without food for a long time and to devour large amounts of it in a short time. This is certainly a great advantage in the hard conditions in which they often have to live, and this is one of the reasons wolves used to be so widely dispersed.

HUNTING AND KILLING TECHNIQUES

Another thing that enables the wolf to live in very different ecological conditions is its way of hunting. Wolves always hunt. They use every opportunity to hunt, whether to catch a mouse or to chase a moose, and they have developed a definite technique of hunting and killing for every size and kind of prey. In the case of the mouse, they leap at it in a high arc like a fox, seize it with their forepaws, and follow up with the muzzle. The mouse is chewed a few times and then swallowed. With my wolves, it was mostly cubs that hunted mice or insects on the wing, and they often went on doing it for hours; and the same is reported of wolves in freedom. They catch rabbits or hares in the same way as they catch mice. When they have overtaken the fleeing prey, they pin it to the ground with their forepaws and follow up swiftly with the muzzle. The killing is not done by shaking, but by a series of bites in various places. I have only seen young cubs briefly shaking prey that is relatively big for them, such as a young guinea pig or rabbit. Adult wolves seem to use this method of killing only with prey capable of defending itself. Two cats that jumped into the enclosure at Rickling were killed in that way, and I once saw the same thing happen to a tame fox. It had been reared with a dog and was then sent to the fox enclosure at the National Park in the Bavarian Forest, from which it escaped. Obviously seeking company, it climbed the fence into the wolf enclosure and was immediately seized and killed by powerful shaking movements.

Still bigger animals such as roe or sheep are killed by bites in the area of the throat (see figure 30). This happens very quickly and, though the wound generally looks relatively harmless, the animal dies in a few seconds to a minute. Presumably vital nerve tracks are destroyed in addition to the carotid artery. Wolves do not have to learn how to do this. The animals that escaped from the enclosure in the Bavarian Forest who had never before hunted larger animals

217

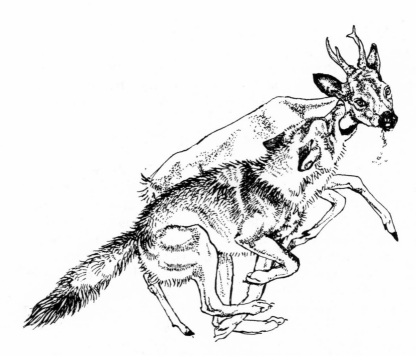

Fig. 30. The death bite. How middle-sized prey is dealt with.

learned in the course of a few days to catch roe, all of which they killed by a bite in the throat. As this method of killing is very quick, wolves can kill many animals in rapid succession if the opportunity presents itself as, for instance, in a sheep pen.

But the big animals preyed on by the wolf die slowly. Dave Mech has described in great detail how they hunt whitetailed deer and moose. He divides the hunt into several phases: the locating and spotting of the prey; the stalking and creeping up; the confrontation, when predator and prey become aware of each other; the quick spurt toward the prey; the chase that follows if the prey takes flight; and finally the kill, when the animal is brought to bay. Contrary to previous ideas, according to which wolves wear down their quarry by long pursuit, Dave believes that wolves use the short, swift attack. If this is unsuccessful, they quickly give up; and the quarry stops quickly too when it realizes that it is no longer being pursued. Caribou can actually tell whether a wolf is hunting or is merely trotting through the herd. In the latter event they let it approach within a few yards, and when it is hunting they take only the minimum evasive action that is necessary. Like wolves, the animals on which they prey have to be economical with their strength.

I have never myself seen wolves successfully hunting large animals. But in East Africa I once witnessed a hunt by Cape hunting dogs and, as these animals are similar to the wolf, I shall describe it. We were observing the dogs north of Governor's Camp in the Masai Mara Game Reserve in Kenya; there were three males, a female, and nine cubs aged about three months old. The four adults would leave the den where the cubs were and go out hunting in the morning and evening twilight. One evening we followed them in a Jeep, of which they showed no fear. We continually passed big herds of gnu, mingled with small groups of zebra. The dogs, running widely separated from each other, approached a herd of gnu. The animals took evasive action without taking flight. One of the four dogs, immediately followed by the others, suddenly dashed toward a group of gnu; they scattered, some running in the opposite direction from the dogs. We hurried after them and saw that the dogs had picked out a younger gnu, about eight months old. They separated it from the herd and soon overtook it. Two bit its hindquarters, causing it to stop, and one immediately went and bit the animal's snout, causing it to yelp loudly. The other gnu had stopped running away surprisingly quickly, and some of them were standing not a hundred yards away, looking on and complaining. While the victim was held fast in front by one dog, the others tore large lumps of flesh from its hindquarters. One bit a large piece from the anus and swallowed it immediately, while the dog next to it tore out the intestines. The animal was still standing with wide-open eyes, uttering low, moaning sounds. Eventually it collapsed to its knees and then on to its side; it died after about eight minutes. The dogs quickly ate their fill and one after the other left the body, for which a number of jackals, a hyena, and many vultures were already waiting. The dogs went back to their cubs and regurgitated, a little at a time, a large part of the food they had swallowed. When it was dark we drove slowly back to our camp, feeling very weak in the knees.

Wolves hunt big animals in a similar way. They also use different tactics, such as driving an animal toward other members of the pack who are lying in wait. They are especially likely to do this on the open tundra. A Canadian documentary film taken from an aircraft showed some wolves driving a reindeer down a slope at the bottom of which two other wolves were waiting. This method is presumably used less frequently in thickly wooded areas. But Doug Pimlott was able to reconstruct successful deer hunts by wolves with the aid of tracks in the snow and thus demonstrate something in the nature of an ambush.[10]

ENERGY BALANCE SHEET

Success at hunting is dependent on a number of factors, of which the most important are the nature, age, sex, and physical condition of the prey, the nature of the country, the snow conditions, and finally the number of wolves involved. In Ontario a wolf pack consisting of from seven to nine animals succeeded in killing 25 percent of the whitetailed deer that it started. In the following winter the success rate of what was presumed to be the same pack, now consisting of eight animals, was 63 percent,[11] an unusually high figure, obviously due to favorable snow conditions for the wolves that winter. An interesting fact was that in spite of this high success rate the killed animals were completely consumed down to the skin and bones. Sometimes nibbled pieces of meat were left, but the wolves always came back for them days or weeks later.

These figures were obtained with the aid of tracks in the snow, and some unsuccessful hunts may have escaped notice. Nevertheless the wolves' success with whitetailed deer weighing about 150 pounds should be much higher than with the much heavier moose. Dave Mech reconstructed 131 moose hunts by a pack of fifteen or sixteen wolves on Isle Royale. Only six moose were killed—a success rate of barely 5 percent. Most moose were able to escape. If they were overtaken they went on running without the wolves bringing them down. Some stopped and defended themselves with powerful kicks of their forelegs.

It also was plain on Isle Royale that single wolves or small packs found it much harder to kill enough animals for their needs. They seemed to have lived partly on the leftovers of the big packs.

It is obviously more difficult for wolves to kill a moose than a deer. In areas where there are both, they therefore prefer the smaller of the two. On Isle Royale, where there are moose only, the young are hunted soon after they are born. The smaller yield of meat is compensated for by the smaller amount of energy spent in obtaining it. Thus wolves seem to be able to draw up a kind of energy balance sheet for different kinds of prey, in which other factors, such as the size of the prey, the nature of the country, and other conditions, as well as an assessment of their own capacities, seem to be included.

Effects on Prey Populations

Let us now take a closer look at the influence that wolves have on the animal populations on which they prey. This is a complex question, for it varies from place to place and also changes with time. Here I can only try to indicate the most important effects quite briefly and schematically. These are (1) the age structure, (2) the health, and (3) the continued existence of the populations in question.

If the hunting success of wolves depended solely on chance, external factors such as the nature of the country or weather conditions, or on their own varying inclinations, the animals they killed would be a reflection of the prey population as a whole. But the wolf's "hit or miss" method of hunting suggests that it is above all the weaker animals that are killed, that is, the very young and very old, as well as those weakened by disease or hunger.

This is confirmed by all the studies of the subject. In the first place, there are Doug Pimlott's findings in Algonquin Park. He compared the ages of 331 whitetailed deer killed by wolves with those of 275 killed in the same area by shooting or road accidents. In the second group of deaths chance was the decisive factor, and the ages of the dead animals could be regarded as roughly representative of the age structure of the population. It turned out that 50 percent of the population was aged between one and four, while this age group provided only 15 percent of the animals killed by wolves. In other words, 85 percent of the deer killed by wolves were younger or older animals.[12] The age distribution of the moose killed on Isle Royale was even more striking; in the early years of the inquiry nearly all the animals killed were young or old animals.[13]

The influence of disease appears very plainly in the study by Murie on Dall's sheep in the Mount McKinley area.[14] Among

221

animals aged from one to eight years, the mortality rate (mainly caused by wolves) was 14 percent; in other words, by far the greatest proportion of animals killed were either young or old. But 68 percent of the sheep of medium age that were killed were suffering from actinomycosis, an infection of the jaw bones that among other things makes the chewing of food very difficult. Only 20 percent of the young and old animals had this disease. So it is obviously difficult for wolves to kill adult wild sheep.

The health of a population depends on a variety of factors, of which the food supply is of outstanding importance. The amount available to each individual depends on the population level. Excessive density of population leads to the destruction of vegetation and a consequent decline in the amount available. The animals grow weaker and more susceptible to disease and are thus easier prey for wolves.

That is exactly what has happened on Isle Royale in recent years. Since studies began there the moose population has increased greatly and the vegetation has suffered accordingly. A "moose-spruce-savannah" developed, with a consequent deterioration in the food supply and hence also the health of the still very numerous moose. Many fewer twins are born now, and thus reproductivity has declined. More and more animals, especially young ones up to the age of six months, die of undernourishment or wounds, and others die by drowning. The proportion of young animals killed by wolves has greatly increased as a result, though the deep snow that has lain in recent years has also contributed to this. But more than undernourishment has been the direct cause of the big increase in the killings of moose in the one-to-five-year age group. Between 1959 and 1964 Dave found only four moose in that age group killed by wolves, or 5.6 percent of the total. But between 1970 and 1974 the proportion increased to 52.9 percent—a truly enormous jump.[15]

Thus we see that so far as the age and state of health of their prey is concerned, the selection made by the wolves depends largely on the general state of the prey population. In healthy populations young animals are preferred, as well as those in the second half of their natural life expectancy. The bigger the species, the more marked is this tendency. In favorable conditions wolves can sometimes kill healthy animals in the prime of life, but this is rarer with bigger species. However, it is true of animals of all sizes that the proportion killed by wolves increases with increasing disease and undernourishment. As both factors are directly dependent on the density of the population, when this density is high or excessive a larger proportion are available as prey. This must be taken into account in considering the question of possible population regulation by the wolf.

Ironing Out the Swings

The question of the natural regulation of the population is one of the most difficult and controversial in ecology. This also applies to the question of whether the wolf exercises a regulating or limiting influence on the population of animals on which it preys. By regulation in this context I mean that as a result of the influence of the wolf, the composition, numbers, and development of the population differ from what they would be in its absence. Limitation would occur if wolves kept the population lower than it would be without them, in other words, lower than the limit that would be imposed by the food supply or other factors.

The best work on this subject has again been done on Isle Royale. At the beginning of the century the first moose swam to the island from the coast of Ontario fifteen miles away, where the moose population was increasing at the time. As a result of the almost untouched vegetation and the absense of enemies, they multiplied rapidly, and by the end of the twenties they numbered between 1,000 and 3,000. By that time the vegetation had suffered severely and, presumably as a result of undernourishment, the population collapsed to a few hundred by the beginning of the thirties. This enabled the vegetation to recover, and in 1936 two big fires destroyed more than forty square miles of forest, thus further improving grazing conditions. Another big increase in the moose population took place, followed at the end of the forties by a big reduction as a result of food shortage and undernourishment.

Thus until wolves, making use of an ice bridge from the mainland, settled on the island in 1949, the size of the moose population was marked by big periodic swings. Eleven years after the arrival of the wolves Dave estimated that the size of the winter population was about 600 moose and 23 wolves. Calculating the number of free-

223

living animals in an area with some degree of accuracy is one of the most difficult tasks in game biology, in spite of the development of a number of refined methods, but Dave's estimates seem to have been very accurate so far as the wolves were concerned. His figures for the moose were quite accurate too, as was shown by later investigations, though perhaps they were rather on the low side. In any event, he concluded that there was an annual increase of 225 young moose; only 85 survived the first year of life and were thus added to the population, while the remaining 140 succumbed to the wolves. He also estimated the yearly number of killed adult animals as 83. Thus the natural increase was skimmed off by the wolves, with the result that the moose population was stabilized at about 600 animals.

These figures, as well as the healthy condition of the moose, the high proportion of twin births, and the apparently intact vegetation, led him to the assumption that the wolves would limit the moose population. According to his calculations, a predator-prey relationship of wolf to 30 moose (or about 10,000 kilograms of moose) prevailed. Figures from other areas reinforced this assumption. In Algonquin Park, for instance, the deer population was limited by an estimated predator-prey relationship of 1 wolf to between 100 and 150 deer (or from 7,000 to 10,000 kilograms). In contrast to this, in another area farther to the west, Jasper National Park in the Rocky Mountains, where there was a very favorable biotope for big herbivores, it seemed that wolves did not limit the population of the animals on which they preyed. Six different kinds of ungulates lived there in much greater density than in the forest areas in the east (see table A, page 215). A predator-prey relationship of 1 wolf to 300 or 400 animals of different species was assumed (or 1 wolf to 40,000 or 50,000 kilograms).[16]

On the basis of this and other examples Dave suggested that wolves might limit the size of the population when the predator-prey relationship was 1 wolf or fewer to 10,000 kilograms, but that when this ratio was exceeded they had less and less influence.[17] This turned out to be not quite correct, as was shown by further developments on Isle Royale.

In spite of the difficulty of accurately assessing the numbers of a moose population, a further increase in the population seems now to be assured. At the end of the sixties the population was estimated at about 1,500, and the number of wolves was believed to have increased to about 28. But in recent years the moose population has again declined to 800 or 1,000, while the wolf population increased to 44 in 1976. While there used to be only one pack on the island as well as a few individual animals or smaller nonterritorial groups, after 1972 there were two territorial, cub-producing packs, and in the winter of 1977 there were actually three.[18]

What do these figures tell us? Let us once more recall the moose-spruce-savannah. The wolves obviously did not limit the moose population in the early sixties. It continued to grow, more slowly, perhaps, than if no wolves had been present, but it again reached and for a time exceeded the limit imposed by the food supply. The vegetation was impoverished and there was less for the moose to eat. Consequently there was a big increase in mortality from food shortage, accidents, disease, and an increased liability to be killed by wolves, as is clearly shown by the increase in the numbers of killed young adults mentioned above. This enabled the wolves to go on increasing in numbers in spite of the decline in the moose population, as a higher proportion of moose were available to them and because a smaller area was sufficient to secure the food supply of an additional pack. An increase in the beaver population presumably also benefited the wolves.

What does this imply for Dave's theory of the restricting influence of the wolf on the numbers of the animals on which it preys? In the first place, as Dave has himself pointed out, a limiting influence should tend to be the exception in special situations that themselves are presumably not stable. The decisive factor that governs the size of the ungulate population is the food supply. The influence of the wolf is limited to selective killing and a moderating effect on the fluctuations of the prey population.

This influence is to a large extent dependent on the quantitative relationship between predator and prey. The more this favors the prey, the smaller is the influence of the predator. But if the situation is reversed and it becomes unusually favorable to the predator, the result may be severe restriction or actual extermination of the prey animal. This seems to have been the case a few years ago in a hunting area near Fairbanks, Alaska. Presumably as a result of excessive hunting, the moose population had greatly declined, and it was feared that the wolves, which were still present in large numbers and also still hunted reindeer, would greatly retard a resumption of growth in the moose population. So a large-scale operation to reduce drastically the numbers of wolves was undertaken. This caused a storm of protest throughout America, but the wolves were shot in spite of it.

Our second example of the wolf's influence on a prey population was in a system greatly disturbed by human influences. In the Abruzzi deer and roe have been exterminated. The native chamois survives only on a mountain range in the National Park there, and it has multiplied in recent years as a result of strict protective measures, though it has not spread to neighboring mountains as was expected. Competition with domestic animals (sheep and goats) certainly plays an important part in this, but it cannot be the only explanation, as the grazing of domestic animals has greatly declined in some areas of the National Park where there are no chamois. Hence the chamois's failure to spread is presumably caused by the wolf. In the high mountains above treelevel the wolf seems to represent no danger to the chamois, but in the lower wooded areas that separate the various ranges it has been able to exercise such high pressure on the few chamois present that no expansion of the population has taken place.

THE ENEMY OF ITS PREY?

The wolf seems to exercise such a restricting influence on the numbers of the animals on which it preys only in environments that have been greatly changed by man. The relationship between wolf and prey in relatively primordial, ecologically intact areas has been clarified in model form by American colleagues. In the extensive mixed forest areas north and west of the Great Lakes, the ungulates (moose and/or whitetailed deer) attain a density of the order of magnitude of 300 kilograms per square kilometer (see table A, page 215). This seems to be the ungulate biomass sustainable in the long term in this area by the vegetation, the primary biological production. The maximum wolf density is 1 to 25 square kilometers. This gives a predator-prey relationship of 1 wolf to 7,500 kilograms—an order of magnitude that is in fact found in different areas that have been investigated.

Since the Ice Age a close and stable interrelationship has clearly developed between vegetation, ungulates, and the wolf. We now know the influence of the wolf on the population on which it preys. Mostly it kills young, old, sick, and weak animals, not out of choice, but because these are the only animals it is able to kill. This has a healthy effect on the population. Also it shifts the age structure in favor of the reproducing age group, with a higher reproductivity rate as a consequence. Finally, the regulatory influence of the wolf seems to even out fluctuations in population, thus making an important contribution to the stability of the system. As a result of its selective hunting methods, its influence on all animals of the prey population is not the same, and we must therefore inquire into the importance of the wolf to the individual prey animal.

The wolf is especially dangerous to the young. Once discovered, they have no way of escape if unprotected by their parents. At this age the behavior patterns that are selectively advantageous both to offspring and mother (who from the standpoint of her own fitness has a great interest in the survival of her young) are those that make the young hard to discover or actually inaccessible to the predator. During their first days and weeks of life young roe and young deer live in remote places that are very well concealed. Among species that live in mountains the mother gives birth and rears her young in steep places inaccessible to wolves. Young reindeer on the tundras are soon able to outdistance any wolf. Two other species that live in open country, the bison and the musk-ox, have developed different forms of collective defense strategies for their young. The wolf's only chance is to find a young animal, or a young animal with its mother, separated from the herd.[19] A healthy female moose seems to be able to defend her young against a big wolf pack.

A young animal's chances of survival depend largely on the behavior of its mother. Chance and luck also play a big part at that age. Nevertheless, the calf of an experienced, alert mother has a better chance of surviving and thus passing on his gene material to the next generation.

As it grows older its chances of survival and of reaching the age of reproduction depend increasingly on the animal itself. As long as it has enough to eat and remains healthy, its chances are good. It must be perpetually on the alert. Its strength and health are likely to be tested by wolves several times in the course of its life, and that costs energy. This also means a more widespread distribution of

227

forest-living herbivores, which prevents excessive concentration and overgrazing of favorable winter grazing grounds. The stronger animals are "freed" from their weaker and sick competitors, which means more space and more food for them, besides diminishing the likelihood of being weakened by internal and external parasites. Thus their chances of reproduction are increased, while the killed animals would in any case have had only a small chance of passing on their genes to the next generation, being either too old or too weak for successful parenthood. To them death means only a quicker release from suffering.

The traditional approach to the question of predator-prey relationships concentrates on the influence of the predator on the population level of the prey. But from the evolutionary aspect it is not the nature or level of the population that matters, but that of the genes, or, as R. Dawkins calls it in his very valuable book,[20] the individual as the genes' "survival machine." It would be interesting to pursue the question of predator-prey relationships from the point of view of individual interests, but this is not the place for it. For us it is sufficient to note that the favoring of healthy prey animals capable of reproduction increases their chances of multiplying their genes in the gene pool of the population. Thus the predator confers a selective advantage on the surviving individuals of the prey population, and it is therefore wrong to describe the predator—in this case the wolf—as the enemy of his prey.

The evolution of predator and prey took place in close reciprocal dependence and affected a large number of anatomical, physiological, ethological, and ecological characteristics of both. If this closely geared relationship is interfered with, as it has been in the past few centuries under human influence, this must necessarily be disadvantageous in the long term not only to the predator but to the prey also.

MAN AS REGULATING FACTOR

In many areas the human hunter has taken over the function of the wolf. Can he do this? Let us briefly compare man's influence with that of the wolf on the animals on which both prey.

In traditional societies integrated into nature, such as those of the

North American Indian or the Eskimo, hunting served primarily to procure food. The influence of these human hunters on the hunted animal populations was similar to that of animal predators. The animals that were killed were mostly inattentive or weak, the killing was done with simple weapons, and only as many were killed as were needed to keep the hunters alive; man was an integrated part of the living community. Interestingly enough, the predators who competed with these hunters were not regarded as enemies to be destroyed. The Indians, for instance, spoke of the wolf as their brother.

The transition to nature-exploiting societies went hand in hand with the invention and development of long-range firearms, and the attitude and influence of hunters changed. Primitive man hunted to feed his family, but with the division of labor other motives came to prevail. To peasants the wolf, the bear, the lynx, and wild ungulates were harmful creatures that either killed and ate their domestic animals or competed with them for grazing grounds, while to the privileged classes hunting became a form of sport. This led to an overexploitation of wildlife, resulting at worst in local or world-wide extermination. The aurochs and the wild horse disappeared completely, and the bison, the ibex, the red deer, and the moose, as well as the big predators such as the wolf, the bear, and the lynx, were reduced to a few individuals in remote or specially protected areas.

In many parts of the world the process of extermination still continues. However, in North and Central Europe and in North America an opposition movement developed during the middle and the end of the last century. Free-living animal populations were "preserved" for sporting purposes. Competing predators, the so-called "harmful" animals, continued to be vigorously hunted down, while the shooting of "useful" animals was subjected to strict regulation, and in many places winter feeding arrangements as well as veterinary care were introduced for their benefit.

The consequence was a rapid reexpansion and a notable increase in the number of ungulates. Today there are probably more roe in Germany, more elk in Sweden, and more whitetailed deer in the United States than there have ever been before, and this in spite of a large reduction in and also a qualitative deterioration of their living space. The results are grave damage to vegetation and an increasing instability of the forest ecosystem, which has important economic consequences for silviculture.

As a consequence of the non-hit-or-miss methods of the human hunter, the lack of regulation by the natural predator is supplemented by the absence of the predator's selective influence. Winter feeding and veterinary treatment result in the loss of other essential selective factors such as the winter food bottleneck and diseases. The cult of trophies, artificial regulations, as well as steps taken to refresh the blood, as it is called—animals from different areas are put in with the home stock in the hope of producing bigger and better antlers—result in artificial selective processes that are sometimes in conflict with the conditions of natural selection.

DOMESTICATED GAME?

These are processes comparable to those of breeding domestic animals, and there is a great deal of talk in this connection about the "domestication of game," of the development of domesticated roe or domesticated deer serving the sole purpose of providing sportsmen with living targets. Studies of domestication have taught us the conditions that are necessary if a population of wild animals is to develop into a population of domestic animals. As a result of human influence some essential factors in natural selection are necessarily absent. The consequence of the provision of food and protection is that the animals become more and more dependent on human beings, who by definite breeding and slaughtering principles exercise selective influences that differ from the natural ones. Finally, these changes must necessarily take place in small, isolated populations.

If we look at the present situation of wild ungulates in many parts of Europe and North America, we see that all these factors are present, at least in embryo. Covering the open landscape with buildings, highways, roads, and fences splits up wildlife populations into smaller and smaller isolated groups. If we consider the most striking sign of domestication, the increase in the variety of individual characteristics, this should apply to many of our game populations in regard to size and shape of skull or antlers. Nevertheless, I do not think that a domestication of game has yet taken place. Natural selective influences still presumably have great influence. Mod-

230

ern studies show that a high proportion of the weak and the sick still die a natural death. Also the modern sportsman has grown more aware of the counterselective effects of his earlier practices and now at least tries to kill weaker animals, even though he is not able to chase his prey and to really separate the weak from the healthy. Also excessive winter feeding, treatment with drugs, hatred of predators, and excess populations are coming under the cross-fire of criticism within the sporting community itself. Thus in comparison with the exterminatory practices of the old days, the efforts of present-day sportsmen to act in accordance with the principles of game biology and the conservation of nature represent a substantial advance. (In many countries such as France, Spain, and Italy, where purely exploitative hunting methods are still practiced to a degree, there is still a substantial leeway to be made up.) But there is still a long way to go until sportsmen learn "to hunt like the wolf"—not for the purpose of reestablishing paradise but to give wild animals a chance to adapt in good health to the environmental conditions brought about by human influence.

II

Regulation of Pack Size and Population

So far we have considered only the influence of the predator on the prey, and not that of the prey on the predator. How, for instance, is the spatial organization of the wolf influenced by its prey, and how is the size of the pack determined in different environmental conditions? These questions lead to the issue of the regulation of the wolf population as a whole. What are the factors that govern the population level, and how is this level regulated over the years?

Spatial Organization

We know that a large proportion of the wolves in a population live in packs. These hunt to a large extent in territories separated from each other, though minor overlaps are possible. Their dwelling areas are marked off olfactorily and acoustically, and intruders, when they are discovered, are generally attacked and driven away. There are numerous accounts of border conflicts between packs with a fatal outcome.[1] Wolves normally avoid meeting neighboring packs, no doubt in order to avoid such clashes. As a consequence the border zones of territories tend to become a relatively unfrequented no-man's-land. At all events, Dave Mech found a greater density of whitetailed deer in those areas, and attributed this to their being less frequently hunted by wolves, giving them a better chance of survival.

232

Because of the large size of the territories, their "owners" cannot drive out every intruder immediately. This enables solitary animals or smaller nonterritorial groups to live in or between the territories of bigger packs. Dave Mech distinguishes three kinds of what he calls dispersers, that is, wolves that leave an existing pack. Some animals stay in the territory of the pack from which they come. They often follow the pack at a distance, and on Isle Royale they are consequently known as trailing wolves. They feed partly on the pack's leftovers, and they rejoin the pack if an opportunity arises. Other wolves move farther from their original territory and thus live in the territories of several packs. A third group consists of animals that leave the pack and the territory and go off in a definite direction, sometimes continuing for hundreds of miles before coming to a stop. In Minnesota Dave noted that they mostly went southwest. His explanation was that the present distribution area of wolves was limited to northern Minnesota, and that it would be to the south and west that they would have the best chance of finding places where they might be able to establish a territory of their own, while to the north, in the direction of Canada, the density of the wolf population was similar to that in the area where Dave was carrying out his studies. Certainly the chances of being killed by men were incomparably bigger to the south, but it nevertheless seemed advantageous that wolves should at least try their chance there. The question of a possible genetically fixed migratory trend is still open, but this behavior of some emigrants from the pack is certainly interesting.[2]

In favorable biotopes in North America maximum wolf densities of 1 animal to 25 square kilometers have been recorded, while in the barren areas of the north the density has been estimated at 1 wolf to 150 square kilometers. Pack territories in the north are very much bigger than they are farther south.[3] The packs follow the migrations of the caribou and range over areas of 10,000 square kilometers or more, while in areas of stationary prey populations farther south they occupy territories of up to 200 square kilometers.

The prey's density of population and behavior has a vital influence on the predator's density of population, and behavior. The size of a wolf pack also seems to depend on the nature of the prey. Comparison between the moose-hunting packs on Isle Royale and the deer-hunting packs in Minnesota, where conditions are otherwise similar, shows that the average size of packs is bigger in areas where the prey is bigger. Statistics from Mount McKinley, where both moose and caribou are hunted, and from the Abruzzi, where sheep are killed, show a similar tendency—the bigger the prey, the bigger the pack.[4]

OPTIMAL PACK SIZE

The figures are in accordance with what one would expect of a predator that hunts in groups. The bigger and heavier the quarry, the bigger the pack has to be. Dave Mech reports from Isle Royale that often the whole pack does not take a direct part in the hunt, but that only five or six wolves actually attack the moose.[5] He could not make out which members of the pack carried out the attack, but they could be expected to be chiefly older, experienced wolves. Such an attack might have fatal consequences for a novice who failed to evade the moose's hoofs. The optimal size of a pack whose chief quarry was moose would have to allow for one or two reserves to replace casualties or temporary absentees, as well as some younger animals who would eventually take over from them. The optimal number cannot be fixed exactly, but it could be expected to be between ten and fifteen. From the point of view of long-term hunting efficiency more are not necessary, though they would not be disadvantageous. A large number is a disadvantage only when it comes to distributing the dead prey, though a dead moose can certainly satisfy a large number of animals.

Two or three assailants seemed to be able to kill a whitetailed deer as successfully as a larger number. Here too, from the point of view of efficiency, more animals are not disadvantageous. If one ignores the skin, the biggest bones, and the contents of the stomach, a deer weighing from 110 to 130 pounds cannot satisfy more than ten hungry wolves on a single occasion. So the optimal size of a deer-hunting pack should be from seven to ten animals.

Packs that live on roe or sheep can be even smaller. Some experience is needed to kill a healthy roe, but a wolf no older than eighteen months has no difficulty in killing a sheep. All that matters is knowing by experience when and where sheep can be attacked with a relatively high degree of immunity from human interference.

A further factor that seems to play a part in influencing pack size is the biomass of the available prey. I have already mentioned Dave's observations in Minnesota, where packs grew smaller and smaller as the deer gradually diminished in numbers while the size of the territory remained constant.[6] Similar findings are available from Isle Royale where in the spring of 1960, for instance, the number of young was unusually low. In the following winter less prey was available, so the big pack continually split into smaller groups that hunted separately.[7] The strategy of compensating for food shortage by reduction of pack size instead of attempting territorial expansion seems thoroughly sensible for reasons of conservation of energy. As we have seen, this avoids energy consumption and dangerous conflict with neighboring packs, though there is a danger that the pack may end by becoming too small to be able to hunt effectively, rear cubs, and maintain its territory.

Finally, there is a close connection between pack size and density of population, as is shown by the figures from Game Management Unit No. 13 in Alaska. But in this case human influence plays an important part, and so for the time being we shall not concern ourselves with it.

Regulation of Pack Size

How does adaptation of pack size to different sizes of prey and changes in the food supply take place? Having no knowledge of energy input-output relationships, hunting strategies, or long-term recruiting needs, wolves do not consciously decide what the size of their pack should be. But the size of their prey and the state of the food supply must have some influence on the variables—the death rate, the birth rate, emigration and immigration—that govern the size of the pack. Let me explain with the aid of a hypothetical model how this could take place.

The problem (see figure 31[8]) is: How does the factor of the biomass of the prey as well as its size (weight) influence the size of the pack? We have seen that not all ungulates can be killed by wolves. The proportion of the total population of prey animals in the pack's territory that are able to be killed by it depends on a number of factors. One is the state of health of the prey population. If that population is very large, exceeding the capacity of the vegeta-

235

tion to support it, a higher proportion of the population is available to the wolves, and it is now easier for them to kill animals of medium age. Another factor is the size of the pack. The hunting capacity of a big pack is greater than that of a small one, but an increase in numbers means more mouths to feed, or in other words less food is available for every wolf, both in general and on the occasion of every kill. Up to a certain point an increase in its size benefits all its members, because their hunting efficiency is increased. At the same time it is also a disadvantage because food has to go further.

The total quantity of food available to each member of the pack as well as the amount available after every new kill must be the ecological factor that affects the death and birth rates as well as emigration and immigration and thus determines the size of the pack. How does this come about? (See figure 32.)

The death rate is certainly directly dependent on the food supply. But the chances of dying as a result of food shortage are unequally divided in the pack. Cubs, for instance, with their big requirements, are much more at risk than adults, and among the latter superiors must have a better chance than inferiors of gaining access to what food there is. Age and social factors thus play an important part. This also applies to the influence of the food supply on the three other variables that govern the size of the pack, and so we must consider the influence that the structure of the pack has on its size before returning to the influence of the food supply.

SOCIAL FACTORS

First of all, aggression forces certain members of the pack to emigrate (see figure 33). We know that aggression in the pack depends on the season and also on the age, sex, and ranking structure of the pack. Aggressiveness also depends on the size of the pack itself; it increases with increasing pack size (see figure 34). Increased aggressiveness increases the probability of individual members of the pack being forced to emigrate. Whom this happens to depends on age, sex, and rank. It is unlikely to happen to a superior adult male or a cub, but likely to happen to an inferior adult female. The greater aggression among the females can lead to an excess of males in the pack.

The situation in regard to bonding is similar. Increasing pack size

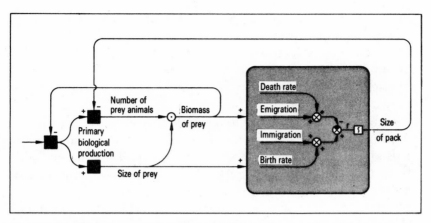

Fig. 31. Model. Influence of biomass and size of prey on size of pack. For explanation of symbols see appendix 8.

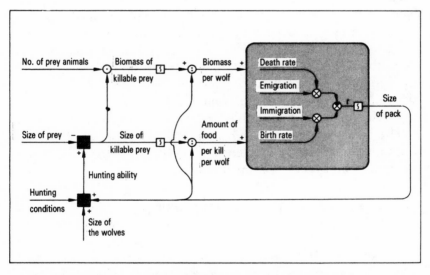

Fig. 32. Model. Pack size is governed by biomass per wolf and the amount of food available to each wolf per killed animal.

necessarily involves an increase in the number of inferior adults, whose bond to the pack is weak. Hence the probability of their voluntary emigration increases. The size of the pack is then reduced, resulting in a strengthening of the average social bond and enabling the pack size to increase again in the long run; and so the cycle continues.

Aggressiveness to strangers to the pack probably increases with increasing pack size, and this diminishes the chances of strange animals joining it; conversely, with diminishing pack size the probability of strange animals joining it increases. The consequent increase in the pack size leads to increased aggression in the pack and against strangers. Immigration again becomes improbable while emigration becomes probable, and so it continues.

In captivity also pack size does not increase indefinitely; the pack in our enclosure did not exceed a certain size. These social feedback mechanisms must be sufficient, in themselves to limit membership. There was ample food in the enclosure, so food supply played no part. It seems that social behavior alone imposes an upward limit, independent of the food supply. The biggest stable pack that has been observed in the wild consisted of twenty animals. In our pack the limit was about fifteen, including cubs. Presumably the small size of the enclosure and the nonuse of their full capacities by the captive animals was responsible for this rather low limit.

The only factor that is largely independent of the size of the pack is the number of cubs. Generally only one female has cubs, whether in a big pack or a small one.

THE FOOD SUPPLY

What influence does the food supply have on this system of social self-regulation? As we have seen, mortality in the pack chiefly affects the cubs. The food supply may also have a certain effect on the birth rate.

Restriction of sexual activity resulting from food shortage is especially likely in very small packs that have difficulty in procuring food. However, this should play no part in big packs that are able to kill plenty of prey but where the average availability of food is small because of the large number of mouths to be fed; for the animals

238

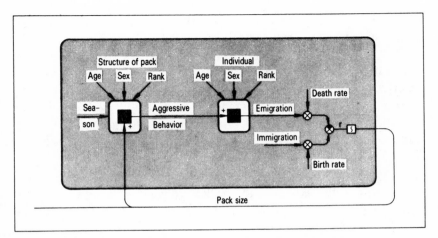

Fig. 33. Model. Increasing aggressiveness in the pack leads to increased probability of emigration.

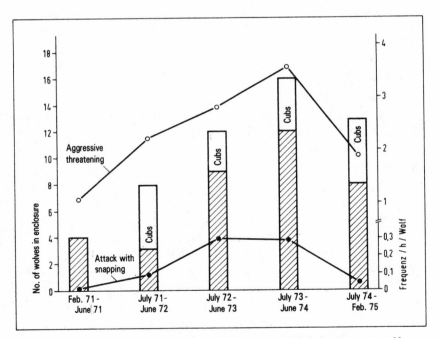

Fig. 34. With more wolves in the enclosure aggressive behavior per wolf increases.

that will reproduce come from the group that gets to the food first and is able to eat its fill.

The food supply can be expected to have no direct influence on emigration and immigration rates. A wolf is not expelled from the pack for being hungry and does not stay in it voluntarily just because it has a full belly. Emigration is governed by aggressive behavior and bonding behavior. If the food supply has any influence on emigration, it must be by way of those two important behavior complexes.

To find out more about this I tried an experiment. For ten days in succession the wolves in the pack were given nothing to eat. This was tough, and so I carried out the experiment only four times altogether, and only in the autumn, when the cubs were big enough to stand it and the mating season could not be affected by it. As wolves can go for a long time without food, I do not think it worried them excessively. I observed the pack as usual before the experiment and then all day long during it.

The results showed (see figure 35) that aggressiveness increased with increasing hunger. As there was a substantial diminution of other social behavior patterns, play in particular, the proportion of aggressive behavior in relation to all other kinds of social behavior was very high. For one thing, the animals were noticeably more "impatient" with one another and threatened at every attempted approach, and, for another, group attacks on inferior or expelled animals greatly increased. We observed a distinct increase in aggression, both between animals of equal status and between all members of the pack and inferiors.[9] So hunger leads to increased conflict in the pack, which can lead on the one hand to enforced emigration and on the other to a stronger structuring of rank relationships including those between cubs and juveniles. Conditions are created that lead to subsequent departures from the pack.

I was not completely satisfied with the data gained from this experiment and, as it was connected with a point of vital importance in relation to our model of the regulation of pack size, I wanted to repeat it. As I was busy working on this book, I had it carried out by a party of students from Berlin who were doing eco-ethological work with me in the Bavarian Forest; and in my new role as observer instead of note-taker I noticed something that had not previously struck me. The animals moved about in the enclosure much more

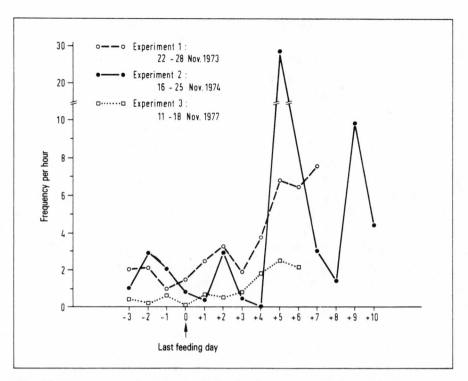

Fig. 35. Frequency of aggressive behavior increases with increasing hunger.

separately and independently than before. This was especially noticeable with the four cubs, who previously had nearly always stayed
together and kept away from the visitors' platform. But now that
they were hungry they roamed all over the enclosure, and in spite of
their great shyness came quite close to the platform. There were a
great many mice that autumn, and the cubs hunted them among
the tangled raspberry bushes. They must have caught a crow, for I
found the feathers. They also looked for old bones to gnaw and ate
raspberries. Each wolf did all these things each for itself alone.
Thus, to make free with a quotation from Brecht, "filling your belly
comes first, and bonding only second." That obviously applies to
wolves also.

Snow fell early that year. It was nearly three feet deep in the wolf
enclosure, and there was no way to get at mice, berries, and old

241

bones. As the students took no measurements of the distances between the animals, I wanted to repeat the experiment. I left my desk, dressed our son up warmly—by now he was nine months old—put him in a rucksack, and spent several hours every day with the wolves. The small boy enjoyed this; he called the wolves "oov" and when they howled, he laughed. Sometimes I actually imagined that when the wolves, Flow, and I howled, he joined in.

But back to my findings. I was very surprised that in the earlier experiments I had not noticed the distinct tendency of the wolves to move about separately in the enclosure. So far as Alexander and Türk, the two exiles from the pack, were concerned, there was no change in this respect, though they were more active in their roaming. But Ho, Tschi, and Tatra, the top-ranking trio in the pack, now tended to go about separately (particularly Tschi, for Ho and Tatra still stayed together a good deal). The tendency to independence was most marked among the eight-month-old cubs (see figure 18).

This showed that wolves' social behavior is influenced by the state of the food supply. Hunger leads to an increase in aggressive behavior and to a weakening of social bonds, and both factors favor emigration from the pack. Murie suspected something of the sort when he raised the question of the regulation of pack size in the course of his work at Mount McKinley. He assumed that not enough animals would be killed to satisfy the hunger of inferior animals, which would be forced to go hunting again, while those members of the pack whose appetite was satisfied would stay behind and sleep. Such repeated separations would ultimately lead to a permanent breach and thus to a reduction in the size of the pack.

SIZE OF PREY AND AGGRESSION

At first I considered this theory rather questionable, as a dead moose, or even a caribou, can satisfy the appetite of a large number of wolves. Also major aggressive clashes over killed prey have not been reported. Perhaps the explanation lay elsewhere. In feeding my wolves it struck me that aggression seemed to be related directly to the size of what they were offered. The pack wolves tended to be very friendly with each other at the big feeding place in the enclosure, but they often quarreled about a dead rabbit or a piece of meat separated from the carcass of a roe. So for a time I recorded their reactions to others who approached their feeding place. I made sure that on each occasion roughly the same amount of food was put in the enclosure. Rabbits or pieces of pig meat were provided, they were given either two or only one roe in addition to the usual butcher's leftovers, and when deer were on the menu only one was provided for them.

The results were very clear (see figure 36). The smaller the piece of meat, the more frequently did its "owner" react aggressively to a new arrival. A rabbit would almost invariably be defended by threats and snapping. Only superiors were able to take such food away from an inferior or an outcast. Young cubs also managed sometimes to beg a rabbit for themselves. When food items were larger, reactions were noticeably weaker. A roe would be quickly torn to pieces by a number of animals, the pieces would be taken a few yards away, and then, if necessary, treated like small prey animals, that is, vigorously defended. But a deer might well be eaten by seven or eight wolves simultaneously without very much aggression. Things were just as peaceful at the other feeding places. Only the outcasts would be robbed of food there too.

OPTIMIZATION OF PACK SIZE

These findings show that aggressive behavior in the pack is influenced not only by the total amount of food available but also by the size of the actual food items, that is, temporal and spatial distribution of the prey that is killed. The question of optimization of pack size in accordance with the prevailing nutritional-ecological conditions that we meet with in all its chance-governed variety among animals in the wild can thus be answered as follows.

In areas with predominantly large prey animals, such as the moose, for instance, packs can be large when prey is abundant. The upper limit is governed only by social factors. When the food supply is short, aggression in the pack increases. True, if a moose is killed all the animals can eat their fill, so aggression in relation to food plays no part, but a long time may pass before the next kill. As a result of hunger inferior members of the pack are driven out or go their own way, and the oversized pack is reduced by a few animals.

As long as the food situation is marked only by brief recurrent

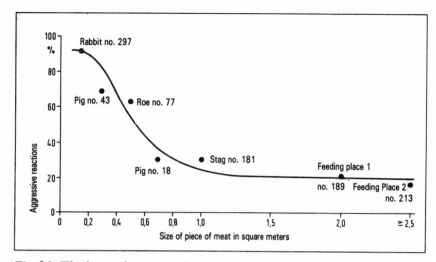

Fig. 36. The larger the pieces of meat, the less aggressively wolves behave to their competitors.

bottlenecks, and cubs can continue to be reared successfully, emigration by a few older animals remains the essential regulatory factor. Only with increasing food shortage—whether because of a big reduction in the number of moose or because the pack has reached a size at which hunting can no longer be done with optimum efficiency—does an increase in cub mortality take place. Things may go so far in this respect that no cubs are successfully reared for several years in succession, with the result that the pack dies out.

But with medium-sized quarry, such as deer or caribou, even if these animals are present in large numbers, oversized packs are inherently impossible because of the limited amount of food available when one of these animals is killed. Inferiors are prevented from getting at the food. But, in addition to two or three adults, the surviving cubs, the juveniles, and perhaps a few other subdominants can eat their fill, so that pack sizes of from ten to fifteen animals are attained. If a moose can be killed occasionally the pack may actually grow bigger, but its division into small hunting units of varying composition is now to be expected. If the food supply continues to decline, particularly in areas where there are only deer, this leads to premature emigration, first by younger adults and ultimately by individual juveniles and cubs, unless they have already died of under-nourishment.

In areas where the prey is even smaller—as in the Abruzzi, for instance, where wolves live on sheep and other domestic animals such as dogs and pigs as well as domestic refuse—competition for food sets in at a very early stage. Even when the food supply is adequate, a dead sheep can feed only a few animals. Juveniles have to fend for themselves. Generally the chances of getting at a sheep are small, particularly in winter, and even cubs have to learn to search for food on rubbish heaps. In the mating season their elders are interested principally in each other, the previous year's cubs have to fend for themselves more than ever, and when new cubs arrive a few months later they are left completely to their own devices. Sheep are easy for them to kill, but they lack the experience to get at them safely, so they have to continue to live on refuse, which each animal must search for on its own. Elsewhere juveniles take part in the rearing of their younger siblings and thus benefit from the pack's shared life and food procurement.

In any event, in the Abruzzi most young wolves from ten to fourteen months of age leave their parents and leave the area in which

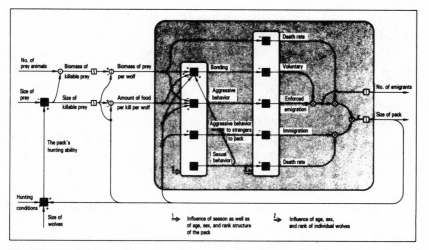

Fig. 37. Model of pack size regulation. Explanation of symbols in appendix.

they are reared. We do not know whether this is caused by aggressive behavior on the part of the older animals or by weak bonding to the pack on the part of the young, but the result is a small pack, consisting only of a single couple and its cubs—a form of social organization that is much closer to that of the fox, the jackal, or the coyote than it is to the big hunting communities of the North American wolf. The basic family unit is maintained, but the extent to which it develops and remains together depends on external circumstances. The essential factor that governs its size is the length of time the new generation remains in the pack. This regulatory system results from the behavior of the animals among themselves and from the complex structure of a form of social organization that is dependent on both external and internal factors. In the past the plasticity of this form of social organization made a vital contribution to the wolf's wide distribution, and—notwithstanding all the opposing factors—it has enabled him to put up a tough defense of his living space to the present day.

Regulating the Wolf Population

Before we take a closer look at the present-day situation of the wolf, its distribution, ecology, and the threats to its continued existence, I propose to go briefly into the question of the reciprocal relations that exist in nature among vegetation, the bigger ungulates, and the wolf in areas that are still largely unaffected by man and consider how the number and/or density of the wolf population are regulated in such areas. It is by no means a simple question, since the number of factors involved and their interdependence is great and variable. Our theory of the regulation of pack size can be applied to a degree, to the regulation of the size of a whole population. If we assume that this population is isolated from external influences, the birth and death rates remain as the two variables governing the population level, and the question is: What are the factors in the population that influence these variables?

We already know one of the vital factors affecting the birth rate: the number and size (if the population remains constant) of the social units into which the population is divided. These units tend

246

to produce one litter a year, regardless of the size and number of sexually mature females. We can disregard the proportion of female animals, in the population, their age structure and reproductive potential, and other factors which sometimes have a bearing on the birth rate. The sex ratio among the cubs, which may be dependent on the density of the population, need not concern us here.

It is not only in the sphere of reproduction that the pack is an exclusive unit. Hunting and food distribution also take place in the pack, and matters of such importance to the death rate as the amount that each animal has to eat are decided in it. We have seen that mortality affects cubs before they leave the pack and after they have been added to the population, while older animals generally die as outsiders, after they have left the pack. The important processes that govern the population level take place inside the pack. Packs occupy relatively large and stable territories. Hence the level of the total population is governed by the size of packs and their territories. Regulation of the population is dependent on events in the pack, as the territories remain constant.

If the number of wolves in the population rises, this means an increase in the size of the social units and/or in the number of emigrants from them. The result is a decline in the birth rate, since the bigger packs now include more sexually mature females that produce no cubs. The death rate again increases, since emigrants can be presumed to have a shorter expectation of life. Thus both birth rate and death rate, the two variables that govern the size of the population, depend on the density of the population. When density increases the birth rate falls and the death rate rises. The essential regulator of this negative feedback is the food supply available to each wolf. But this factor does not directly affect the birth and death rates, but only by way of a complex social structure that leads to an unequal distribution of the food supply. This enables the wolf population to adapt very quickly to changed conditions, since the important reproducing animals in a territorial pack are independent of the food supply, while the age and sex groups that have little reproductive potential, such as juveniles and subdominants, are affected much more seriously. When its density is high, stabilization of the population takes place at their expense. But when it is low, as a consequence of a drought or as the result of human influences, they

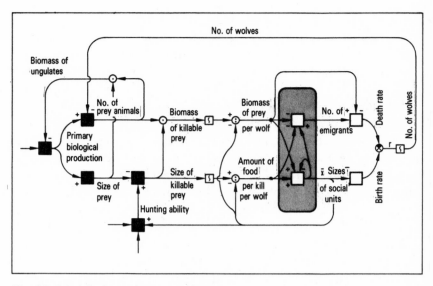

Fig. 38. Model of population regulation.

can settle new territories and contribute to a rapid revival of the population. They form a kind of buffer that absorbs changes and contributes to the stability of the whole system (see figure 38).

This model enables predictions to be made that can be used to test its correctness. Future ecological studies should show whether the following assumptions are correct:

1. The death rate and above all the birth rate are dependent on density of population.

2. The mortality of cubs in very big and very small packs is higher than in packs of optimum size.

3. The birth rate in areas with big packs (e.g., in moose areas) is smaller than in those with small packs (e.g., in deer or caribou areas).

4. In undisturbed high-density populations the proportion of adult females both in the pack and in the population as a whole is less than 50 percent.

5. In areas with small prey animals, as well as in populations undisturbed by man, there are more solitary animals than in areas with big prey animals.

248

6. In the areas where hunting of wolves by man is moderate, the birth rate is higher than in areas where there is no such hunting. The increased mortality is compensated for by a higher birth rate, so the ultimate effect is that the density of the wolf population does not decline as a result of the hunting.

This last point brings us back to the question raised at the outset, that is, the relationship between wolf and man. So far we have to a large extent considered the wolf in terms of his interrelationship with the natural environment as it is to be observed in the few relatively unaffected areas in North America. But even in America these areas are shrinking, and it has been a long time since any areas like them existed in Europe.

The tradition behind the hard struggle between wolf and man for living space and prey goes back thousands of years and it is with this struggle that we shall concern ourselves in the last two chapters.

12

The Abruzzi Wolf Project

The World Wildlife Fund (WWF) is an international organization with branches in many countries devoted to the conservation of nature. The Italian branch is one of the most enterprising and active of these, and it is now the most important organization of its kind in Italy. A list of endangered animals and plants in that country was drawn up in 1972, and one of the most endangered species was the wolf. It was not legally protected and could be shot, poisoned, or trapped by anyone anywhere at any time, but the Italian government reacted with surprising speed to a campaign conducted by the WWF and made the wolf a protected animal for two years. There was a great shortage of information; no one knew where the wolves lived, let alone how many still survived.

It was therefore agreed that the WWF should conduct an inquiry into the distribution and approximate numbers of wolves in Italy. When the WWF offered me the job I did not hesitate for long. It was a chance to supplement my investigations of captive wolves with observation of wolves living in freedom. Also I had often criticized biologists for making scientific studies of different kinds of animals without bothering about the question of their being threatened with extinction. There is plenty of time for academic inquiries when the urgent practical problem of protecting such animals has been solved.

So I agreed, on the condition that the WWF provide me with a counterpart, namely an Italian colleague. Luigi Boitani had just returned from the United States, where he had spent several years devoting himself mainly to ecological questions. He spent a few days with me in the Bavarian Forest, where we discussed the project. I soon realized he was the right man for the job. We became friends and worked very well together in the next few years, and this certainly contributed to the success of the project.

The conditions in which wolves live in the Abruzzi must in many respects be typical of those that prevail in areas inhabited and farmed by man—conditions that, as we shall see, differ greatly from those I noted in America.

Italy's Wolf Population

Luigi and I agreed that attempting to count the wolves in Italy would be a hopeless task. The area that would have to be investigated was far too big. In the Alps wolves were exterminated by the end of the nineteenth century, and no one knew where they still survived in the Apennines, which stretch all the way from south of the Po Valley to the southern tip of Calabria. Even if we confined ourselves to the higher altitudes, that would still mean an area of about 27,000 square miles. So we agreed that Luigi should first visit all the areas where wolves might still be expected to exist and gain an impression of their numbers and distribution by questioning local people. Then we should go together to one of the areas where wolves were said to survive and check the reliability of the information by an actual count.

Luigi soon found that most of the information he was given was useless. Too many prejudices and lively imaginations led in most cases to the wildest exaggerations. Finally he concentrated on questioning people who had had direct contact with wolves, such as foresters, road workers, sportsmen, and shepherds, though still much of what he was told was contradictory. Unfortunately this form of indirect inquiry could yield only very unreliable results.

The only certainty seemed to be that for several years the wolf had been extinct both in the northernmost and southernmost parts of the Apennines and had also been exterminated in Sicily. Elsewhere its distribution seemed to be restricted to about ten enclaves in the higher parts of the Apennines (see figure 39). Luigi felt that because of the density of human settlement, the many roads, highways, and railway lines in the lower areas, there could be no connection among the wolves in these various enclaves. As the estimated number of wolves in some of these areas was very small, it looked as if their extinction there could be only a question of time.

In the only distribution area outside the higher areas of the Apennines, the Tolfa, just north of Rome, wolves' days seemed to be numbered too. It was surprising that they had survived at all. The Tolfa is an extensive but thinly inhabited farmed area in which good refuge areas for wolves seemed to be completely lacking. The fact that they did exist, however, was shown by the examination of a young wolf that was run over within the city boundaries of Rome.

THE ABRUZZI

Where else in Europe are wolves still to be found in the immediate neighborhood of a big city? I was eager to begin the actual count. Luigi suggested the Abruzzi, a manageable area easily accessible from Rome. On the basis of his inquiries he estimated that there must be about twenty-five wolves in an area of about 650 square miles.

The Abruzzi constitute the central portion of the Apennines. The area is limited by the Gran Sasso, with Monte Corno (9,560 feet) in the north, Monte Velino (8,159 feet) and Monte Sirente (7,546 feet) in the west, the Maiella massif in the east—on a clear day you can see the Adriatic near Pescara from Monte Amaro (9,170 feet)—and on the south by the Abruzzi National Park, with Monte Petroso (7,379 feet). It belongs mostly to the province of Abruzzo, the capital of which is L'Aquila.

There is a strong maritime influence on the climate, and at higher altitudes there is an annual precipitation of 51 inches (based on average measurements over the past five years in eight villages in the National Park). There is precipitation on about 110 days annually, and in winter there is generally permanent snow cover above the 3,000-foot level.

While the northern part is to a large extent unwooded, thick beech forests cover the steep mountain slopes from 3,600 to 6,000 feet. In some places in the National Park area primeval pine forests still survive. Above the forested area there is extensive open pasture

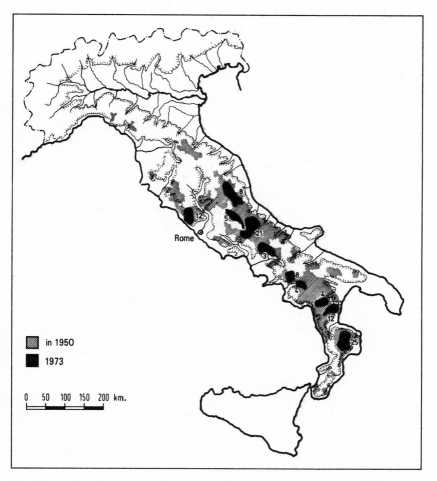

Fig. 39. The wolf in Italy. The figures show estimated population in different distribution areas.

land that finally gives way to a bare, rocky, high mountain zone. Below 3,600 feet the common beech gives way to hornbeam and oak. Here too there is extensive pasture land, and in the valleys corn and wheat are cultivated. At still lower altitudes below 2,000 feet grapevines as well as fruit, vegetables, and wheat are grown.

At altitudes of over 2,500 feet sheep are kept. The local flocks are small, seldom exceeding one or two hundred sheep and a few goats. The sheep are kept at night in stone sheds in the villages, and when there is no snow on the ground they are driven out to pasture close to the villages. In summer some are taken higher up into the mountains, where they spend the night in fenced pens. In addition to these local flocks, big flocks from the plain are driven into the mountains where they graze from the middle of June to the end of October. These flocks can consist of several thousand animals, and they too are guarded by shepherds and dogs in the daytime and kept in pens at night. Thus there is no grazing of the kind practiced in Scotland, for instance, where sheep are left to graze over wide areas unguarded day and night. In the past fifty years there has been a steady decline in the number of sheep and a slight increase in the number of cattle. The latter graze freely in the mountains in summer, like sheep in Scotland.

The human inhabitants live chiefly in villages, many small towns, and a few bigger ones in the lower-lying areas. The population density of the whole of the Abruzzi is 202 per square mile. At higher altitudes small villages lie at the foot of the mountain ranges up to heights of 3,600 feet. Here there is an average of 75 persons to a square mile. Up to the middle of this century there was a high rate of emigration from these areas, and some villages were completely abandoned, but in recent years the development of tourism has led to a movement in the opposite direction, and many emigrants now return from Britain, the United States, and Australia. The big skiing resorts are Roccaraso (south of the Maiella) and Pescasseroli in the National Park.

In the Southern part of the Abruzzi there is a small surviving population of about 60 to 100 bears, the last in the Apennines. The chamois has been exterminated, apart from about 500 animals in the National Park. Roe and deer were exterminated, and attempts to reintroduce them began in the National Park in 1972.[1] Wild swine similarly had almost completely disappeared, but a slow natural

254

increase in their numbers has now begun. As far as the wolf was concerned, Luigi had reports of them only from the more densely wooded areas of the Maiella and the National Park area, and it was there that we proposed to begin our work.

THE FIRST WOLVES

Luigi had made his preparations well. We went to an isolated mountain hotel on the San Leonardo Pass (3,400 feet), where we wanted to spend a few days looking for tracks alone until we were joined by ten more colleagues—zoologists and conservationists from many parts of Italy (including some game wardens from the Gran Paradiso and Abruzzo National Parks). It had been snowing on the day of our arrival, and the next morning thick mist lay over the pass. We set out to look for tracks immediately. Luigi was enthusiastic about the beauty of the surrounding mountains, but unfortunately they were invisible, and not much else was visible either. We followed a narrow, curving road that led downhill in a northerly direction across broad open slopes that occasionally appeared out of the mist and were evidently used in summer for grazing sheep and cattle. Suddenly we saw a big, fresh trail right across the road. We were thrilled. Could we really have come across our first wolf so soon?

We followed it on snow shoes down into a hollow, then uphill again, then down again in a circle, and we carefully examined every slope. Another trail appeared in addition to the first, and we decided that the wolves had been here during the night. They must have been looking for something, because the trail was never straight for long, but curved and often came back on its tracks.

If we had had more experience, we should have realized at once that we were following the tracks not of wolves but of dogs, but as it was we followed them in the thick mist all the way down to Santa Eufemia, a small village on the road below the Maiella massif, where we discovered our mistake. Some big, nearly white Abruzzi sheepdogs barked at us. Our laughter was equaled only by our disappointment. Many of the dogs that approached us out of the mist wore collars fitted with two-inch steel spikes, which could only be a protection against wolves. So the creatures we were seeking must exist.

255

In our defense I must plead that it is impossible to distinguish a dog's footprints from a wolf's when they are of similar size. There are many dogs whose paws are rounder than a wolf's and can be identified by that (or by their size), but some leave footprints exactly like a wolf's.

It snowed without interruption for the next two days, which made searching impossible. Meanwhile our aides arrived, and we sat about the otherwise empty hotel and waited for the weather to improve.

Then at last one morning there was a bright blue sky. Luigi was right; the view was truly magnificent. We were at the edge of a big plateau with the Maiella massif to the east and Monte Morrone to the west. The plateau was largely unwooded, but a thick beech forest extended up the slopes to about 6,000 feet. In steep places exposed to the sun the first avalanches came thundering down, though it was still early morning. Nearly two feet of snow had fallen around the hotel, and the noise of the avalanches accompanied us all day.

We had made our plans the day before. Everyone had a definite area to search, either on skis or with snowshoes. The few who were unwilling to face the effort of searching in deep snow were to drive along the road and look for tracks. But there could be no thought of driving yet; the snowplow had to be awaited. This arrived just when we were about to leave, and a huge machine it was; obviously a great deal of snow was expected in these parts. Some road workers told us there was a wolf trail across the road down below, in the direction of Pacentro, which was my area. I found it hard to gain height on skis in the deep snow above the hotel, but then I kept to the same height along the southern foothills of Monte Morrone. Soon I found a trail. How different it was from that of the dogs a few days before. Two animals, one behind the other, had made their way purposefully along the slope without many detours or unnecessary movements in the deep snow, making use of all the places from which the wind had cleared the snow. Two places along the trail where the animals had urinated, obviously crouching, showed that there were probably young.

More trails appeared. A whole pack seemed to have come down from Monte Morrone early that morning (during the night it had still been snowing). The animals had run in various changing groups, but always scattered over the mountain and never in a single line. They had all met in a steep ravine above the Pacentro refuse pit. To judge from the urine markings, at least one adult animal must have been with them.

I followed the trail all day long. It was hard work in that steep country and in the deep snow, but it was a wonderful experience. There seemed to have been six wolves altogether, and I was thrilled when I returned in the evening to the hotel. No one else had found a trail. Some were still out searching, but I wanted to show my discoveries to those who had returned, so we drove to the place above the ravine in which the wolves had disappeared that morning. Suddenly I heard the beginning of a wolf's howl from below, so I began howling myself, and within seconds there was a multivoiced reply from the ravine. From where we were we could make out six wolves in the fading light. After they had finished howling they went on playing vigorously for a long time.

My companions were as thrilled as I was—and my "authority" as a wolf expert was assured for the rest of our stay. The next day we discovered that after we had left them in the ravine and it had grown dark, the wolves left the ravine and took the road to Santa Eufemia, passing the hotel where we were having dinner. As the snow was still soft, they preferred to use the road, where the going had been made easier by the snowplow. Later that night, when the snow had frozen hard, they made off from Santa Eufemia in the direction of the steep slopes of the Maiella massif.

The party that followed their trail was unable to discover whether they had found anything to eat. That day I spotted another trail high up on the mountain. I painfully made my way up it on snowshoes, to which pounds and pounds of wet snow clung at every step, only to find that the broad trail in the deep snow had been left by a marten.

WOLF HUNT

News of what we were up to soon spread in the villages. The teacher from Santa Eufemia came to see us and complained that on the night before the snowstorm wolves had killed his dog and two puppies; he expected to lose a pig from his sty almost every night because of the wolves. His complaints about both the wolves and us grew more and more vociferous and expressive.

We went and had a look at the remains of the dog and at the pigsty. The dog really seemed to have been killed and eaten by wolves. The pigsty was an appallingly filthy ramshackle hut. The doors and windows were nailed up with boards, pieces of cardboard, and corrugated iron. We clambered in through an opening that was made for us and were confronted by about fifty pigs of all ages moving about in the dirt. The teacher complained that his losses amounted to millions (of lire). He insisted that wolves broke in and helped themselves to one of his pigs nearly every night. We could not see how wolves could possibly get into this curious structure, but the man swore that they did so, though he couldn't explain how they managed it.

We went back to the village. A number of men, thickly swathed in overcoats, were sitting in the cool, neon-lit bar, the only one in the village. We drank *centerba*, a green liquor made of a hundred local herbs, and talked to them. They too had heard a great deal about the teacher's woes. They had only sheep and cows, but they had suffered no damage from wolves. What the teacher said about his pigs struck them as rather exaggerated too. Wolves had broken into the pigsty once and killed a few pigs, whereupon the men had fetched their guns and gone off in the direction of the Maiella, from where they sometimes heard wolves howling. But the road had been too difficult, and they returned to the village in the evening. Whether the wolves had done any damage after that they could not say.

Then they wanted to know why we wanted to protect wolves. "What's the use of a wolf?" they asked, and were we not afraid of them? "Why afraid?" we asked, not so much to convince them that wolves were not dangerous as out of surprise that these people regarded them as dangerous. Had they ever heard of a wolf attacking anyone? "No, but one hears so much about them, on television, for instance, from America and Russia, and from books." At all events, they wouldn't go alone at night along the road over the Passo San Leonardo, and if we did that without being afraid, "Well, you're townsmen, you don't understand," they said. Only the shepherd who took these men's few sheep out to graze on the mountains in

258

the morning and brought them back again in the evening said he would go along the road at night. "Afraid of wolves?" he said. "No, *mai*."

I realized only years later how much we discovered about the ways of wolves and the attitude of the local people toward them in those first few days. At the time everything was still strange and puzzling. Why had the men of the village not pursued the wolves more vigorously that day when they went out after them with their guns? Had the little bit of snow stopped them? In Lapland hundreds of men go off hunting wolves for weeks in the most intense cold. These men did not look soft, as if all they wanted was domestic warmth. And why did they show such respect for wolves, while the shepherd in the same village and the road workers who had shown us the wolves' trail spent every day of their lives working unarmed in the area where wolves roamed?

During the next few days we combed the area south of the Maiella region. We found no wolf trails on the higher slopes covered in deep snow, and only a few single trails in the valleys. Above the village of Rocca Pia we found the tracks of several wolves in steep ravines and rocky areas in close proximity to the thick beech forest on the mountain slopes, as at Santa Eufemia and Pacentro. Here too they led toward the village and back again. Because of the many tracks left by dogs, sheep, and humans we could not establish how close the wolves had gotten to the village or what they had been doing there.

THE NATIONAL PARK

More helpers awaited us in the Abruzzo National Park in the southern part of our area. Franco Tassi, the head of the park, put all his game wardens at our disposal. We lost two days because of heavy snowfalls, but then fine weather returned, so we were able to comb the whole area and the surrounding districts in a single day. As before, we found hardly any trails in the higher areas covered in deep snow. The wolves kept below 4,600 feet. At night they seemed to use the well-cleared valley roads whenever possible, and they obviously did not stray very far from human habitations. Again we found tracks near three high-altitude villages that led to rocky, wooded mountain slopes almost inaccessible to human beings, where wolves apparently spent the day. At one point the National Park people had established a feeding place for wolves where they put slaughterhouse refuse from time to time. There too we found tracks, and once, when we howled there in the evening, we were answered by about four or five wolves from the thick forest overhead.

Unless we assume that the six wolves frm the Maiella accompanied us to the National Park, which is extremely unlikely, we could assume that there were at least sixteen wolves in the area under investigation. The actual population was presumably higher, say about twenty or a few more. The two snowfalls greatly facilitated our task; in the years that followed we never had such conditions again. Luigi's previous estimate had been twenty-five, so the outcome was very satisfactory to him. Both figures could be regarded only as rough approximations, but one thing they showed clearly. In view of these small numbers, the wolf in Italy was a highly endangered species.[2]

THE NEXT PROJECT

We discussed the next step to be taken together with Arturo Osio of the World Wildlife Fund in Rome. The work we had done so far had cleared up the most important questions concerning future protective measures. We now knew roughly where the wolves lived, how many there were, and to some extent what they lived on. The WWF decided to continue the project on an international scale with a much bigger budget. The aim was not only to gain a more accurate knowledge of the wolf's living conditions but also to get useful publicity for the wolf and the aims of the WWF and the International Union for the Conservation of Nature and Natural Resources (IUCN).

The IUCN, whose headquarters are at Morges in Switzerland, is an international agency associated with the United Nations, and it works closely with the WWF. It has set up a number of expert committees for a large number of endangered animal species, including one for wolves, the chairman of which is Doug Pimlott. The IUCN backed the international wolf project in the Abruzzi jointly with the WWF.

After a long discussion with Luigi, Doug Pimlott, who came to

260

see us in Italy, and other members of the IUCN wolf committee, I worked out a detailed plan after a meeting in Stockholm. Our project was to be divided into three parts.

1. Study of the ecology of the wolf in the Abruzzi, with emphasis on the development of population, migratory activities, size of home territory, food, interactions with human beings and domestic animals, and relationships with the fox.

2. Reintroduction of roe and deer. On the basis of experiments carried out in the Abruzzo National Park, the possibility of large-scale reintroduction of ungulates into Italy was to be studied.

3. Ecopolitical studies. Here the primary aim was to discover the attitude of the local population directly affected by the wolf and to find out on what conditions they might be prepared to accept the wolf as a neighbor. Second, the Italian public should be given information about the wolf in order to establish a favorable basis for legislative measures at the local and national level. The most important objectives were clear to us already. The wolf should be fully protected throughout the year and—even more important—the use of poison in combating the fox, for instance, should be prohibited, if possible throughout Italy, but at least in the areas in which wolves lived.

Winter after winter local shooting clubs, aided by the state forest police, laid out vast amounts of poisoned bait for foxes. In the few days of our work in the field we had already been struck by the many fox trails that we came across, and the fox population must indeed be high, presumably because of the large amount of domestic refuse to be found around every village. Local sportsmen tried to cope with this with the aid of strychnine, which apparently did not worry the fox very much but had devastating effects on more sensitive species such as falconiformes, bears, and wolves in particular. We had no exact figures, but Franco Tassi's reports from the Abruzzo National Park were alarming. In the course of our work, poison turned out to be the principal cause of death of wolves in the Abruzzi.

From the work point of view our project was anomalous; it was intended to be both scientific and to serve the practical purposes of nature conservation. We called our project the study of nature conservation, which of course involved a certain inconsistency, since as scientists we wanted to exercise as little influence as possible on the

261

system we were examining, while as conservationists we wanted to improve it. When we observed that wolves were getting too little to eat, the scientific attitude required us to observe their behavior and find out what influence food shortage had on the death rate and so on. But as conservationists we wanted to help them by laying out food. Nevertheless, as far as the first objective outlined above was concerned, I think we obtained useful results, both in regard to the scientific and to the conservation aspects. As for the second purely practical objective, the reintroduction of deer and roe into the National Park, we were successful. The more general goal of fact-finding with a view to further reintroductions in other areas of Italy remained largely unfulfilled.

First Catch Your Wolf

On my first visit to Minnesota in 1973 I succeeded in persuading Dave Mech to come to Italy to show us his methods of catching and drugging wolves and following them up by telemetry. In view of the animals' great shyness and their secretive way of living, there was no way of studying them other than with the aid of telemetry. Hence enlisting Dave's aid was invaluable to Luigi and me, neither of whom had any experience in the matter. Dave had been struggling with the technique for five years and had now reached the point where it worked.[3] We were able to take over a ready-made system and were able to greatly reduce the running-in period that is usual in telemetric studies.

At the beginning of April 1974 Luigi, Dave, Hartmut Jungius of the WWF, who was to make preparations for the reintroduction operation, and I all gathered at Pescasseroli, the headquarters of the Abruzzo National Park, and in the course of the month were joined by others who helped in the project for different periods. Dave had brought everything necessary from the United States: the traps, the equipment for anesthesizing the wolves and taking samples from them, as well as transmitters, aerials, and receivers. Luigi had obtained approval for the setting up of traps in the province of L'Aquila as well as authority from the Post Office to use radio equipment—no mean achievement in bureaucratic Italy. He actually managed not just to get Dave's equipment through customs at the airport without paying duty, but actually to take it away with him immediately. But there were some anxious hours during which Dave and I observed with astonishment Luigi's negotiating skill and learned to admire the adroitness with which he picked his way through a jungle of laws, rules, regulations, and neverending bureaucratic operations with documents and stamps conducted by officials who seemed totally indifferent.

During the autumn Luigi had chosen two places at which game wardens had laid out food throughout the winter as suitable for laying traps. We found many tracks in the still sparse snow showing that wolves, dogs, and a great many fox had visited them, and Dave set his first traps immediately. These were ordinary spring traps such as those used by North American trappers, dreadful things that would cause any animal conservationist to protest vigorously. In particular the sharp spikes on the jaws looked fearsome. But Dave assured us that they prevented injury, as the captured animal's foot was held firmly instead of moving this way and that, which could cause serious flesh wounds. At all events, no serious harm had been done by these traps to the wolves he caught in Minnesota. This was assuming, of course, that all the traps were checked every morning.

Dave began by setting twelve traps. As a boy he had trapped muskrats to supplement his pocket money. An old trapper had shown him all the best ways of trapping wolves, and now he demonstrated his skill. First of all the trap was boiled for hours in a concoction of leaves, beechnuts, and brushwood, and subsequently it was handled only with gloves that had been well boiled. Then a hole was carefully dug and the trap was set in it. Earth was then carefully strewn over it, and the place was prepared in such a way that it seemed impossible for even the wariest wolf to detect anything suspicious. The important points were the thorough covering of the trap and of the place where it was hidden. The plate that caused the jaws to snap together was not much bigger than a small coin, and if it had been put just anywhere we would probably have had to wait for years before a wolf happened to tread on it. So Dave placed his traps close to especially tempting morsels, such as the carcass of a whole cow, which was to serve as bait. All this quickly turned out to be ineffective.

We set new traps every day, with the result that we had between twenty and thirty out every night, but the wolves refused to walk into them. We found their tracks at the feeding places, and nearly every night they ate all the food except the bait, which they left untouched. It seemed inconceivable that they should be able to detect where the traps were in this way, and for a time Dave actually doubted whether they were wolves, until one morning we saw a wolf at one of the feeding places. Obviously we were doing something wrong, and obviously these European wolves differed from their North American counterparts. In Europe they had been hunted down for thousands of years, and only the shyest and most cautious had survived and multiplied. Perhaps we were being confronted with a result of this process of selection. Though the wolves were familiar with human scents and human equipment, they spotted the traps—and this in spite of the fact that in this area they had not been hunted for years. Dave grew visibly upset and staked his reputation on finding ways of outwitting them, but in vain. Ursitti, now a game warden in the National Park but formerly the best-known wolf hunter in the area, assured us he was doing a good job, and only his lack of success would seem to have contradicted this.

HUMAN PROBLEMS

Meanwhile new problems arose. We found ourselves in the crossfire between the National Park authorities and the forest administration. I was familiar with such rows from the Bavarian Forest; for years I had been able to observe the authoritarian manner in which the forest administration tried to defend traditional rights against the incursion of new ideas. Here the warfare was not without its amusing aspects, but for us it was not so amusing. Dave had to return to the United States at the end of April, and it was essential that he should catch a wolf first.

Trouble started when a party of well-armed forest police in uniform came to see us and asked to be shown the traps. At first we thought they were merely curious, so we showed them where the traps were and how we laid them. The next morning they went to the traps before we did, which did not please us very much, and a few days later they again insisted on being shown all the traps; they also told us we were under arrest for setting traps in the National Park without authority.

We really had more important things to do than to act as dummies in a long-term dispute between rival administrations. We had been told in the village that there had been actual frays between the National Park game wardens and the forest police, both of whom had police privileges. But the reason for the quarrel lay deeper. In the interests of conservation the National Park authorities had to engage in frequent battles with local and national groups who wanted to build more ski lifts, hotels, and private villas. Pescasseroli, which had once been a poor mountain village, had become a fashionable ski resort, and it was the scene of frenzied building activity. The native population had little share in the profit from all this, but many villagers hoped for better times as a result of the activities of capitalists from Rome and Milan. The National Park authorities had not only to oppose powerful economic interests, but were often faced with opposition from local people who objected to the National Park. Meanwhile the crystal-clear stream that had run through the village had turned into a drain, the hills above Pescasseroli were full of big, ugly hotels, and the many villas around the village were occupied by their owners only for two or three weeks in the year, at Christmas, New Year's, and for the *ferragosto* holiday in late summer; for the rest of the year they were empty. Blame for this was attributed solely to the National Park, which had prevented a funicular from being built on Monte Marsicano, right in the middle of the area where the last surviving bears in the Apennines lived.

Thus there was a conflict of the kind that exists everywhere between business interests and conservationists. What was overlooked was the fact that the National Park had created more jobs than would be created by a skiing circus on yet another mountain and that in the long run it would attract more tourists to the area throughout the year. Conservation calls for no large capital investment and thus produces no big profits for outside capitalists; that was the real trouble. Meanwhile the conservative mayor of Pescasseroli had been sent to prison because of some speculative activities and a new mayor had been elected, this time a Communist, who promised better relations with the conservationists. But, as before, the forest administration was opposed to the National Park, not least because the conservationists were more and more insistent that no more forestry work should be done in the National Park. Private feuds were also presumably involved, and we were in the middle.

Luigi showed the police the official approval we had for our traps,

265

but this made no more difference than the long telephone conversations we had with the WWF in Rome, with Tassi, who was on leave, and with the head of the forest administration for the whole of the Abruzzi, who was a great supporter of our project. The policeman had the right to bring charges against us, his superiors could not stop him, and he maintained his stand.

Well, we were not locked up. We handed over some traps to the police and simply continued as before. But again we found the police hanging about the places where our traps were, and this time I exploded. I spent several minutes flinging at them all the Italian expletives I had picked up, and they departed obviously embarrassed. Subsequently they were very polite, and we explained all our equipment to them. A few days later, after half the WWF committee came from Rome to support us, the nonsense came to an end and we were allowed to carry on without police interference. But two years later Luigi, Dave, and I had to appear in court on a charge of laying traps without authority. We were all acquitted, of course, but in the meantime the forest people had become great friends of ours.

But our difficulties were not over yet. First of all, several of our traps were stolen. Then something really remarkable happened. One morning we found Jeep tracks in the fresh snow near one of the places where we had lain traps—its whereabouts were known to very few besides ourselves. The Jeep had drawn up about ten yards from a dead sheep next to which two traps were buried. Footprints led from the vehicle through thick undergrowth directly to the traps, where distinct traces showed what someone had been up to; he had simply urinated on our traps.

The tire marks showed that the Jeep belonged to the National Park, and there was no difficulty in establishing whose boots had left the tracks in the snow. They belonged to someone from the National Park office. We were obviously under fire from both sides. But why? Sometimes the struggle assumed strange forms.

THE FIRST WOLF

Meanwhile we had caught several foxes and a bitch in our traps. The bitch had gone straight for the bait, was caught in two traps, and went on eating it lying down, but the foxes were caught only in traps in paths leading to the feeding places. It had become clear to us that wolves too were extraordinarily cautious in the immediate vicinity of food, so we started laying traps farther and farther away from the bait. The probability of a wolf's being caught was much less than if it were closer to the food, but we hoped that they would be less cautious; after all, they could not watch every one of their footsteps everywhere. We also left artificial scent markings, using a "secret recipe" of the old trapper who had been Dave's instructor; it was a foul-smelling concoction of rotten fox meat, fresh wolf feces, the putrefying innards of deer, and other things of that kind. Disgusting though the stink was to us, Dave insisted that the wolves would take a different view.

We caught our first wolf, a male, sixteen days after the first trap was laid, which was the longest wait that Dave had ever had. Naturally we were thrilled. Dave showed us the best way of immobilizing a wolf with a syringe fixed to the end of a long stick. American wolves were apparently completely intimidated in such circumstances and allowed people to approach without defending themselves. So I calmly approached the wolf with the stick and the syringe, but it leaped at me and its open mouth snapped right in front of my face. The chain fixed to the trap stopped it only a few inches away. Dave and Luigi had to distract it while I gave it the injection from behind.

It lost consciousness in a few minutes. It weighed only 52 pounds, and it was measured and a blood sample was taken for some tests on free-living wolves that were being carried out by one of Dave's colleagues. As it was so aggressive, we fitted it with a muzzle as a safety precaution. No other wolf subsequently behaved in this way, and the muzzle was never used again. The only real difficulties we had were with the dogs that were caught in the traps. They generally bit wildly all around, though they were always quiet when they first fell into the trap. Wolves, however, vigorously fought the trap, and that involved a risk of injury. With the single exception of our first catch, once they were surrounded by human beings they were completely intimidated and remained crouching on the ground, often excreting and urinating, enabling us to approach and use the syringe at close quarters. Finally Dave showed us how to fit the collar with the radio transmitter. While the wolf was slowly recovering consciousness we carried it up to the wood

267

above the feeding place, where it slept for a few hours. In the evening it moved a short distance (as we were now in a position to find out) and two days later it was miles away.

Before Dave left we caught two she-wolves, which made his stay with us a complete success from that point of view also. He gave us an excellent introduction to the whole technique of telemetry. Also we enjoyed ourselves immensely, and not only while setting traps for wolves.

Until the end of the year Luigi and I took turns in following up the three marked wolves. Then we left the National Park to continue our work in the Maiella region farther to the north. The feud, by which we were increasingly mystified, was not unconnected with our departure. Also the National Park authorities did not extend our permission to set traps and, apart from that, we preferred to study wolves living in conditions more typical of those prevailing in Italy, unprotected by game wardens and with no winter feeding arrangements or reintroduced prey animals.

PASSION OF THE HUNTER

On the third day of our first independent trapping operation in January 1975 we caught a she-wolf with the aid of Dave's foul-smelling concoction. Luigi's time was increasingly taken up with "ecopolitical" tasks, so I continued the trapping operation myself, now aided by Paolo Barrasso, a young Italian biology student from the Abruzzi who had joined us. We caught eleven wolves altogether, as well as many dogs and perhaps about thirty foxes. The wolves were still extremely cautious. Sometimes we were almost tempted to attribute "supersensory" abilities to them, but in the course of time we too grew more skillful. During the mating season I once found some fresh wolf's feces. Instead of putting it in a plastic box as usual and adding it to the many hundreds of boxes with similar contents, I carefully laid it aside, prepared a trap, and put the feces quite close to it. The next day we had a she-wolf in heat in the trap.

Setting traps ended by becoming practically a mania with me. The problem of outwitting the wolves preoccupied me day and night. Sometimes the others had practically to force me to give up when it turned out after months of effort that the wolves were not to

268

be caught by the usual traps or the snow conditions made further efforts futile. The motivation, the passion, of the hunter who spends days, weeks, or even months pursuing a particular quarry became perfectly clear to me during that period, though I was glad that the satisfaction of my hunting instinct did not have to be paid for by the animal's death.

To fix the wolves' position and follow them in their roamings we had portable aerials that we could attach to our rucksacks. We procured a Land Rover from England on which we mounted the directional aerial so that it could be turned 360 degrees from the driver's seat. Tracking the wolves was done chiefly with the aid of that vehicle. At first we also had the two Norwegian horses that I had brought from Germany, but they turned out to be useless. There was nothing wrong with them, but the wolves did not behave as expected. The day-long or week-long pursuit over the mountains for which we had intended them did not take place, for the wolves turned out to be definitely loyal to a single locality. The range of the wolf's radio signals was at least twelve miles as the crow flies, but in the forest it was greatly reduced, and a mountain range or even a small hill between us and the wolf meant that reception ceased. Sometimes a wolf had to move only a few yards for the bleep in our receiver to cease abruptly. How many days we spent going uphill and downhill, how many thousands of miles we drove to track down wolves that had disappeared from our receiving sets, is a matter I do not care to think about. On one occasion three of us spent ten days in the mountains looking for the first wolf we caught, only to find out that he had moved his usual daytime resting place to a ravine only about 600 yards away. There was another young wolf that emigrated from the Maiella area at the age of fourteen months for whom we searched unsuccessfully several times a week over half the Abruzzi. Then one day I found him in a few minutes when I went out in a helicopter.

Luigi had succeeded in securing one for us. Another police force in the area—had two helicopters at Pescara. A talk at the Finance Ministry in Rome brought results, and one of them was put at our disposal. On paper. For the cost of all the useless telephone calls we had with Pescara we could have chartered a commercial aircraft for many hours, if one had been available. There was always something wrong with the helicopter. Either it was out of gas, or it had broken down, or the weather was bad, or the pilots or the airport firemen were on strike, or it was required for police purposes, or some new authorization had to be obtained from Rome. Therefore, we used it only a few times. As far as private aircraft were concerned, things were no better. One pilot lacked authorization for airborne radio transmission, another did not dare fly in the mountains, and so on. I ended by having enough of all this, so I learned to fly in Germany, chartered a small Cessna 150, and flew with Dagmar over the Alps and the Adriatic to Pescara. For the last six months of our work we had an aircraft at our disposal, unfortunately much too late.

We tried to locate each of the marked wolves every day, but often, as I said, we were unsuccessful. There were times, however, when for weeks on end we were able to locate the exact spot where they stayed during the daytime, and we also followed a number on their nightly excursions. Sometimes we split up into two parties for this purpose. One party would spend weeks camping up in the mountains spotting a wolf's whereabouts in the daytime, and in the evening, when it came down to the valley, the second party would take over and follow its nighttime movements from the Land Rover until it went up into the mountains again at dawn. We tried to keep every wolf under continuous observation like this for several days and nights in succession at least once a month.

STAR-SHAPED MOVEMENT

The results[4] of following up radio-marked wolves like this for two and a half years in the Abruzzi showed us a way of life markedly different from that of their counterparts in the wild in North America. We know that North American wolves travel long distances in their territory generally in packs and sleep in a different place every day. Only during the cub-rearing period in summer are their movements star-shaped, so to speak, to and from the place where the cubs are. In the Abruzzi this star-shaped activity continues throughout the year. Every wolf (or small pack) had a few places in its territory to which it returned day after day, sometimes to the same place for weeks on end. These "traditional resting areas," as we called them, were in places that were to a large extent inaccessible to human beings, on steep slopes covered with thick beech forest. The distance to the nearest village was not necessarily great, but the places were such that humans rarely went to them. In winter the wolves kept to rather lower altitudes, and in summer they went higher up the mountain. We also noticed that in many areas they stayed higher up the mountain on Sundays than on weekdays. Many of the lower-lying areas where cars could go were overrun on fine Sundays by crowds of picnicking Italians, so it was sensible on the wolves' part to keep out of the way. Sometimes we actually had the impression that they withdrew higher up the mountainside early on Sunday mornings before the picnickers' invasion began, as if they knew that it was imminent. But that could have been chance.

When darkness fell the wolves emerged from their refuge areas and set out on roamings that took them from one place where food might possibly be found to another. First they might go to a refuse pit, then a village, then a sheep shed, then another refuse pit. In the morning they withdrew again, often to the place where they had spent the previous day. This was also the time of day when we were most likely to see them. In the evening they nearly always waited until it was quite dark before coming down, but in the morning they often stayed below until the first peasants appeared in the fields. Thus they adapted themselves to a large extent to the rhythm of human activity, which generally lags a few hours behind the state of the sun.

Sometimes they would be late in returning to the mountains from areas in which human beings lived. In that case some wolves would stay in a hiding place all day long and not move on till darkness fell. Wolf 1/2, for instance (this was the first male we captured, whom we marked with a "1" in his left ear and a "2" in his right ear), sometimes spent the day in a small wood below a village not a hundred yards from the nearest house, while wolf 9/10, a female in the Maiella region, made great detours in order to return to her daytime territory, the steep rocky slopes at the foot of the Maiella above Santa Eufemia.

KNOWLEDGE OF HUMAN WAYS

The wolves seemed to have an excellent knowledge of human habits. Though they avoided contact with human beings as far as possible, food was to be found only in the neighborhood of humans. In

271

summer they hardly ever used tarred roads but made good use of tracks and paths. In winter roads that had been cleared of snow were their favorite routes. They avoided open, unwooded country where they were likely to come across human beings in the daytime, but used it at night or very early in the morning. This applied particularly to the summer months, when human activity in the country was very much greater than in winter.

One morning in January 1976 when I was driving the Land Rover from Campo di Giove toward the Passo San Leonardo I picked up the signal of 9/10 and two of her nine-month-old cubs from Fonte Romana. Presumably the whole pack was resting in the forest only a little way above. I drove on. Before the Passo San Leonardo the road was blocked by huge snowdrifts, so I returned to Fonte Romana. I could tell that the wolves were getting restless, and after about twenty minutes they went off in the direction of the pass and their traditional daytime territory of Santa Eufemia about five miles farther north. On such daytime roamings they always kept to the forest at the foot of the Maiella. At all events, I had never seen them crossing the open country around the Passo San Leonardo in daylight.

As soon as they left Fonte Romana I put on my skis and climbed up the slope to find out how many of them there had been. I soon found the tracks of six wolves, and I followed them in the direction of the pass. They had a head start of perhaps thirty minutes. But this time when they reached the big plateau they left the edge of the wood and made for the road—in broad daylight. Previously I had not seen anything of the sort. Somehow they must have known that no cars were being driven or could be driven along the roads that were blocked with snow. At that time of year traffic was minimal in any case; on a normal day you would expect to see no more than three or four vehicles, perhaps. But on such days they did not leave the forest. So they must have realized from the state of the road that they could move across the open country without risk. No car traffic was possible, so there would be no human beings.

I admit that this is a bold hypothesis, for it assumes intelligence on their part. But I cannot think of a better explanation—their crossing the open plateau was too unusual to have been due to chance. At first they used the road and then they made a detour to a small hut in which we had previously lived. They approached it

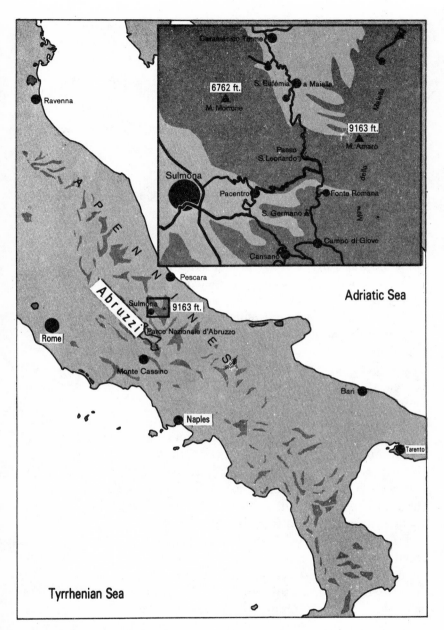

Fig. 40. The Maiella study area.

from behind, obviously sure that it was uninhabited. Then they crossed the road and the pass again a few hundred yards from the hotel. Below the pass the road was clear again, and the wolves' tracks led away from it up in the direction of the steep slopes. I struggled along in their tracks, and I howled in their direction from an eminence. The answer came at once—the howling of a whole pack barely five hundred yards away in the forest. They were so sure of themselves that they had not even hurried.

Many such observations could be described. In stormy weather they generally spent the night in their refuge area and began to move again only when the storm was over. Sometimes they did not leave in the evening even when the weather was fine, and then we always betted on whether or not there was going to be a storm—and those who betted that a storm was on the way generally won. But how did the wolves know that bad weather was imminent?

I had another interesting experience with wolf 5/6, a young female in the National Park. She was definitely a "refuse-pit wolf," and her favorite daytime resting place was at a steep spot above the Pescasseroli refuse dump. One summer evening in 1974 I followed her from the refuse pit to the ruins of a big hotel above Pescasseroli. The village lay beneath us. I took care not to approach too closely in the car. In the village everything was quiet, except that music was still coming from Pepe's bar. The she-wolf remained above among the ruins. Only when the light went out at Pepe's did she come down past the slaughterhouse and right into the village. I could not believe my eyes, but she went right on through the sleeping village. Dogs howled frantically all over the place. She was on the west side of the stream, so she had to cross the village square and go down the main street past the National Park headquarters before making off in a southerly direction.

In spite of such behavior, few people in the Abruzzi have ever seen a wolf. Sometimes wolves are surprised by headlights on the main road. Only game wardens, forest police, and of course shepherds see them from time to time, and even we, who followed so closely on their heels, saw them relatively rarely. My wife, Dagmar, had been in the Abruzzi for a long time before she saw her first wild wolf on an autumn evening between the tennis courts and the empty swimming pool in the middle of Campo di Giove. We had followed 7/8, an old she-wolf, right into the village, and suddenly the signal became very loud. I switched on our big spotlight and soon caught her in its beam. She took no notice of it, but that was quite normal. We watched wolves for hours at refuse dumps in the beam of our headlights without their seeming to take any notice. To them headlights obviously did not mean danger. At Campo di Giove the she-wolf was looking for something to eat. Down in the valley a passenger train slowly worked its way up the mountain from Cansano, and the illuminated carriages clattered noisily by. The she-wolf was directly below by the rails, but she did not even look up at the passing train.

Dagmar saw her second wolf at the Caramanico refuse pit. A fox and a cat were present in addition to the wolf. The cat obviously kept its distance from the fox, and the fox obviously kept its distance from the wolf. The next morning we found that the animals had been eating a big load of slaughterhouse refuse that had been dumped there. Much of this refuse, in contrast to what happens to it in Germany, is not sent to the knacker's yard. At refuse dumps we found liver, for instance, full of echinococcus (dog tapeworm) and liver fluke.

DOMESTIC ANIMALS AS PREY

Thus the wolf seems to have adapted itself admirably to man—its only enemy and at the same time its food provider. It is active when man is either asleep or—as a creature that orients itself chiefly by sight—is visually restricted. This applies not only to nighttime or the season of deep snow but also when daytime visibility is restricted by mist. Thick mist is frequent on the Passo San Leonardo, and in summer, when sheep graze in the area, it is the time for wolves. When mist appears the local shepherds immediately take their small flocks down into the valley and, if visibility is no better there, put them back in their sheds. But shepherds from elsewhere, who are often inexperienced with wolves and have big flocks and inexperienced dogs in the bargain, do not always appreciate the danger or fail to collect their many sheep and drive them down to the valley in good time. Sheepdogs here are used only as a protection against wolves; shepherds keep their flocks together and drive them themselves.

It was in such a situation that the first wholesale killing of sheep during our work in the area took place in the summer of 1974. Luigi and I were informed in the National Park that 300 sheep had been slaughtered by wolves in the Maiella area. We called the carabinieri station at Santa Eufemia who confirmed the information, whereupon we went to the spot immediately. Unfortunately, we were too late. Because of the danger of an epidemic 150 dead sheep had already been buried with the aid of a bulldozer. A shepherd who had been present told us that late on the previous afternoon there had been a sudden thunderstorm, accompanied by a thick mist. Two flocks, each of 500 sheep, had been grazing around Roccacaramanico, a half-deserted village on the slopes of Monte Morrone, and they were at once driven down toward the valley. Just when the shepherds were driving the sheep into the pens from five to seven wolves had suddenly appeared. The dogs had run away and the wolves had scattered the sheep.

When the storm was over the shepherds had counted 150 dead sheep in an area of about 250 acres, and the same number had disappeared. The official veterinarian and the forest police who investigated the incident confirmed this story, so we had no reason to disbelieve it, though the 150 vanished sheep struck us as rather strange. Why had they not been found? They belonged to one of the biggest sheep owners in the Abruzzi, a businessman with a doubtful reputation.

At the insistence of the World Wildlife Fund the Abruzzi authorities had decided that year for the first time to pay compensation to sheep owners for damage caused by wolves, as it was obvious to us that wolves should not be protected at the expense of private individuals. This sheep owner was entitled to full compensation for his losses. As the sheep in question were stated to be especially valuable animals imported from France, the amount involved was not small.

Two days later news arrived that forty of the vanished sheep had been found. This time we were not too late. The animals were lying close by the roadside below the Passo San Leonardo, all dead, and a bulldozer was busy making a big hole under the direction of the forest authorities, some shepherds, and the owner of the sheep. We were just in time to stop the burial and have a look at the dead animals. The fraud was evident immediately. The sheep allegedly killed by wolves all had a nice clean slit in the area of the throat, not caused by teeth, but obviously done with a knife. Also the gastrointestinal tract, which putrefies rapidly, had been removed by human agency in each case. Some of the animals had certainly been gnawed at, but they had all been killed by a human hand. Wolves, foxes, or dogs had been able to eat their fill subsequently.

We passed on these observations to the forest police, who were very astonished. The owner of the sheep tried to explain to them that it was all the work of the wolves, but the whole thing was too obvious, and a new report was drawn up. The man, who had greeted our arrival in a rather unfriendly fashion, seemed suddenly transformed. A long conversation followed in which I used very hard words indeed, but Luigi asked me to let him speak to him alone, and in fact he was much better at that sort of thing than I was. After a talk that lasted for many hours, and a good dinner at the hotel up on the pass, the truth came to light. It was agreed that for our part we would not make a fuss about the matter, while the sheep owner would not put out poison for wolves. Additionally, he would support our efforts to secure the establishment of a big protected area in the Maiella region, which could be of great importance in view of his political influence. I must admit that I learned a great deal from Luigi in the course of that year.

What had happened? The story of the storm and the raid by the wolves was correct. The wolves had managed to kill some sheep, but not 150, and they had not driven away another 150. To double the compensation the shepherds had killed a number of animals and claimed they had been killed by the wolves, but they had not had them buried. These and the sheep that had allegedly disappeared had been sold on the black market to local butchers, one of whom had suddenly grown nervous when he saw a number of forest police while driving over the pass. In his anxiety not to be found out he had dumped his "hot" merchandise, and later the stinking sheep had been scattered about to make it look as if they had been killed by wolves.

This was certainly not the only attempted fraud in this first year of compensation. Altogether nearly 38 million lire was paid out in the Abruzzi in 1974.[5] We estimated that at least half of the reported kills were the work not of wolves but of dogs, or were simply invented. Franco Tassi of the National Park, who had a great deal of experience in such matters, as in his area compensation for damage done by bears and later by wolves had been paid for many years, estimated that the real damage done was from 20 to 30 percent of what was claimed. In following years the conditions for paying out compensation were made stricter at our suggestion. Only killings actually identified as such would qualify. Shepherds must have a sufficient number of dogs, and one shepherd must not be in charge of more than a hundred sheep. This last requirement could easily be met by the local shepherds, but it was hard on those who came with their big flocks in summer, so it was not too strictly enforced. Also the forest administration began building big, secure pens in the mountains that neither wolf nor bear could enter. The result was that compensation payments greatly diminished.

While sheep are constantly watched, cows and horses graze freely. Several times I saw wolves making their way through herds of cattle or horses without the animals taking any notice or the wolves showing any sign of wanting to attack them. To the wolves, which are relatively small in the Abruzzi and run only in small packs or alone, these animals are simply too big. It was only rarely that we could be sure that a dead calf or foal had been killed by a wolf. In most cases the young animal had been separated from its mother. With horses, the mother was always hobbled. This is a usual practice that enables the animal to be caught more easily, but it is a handicap against wolves, and many foals have paid for it with their lives.

Apart from domestic animals, occasional wild swine are to be found in the Maiella. We once saw a herd of sixteen animals and found tracks up to an altitude of 6,000 feet. Single large animals, presumably boars, had been moving about in deep snow in winter while most of the herd remained in snow-free areas lower down. It is reported from Turkey that wolves there chiefly hunt wild swine, but in the Abruzzi we found none that had been killed by wolves and their hair was never found in wolves' feces. Presumably the small packs are not dangerous to them.

By far the largest number of sheep that were killed while we were working in the area were solitary animals. At night wolves crept up to the fenced pens and helped themselves to a sheep, which they generally dragged outside and ate there. Local shepherds also reported the loss of single animals that went astray on the way home or in a thick mist. Many of these were eaten on the spot. All that was left were the heavy bones and the skin. But it was not uncommon for wolves to leave behind animals that had been only nibbled at, no doubt they had been disturbed. The remains were generally left and the dogs ate them the next day.

Yet we also saw damage on a larger scale. It was not uncommon for as many as ten sheep to be killed, and on two occasions there were more than a hundred. This seemed always to happen when panic broke out among the sheep and a large number ran about bleating wildly. To the wolves this was an only too irresistible signal to catch and kill, and they killed everything they could, like a fox in a chicken run. A bear was said to have broken into a sheep shed in the National Park and to have killed all the sheep in it—there were said to have been more than a hundred—and then to have gone to sleep out of sheer exhaustion. The next morning the shepherds found him asleep in the middle of the dead sheep.

This wholesale killing occurs among many predators. Penned animals that cannot escape become such an obvious target of the drive to kill that the predator does not get around to eating. In his detailed study of the killing behavior of cats, Paul Leyhausen has drawn up a so-called "relative hierarchy" of feeling according to which the separate phases of the hunt, such as the creeping up, the killing, and the eating, each has its own impulses and objectives. Each has to be satisfied before the next phase in the sequence is triggered off. Thus the killing of the prey is motivated not by hunger but by the key stimuli that arise when the prey is brought into a particular situation as a result of the early stages of the hunt. If more and more new key stimuli to kill keep arising, the animal reacts accordingly. Going out to hunt and searching for prey—"appetence behavior"—is only motivated by hunger.[6]

Such excesses of killing can therefore arise only in the unnatural situation in which a predator is confronted with a large number of prey animals whose movements are restricted. In complete contrast to the situation when they hunt wild prey, nearly all of which they eat when they have killed it, predators kill more domestic animals than they can use. Erki Pulliainen reports the same thing from north Finland. Of 149 dead sheep, 9 cows, 15 calves, and 3 horses, only 31 sheep, 3 cows, and 5 calves, and 1 horse were eaten.[7]

It is this behavior that causes the very understandable hatred of shepherds for these predators, the wolf in particular. A single sheep, a single foal, or a single calf occasionally would perhaps not be so bad. But killing a hundred or more and then not even eating them is too much. Whenever this happened it was widely reported in the newspapers, and hostility both to wolves and to the movement to protect them became vociferous.

WOLF MORTALITY

When the opposite takes place and a wolf meets a violent death, newspapers and television also report the event with horror, as happened, for instance, when Luigi and I found our first wolf, 1/2, dead in a stream in the National Park area. The animal had obviously been killed with a shotgun by a poacher who had been shooting birds. It must have taken some time to die, and its body was carried along by the stream and finally ended up in the undergrowth by the bank, where we found it, guided to the spot by the transmitter.

Other wolves marked by us also died at the hands of man. At the very beginning of our work in the Maiella area we caught two adult females from neighboring packs. At least four other wolves were living with one female (7/8), presumably an adult male and three cubs. She had cubs again in the spring in a thick wood on the Cresta Maggiore above Cansano. Luigi found the den and saw two cubs, though there may have been more. This den was the pack rendezvous throughout the summer. In the winter that followed I succeeded in catching two adult males and two nine-month-old cubs, so there were four members of the pack we kept track of.

Together they roamed an area of about seventy-five square miles between Sulmona, the Passo San Leonardo, and Pescocostanzo. It was not long before we found one of the cubs dead; it had swallowed strychnine hidden in the carcass of a sheep. The adult male died soon afterward, also of strychnine.

For an experienced wolf this was unusual. He was very emaciated when he died, and perhaps hunger had made him incautious. But we may have been responsible for his bad physical condition. He had hurt himself badly in the trap, and the wounds had not yet healed. We sewed them up and gave him a penicillin injection, but this had not helped. So in the very course of our efforts to preserve the wolves of the Abruzzi we may have been responsible for the death of one of them.

280

This incident, as well as the many bad wounds suffered by foxes we caught, made me decide not to go on using these spring traps, and in a recommendation to the World Wildlife Fund I proposed that in future projects wolves should be caught by other methods.

Luigi made an interesting observation on adult wolves' reaction to the presence of strychnine. In the autumn of 1975 he was following she-wolf 7/8 near Campo di Giove when he came across a dead dog. When he got back to the village he discovered that poison had been laid in the neighborhood and that a dog that fit the description was missing. He went back to fetch the body next day, but all he found was some remains. Presumably the she-wolf had eaten the animal but, quite contrary to her usual habit, she had left the gastrointestinal tract untouched and had not even torn open the abdominal cavity.

That is certainly no proof that she "knew" that those parts were dangerous to eat. Strychnine is said to have no odor, even to wolves. Nevertheless, healthy adult wolves are extraordinarily cautious in dealing with poisoned meat, though the young easily succumb to it. There are similar reports from North America, where the quantities of strychnine used in the past century to combat wolves and other predators by far exceeded those used anywhere else.

The second marked wolf left his mother and the area in which he was reared in the spring of 1976 when he was twelve months old. After protracted wandering he came "home" eight weeks later, only to move on again straight away. Our last radio contact with him came from the National Park area. We would have liked to have found out more about him, particularly the direction in which he went, but we had no aircraft. When we finally had one either his radio was no longer working or he too had died concealed in some place from which his signal could no longer be received.

His mother's radio also stopped transmitting after eighteen months. I saw her once with another wolf, presumably a male, perhaps one of her sons whom we had not managed to catch. She had no cubs in 1976, and when I howled at her old den in the summer of 1977 there was no answer. Presumably the pack no longer existed.

Of the total of twenty-five dead wolves known to us in the Abruzzi from 1974 to 1976 at least nine, chiefly young ones, died of poison. Three died of shot wounds and one was run over. The cause of death of the remainder could not be established. Thus human influences were by far the most frequent cause of death. We have no information about wolves that die of natural causes—illness, old age, wounds, or undernourishment. But in view of the fact that of an estimated total of twenty-five wolves at least fourteen and probably more were killed in the course of two years, the chances of natural death are obviously not very high.

SPATIAL ORGANIZATION

Because of the wolf's secretive way of living, we were not able to obtain an accurate picture of the nature of the population, that is, its age structure, size of groups, reproduction rates, and so on. But observation of 7/8 and her pack showed that wolves in this area were able to form small packs that remained stable for a time and lay claim to a territory that was defended against strange conspecifics. But the high death rate due to human agency, as well as living conditions that are greatly dependent on human beings and thus affect the spatial organization of the population, do not allow such packs to survive for long. The large amount of food required by young animals and the consequent increased pressure on domestic animals (when cubs are present) results in an increase in human persecution when a pack has been formed. The result is a surviving wolf population largely split up into small groups or individual animals that generally live on refuse and are able to reproduce and rear cubs successfully only in exceptionally favorable circumstances.

That is the explanation of what is presumably a very low birth rate and of the fact that in many parts of the Abruzzi the wolf appears only sporadically. When we began work in 1973 there were no reports of wolves in the Gran Sasso area, but two years later substantial damage was reported and everything pointed to its having been caused by wolves. In the Maiella area wolves were also unknown or at any rate very rare for many years. Many shepherds who had suffered losses in recent years told us that this was the first time in their lives that such a thing had happened to them. The World Wildlife Fund actually had to take vigorous steps to counter rumors that we had introduced wolves. We were said to have imported them from Canada and dropped them by parachute; that was the most common version of the story. Single wolves had always appeared from time to time, but only the successful rearing of at least three litters known to us caused any perceptible pressure on domestic animals. By now most of these wolves have either died or disappeared, and there have been no more reports of damage. But, as Luigi reports, wolves have appeared farther west in an area where none were reported at the time of our work. Obviously a new pack formed as a result of successful cub rearing. But the local population has not been inactive; four of these wolves have since been killed.

WOLF-DOG HYBRIDIZATION

In an area of low density and intensive human exploitation wolves are subject to an additional hazard over and above that of direct efforts at extermination; that is, hybridization with dogs. We caught she-wolf 9/10 in the winter of 1975 in the area where we had previously caught 7/8. We do not know whether she came from 7/8's pack or whether she had been driven out of it. In any event, she kept away from 7/8 and her companions and lived in the area north of the Passo San Leonardo. During the winter everything pointed to her being on her own. Then in the summer Paolo was the first to see her accompanied by a black cub. The next winter we heard several times distinct barks mingled with the howling of a pack above Santa Eufemia, so we were not surprised when we caught the first hybrid, a black creature with white spots on its legs and breast. A few weeks later two more of these creatures, which otherwise behaved completely like wolves, were caught in our traps; one was a black female with white spots and the other was a female with the coloring of a wolf that only an expert would recognize as a hybrid. At all events, a shepherd could see nothing unusual about her; to him she was a wolf. Soon afterward I saw the whole pack together. Apart from the she-wolf and a male that presumably joined her subsequently, it consisted of six cubs, four black and two wolf-colored.

We had a long discussion about what to do with the cubs. After we caught them I fitted all of them with collars with radio transmitters and let them go. That exhausted our possibilities of influencing them, because in spite of my efforts I did not succeed in catching

283

any more cubs. They were so shy that there was no chance of shooting them, and in no circumstances were we willing to use poison—and not only because of the danger to the two "real" wolves. So we had no alternative to adopting what in any case seemed to be the best course, namely doing nothing at all.

My argument was as follows. It was not to be assumed that the incident we had observed was highly exceptional. A similar instance was reported from Israel, where a she-wolf was said to have joined forces with an Alsatian and to have had cubs by him.[8] There were also similar reports from America.[9] Thus it seemed that hybridization between wolves and dogs must also occur in Italy. A wolf in a group will eat a dog, but alone it will mate with it.

Nevertheless, the wolf population in the Abruzzi has hitherto apparently not been influenced by hybridization. So far as we can tell, the wolves there are pure wolves. The same applies in North America. Thus crossings between hybrids and ordinary wolves most probably do not occur. Though in their behavior toward human beings the hybrids do not differ from wolves, they are not conspecific. So the hybrids remain among themselves or go on multiplying with dogs. Thus hybridization represents no danger to an otherwise viable wolf population. For a population endangered by further crossings or by competition with hybrids, it is presumably too late in any case. Mating with dogs is only the final act in their disappearance.

THE WOLF IN ITALY

Our work in the Abruzzi showed very plainly the demands that the wolf makes on the living space it shares with man. Apart from a sufficient food supply, a matter on which it is not exactly choosy, the wolf needs refuge areas to a large extent undisturbed by man. These can be either undeveloped forest areas or mountainous regions with forests and steep ravines. At all events, in the Italian distribution area we found nowhere where wolves survived and woods or mountains were lacking. In this connection the efforts of the forest administration to reforest many of the Italian mountans that have been cleared are certainly a positive factor.

Observation of the nightly activity of wolves also showed that they are well able to make their way into areas more thickly populated by human beings. Twice I followed wolves into Sulmona, a town of some 30,000 inhabitants; they had to cross railway lines and roads on which there is a great deal of daytime traffic several times. This seemed to cast doubt on our original idea that wolves in the Apennines lived in isolated enclaves.

To conclude our work in the Abruzzi, Dagmar and I flew along the Apennines from Florence in the north to Calabria in the south. We wanted to find out what the country looked like between the high mountain areas where Luigi had originally concluded that wolves still survived. We spent four days criss-crossing the mountains, and found no distribution area that seemed to be completely isolated from the rest. Thus, according to the present state of our knowledge of their behavior, wolves should be able to roam from Monte Sibilini in the north of the Abruzzi to Monti della Sila in the south. That would make their final extinction in Italy more difficult than we had originally supposed.

Reintroduction of Natural Prey

It soon became clear to us that their survival, whether they lived in isolated enclaves or in contact with one another, depended on doing away with their total dependence on man. This could be done only by large-scale reintroduction of their natural prey. The red deer was exterminated in the Abruzzi in the nineteenth century, and a small population of roe survived in the National Park area up to the sixties, but then died out too. The principal cause for the disappearance of both species must have been hunting, though the competition resulting from overintensive grazing of domestic animals may also have played a part.

In 1971 and 1972 a total of forty-five deer from Yugoslavia and twenty-one roe from northern Italy were set free in the National Park. Little was known about their whereabouts when our project began a year later. The deer had established themselves around about the area where they were released, but the roe seemed to have disappeared again.

We therefore proposed that more animals of both species should be released and that they should be followed up with a view to gaining knowledge and experience for further large-scale reintroductions. We were particularly interested in how they would multiply, the influence they would have on the vegetation, and their interactions with domestic animals, as well as with the wolf and the bear. Unfortunately, this object was not achieved. Luigi and I concentrated on the wolves and left work with the deer to the National Park people. The latter, as was to be expected, were chiefly interested in the reintroductions into the National Park, and the acquisition of knowledge for further reintroductions took only second place. So our telemetric collars for deer remained unused, and an opportunity was missed. Between 1974 and 1977 a total of twenty-eight deer and sixteen roe were released at various places in the National Park. The deer all came from the Bavarian Forest. They were presented by the Bavarian Ministry of Agriculture as part of a joint operation between the Abruzzi and Lower Bavaria and the two national parks. This certainly reflected credit on the minister, Herr Eisenmann, who exposed himself to severe criticism from the political environment from which he himself came. The gutter press talked of "German deer for Italian wolves," and the sporting community were not exactly friendly in what they said about him either.

An argument that was frequently used by critics was the "massacre of birds" that takes place in Italy. It was claimed that as long as such a disgraceful state of affairs prevailed "ecological development aid" should not be granted in other fields. But these arguments do not hold water. Certainly a stop should be put to the shooting of millions of birds, including migratory birds, that takes place in Italy. Nobody is more aware of that than the Italian conservationists. The Italian shooting of birds has become ecologically intolerable. But even this massacre is not as bad as depriving animals of their living space by draining the last marshes, straightening the course of rivers, turning natural forests into pine plantations, and the wholesale use of poison in agriculture and forestry—all because of the compulsion to exploit every last square foot of our soil. In this respect, I believe, we humans are in need of "development aid."

Our object in introducing deer was not to supply wolves with living meat, but to reestablish ecological relationships destroyed by men, including sportsmen. Not only should wolves have their natural prey, but deer and roe should get back their natural predator— an ecological act of "reparation" that, we hoped, would benefit the disrupted living community of the selected territories.

The deer established themselves excellently. In the summer of 1976 there were already 130 of them, and by now they must number over 200. At first they settled in the surrounding valleys, but soon some individual animals had advanced to the neighborhood of Sulmona. We know little about the effect they have had on the vegetation. In the National Park area I saw large areas of willow herb that had been stripped bare. But in areas where there is no grazing of domestic animals, the vegetation is so luxuriant that there would still be a place for a great many more deer, and even in grazing areas it should be possible to maintain a limited number of them by winter feeding.

During the years of our work in the National Park we found the remains of three deer killed by wolves. One weak female was killed soon after being released, and the other two were young males that were cornered by the wolves in impassable woodland. But the growth of the population shows that the wolves exercise no regulatory influence. Presumably the deer are generally too big for single wolves or small packs. It would therefore be very interesting to investigate possible changes in the social organization of the wolf as a result of adaptation to the new kind of prey.

The reintroduction of roe has not been successful so far. These animals are much more locality bound, and they stayed close to the enclosure in which they were put before they were released. Of the sixteen released while we were there few survived; most presumably fell victim to the wolves. A much larger number of animals will be required if reintroduction is to succeed. The numerical proportion between roe and wolf will have to be so changed in the roe's favor that even a great deal of hunting of the newcomers by wolves will not eliminate them or reduce their numbers as drastically as has happened so far. Further experiments are necessary in this respect.

Because of the great importance of the matter a follow-up project concentrating on reintroduction was agreed to by the World Wildlife Fund when the wolf project came to an end in 1976. Luigi is in charge of it. To secure independence from imports, a big breeding enclosure was established in the Maiella area with the aid of the Italian forest administration. Deer from the National Park in the Bavarian Forest, which now unfortunately have to be bought—and they are very expensive—were to be brought there in 1978, and roe were to follow later. The animals born there were to be introduced first in the Maiella region, then elsewhere in the Abruzzi, and later perhaps in other parts of Italy. Luigi's task is to make a close study of the reintroductions in the Maiella region and gain knowledge and experience for subsequent operations.

Political Ecology of the Wolf

There is no doubt that unless fundamental changes are made soon the days of the wolf are numbered in the Abruzzi, as elsewhere in Italy. In the course of our fieldwork the necessary changes became very clear to us. All hunting of wolves would have to cease, and the use of poison in combating foxes or other wild animals would have to be done away with. Also no more refuge areas vital to the wolf could be destroyed by the building of roads and ski lifts. Thus our primary concern was to secure action at the legislative level, though it was clear to us that the best laws would be of no avail unless the wolf were accepted by the local population. Hence we had to investigate the attitude of people in the locality and discover the conditions under which they would be willing to accept the wolf.

We made our first efforts in this direction when we began work in the area in March 1973. Our methods of interrogation would not have been regarded as scientifically acceptable in sociological circles, but we asked a number of people whether they thought wolves were dangerous to human beings. Our "impressions" (I use the term to avoid saying "findings") were very interesting. The farther we were from the areas in which wolves lived, the more dangerous they were believed to be. In areas inhabited by wolves those least impressed by their alleged dangerousness were those who had direct contact with them. All the shepherds we asked agreed that the wolf was not dangerous to human beings. The occupational group that regarded the wolf as especially dangerous was, interestingly enough, innkeepers, an impression that did not exactly surprise us.

Our impressions were confirmed two years later by a proper scientific inquiry conducted in cooperation with us by the sociological institute of the University of Rome. The questioning took place in a number of villages in the Maiella area. It should be mentioned that by that time our work with the wolves had been given a great deal of publicity, most of it favorable. A number of television films were made, and many of them were broadcast in the evening. Also there had been many reports in the press, the local radio station had shown a great deal of interest, and Luigi had delivered a number of lectures. So there was practically no one in the area who did not know us, or at any rate our Land-Rover with its array of aerials, which was on the move by day and night. Our campaign as well as that of the World Wildlife Fund against plans to establish a new ski resort on the Passo San Leonardo, together with ski lifts, a golf course, hotels, and holiday homes, was also known. Instead of a ski resort, we proposed that another national park should be established, or at least a regional park in the Maiella. Hunting should be forbidden, and deer and roe should be reintroduced. Instead of building big hotels financed from Rome and Milan, the beautiful old villages should be restored, facilities for overnight visitors extended, and small *pensions* established. Our proposals certainly looked rather unfashionable in comparison with the spectacular plans to develop the Maiella with ski tracks and concrete, but they had the advantage that they would benefit the local population and that the kind of tourism that they would attract, though it would bring in less money, would not be so seasonally limited.

The inquiry showed very clearly that people's attitude to the wolf largely depended on their interest in the various possible alternatives for the future development of the area. Those who lived in the lower-lying areas, who would neither suffer damage from the wolf nor benefit from the development of the Maiella into a ski track, were generally in favor of the wolf and its protection. The cultural aspect, the desire not merely to exterminate a creature that had made such a mark on the history of the area, played an important part. Even shepherds were surprisingly favorably inclined to the wolf. They had no objection to it as long as they were compensated for any damage they suffered and the number of wolves did not get out of hand. They also favored the idea of introducing deer and roe, which would relieve the pressure of the wolf on their sheep.

I find this attitude on the part of the shepherds quite remarkable. In spite of the millennial traditional warfare between wolf and bear on the one hand and shepherd on the other, their attitude was one of tolerance. Sportsmen, however, were less favorably inclined. Though the wolf was hardly a competitor of their "prey," their attitude was negative, and they frequently produced the argument of the damage done to domestic animals. Finally, those who hoped to benefit from a skiing circus on the Maiella were definitely opposed, whether because they wanted to build hotels or merely because they owned land they hoped to be able to sell at a high price. The people of Pacentro, in whose communal area the ski lifts and hotels were to be built, were especially hostile. The woman who conducted the inquiry was once actually thrown out of the village as a Communist agent; a story soon evolved, embellished with many variations.

People in the villages through which we often drove, many of whom knew us personally, were much more favorably inclined, though here too their attitude basically depended on where their interests lay. This shows the limitations of all public relations work, in my opinion. There were people with whom we were on the best of terms and who were accessible to our arguments who nevertheless would shoot or hunt down every wolf they could.

The inquiry showed plainly that conservation work cannot succeed in the long run if it is against the interests of the local population, however questionable those interests may be. It must attempt to get the majority of the population on its side by a conciliatory approach, by putting forward alternative development plans, by a willingness to pay compensation for lost rights, and by a great deal of factual explanation that does not attempt to conceal the existence of opposing interests. People should not be allowed to feel that conservationists are going to decide what is to happen in their neighborhood without consulting them. Instead they must be persuaded that conservationists consider their own interests also. This may prove to be a long, difficult, and thoroughly political task, a fact that is not always sufficiently understood in conservation work. I believe that in the Abruzzi we succeeded at least in making a start at integrating our conservationist aim of the preservation of the wolf into an alternative view of ecological and economic development that will ultimately turn out to be more beneficial to the people of the area.

But it is not only at a local level that the future of the wolf and the values for which it stands will be decided. An essential role belongs to legislation. In this respect Luigi and the World Wildlife Funds succeeded in attaining two objectives that are vital to the survival of the wolf. Shortly before my departure from Italy in December 1976 the Agriculture Ministry in Rome made the wolf a permanently protected animal throughout the country, and the use of poison for keeping down animal populations was prohibited throughout the country. We were especially pleased by this last prohibition, because it was so unexpected and so important, not only to the wolf.

What does the future hold for the wolf in Italy? Everything depends on how these two laws are observed. And that depends on the attitude of the local population, which in turn depends on the future economic development of the higher-altitude areas in the Apennines. If compensation regulations were introduced in the southern provinces, as they have been in the Abruzzi and now in some other provinces, that would represent another step in the direction of tolerance. A reasonable development of tourist facilities would presumably also be beneficial, since the economic base would be broadened and the great dependence on the sheep that has prevailed in the past would be diminished. Economic prosperity is certainly one of the essential conditions for the preservation of the wolf. But every mountain need not be equipped with skiing facilities and every village need not have a big hotel. Not only would that be an ecological disaster to the wolf and other free-living animals, but it would certainly also be an economic cul-de-sac for the people of the area.

Finally, the future of the wolf depends on the success of the reintroduction program. Whether deer and roe will be able to survive outside strictly protected areas such as the National Park depends on Italian sportsmen. This is certainly a factor of great uncertainty, and I must admit that my hopes in this respect are not very high. Roe, deer, and chamois are strictly protected, and the penalties for shooting them are severe. But who is to ensure that the law is enforced? Our hopes lie with the forest administration, whose attitude toward reintroduction is very positive. Also the sportsmen of central and southern Italy do not have a tradition of shooting ungulates. They only have shotguns, and shooting in the forest is prohibited. Perhaps, after all, there is a chance that deer, roe, wolves, and human beings will be able to coexist in an area developed and cultivated by man.

Our project in the Abruzzi showed that the wolf can live in areas settled and exploited by man. It is now up to man to show whether he will let the wolf live in them.

291

13
Wolf and Man

Two notable facts emerged from our work in the Abruzzi. The first was the wolf's great ability to adapt to human ways, and the second was the surprising amount of tolerance shown by people who suffer from its depredations. In comparison to the deep hatred reported from other areas where it lives, the shepherds of the Abruzzi seemed actually indifferent. Above all, it is surprising that the wolf should have survived in an area with a relatively high population density while it has disappeared in the inaccessible, almost uninhabited, tundra regions of northern Scandinavia, for instance, where one would be much more likely to expect it. Its present-day distribution is obviously not dependent only on the nature of the country, its types of forests, supply of prey, and other ecological factors, but also to a quite vital extent directly on man.

To what animal species does that not apply? Man is part of the environment and its ecology. He affects and is affected by wild animals. This relationship arose historically, independent of economy and culture. For a complete understanding of the behavior and ecology of any species, this relationship between man and his environment must be taken into account. For a biologist, however, that is a rather unusual task. It is forced on us by the wolf, who has engaged our imagination and our fears as no other animal has.

The Wolf's Historical Image

I have already mentioned the favorable idea of the wolf that prevails among the Indians and Eskimos of North America. They hunted the same prey and so were ecologically its competitors, though the hunting of each could hardly diminish the prey of the other. But even then man was the wolf's enemy. The Indians of the prairies hunted it occasionally for the sake of its pelt and perhaps in bad times for food also. Nevertheless, they called it their "brother," no doubt in recognition of their similar ecological situation. To hunt bison they often disguised themselves in wolf skins. Adult bison or herds of bison allowed wolves to approach, as they hardly represented a danger, and the distance at which they took flight from human beings was much greater. By disguising themselves in this way the Indians were able to reduce the distance to such an extent that they were able successfully to use bow and arrow or missiles. [1]

The religious and mythical ideas of the Indians of the west coast of Canada are well known to us nowadays. They carved the celebrated totem poles on which their legends and beliefs are represented. At the top of the totem pole at Wakias, in British Columbia, which was once more than forty-five feet high, there is an eagle, king and ruler of the air; underneath it there is a killer whale, the ruler of the sea; and then there is a wolf, the ruler of the land, who was believed to be courageous and wise. [2] According to the myths of the Columbia River Indians, which were handed down orally, in a previous age human beings were animals. [3] There were deer men and beaver men and bird men, as well as many others. There were also monsters, who lay in wait in shallow rapids and dragged passing animal-men into deep water. All these creatures were made of earth, and these animal-men were ignorant and selfish, so the earth sent them a coyote (the coyote was presumably synonymous with the wolf). The coyote killed the monsters, combated evil, showed the animal-men how to behave, and taught them many useful things. It was continuously on the move, performing good deeds, and eventually created man out of parts of the body of a dead monster. It used the legs to make the Klickitat tribe, who were able to run especially fast, the body to make the Indians who lived by the river, and the arms to make the Cayuse Indians, who were especially skilled with bow and arrow. Thus each part of the body was used to make the different tribes with their different characteristics. But one thing the coyote overlooked—it forgot to give the men who lived on the coast a mouth, and when it visited them they were all very thin and hungry, so it took a knife and cut a mouth for them. But, as it was in a great hurry, it did the job badly, and all coast Indians are said to have had ugly mouths ever since.

In all this the wolf is a good, almost divine creature, rather slovenly and overhasty and impetuous, but kind, sympathetic, and wise. One very celebrated totem pole, that at Gitlatedanix, tells a story that continually recurs with modifications. A man helps a wolf that has a bit of wood stuck between its back teeth, and later in a time of famine the wolf repays this by killing a deer for the man and his tribe.[4]

Such splinters can indeed cause a wolf great trouble. When Näschen returned four months after running away he ate a great deal, but soon seemed to be ill. The veterinarian could find nothing wrong with him and attributed his weak state to undernourishment while at liberty. But he grew worse, his mouth stank, and eventually I found the cause of the trouble—a bit of wood fixed between the upper back teeth. After this was removed he recovered in a few hours.

One might be tempted to interpret this legend of aid for a sick wolf that later reciprocates by procuring food for hungry human beings as representing a first attempt at domestication but, so far as we know, neither Indians nor Eskimos have ever tried to tame wolves by rearing cubs that they found. Presumably they brought their dogs with them from Asia.

Stories told by aged Eskimos show a surprising knowledge of the ecology and behavior of the wolf.[5] They too hunted it for its pelt and later for the bounty paid by the government for dead wolves. But, like the Indians, they do not share the hatred of the wolf that is so evident in other societies. Their idea of the wolf coincides to a large extent with ours of the present day. There are differences only on a few points. According to the Eskimo, the wolf is not only highly intelligent and social, which rouses their admiration, but frequently acts with insight and deliberation—an idea that after four years' work in the Abruzzi no longer seems to me to be so completely off the mark.

We have every reason to believe that this positive attitude to the wolf was typical of all societies at the food-gathering and hunting stage and at the first beginnings of agriculture. It changed only with the extensive keeping of domestic animals, when the wolf became an enemy. In ancient Teutonic mythology the wolf became a symbol of the powers of evil, and in the picturesque language of the Old Testament it has negative characteristics, often already standing symbolically for the devil.

CLASSICAL ANTIQUITY

In the religious and mythological ideas of the Greeks and Romans animals no longer played as big a part as in societies that were completely integrated into nature and were characterized by animistic beliefs. The pre-Socratic natural philosophers sought rational explanations for astronomical, physical, and biological phenomena. Agricultural improvement depended on favorable climate and fertile soil, and as a result of this a class society developed in which peasants, women, and slaves contrasted with a small upper class possessing a monopoly of economic and political power. The latter lived increasingly apart from the places where agricultural production took place. Towns arose that became the centers from which trade as well as all important religious, scientific, and philosophical impulses radiated. Slave keeping provided both the condition and the motivation for the many wars that ultimately led to the Roman Empire.[6]

Roman prosperity depended on high agricultural productivity, but the landowners as well as the domestic animals and the means of production led a totally urban life. To the urban Roman hunting played a merely subordinate role. Roe and fallow deer, which were introduced from Mesopotamia, were hunted, and so were wolves, but no attempts at systematic extermination were made. To the sheep owner the wolf was only one of many hazards to which his prosperity was exposed. He seldom saw sheep that were killed and eaten, and what the rural population thought has not been handed down to us. In spite of large-scale forest clearances, there were still plenty of refuge areas and an ample supply of prey for wolves. So the damage caused by them presumably remained within bounds. The legend of the foundation of Rome by Romulus and Remus, who were reared by a she-wolf on the Capitol hill, actually shows us a positive picture of the wolf at that time (the Italian word *lupa*, she-wolf, still implies great motherliness, and also extends to prostitution; a *lupanar* is a brothel). (See figure 41.) The great clash between the interests of man and wolf had obviously not yet taken place.

THE MIDDLE AGES

The battle between man and wolf arose only after the collapse of the Roman Empire. Great marshes had developed and the forest had to a large extent replenished itself, perhaps as a consequence of a deterioration of the climate. During this period stories of havoc brought by wolves on domestic animals became more and more frequent, and for the first time there are accounts of attacks by wolves on human beings. The first reports of organized wolf hunting date from the time of Charlemagne; professional wolf hunters were employed, dogs were specially bred, and a number of different methods of hunting and killing wolves were developed.[7] How did this change in the relationship between wolf and man take place?

In ancient times the living space of wolf and man were to a large extent separate. At the beginning of the Middle Ages a number of innovations, such as the heavy plow, the horseshoe, and the three-field system, greatly affected agriculture, which was intensified and expanded into mountainous regions to which access was difficult. Increased food production led to a big increase in population around 1,000 A.D. Forests were cleared again, and hunting, both as a source of food and as a sporting activity by the nobility, who mostly lived on their estates, greatly increased in importance.[8] Competition for game that grew rarer and rarer drove wolves into areas of human settlement, where they exercised increasing pressure on domestic animals and finally became a nuisance.

Whether they really attacked human beings cannot be established. It is hard to distinguish among reality, invention, and magic in the literature of the period. Under the influence of Christianity the rational outlook of antiquity had given way to a magic mode of thought in which a dominant role was played by the mythological, the supersensory, and the mystical. A duality between good and evil, God and the devil, served both as a means of oppression in the country and as a justification for brutal acts of warfare.

Fig. 41. Romulus and Remus.

The rulers claimed God for themselves alone, while their enemies, whether Mohammedans, unfaithful wives, or harmful animals, belonged to the devil. The east was plundered, witches were burned, and in illustrations of the period Christ is to be seen fighting wolves in person (see figure 42). The idea of the werewolf, which in antiquity had been only very vague, now had its heyday (see figure 43). Werewolves were people disguised in wolf skins who, often in a state of trance under the influence of drugs or magic rituals, carried out vampirelike abductions or human sacrifices. In the Middle Ages their existence was not doubted; the only doubt was whether they were really men or really wolves. Like witches or persons possessed by the devil, when they were caught they seemed themselves to believe what they were accused of. Wolves in human clothing are to be seen hanging from gallows in medieval illustrations. Obviously no real distinction was made between wolves and wolf men, and presumably many of the reported attacks on human beings were attributed to these werewolves.

In many of these illustrations the wolves are black, though there are no black wolves in Europe. Presumably they were confused with dogs, which does not seem at all improbable after our experiences in the Abruzzi. During our last summer there, for instance, we were told a dead wolf had been found near Campo di Giove. We went there, and it was immediately obivous that it was a perfectly ordinary dog, though it had the coloring of a wolf. But we completely failed to persuade the many curious villagers who came to see it of the fact. They were convinced that it was a wolf—in an area where men and wolves had lived side by side for thousands of years.

In spite of such confusions and magical thinking, the reports are too numerous, fear of the wolf and the forest too strong, the mythology of the wolf too dominant, for the idea of attacks on human beings by wolves to be entirely without foundation. With the human invasion of the wolf's living space, the settlement of mountainous areas and the clearing of forests, with human hunting and large-scale extermination of game, confrontation undoubtedly arose. Men living in small hamlets and villages had poor weapons or none at all. In wars and epidemics men died outside inhabited areas, and the wolves no doubt exploited this source of food. As early as 500 A.D., the Latinized Germanic word *wargus* is used for dese-

Fig. 42. Jesus and the wolf. A medieval engraving.

Fig. 43. Wolf in human clothing or werewolf?

crator of the dead in the Merovingian *Pactus legis salicae:* "If he digs up and plunders a buried corpse, which is called grave robbery by the courts, and this is proved against him, he shall be a *wargus* until the day on which he reaches a settlement with the relatives of the deceased."[9]

The use of the word *wargus* for a person who exhumes a dead body—in Swedish the word for wolf is *varg*—is not of course conclusive evidence that wolves ate human bodies, but it is a pointer. In modern times many accounts of attacks on human beings by wolves coincide with wars; and during the westward movement in the United States—particularly after the discovery of gold in California in the middle of the nineteenth century, when many died of yellow fever—wolves were also reported to have eaten corpses.[10]

Many assumed killings of human beings by wolves can probably be attributed to their eating of corpses. But it would not be surprising if some wolves, having grown accustomed to men, both living and dead, and having learned to distinguish between dangerous and nondangerous ones, should have learned to kill them. Children above all must have been easy prey. So it is not surprising that every conceivable form of wickedness should have been ascribed to an animal that was both a competitor for food, a destroyer of domestic animals, and on top of that was now an enemy of man himself.

The Germanic word *wargus* or *varg* for wolf was also used in other connections. Diphtheria, for instance, an illness that restricts the throat, was called *warcgingil*, and an outlaw was a *warg, warag, wearg, wearh*—robber, criminal, evil, and damned. He lived a harassed life in the forest, just like a wolf. The law forbade anyone to give him aid or shelter, and anyone could kill him. The use of the same word for wolf and for outlaw has attracted a great deal of attention from philologists and legal historians, the chief question being which was named after which. W. Grimm believed that the application of the term to the outlawed criminal derived from the outlawed wolf, while modern philologists take the view that the animal took its name from the human outlaw.[11]

THE WOLF IN FABLE

But the wolf did not stand only for evil in the imagination of the time. In medieval animal fables he was strong and powerful, but also rather slow-witted and ignorant, actually a kindly but rather stupid creature. These fables originated in the east and in the ancient world and kept recurring, with modifications, in later times. Many were attributed to the clever and resourceful slave Aesop.

> Aesop probably never existed. Popular imagination invented the kind of hero that it needed, and he was imagined to be short, hunchbacked, blubber-lipped and a stammerer; in fact, his external appearance was the very opposite of the Hellenic ideal of beauty of the Greek upper class. His inner greatness derived from the suffering and maltreatment to which he was exposed as a slave and which he put up with patiently or evaded thanks to his quick wit and presence of mind. [12]

Aesop's fables made their way out of Italy into the Germanic world, where they were first told for entertainment at courts and in monasteries. But a resurgence of the art of the fable took place when it was adapted by the people who began humorously and often satirically spinning pearls of practical wisdom, often related to dealings with the upper class. Alien animals such as the lion and the jackal were transformed into familiar ones such as the bear, the wolf, and the fox, and the action and point of the story as well as its moral were adapted to the living conditions of the time. One of the most popular animals in these fables, together with the fox, was the wolf. In the perpetual duel between various animals and man each was sometimes the winner and sometimes the loser. The wolf won when he met someone even stupider than himself, and the fox lost when he came up against someone even cleverer. But in their encounters with each other it was always the weaker but more cunning fox that won at the expense of the stronger but stupider wolf.

Perhaps the wolf here stands for the all-powerful upper class and the fox for the weaker but subtler inferior (Aesop), who always adapts himself to the immediate situation but is often able to exploit to his own advantage the rivalries of those stronger and more powerful than himself. The wolf may also symbolize nature, the strength and arbitrariness of which is circumvented by weaker but thinking man. What is of special interest in this respect is the purely individual nature of the defense against the arbitrariness of the powerful. Existing power relations as such are not questioned, and everyone has to adapt himself as well as possible to divinely established living conditions. Only later, for instance in the fables of the enthusiastic Lutheran Hans Sachs of Nuremberg or in those of Heinrich Steinhöwel, the town doctor of Ulm, are fables given a political dimension. This was the age in which the bourgeoisie, which by now had attained considerable economic power and was receptive to the new ideas of humanism and the Reformation, turned against the ecclesiastical and feudal system of government. However, its attitude toward the revolutionary peasant movements that followed was skeptical or actually hostile, as was that of Martin Luther himself, who also wrote some fables. The wolf now became a symbol for the "loutish, crude, or stupid" peasant who was a threat to law and order, as, for instance, in Burghardt Waldis's fable of the wolf and the hungry dog that dates from about 1540.

In this fable the dog is badly fed by its master and is very thin. As a result of the wolf's cunning it gets better treatment, and as a reward the dog allows the wolf to take a lamb from the flock. But when the wolf comes and asks for another lamb, the dog refuses. Its task is to guard the sheep and not the house, and so it shows the wolf the way to the larder. The result is that the wolf is discovered and beaten up terribly. The moral is:

> We learn here about the miserly master
> Who dislikes supplying the members of his household
> With the food to which they are rightly entitled
> And himself suffers loss as a result.
> The wolf shows us that it is harmful and not at all good
> When someone is not satisfied
> With what God grants him.
> From this we learn
> That in good times
> Stupid, impudent, crude people
> Refresh themselves with food and drink,
> Live entirely without fear of the Lord
> And ignore good advice.[13]

PRESENT-DAY IMAGE

It is not only in fables that human fears, needs, and political ideas have been projected onto the wolf, who has not always been an object of hostility. Indeed such hostility seems to have been the exception rather than the rule. In many refuge areas such as the Alps, the

Carpathians, or the Bavarian Forest he was for a long time a competitor only of the sportsman. The deep winter snow made it impossible to keep domestic animals in the open for many months of the year, and the wolf retreated or fed on wild game as long as there was any. But in areas where domestic animals grazed in the open throughout the year, particularly where farms were small and domestic animals few, the situation was worse. Damage caused by wolves could threaten the livelihood of whole families. The worst places for coexistence with wolves must have been those where the keeping of domestic animals was the only source of livelihood, as it was with the Laplanders in Scandinavia with their reindeer. There wolves were a threat to human survival. Not only did they kill reindeer but, even worse, they continually scattered the half-tame herds that were kept together only with difficulty, and collecting them again meant days or weeks of hard work and the additional loss of many animals. Hatred of this enemy must have been as intense as the campaign mounted against it.

In spite of such local differences, a very uniform idea of the wolf has survived throughout the European cultural area to the present day; it is exemplified in Hobbes's phrase *"homo homini lupus"* ("man is a wolf to man") and in a large number of other proverbs, allegories, book and film titles, in which the wolf is used as a graphic symbol of evil. The evil wolf appears in fairy tales such as Little Red Riding Hood and Snow White. The idea of the evil wolf is very much alive even in countries where there have been no wolves for centuries. A few years ago I gave some lectures in Sweden about the possibility of reintroducing the wolf. One evening after such a lecture I switched on the television, and a talk show was being broadcast. In spite of the lateness of the hour, the guest was a little girl of about five. The show master asked her what she was afraid of, and she quite spontaneously answered: "Wolves and evil spirits in the wood."

She had adapted from her parents an attitude nearly all European children learn and later pass on to their children—fear of the wolf and the big, mysterious forest. I actually know foresters who dislike going alone into the woods at night, because they are afraid of what are now the safest places to be found in Europe.

Ancient fears inherited from our remote ancestors survive, in this totally irrational attitude to an animal species and its living space.

Fig. 44. Little Red Riding Hood.

Fears of being the hunted, not the hunter, the prey, not the predator, fears that were perhaps appropriate to the real dangers faced by *Homo erectus* or Neanderthal man, and perhaps also by the men of the Stone Age, but are insignificant in comparison with the dangers of contemporary civilized life. More people probably die every day in road accidents than have been killed by wolves during the past few thousand years. Yet it is the wolf, not the automobile, that we are afraid of. Nothing shows more plainly how hopelessly our biological evolution lags behind the development of civilization.

But these atavistic fears and the mythological transformation of the wolf into an approximation of the devil are not our only reaction to it. In Jack London's work, for instance, or Rudyard Kipling's children's books, the wolf is the king of the forest, not a symbol of evil, the opposite of the usual myth.

The nineteenth century was an age of great technical discoveries and of tremendous development of the capitalist system. In the middle of the century Darwin revolutionized the foundations of biology and the ideas of human origin connected with them. The modern theory of evolution with its basic proposition expressed in the phrase "survival of the fittest" (wrongly translated into German as "survival of the strongest") was extended to the social and economic activities of human societies. "Social Darwinism" was an attempt to justify the appalling poverty of the exploited masses and the great injustices of early capitalist conditions by the struggle for survival; the victory of the better and stronger over the weaker was claimed to be the sole guarantee of continued improvement in human conditions. Jack London called himself a socialist (and perhaps he was one), but in his books he adapted himself to the heroic spirit of the age. The wolf was transformed from criminal predator to ruler whose strength guaranteed the downfall of the weaker who were its prey.

This changed image of the wolf also motivated the breeding of a dog that looked like a wolf. Crossing and careful breeding at the end of the nineteenth century resulted in the Alsatian, or German shepherd dog. This is not, as is so often assumed, an ancient breed closely related to the wolf, but a breed of very recent date. The breeders were actually guided more by their own image of the wolf than by its real appearance. Thus the Alsatian was developed into a broad-chested, bulky creature with relatively short legs, in contrast

306

to the slim, long-legged wolf. Many Alsatian owners have similarly incorrect ideas about wolf behavior. Many want an especially "sharp, spirited" dog that will accept only one master, to whom it will subject itself completely. The result is that the familiar problems with the Alsatian—no breed bites the wrong person so frequently and so hard—are programmed into it, both by breeding and by training and attitude. If breeders' expectations are not realized, many of them believe they will be able to make it still "sharper" and more spirited by crossing it with a wolf. This is wrong. The results are precisely the opposite of what they are intended to be—that is, the animals are nervous, some say cowardly, and unteachable, but they are independent, meaning they have a weaker bond to human beings.

How completely deceptive this image of the wolf's "loyalty" and its alleged "social monogamy" is is shown by Konrad Lorenz's theory about the origin of the dog. As we know, he distinguished between "*aureus* dogs" and "wolf dogs." He suggested that breeds that tended to be friendly to everyone were descended from the jackal (*Canis aureus*), while those that accepted only one master were descended from the wolf (*Canis lupus*).[14] Thus, even a scientist as eminent as Lorenz was mislead by this heroic image of the wolf.

This false idea of the wolf received its ultimate perversion in Fascism. The wolf became the very symbol of authoritarian leadership. Hitler had two dogs, Alsatians, of course, with whom he liked to be photographed and filmed in order to demonstrate his love of animals, and no doubt also his love of humanity. As I've mentioned, his headquarters in East Prussia was called the Wolf's Lair, and the U-boat squadrons he sent to hunt down allied ships were known as wolf packs. The wolf was chosen to symbolize strength, not so much superior physical strength as *esprit de corps* and unconditional subjection to the elitist will of the top wolf, the leader of the pack, for the alleged benefit of all.

Thus at the present time there are two contemporary images of the wolf, the atavistic and the Fascist. In our culture no other animal simultaneously arouses fear and terror on the one hand and fascination and admiration on the other. No animal is so unselfishly loved as the domesticated wolf, the dog, and none is so mercilessly hunted down as the real wolf.

Hunting alone has affected the wolf's numbers only locally and temporarily. It has led to its extinction only where there is large-scale human interference with the structure of the landscape and the game populations on which it preys. This is plainly illustrated by the history of its extinction in the British Isles. [15]

In England and Scotland the systematic hunting of wolves began in Celtic times and was continued by the Anglo-Saxons, though without great success. It was easy for the wolf to take refuge in the big forests and broad moors that still covered the British Isles. In the Middle Ages hunting was stepped up, as is shown by many historical accounts, as well as by new laws and regulations. Nevertheless, the wolf became a pest, and fear of it was great. Information about how wolves lived at the time can be gleaned from old maps of hunting grounds. Wolf howls, howl moors, wolf pits, or wolf dales presumably described areas or places to which wolves were known to withdraw. These refuge areas were sometimes not far from the nearest village, as they still are in the Abruzzi. England at the time was covered with dense vegetation, ravines, and marshes, which hampered access to these refuge areas.

The wolf was hunted in various ways. Poison must still have been used only rarely, and steel traps were presumably seldom used because of the expense. Wolf hunters seem to have known that it was difficult to trap wolves with meat—a fact that we discovered for ourselves several centuries later. Also "wolf hooks" do not seem to have been very successful, though their use was widespread. These were devices similar to meat hooks; bait was hung on them and they were suspended from a tree about six feet above the ground. The wolf jumped to get at the meat and was supposed to be caught like a fish on a fish hook (see figure 45). Wolf pits and a variety of devices for trapping wolves alive, in which living animals were often used as bait, seem to have been more successful. Hunts with beaters were arranged in which various breeds of big wolf-hunting dogs such as the Irish wolfhound were employed. The nobility hunted the wolf *par force*, on horseback with a pack of hounds, like fox hunters of the present. This was regarded as the feudal manly sport *par excellence*, the supreme form of hunting, so much so that in spite of

Fig. 45. The "wolf hook."

all the trouble wolves caused, the common people were forbidden
to hunt them in the forest. They were allowed only to act as beaters.
Perhaps that contributed to the wolf's surviving for so long.

The decline of the wolf began only with the clearing of the forests
that followed rapid population growth. By the end of the Middle
Ages most of England had been brought under cultivation, and the
wolf, deprived of its refuge areas, was in a serious plight. Finally, a
closed season for hunting the wolf—as game reserved for the nobility—was proclaimed, but it was too late; popular hatred was too
great for it to be able to survive for the sporting entertainment of the
feudal class. By the beginning of the sixteenth century it was extinct
in England.

In Scotland, where sheep and cattle were so important, wolves
became an even greater pest with the progressive disappearance of
game. Under James I wolf hunts were ordered by law; these were
carried out at the cub-rearing time in early summer. In Mary
Stuart's time the situation became so serious that in some places the
dead were no longer buried in churchyards for fear they might be
dug up and eaten by wolves; instead they were buried on islands in
the sea, or so it is reported. Some years later, under James IV, all
men of military age were legally obliged to take part in wolf hunts
three times a year. The necessity of perpetually guarding domestic
animals was felt to be especially irksome, and it was only after the
disappearance of the wolf that the typically Scottish method of free

309

Fig. 46. Death of a hated competitor.

grazing by day and night was adopted. In comparison to traditional labor-intensive methods of grazing in areas where wolves survive, such as in the Abruzzi, this was certainly a great relief.

As in England, hunting alone failed to exterminate the wolf in Scotland. Forests had to be cleared before it grew rarer in the middle of the seventeenth century. The last wolf was not killed till a century later, apparently in 1743.

The extensive mountainous regions of Scotland that were cleared of trees are today being reforested at great expense, and several species that were exterminated, such as the capercaillie, have returned. After the grim experiences the Scots had with wolves, they can hardly be expected to agree to having them back. In England a certain Colonel Thirton of Thornville Royal—an enthusiastic follower of hounds for whom fox hunting was obviously not exciting enough—suggested in 1800 that wolves should be bred and released for hunting purposes, but the indignation of his farming neighbors caused the idea to be nipped in the bud.

On the European continent the extermination of the wolf took a rather different course. At the beginning of the eighteenth century only the intensively farmed plain along the North Sea coast was free of wolves. In Denmark, for instance, the last wolf was killed in 1772.[16] Elsewhere in Europe there were still big forests and inaccessible mountainous areas in which the wolf could take refuge. The way in which the extermination of the wolf came about in spite of that is well illustrated by the example of Sweden.

At present, Sweden is still 55 percent wooded, and lakes, mountains, and uncultivated land constitute another large part of it. Only 9 percent of the country is farmed. Thus there was plenty of cover for the wolf right down into southern Sweden. Its chief prey was the elk, which competed for pasture with many domestic animals and was also hunted for the sake of its meat. By the beginning of the nineteenth century there were only a few survivors in the north. So the wolf had no alternative but to kill domestic animals.

Intensive hunting of the wolf set in. There are accounts of hunts in which more than a thousand men took part. In every village there was a chief beater who called the men out and led hunts that sometimes lasted for days or weeks. At least one man from every farm had to take part, and every farm was put under an obligation to keep nets and other equipment. The wolves, intimidated by long lines of beaters, were driven into the nets and then shot, stabbed, or simply beaten to death.[17]

In the thinly settled north of Sweden another method was employed, particularly by the Laplanders, whose day-long pursuit on skis on the open fjeld wore wolves down to such an extent that they came within range and could be shot or stabbed with ski sticks specially made for the purpose. This way of hunting was carried out on deep newly fallen snow; the hunters took turns on specially made broad skis. Wolves were also caught in traps that were often kept by generations on the same farm. Also in different areas traps of various shapes and sizes were used in which living bait was used. Steel traps and hides were used, and finally poisoned bait was put out. Strychnine and arsenic were used, as well as homemade poisons derived from various plants. Apart from state bounties, which sometimes reached considerable amounts, the successful hunter could keep the skin, which was highly valued as material for coats.

Another method of driving the wolf away was for a large number of men, women, and children to make their way through the areas in which domestic animals grazed, making a tremendous din. This was done in the spring, when the cattle were driven out, and was sometimes repeated in the course of the summer if wolves were still in the neighborhood. This acoustic method of driving wolves away was said to have been very successful. But the wolves had to live on something, and quite frequently this was its neighbors' sheep.

But in winter domestic animals were kept securely indoors and, as the numbers of natural prey animals had been greatly reduced, the wolves suffered from acute food shortage. This, combined with the enormous pressure put upon them by hunting, resulted in a drastic reduction in their numbers within a few years. Between 1827 and 1839 about 500 wolves a year were killed in Sweden (see figure 47), but twenty years later, in 1860, the figure was only 100. A similar drastic reduction in the wolf population took place in Norway and Finland between ten and twenty years later. In 1860 there were no more wolves in the southern provinces of Skåne and Blekinge. Thirty years later they had disappeared from all the provinces of central Sweden, and after another twenty years the wolf was restricted to his last refuge areas in the wide, treeless, mountainous areas of the northwest.[18] The wolf, originally a forest animal, found security in these almost uninhabited and inaccessible regions and, thanks to the reindeer, plenty of food. But the Laplanders' campaign against him continued.

There are innumerable stories about the almost superhuman efforts of the most celebrated wolf hunters who kept on the wolves' heels by day and night. When the open fjeld was finally made accessible by new roads, aircraft, and above all the snowmobile with its ecologically devastating effects, the days of the wolf were numbered.

The Swedish nature conservation office headed by Bertil Haglund conducted an inquiry into the distribution and numbers of the four big predators, the wolf, the lynx, the wolverine, and the bear, between 1960 and 1964. They found that the wolf was gravely endangered. The few survivors traveled great distances, no doubt an adaptation to the perpetual hunting. The result of the inquiry was a public debate on whether the wolf should be protected. Surprisingly enough, many Laplanders came out on the wolf's side. In spite of their traditional hostility to the wolf, they must have felt respect and admiration for it. Per Blind, the best-known hunter of the last wolves in Lapland, joined with biologists and the Swedish associa-

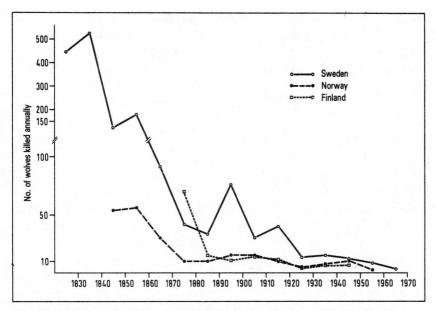

Fig. 47. Number of wolves shot annually in the Nordic countries. (From Haglund, 1975.)

tion for the conservation of nature in advocating protection for it, for the time being without success.[19]

At the end of January 1965 what was claimed to be the trail of a wolf was found near Östersund in central Sweden, and the result was a popular rising against the wolf. No wolves had been seen in the area for years, but the news caused hundreds of armed men to set out on the predator's trail, together with a large escort of police and journalists, some equipped with helicopters. This way of hunting the wolf was of course futile, and it was not even certain that the trail was that of a wolf, but the incident illustrated an attitude that still survived. On this occasion it was chiefly sportsmen who issued the call to the chase. Swedish sportsmen have a special attitude toward the elk, which can be appreciated only by those who have been present at the time of the traditional elk hunt in the autumn. The elk has fully recovered from its former severe population reduction and is now distributed all over Sweden in unprecedented numbers. Swedish forestry, which offers it the best possible grazing con-

313

ditions because of the big clearing operations that take place, has presumably made a big contribution to this. The creature does considerable damage to the forestry industry and to human beings by colliding with cars. Every year about 70,000 are shot in Sweden, but its numbers continue to increase, and in many areas there is talk of a plague of elk. Nevertheless, the thought of a possible competitor, and even the trail of a suspected wolf, rouses emotions in many sportsmen the irrationality of which would be comic if these people were not equipped with deadly weapons.

Perhaps shame at this mass hysteria contributed a few months later, in the summer of 1965, to the wolf's being put under complete protection throughout Sweden. But it was too late to save it. In 1968 Haglund estimated that six animals remained, and a few years later it was thought that there might possibly be one. As the wolf had in the meantime also disappeared from Norway, its extinction seemed to have been completed. One last wolf was said to have survived south of the reindeer area in the frontier zone with Norway—both symbol and accusing finger pointed at man's claim to monopoly.

It was therefore all the more pleasing when news came in 1976 of a wolf pack on the Norwegian side of this central Scandinavian wilderness. Colleagues there had kept the discovery quiet for a long time for fear of "popular indignation." Had that single wolf succeeded in finding a partner somewhere and rearing cubs? Or had it mated with a dog? The big Pomeranian breeds that are native to the area are very similar to wolves, and wolf-Pomeranian hybrids are difficult to distinguish from real wolves, at any rate from a distance; it is to be hoped that this is not the case.

Meanwhile there has been news from Norway. Svein Myrberget reported that in the winter of 1977–1978 there were perhaps from six to twelve wolves in Hedmark, in the central part of the country. The animals were very shy and cautious and were said to run chiefly alone. More information was not available, and it is not even certain that they were pure wolves.[20]

Wolves certainly penetrated into north Sweden again during that winter. Presumably they came by way of Finland from Russia, where the wolf population has apparently increased again in recent years. A wolf was shot with the approval of the nature conservation authorities soon after Christmas 1977 in a wintering area for rein-

314

deer; it had caused considerable damage in the course of a few weeks, and therefore its death was deemed necessary. Perhaps as a consequence of the authorities' understanding attitude to their needs, the Laplanders seemed to be tolerating another group of three wolves further to the west, in the area of the Padjelanta and Stora Sjöfallet national parks, that were living chiefly on elk and reindeer that had remained behind. Anders Bjärvall, who was studying the numbers and distribution of predators in Sweden and was in contact with the Laplanders, believed that other wolves were in the neighborhood that winter, and he regarded it as possible that breeding had taken place. Tracks in the snow indicated the possibility, and that will be good news if it turns out to be correct. But as long as there are wolves in reindeer areas, there are bound to be conflicts with the interests of the Laplanders, and a revival of the wolf in this region therefore seems unlikely. Nevertheless, the increasingly understanding and tolerant attitude of the Laplanders toward their hereditary enemy gives some reason for hope.[21]

CENTRAL EUROPE

As in Scandinavia, the extinction of the wolf in Central Europe seems to have been brought about by food shortages combined with vigorous hunting of the last surviving animals. At the beginning of the nineteenth century the red deer had practically disappeared and the roe had become very scarce. The last deer in the Bavarian Forest was killed in 1809, before the disappearance of the wolf, the lynx, and the bear. The big herbivores competed with domestic animals, and that was reason enough for getting rid of them. As a result of intensive hunting the wolf was forced back into the wooded and climatically more severe highlands and the Alps. Here livestock was kept indoors in winter and sent out to pasture only in summer. Food shortage forced the wolves into more populated areas, where again they were vigorously hunted. In 1847, that is, about forty years after the last deer, the last wolf was shot in the Bavarian Forest, and it disappeared from the northern Alps at about the same time. In the western highlands as well as in the southern Alps it survived for a few more decades. Bounties for shooting twenty-six wolves were paid out in the Koblenz district on the left bank of the Rhine as late as 1871. The last wolf in the Eifel was shot in 1888 and its counterpart in the Saar as late as 1891. By the turn of the century it had also disappeared from the southern Alps. [22]

The fact that the wolf survived longer in those areas presumably was connected with the milder climate. Domestic animals were taken out to graze much longer, and in some areas grazing continued throughout the winter when there was no snow. Thus it was easier for the wolves to survive the winter bottleneck. This no doubt also explains why the extermination of the wolf in France occurred much later. The last wolves in Alsace were killed only in the winter of 1910–1911, and they actually survived in the Massif Central in southern France until World War II. Reports of wolves kept cropping up even after the war, but these animals may have been Alsatians that had run wild after being left behind by the Germans.

The wolf has also vanished from large parts of North America. With the exception of a substantial wolf population in north Minnesota and on Isle Royale, it is practically extinct in the forty-eight states. In Alaska, however, it is to be found almost everywhere, though in some areas in very small numbers, and it is said still to be present in practically 90 percent of its original distribution area in Canada. It has disappeared only in parts of the border areas with the United States in the south, in Labrador in the east, as well as in the prairie region in the west. Finally there are small pockets of survivors in Mexico. [23]

In North America, unlike Europe, the retreat and large-scale extermination of the wolf were undoubtedly chiefly due to the direct efforts made to destroy it. To European immigrants and Americans in their westward advance, the wolf was as great a threat as the Indian. The expulsion and ultimate extinction of both were pursued with equal vigor and brutality, though by different means. The wolves, unlike the Indians, had little opportunity to defend themselves. They lacked the experience of evading human persecution acquired by their European counterparts. Hundreds of thousands walked into the white man's traps or swallowed his poisoned bait. This inexperience was perhaps one of the reasons for their relatively rapid extinction. By the end of the nineteenth century they had disappeared east of the Mississippi, and after the introduction of organized methods of combating them their numbers fell rapidly in the west also. A large proportion of the celebrated buffalo wolves

316

were killed in only twenty years, from 1850 to 1870, and sixty years later they had been wiped out.

Surely no animal species has ever been so vigorously hunted down as the wolf was in North America. In the early stages of British colonial rule bounties were paid for dead wolves. The bounty system was expanded in the centuries that followed, and money was often paid out by several official agencies for the same dead wolf. The rules and regulations were frequently changed, and the sums paid out were raised or lowered according to need. The amounts paid were enormous; they have been estimated at more than $100 million in the United States alone. No wonder innumerable adventurers tried their luck as "wolfers," or professional wolf hunters.

Every conceivable method was used, but the most devastating was poison. A wolfer on the prairie would shoot a few bison or pronghorned antelope and strew strychnine on the still-warm bodies, and the next morning he could be sure of finding dead wolves frozen stiff (as many as sixty at a time, or so it has been claimed) along his poison trail. A large part of the profit would be spent on "Indian whisky," but some of these adventurers grew rich on the proceeds. Apart from earning the bounty, they could sell the skins, which at first had had little value, but by the end of the nineteenth century, after the extermination of the beaver, fetched good prices.

Many of the stories told by Young in his book on North American wolves should be taken with a grain of salt, like many other Wild West stories, but there is no doubt that in the past hundred years more strychnine has been used in North America than anywhere else. The wolf was accordingly eliminated with great rapidity, and not only the wolf. The red fox, the prairie fox, the coyote, the skunk, and a great many birds also swallowed the poisoned bait, and, like the huge herds of bison that were indiscriminately shot and the innumerable prong-horned antelope and pigeons, were reduced to small pockets of survivors or were wiped out for good. It is not surprising that the Indians hated the wolfers, and many of them paid with their scalp, for the ecological and cultural madness of the new Americans.

But not all wolves swallowed the poison. A few experienced wolves survived and, deprived to a large extent of their natural prey, turned their attention to the new animals on the prairie, sheep and

317

cattle. Cattle breeders offered enormous sums for some of the last surviving buffalo wolves. A large number both of private hunters and hunters employed by the state were permanently on the heels of animals known by such nicknames as Three Toes of the Devil, Old Guy Jumbo, Old Doctor, Black Devil, the Traveler, Old Whisky, or Custer Wolf. No less than $500 was offered for the head of the last-named animal. They were too clever to swallow poisoned bait or to be caught in any ordinary trap. After making a kill they often traveled fifty miles or more before returning to the same neighborhood months later. But, like the last free Indians, they finally succumbed to the overwhelming superiority of the country's new masters. No free-living buffalo wolf (*Canis lupus nubilus*), which once shared the wide prairie with the bison, the prong-horned antelope, and the Indian, survives.

The European immigrants' disturbed relationship to everything in the new continent that stood in the way of their ruthless exploitation is illustrated by an example from Australia, where there are no wolves, but dingoes. These dogs, which presumably came to Australia from the mainland of Asia with the original inhabitants and then ran wild, were a thorn in the side of the sheep rearers, and great efforts were made to exterminate them. This failed, however, presumably because the dingoes, who are rather smaller than wolves, can live very well on other prey, including the rabbit, which had been introduced into Australia. To protect the sheep rearers, a number of dingo fences were erected across Australia, one of which is more than 5,000 miles long.[24]

Imagine the trouble and expense of building such a fence over mountains, ravines, and steppes empty of human beings. Recent investigations have shown that there are dingoes on both sides of the fence, and also that they cause much less damage to sheep than the sheep rearers suppose. Nevertheless, the fence is kept in repair, a gigantic monument to human irrationality toward a supposed competitor for food. In the past twenty years the attitude of many North Americans to their environment, and to the wolf, has changed. They are slowly becoming aware of all that they have lost as a result of uninhibited exploitation, and the desire to preserve their last great areas of undisturbed nature is strong. In Minnesota, Alaska, and most of the provinces of Canada closed seasons have been introduced, the use of strychnine and hunting from aircraft has been prohibited in many areas, though unfortunately not in all, and, in spite of opposition from old wolf hunters, the bounty system has been abolished in a number of places. In some parts of his former territory the wolf still has a chance.

ASIA

Finally, it is in Asia that the wolf seems to have done best so far. In many places previous population densities no longer exist, but to a large extent its distribution has been maintained. It has disappeared only from the Arabian peninsula and Japan. Apart from that, its distribution area stretches from Turkey, Syria, and even Israel in the west by way of Iran, Afghanistan, Pakistan, India, and Tibet to north China, Korea, Mongolia, and Manchuria in the east. In Siberia it is to be found up to 75 degrees north, and its distribution coincides with that of the reindeer. Desert and tropical rain forests provide an effective barrier to its expansion southward.[25]

But what has been happening to the wolf in Asia suggests that it may meet the same fate it did in North America and Europe. In the People's Republic of China, for instance, total extermination is the goal,[26] and it is likely that in the next few decades the wolf will be forced back into a few relatively inaccessible areas.

Political Problem

On the strength of what has been said so far it might be concluded that the future of the wolf in Europe depended on the outcome of the conflict of interest between farmer and wolf or sportsman and wolf. But that would be a superficial view. The problem is more complicated. The survival of the wolf, as of many other animals and plants, depends on the future of land use. This makes it an economic and political problem.

PRESENT DISTRIBUTION

The wolf has hitherto survived in Europe only where it has found: (1) refuge areas of adequate size in the form of extensive forest or wooded mountains; and (2) sufficient food throughout the year in the form of wild or domesticated animals. These conditions now

319

exist only in eastern and southern Europe. But there too wolf populations have been rapidly dwindling in recent years.

Perhaps as the result of a brief recovery after World War II, wolves from eastern Europe have made their way into Central Europe from time to time. Five wolves are said to have made their way into Lower Saxony alone and to have been killed there. It has often been assumed that they followed a traditional westerly migratory route, but that is of course nonsense. They made their way through areas that are heavily wooded and relatively unpopulated. The same thing can be observed in the southeastern Alps, where wolves sometimes come presumably from areas in Yugoslavia.

Bigger wolf populations exist today only in the Soviet Union, Rumania, Yugoslavia, and presumably also Greece (see appendix, table 19). The history of their extermination in other countries tells us that if conditions become unfavorable for them, if they have lost refuge areas or prey has disappeared, vigorous action against them

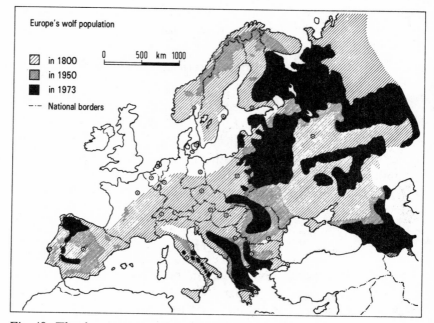

Fig. 48. The drastic retreat of the wolf in the past 150 years.

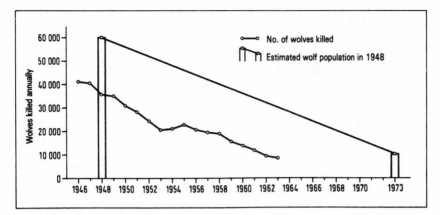

Fig. 49. The number of wolves killed in Russia since World War II. (From Fengewisch, 1968.)

can result in a huge reduction in their numbers. Their future therefore is not assured in these countries either. With the exception of some of the constituent republics of Yugoslavia, they have no legal protection in these countries. On the contrary, official measures, such as the payment of bounties for shooting wolves and the employment of professional hunters, are used to bring about their extinction. As in many areas the bounty far exceeds a worker's monthly pay, the incentive to hunt wolves is great.

Since the denunciation by conservationists of the trade in leopard skins and the change in fashion that favors the skins of long-haired animals, a substantial export trade in wolf skins has developed. Anyone who now wears wolf skin, or sells or deals in it, should be aware that he or she is contributing to the savage reduction and possible extermination of the species. The same applies to the skin of many other free-living animals, such as the lynx, which has also become very popular. If purchasers had any idea of the ordeal of the animals, which are sometimes left in traps for weeks, or of the conditions in many fur farms, I believe many would refrain from buying.

The figures for shootings in Russia, where the biggest European wolf populations still live, point to a drastic reduction in their numbers (see figure 49). Since the end of World War II they have been reduced by about 80 percent. Hunting is still sometimes done from aircraft, though it has been found that elimination of the wolf has unfavorable consequences on the health of reindeer herds.[27] The aim of the authorities is to exterminate the wolf except in a few protected areas. That makes all the more surprising recent reports pointing to a notable recovery in the population in spite of intensive hunting. The wolf is stated to have attained a density and distribution similar to that after World War II.[28]

We know little about the situation in Rumania, Yugoslavia, or Greece, but the yearly figures of shootings indicate that the populations there are still relatively high.

In all other European countries in which wolves survive, the age of large-scale hunting down and drastic decline in numbers is over. But there is every prospect that the survivors will disappear in the next few years unless there is a radical change in government attitudes, for in few of these countries have protective measures been taken. In Norway and Sweden wolves are protected all year round, but in reality they are already extinct. They are similarly protected in southern Finland outside the reindeer areas, but they are still hunted. About twenty wolves were killed in Finland alone in a recent winter. Meanwhile Erkki Pulliainen has estimated the number of wolves that have crossed the frontier from Russia—the last litter in Finland was recorded in 1963—at about eighty. That is a notable increase from the last estimate of fifteen animals in 1973 and is certainly a consequence of the increasing number of wolves in Russia.[29] In Poland, where they also survive only along the Russian frontier, regulations governing the hunting of wolves were introduced in 1975, though these were totally inadequate. In other east European countries they are unprotected. Bounties are still paid for shooting them, despite the minimal populations that survive in protected areas such, for instance, as the High Tatra National Park in Czechoslovakia. In south European countries the survivors are gravely endangered, as we know, but there at least there is some prospect of a change in attitude to them.

VALUE OF THE WOLF

Thanks to the still relatively wide distribution of large populations in North America and Asia, the wolf as a species is not yet directly endangered, though many local populations are under strong pressure. I therefore propose to discuss what we must do to stop its further retreat or, where it seems reasonable, to reintroduce it where it has been wiped out. But that question cannot be answered until we have considered why we should preserve the wolf and what value it has for us.

Now, it is indicative of our relationship to nature that to justify the right to life of species other than our own we always ask what its value to us is. It is as if every species of animal and plant did not inherently possess the right to life. Is our anthropocentric outlook not partly responsible for the looming environmental catastrophe? Nevertheless, an outlook that does not take human interests into account does not help us either. The life of all living things is now to a large extent in man's hands, and we must so arrange things in this world that these living things benefit us. This means all of us, and not only privileged groups who continue to exploit nature in their own interests.

Achieving this is not only politically necessary, but is ecologically an extremely difficult task. We know far too little about the complex interactions of ecological systems to be able to manipulate them successfully. Interference with those systems for the supposed benefit of humanity has only too often had unforeseen negative consequences that turned out to be irreversible. Once upon a time, combating the wolf was an economic necessity, but we now see the ecological and economic consequences to silviculture as a result of its extinction. We also now know that the wolf is a vital part of natural living communities on whose structure and stability it has great influence. If we preserve the wolf we also preserve our last relatively natural biotopes and natural populations of ungulates. Study of reciprocal relationships in these natural ecosystems is essential to an understanding of the ecological links in our own generally very disturbed environment.

The wolf as part of natural living communities also has an esthetic value and a value to the sportsman. The opportunity of observing wolves living in freedom, or at least being able to hear them from a distance, would certainly be a great experience to many; and the wolf would also have a value as game. That statement may seem surprising, but we must recognize that in many areas hunting wolves will not just have to be tolerated, but in certain circumstances may actually be essential.

There are also more subtle arguments, I believe, for the preservation of the wolf. Our environment has a vital influence on our emotional world and our behavior. That has become plain to us only in recent years as a result of the large-scale destruction of living space both in urban areas with great concentrations of population and country areas damaged by the reallocation of land. As a consequence the call for more "nature" in our environment has become more persistent and vehement, and that amounts to a call for a better quality of life. We are becoming aware that we grew up in an environment in which our parents and grandparents lived and in which our children will have to live too. The environment has historical dimensions and is a part of our identity.

Let me give an example. As part of the reallocation program the approach road to our house at Waldhäuser was recently rebuilt. It was once a part of the Guldene Steig, the trade route into Bohemia. Waldhäuser actually owes its existence to this bumpy thoroughfare that threaded its way between high stone walls and cherry trees. It was certainly not suitable for modern traffic, or even as a mere access road to our house. (A modern motor road to Waldhäuser had long since been built.) But was it necessary for that reason to destroy road, walls, trees, the whole of the charming surroundings, with big bulldozers in order to build a "modern" asphalt track across the fields? Not only nesting places and sources of food for birds were destroyed, but also part of a very beautiful cultural landscape. I did not grow up in this area and shall not stay here forever, but I cannot help feeling sympathy for the people of Waldhäuser, who have so thoughtlessly wrecked a part of their environment. But what I feel to be positively disgraceful is that the very same people who decided to destroy this cultural and historical monument in spite of our protests also decided in the course of giving names to the village streets—they want to be urban and modern, after all—to call the new asphalt horror the Guldensteig.

A minor episode in an everyday process, to be sure, but typical of our present behavior toward our environment. We have perfected it from the technical point of view of water supply and facilitating traffic, and degraded it in other respects in order to maximize the production of food and raw materials. Even in exploiting it for rest and recreation we are really dominated by purely utilitarian motives. We forget only too easily that our environment not only has to feed us but is also the living space of many seemingly useless animals and plants, just as it is for us; we forget that it developed historically and that its functions make up an indivisible whole. This dimension is certainly not maintained by borrowing a historical name from structures that have already been destroyed. Konrad Lorenz once spoke of the "education in harmony" that we undergo in experiencing our natural environment,[30] and proved himself once again to be a pioneer in discovering a field neglected by the modern psychology of development and education.

Combating the wolf was once necessary to human survival, but with its extinction part of our historical heritage is lost, just as it would be if we demolished Stockholm's town hall or Cologne Cathedral or the Old City of Bologna. The important thing is not whether we have ever caught a glimpse of a wolf living in a state of freedom, for Cologne Cathedral has a significance for us even if we have never seen it. What matters is not that the wolf should be preserved in a zoo like a museum specimen. What is essential is the preservation of the part of our environment not completely transformed by man. The wolf is only a part of this and it is not for the wolf's sake, or for the sake of any abstract idea, but for ourselves and for future generations that we must preserve them. Without such regenerative areas we should be ecologically and culturally crippled.

DANGEROUSNESS OF THE WOLF

The wolf as part of our traditional environment continues to be persecuted, not only because of thoughtlessness but as part of a framework of specific interests. These interests are frequently camouflaged by new or rehashed stories about the wolf as man-eater which seem to confirm the still prevalent image of the "bad" wolf. Obviously selfish interests are thus made to seem to be for the benefit of us all. Nowadays it is principally the press and books by the sporting community, whether in Germany, Sweden, North America, or Italy, that tell us how dangerous wolves are.

Thus the so-called monster of Gévaudan, about whom several books have been written, keeps being warmed up and served all over again. Then there is the old story of the "wolf years of 1880 and 1881" in Finland, when wolves are alleged to have killed twenty-two children between the ages of two and nine in the thickly popu-

Fig. 50. The celebrated wolf of Gévaudan.

lated area around Åbo.[31] It is very difficult in retrospect to discover the facts because there has been a great deal of embellishment. On November 14, 1880, for instance, a wolf is said to have seized the eight-year-old son of the tailor D. Hornberg at one o'clock in the afternoon on the family farm near Nykyrko and to have carried the boy in his mouth to the woods, where he ate him. We are not told how heavy the boy was, but either he was very thin or the wolf was of gigantic size if it was able to carry such a weight in its mouth for a long distance.

There is no lack of such incredible stories. A celebrated German hunting writer, for instance, describes quite seriously an incident said to have happened in central Sweden in 1727. A minister named Petrus Petri Schissler heard the howling of wolves from a wolf pit he had dug. (Just imagine trapped wolves "making their dreadful lonely voices heard," as it says in the book.) In trying to kill one of the six wolves that ferociously bared their teeth at him, he fell into the pit himself, but miraculously the wolves did not tear him to pieces but used his back to climb out of the pit and escape.[32]

Many stories keep cropping up in different areas in similar form. There is the story of the soldier, postman, or solitary individual who is attacked by wolves on a cold winter night. He defends himself with his sword and succeeds in killing or wounding several of them. The rest withdraw and the man puts his sword back in the sheath. But that is a mistake, because the wolves attack again, and this time the bloodstained sword is frozen in the sheath, with the result that only a few remnants of the man are left, as well as the sword, of course, as "evidence" of the tragic event.

There is a striking resemblance in stories coming from many areas. The Russian version—the troika pursued by wolves on a winter night—has been repeated a thousand times. Its North American counterpart has the hero alone with his dog at a campfire, and he has to defend himself against attacking wolves by swinging his cudgel. All these stories happen on a winter night and in all of them the ammunition runs out, but the hero's courage, resourcefulness, and strength enable him to win against all odds.

In the course of my work with wolves I have heard or read a large number of such stories, told by aged sportsmen in the Carpathians or German ex-service men who fought in Russia. Many of them have exactly the same plot and can thus be dismissed as unimaginative reproductions of the standard repertoire of aggressive tactics attributed to the wolf. Others, though sometimes more imaginative, are so full of phony details about wolf behavior that they are incredible. Wolves are smoked out of their dens in the middle of winter, for instance, or howl while hunting their human prey (they in fact hunt in silence), they bare their teeth while attacking (as if they were attacking a social partner and not prey), they howl in a wolf pit or possess "super-wolfish" strength (as in the story of the boy in Finland). In the great majority of these stories there is a complete lack of critical questioning. If a dead child is found, it must have been killed by wolves. The much greater probability that dogs were responsible is not even considered. If the mangled remains of a man are found somewhere in the wilds, he must obviously have been attacked by a wolf. That he might perhaps have died of heart failure and that much later the remains were nibbled by bears, foxes, or even by wolves—a much more likely eventuality—is overlooked in the general excitement.

I have had several opportunities to see how such rumors arise. There was the eight-week-old Anfa who was turned into an evil Siberian monster, and the boy with a scratch on his bottom in the Bavarian Forest who made the headlines as a child lacerated by a wolf. Once I had the opportunity to follow up one of the news stories that regularly recur every winter, of the type "Wolves Attack Village" or "Bitter Cold Drives Wolves down from the Mountains." In September 1975 I read a story at Waldhäuser about a pack of fifty wolves who were said to be besieging a village in the Abruzzi. A few days later I went to the Abruzzi, and Luigi and I found out what had happened. The German Press Agency message from Rome was based on a long article in *Il Messaggero d'Abruzzo* about one of the usual conflicts between capitalists and conservationists in a village in the Gran Sasso area. Some of the villagers wanted a new skiing resort to be established there, and the World Wildlife Fund opposed this. The article incidentally mentioned that those who favored the project were critical of the WWF commitment to wolves. They had suffered considerable damage from wolves that year (for the first time in a long time) and now had to make extra efforts to guard their livestock. One villager expressed the exaggerated view that there must be at least fifty wolves in the neighborhood and that children were no longer safe.

This single statement among many in an article on a completely different subject was picked up by a journalist sitting at a desk in Rome, and a few hours later a news item about fifty wolves was distributed to German newspapers by way of the German Press Agency teleprinter and was printed as it stood. Editing newspapers and having to fill them daily is a form of business, as is selling information. Who is interested in the truth?

Exaggeration, sensationalism, lies, and business are certainly not exclusive to the twentieth century. Certain expectations in relation to wolves have always existed and have been satisfied in all centuries, depending on the needs of the age and usually taking little account of real wolf behavior. The terror felt by human beings at the nightly howling of a wolf pack, the stories of the wolf's dangerousness, the belief that existed at one time that there was a pact between the wolf and the devil, could be justified next morning only by a story about a bloodthirsty attack.

But the behavior of the wolf cannot have been completely independent of current expectations. Now, as we have already pointed out, it is very difficult or actually impossible to reconstruct in retrospect the truth that lay behind all these stories, and though we have no authenticated account of a fatal attack on a human being by healthy wild wolves, we must nevertheless assume that such attacks have taken place, though rarely. I know from my own experience how much less fear of human beings wolves have under the protection of darkness. The wild wolves in the enclosure in the Bavarian Forest had a much smaller flight distance in relation to me at night than in the daytime, and I could well imagine an attack if their fear ever disappeared completely. Suppose there had been a child, for instance, or a wounded and perhaps unconscious man alone at night in the enclosure. Presumably they would not at first have regarded the object as prey. Then, after long hesitation, as often with strange and unfamiliar objects, they might have begun by cautiously approaching, continually ready to turn and flee, and eventually they might have sniffed at it, and then taken a trial bite. Several wolves might then have approached, sniffed, taken trial bites, and then begun tearing at it, perhaps started fighting about it, and then. . . . A horrifying idea, and purely imaginary. But it would be on such lines that one could imagine wolves developing into man-eaters.

The flight distance at night was much smaller than in the day-time in the Abruzzi too. We seemed to be dealing with creatures quite unlike the wolves, who were otherwise so shy. Nevertheless an attack on human beings by wolves in the Abruzzi is hardly conceivable. When and in what conditions may attacks on human beings have taken place? To gain a more accurate idea on the subject, one would have to collect a large number of accounts of such incidents and subject them to careful analysis in conjunction with changing mythological attitudes to the wolf. My own guess is that attacks might occur if natural prey were lacking, if wolves were too numerous to be able to live on domestic animals, and if human beings were poorly armed, so that they were not very dangerous, and the wolves had got used to human flesh as a result of eating corpses. Such conditions seem to have prevailed above all in the Middle Ages, and most of the episodes of that kind can be presumed to have actually taken place. With the availability of better arms and the increased hunting down of the wolf in recent centuries, the danger can be presumed to have dwindled, and in fact attempted attacks—if there really have been any—have been extremely rare. This would also explain why there are hardly any credible reports of such incidents from North America. The conditions we described above never existed there, either at the time of the Indians or later; and in Europe wolves everywhere live in conditions that make an attack on a human being by a healthy animal extremely unlikely.

The popular idea that hungry wolves might attack human beings is certainly mistaken. As we saw in Chapter 2, wolves discover what is prey and what is not by an individual learning process, and it is therefore extremely unlikely that man, whom the wolf has normally learned to regard as an enemy, would suddenly be treated as prey. Wolves driven by hunger approach human settlements purely to find something to eat, and it is this that led to the idea that when they are hungry they are dangerous.

RABIES

In regard to wolves infected with rabies the situation is rather different. There are a number of apparently reliable reports from North America and Europe of people being attacked and bitten by obviously rabid wolves.[33] The external wounds were generally slight and generally healed quickly, but most of the victims died months later as a consequence of rabies before the vaccine developed by Louis Pasteur came into use. It was very rare for the infection to be transmitted by wolves. Most of the deaths have been caused by rabid domestic animals, especially dogs and cats. The reservoir of the disease lies with wild animals, in particular the fox, which is apparently much more liable to the infection than the wolf. This could be because of the different social structure of the fox and wolf populations. The wolf's exclusive way of life in separate packs probably prevents the transmission and rapid spreading of the disease within the population; difference in size also prevents easy transmission of the infection from the fox to the wolf. In addition there is the much smaller number of wolves, and to an extent there is also the difference in the behavior of the two species when they have the disease. While rabid wolves continue to avoid human settlements, sick foxes tend to move to areas in which they can transmit the disease to domestic animals and so be dangerous to human beings.

With modern methods of inoculation rabid wild animals hardly represent a direct danger to human beings. A fox or even a wolf bite can be treated immediately. The danger is domestic animals, in whom rabies can remain unrecognized in the absence of symptom, so that scratches received from them are not taken seriously.

Thus in the course of the ages there have been many changes in the relationship between wolf and man. First the wolf was only a competitor, and for a time he was actually a welcome prey. He was tolerated and actually admired as a skilled and cautious hunter. He became harmful only with the advent of the breeder of livestock. After the loss of his natural living space he was for a period a danger to human beings. Today in some areas he is still harmful to domestic animals, while in others he is the sportsmen's competitor, though the threat that he once represented no longer exists. Nowadays it is not the wolf that is dangerous to man, but man that is dangerous to the wolf.

METHODS OF PROTECTION

In North America there are still large areas of unused land. The efforts of American conservationists, including Dave Mech, are directed toward preserving the wolf in those areas, while they accept, or actually favor, the disappearance of the wolf from areas of greater human exploitation. Our picture of the wolf as one of the animals of the last wild open spaces comes from North America. But in Europe there is no more wilderness. Practically every square yard of our soil has been subjected for centuries to some form of human use; the landscape has been almost completely transformed into a site for generating agricultural or sylvicultural produce or game. Land use changes, but because of partially similar conditions all production in both eastern and western Europe is subject to the compulsion of maximizing yield.

The big changes in the countryside in recent centuries as well as the changed forms of land use have brought about big changes in the living conditions of practically all our native animal species, in some cases for the better, but in most for the worse. Large-scale forest clearance has provided better conditions for some species, such as the buzzard, the hare, the roe, and the stoat, which flourish in an open agricultural landscape. Some species have become closely associated with man and find it easier to make a living in the new landscape. Examples of this are the blackbird, the crow, the gull, the vole, and the fox. Others, mainly species used for shooting, such as the pheasant, the roe, the deer, or the chamois, receive human aid in the form of food, protection from enemies, etc.

In contrast to this there are a large number of species that have been deprived of vital needs, whether essential articles of diet or areas for nesting or rearing their young. These include many amphibians and reptiles, ground breeding birds, grouse, bats, wild cats, and beavers. Either local or total extermination has resulted from the destruction of nearly all predators as pests as well as ungulates such as wild swine and, in the old days, roe, deer, and elk. Predators were also hunted down as competitors of the human hunter, and many kinds of duck and goose, the aurochs, the wild horse, the bison, and the ibex fell victim to the sportsman. Water pollution and insecticides have caused havoc among many species of insects and fish as well as end links in food chains such as the peregrine falcon, the white eagle, the shrew, and the bat. Finally, increased mobility, including that of the large numbers of people who seek rest and recreation in the country, leads to more frequent disturbances of wildlife, including places that were used as refuge and rearing areas because of the rarity of the human visitor. The otter and the capercaillie are believed to have suffered severely in this respect.

Common to all these species is the fact that their numbers have been drastically reduced by human methods of land use and are still declining. To preserve the last survivors, particularly of the more spectacular species, protected areas have been introduced. When these are above a certain size, they tend nowadays to be called national parks, and the intention is to save endangered species from extinction by the prohibition of certain human activities in those areas. Thus the habitat of these species is separated from that of mankind. They are allowed to live within the prescribed boundaries, while outside them they are deprived of their means of nourishment, important structural elements in their biotope are destroyed, and they continue to be hunted and killed off.

The establishment of these conservation areas and nature reserves is essential to the survival of many species. But this kind of disintegrated conservation that separates human and animal habitats involves great dangers. The question arises, particularly in connection with the national parks that are so popular at the present day, whether they really are the summit, the highest form of conservation, as is so frequently maintained. My misgivings about this kind of conservation are well illustrated by the European national parks.

According to the principles of the International Union for the Conservation of Nature, national parks should be areas largely undisturbed by man in which agriculture, forestry, and the rearing of game would not be pursued. This is an excellent principle, which to an extent is admirably practiced in North America and Africa. But in Europe the reality is different. Because of the extensive use made of the land, economic reasons prevent national parks from being established in areas other than those of low productivity, and these are often marginal areas for the animals and plants they are intended to protect. And in many areas traditional forms of land use continue because of traditional rights. Forestry continues in the national park in the Bavarian Forest, and shooting has not been prohibited there. Critics rightly regard the description of such places as national parks as fraudulent. This is especially clear when one bears in mind that many of them were established for economic and not conservation reasons, in order to improve the living conditions of the local population. The traditional forms of land use in the locality became uneconomic, so they have been replaced by a new use, tourism. There would be no objection to this except for the fact that many species already living in the area under bad conditions are now subjected to an additional threat as a result. Many species and animal communities are not really protected in the national park, but continue to be hunted down or destroyed. I have already mentioned that the Tatra National Park authorities pay bounties for shooting wolves. At one time that was usual in many protected areas.

As a result of the ending of traditional methods of land utilization in many national parks and protected areas, we have actually noted an intensification of those methods in the surrounding area to compensate for lost rights or lost sources of raw materials. Thus the establishment of a protected area has frequently resulted in the escalation of the destruction of nature in neighboring areas. The establishment and maintenance of big national parks has often served as a kind of alibi for the further economic exploitation of "areas between the national parks," and these are often much larger.

In the worst instance, disintegrated land use can lead to the creation of a biological desert with small natural oases isolated from one another. These are museumlike entities in which many species will not survive in the long run in spite of temporary protection. The susceptibility of small, isolated populations to chance events such as epidemics, for instance, or a few years' bad weather at breeding or offspring-rearing time, is very great. The problem of long-term genetic isolation is similarly overlooked. Apart from that, the generally small size of the protected area is insufficient for the effective protection of many species. This applies in particular to those that need a large amount of space and a low density of population, in other words, a large number of the specially endangered species.

One of these is the wolf. A nature reserve big enough to support a viable wolf population would have to be so big as to be unthinkable in Europe. This type of protection for the wolf is therefore not practical. Only coexistence of wolf and man in areas used by both can enable the wolf to survive in Europe. We could call this integrated protection.

That coexistence between man and a species as complicated as the wolf is possible is shown by our experience in the Abruzzi. For structural and economic reasons it is of course not possible for the wolf to exist everywhere in Europe. There are a number of large areas in which it still lives or could live again where there is enough natural prey for it, as well as refuge areas to protect it from mankind. It has now disappeared from many of those areas. The use of land principally for pasture necessitated its elimination, but in recent decades this has ceased in many places, such as the big forested areas of Sweden and in eastern Europe and the wooded mountains of Central Europe. In the Bavarian Forest, for instance, forest grazing has completely disappeared; most livestock is kept either indoors or in the immediate neighborhood of the farm for a few months in summer. As a result game animals have greatly increased in numbers, sometimes excessively so. There are large uninhabited areas along the frontiers of Bavaria and Czechoslovakia that are admirably suited to be refuge areas, and there is no biological, agricultural, or sylvicultural reason why the wolf, the lynx, and the bear should not live in limited numbers side by side with roe and deer. Similar considerations apply to large parts of Scandinavia and Finland (outside the reindeer area), Poland, the Carpathians, the Riesengebirge, and the Erzgebirge all the way to the Bavarian Forest, and from there over the eastern Alps into Yugoslavia. One can imagine a big system of possible distribution areas for wolves in Europe that would run in between the areas of intensive agricultural exploitation and connect most of the principal distribution areas.[34]

Such ideas may be utopian at the present time. The idea of the "wicked wolf" is still too strongly entrenched, and the interests of sportsmen are still too powerful. But the negative image, the fear of the wolf, may gradually yield to increased knowledge. As for the sportsmen, we must seriously ask whether shooting should not be subjected to the same conditions as agriculture and forestry. The maximization of production (which is in any case a highly questionable activity) of kinds of game interesting to the sportsman must gradually give way, in the sportsman's own interests, to the idea of an ecologically functioning living community in which all native animal species will be able to live side by side with man.

So far as the wolf is concerned, we are gradually beginning to learn what demands it makes on its environment and on what conditions it can be accepted by man. In the case of many others of the

335

world's endangered species, what we know about their ecology (if we know anything at all) comes from areas little used by man. Zoologists have gone to the big empty spaces of North America or the huge national parks in Africa, but hardly anyone has studied the ecology of these species in areas used by man or has sought to discover to what extent they are able to adapt to man and the environment shaped by him, let alone investigate the economic consequences imposed on local people as a result. No one has inquired into the cultural and mythological attitudes toward them, or the conditions upon which people would be willing to accept these animals as part of their environment. We often lack the most basic knowledge necessary for the taking of effective protective measures. Keeping them alive in a national park is perhaps easy, but it is not enough. Assuring them of a basis for living in areas inhabited and used by men without harming the local population, and enabling them to benefit from this, is a much more difficult task, but a necessary one.

It seems to me that we urgently need a reorientation of ecological studies in regard to the endangered animal kingdom, studies in which biologists, veterinarians, agriculturists, and sylviculturists as well as sociologists and economists will have to work in close cooperation. Only by means of such teamwork will we be able to work out a policy of integrated conservation and land use that will permit the coexistence of man and animals. Whether such a policy can be put into practice depends not on the work of a few specialists, but on us all. There is no doubt that our nature-exploiting behavior, our economic system of compulsive growth, must be superseded by a long-term policy of regenerative raw material and energy cycles in which human labor and natural resources are no longer treated as commodities. That is an urgent task for us all. Only in such a political framework do I see any prospects of survival for the wolf and other endangered species.

Postscript

While I was reading the proofs of the last pages of this book, the news arrived in January 1978, nearly two years after nine wolves escaped, that the last of them had been shot not far from here on the Czech side of the border.

Even though there is no future for a solitary male wolf, the news saddened me. Have we humans brought nature so firmly under our control that we are unable to tolerate a single "disturbing factor"? Has the exploitation of nature reached such a pitch that only those creatures who seem to be useful to us have a right to life?

And yet, haven't wolves been living in the heart of Europe for two years without attracting any recent attention, without causing panic in the local population, without doing any great damage to livestock, and without outraged sportsmen banding together to hunt them down? And wasn't the Czech press almost apologetic about the shooting of the last wolf?

"The question arises," one newspaper said, "why the last wolf in Bohemia really had to die. Some experts believe that wolves could be actually useful in our forests. In many European nations they are protected animals, and so it is possible that they will reappear on our territory in the future." [1]

That reminds me of what was said at the time of the escape and the big wolf hunt here in the Bavarian Forest. "Wolves are beasts of prey, and beasts of prey are dangerous," a peasant woman said, and many sportsmen said it was wrong to leave useful animals to predators at sportsmen's expense. "The place for wolves is in the zoo and not running wild," one headline said, and another, "Slaughter the wild beasts at last." But there were also other voices. "We sportsmen should welcome the presence of wolves in our forests if our professions of faith in the conservation of nature are not to be mere hypocrisy," one of them said.

Finally a letter to me said: "We are children, and we certainly don't want to be bitten by a wolf. All the same, we wouldn't be afraid to go for walks in our wood if there were wolves there. We believe the likelihood of anything happening to us is not very great. Besides, things can happen to us elsewhere too. One of our schoolfellows had a serious car accident and spent months in the hospital. But all cars are not shot for that reason, though they are obviously dangerous to children. Also children are often bitten by dogs, but they are not shot dead for that reason. Our parents know the dangers, and our teacher is nervous too. Life is a bit dangerous everywhere. But it is only wild animals that are not allowed to be a bit dangerous. If they are, they have to die. But experiences with animals make our lives better and richer. We were really delighted that there were some wolves again in Germany, and are very sorry about their death."

So am I. But, one may well ask, doesn't it almost border on the absurd to waste words on the death of an animal in a world in which millions are suffering from hunger, a world with an ever increasing population, escalating use of energy, and a hyper-exponential increase in destruction of the environment, while all the time the rich grow richer and the poor grow poorer? Certainly—but for the fact that the extinction of an animal species is symptomatic of the threat to ourselves. Once upon a time the wolf was a symbol of our fear of nature, our struggle against it: now it has become a symbol of our fear *for* nature, the environment that is all of ours. In the light of the consequences that are now becoming evident, the worst possible advice that could have been given to humanity was: Make yourselves masters of the world. It is becoming clear to us that it should have been: Adapt yourselves to life in the world. Even though it sometimes takes generations for new ideas to be accepted, there is some hope for us all—as well as for that hunted hunter, the wolf.

Notes

INTRODUCTION

1. A full description of the events that followed the escape can be found in Zimen (1976*a*).

CHAPTER ONE

1. Herre and Röhrs (1971).

The dog belongs to the family of doglike predators (*Canidae*). About thirty-five different species, divided up into thirteen genera, belong to it. The genus *Canis* is especially widespread and rich in species. It includes:

The wolf (*Canis lupus*), once widespread throughout America, Europe, and Asia (down to southern India as well as the whole of Indochina and the archipelago to the south of it (see chapter 13). There is still great confusion about many subspecies, as well as about their status and distribution, particularly about the extremely endangered Indian red dog of the southeastern United States. Some authors (such as Goldmann 1974) describe it as *Canis niger*, a separate species from *Canis lupus*; others (such as Ewer 1973) as a subspecies of the wolf, *Canis lupus niger*. Presumably hybridization has taken place between the Indian red dog and the coyote (*Canis latrans*). Other prominent subspecies of the wolf are the European wolf *Canis lupus lupus*; *Canis lupus lycaon*, the wolf of eastern North America, *Canis lupus pambaselius*, the big Alaskan wolf; and *Canis lupus pallipes*, the small wolf of southern Afghanistan, Pakistan, and India.

The coyote (*Canis latrans*) is still widespread in large parts of North America.

339

The golden jackal (*Canis aureus*) is widespread in southern Asia, southeastern Europe, and in North and East Africa.

The side-striped jackal (*Canis adustus*) occurs in Ethiopia and Somalia in the north, in East Africa, and as far south as northern Namibia.

The black-backed jackal (*Canis mesomelas*) is to be found in East and South Africa.

The simenian jackal (*Canis simenis*) occurs in the highlands of Ethiopia.

According to Zeuner (1963) the domestication of the dog took place either in the Upper Paleolithic or at the beginning of the Mesolithic age, that is, from 10,000 to 15,000 years ago, presumably somewhere in southwest Asia, Europe, or North Africa.

2. Klatt (1921).

3. Silver and Silver (1969), as well as personal communication from Kolenosky (1975).

4. Zimen (1974).

CHAPTER TWO

1. Woolpy and Ginsburg (1967).
2. Scott and Fuller (1965).
3. Tinbergen and Tinbergen (1972).
4. Lorenz (1940 and 1950).

CHAPTER THREE

1. Eisfeld (1966).
2. Cf. Wilson (1975).
3. Schenkel (1947).
4. Peters and Mech (1975).
5. Mech (1974).
6. Mech (1978).
7. Further details in Zimen (1972).
8. Darwin (1872).
9. Lorenz (1963).
10. This interpretation of "offering the throat" differs from that of Lorenz (1943 and 1963), who says that at the end of a fight the inferior wolf or dog averts its head and offers its throat as a gesture of humility and claims that this "attitude of submission" brings the fighting to an end. Schenkel (1967) showed in a very interesting paper that (1) it is the superior that averts its head and (2) the course of the fight assumed by Lorenz and others (e.g., Fischel 1956)—according to whom it begins with threats

and ends with the submission of the weaker—is incorrect. A serious fight between two wolves is not ended by humility behavior but by flight, vigorous defense, or the loser's death. Humility behavior, that is, active and passive submission, does not occur in connection with serious fighting, but only when the superior shows tolerance toward the inferior or when tolerance is to be expected from him. ("Submission can only develop in the inferior when the superior shows tolerance or at least does not destroy in the inferior the expectance of tolerance," Schenkel 1967, p. 324.)

11. Lorenz (1963).
12. Zimen (1975).
13. Schenkel (1967).
14. Kleimann (1967).
15. Theberge and Falls (1967).
16. Joslin (1967).
17. Harrington and Mech (in press).
18. Murie (1944).

CHAPTER FOUR

1. Scott and Fuller (1965).
2. Fox (1972).

CHAPTER FIVE

1. In the rest of this chapter I shall be describing the further development of the pack. The reader uninterested in a detailed description of changing rank relationships is advised to skip the next few pages and read the summary at the end of the chapter (p. 125). The development of the social ranking order is summarized in tabular form in the appendix (table 4). To indicate the status of various animals I use a system consisting of two figures followed by the symbol ♂ for male and ♀ for female. The first figure indicates the animal's age: 3 stands for cub (up to one year old), 2 for juvenile (from one to two years old), 1 for adult (older than two). The second figure indicates the animal's rank in its age and sex group. Thus 1.1 ♂ indicates the alpha male, 1.1 ♀ the alpha female, 1.2 ♂ the number-two adult male, 2.1 ♂ the highest-ranking juvenile male, etc.

CHAPTER SIX

1. In my daily notes I distinguished forty-eight different social behavior patterns (see appendix, table 11 and chapter 9).

CHAPTER SEVEN

1. Eibl-Eibesfeldt (1967), p. 340.
2. Dawkins (1976), Wickler and Seibt (1977).
3. Mech (1978).
4. Jordan et al. (1967).
5. Hamilton (1964). See also Dawkins (1976) and Wickler and Seibt (1977).

CHAPTER EIGHT

1. The question is, what differences are there in the bonds between different members of the pack? Let us take three animals A, B, C. Each is attracted by the other two and itself exercises a force of attraction on them. The strength of these bonds is measured by the distances maintained between them and can be represented graphically by the vector a, b, c. If A is seen more frequently in B's company than in C's, the obvious conclusion is that A is more strongly bonded to B than to C (Ab > Ac). But it could be that A is with B not because he is more strongly bonded to B but because B is more strongly bonded to A (Ab < Ba). The bond between two animals does not have to be equally strong on both sides (Ab ≠ Ba). Also the bond of one animal (A) to another animal (B) does not have to be equally strong at every moment in time (t) or at every place (x, y) ($Ab_{t1} \neq Ab_{t2}$ or AB_x! $\neq Ab_y$). Finally, when one animal (A) is separated from the other members of the group (BC), A's bond to BC does not have to be equal to the sum of the individual bonds of A to B and A to C (Abc ≠ Ab + Ac; and similarly, the bond of the other members of the group to A does not have to be equal to the sum of the bonds of B to A and C to A (BCa ≠ Ba + Ca).

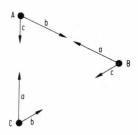

2. Altogether eleven attempts to remove cubs were successful. One cub was removed three times, two cubs were removed five times, and three cubs, three times. Obvious search behavior by the mother after the removal was observed seven times, once when she missed one cub, three

342

times when she missed two cubs, and whenever she missed three cubs. The intensity of the search obviously increased with the number of missing cubs.

3. Van Ballenberghe and Mech (1975).

4. Zimen (1976*b*).

5. To state it in the formal manner described in note 1, in many cases A's bond to B is approximately equal to B's bond to A (Ab = Ba). If A's bond to a third party (C) is weaker than his bond to B, A's bond to C is accordingly weaker than B's bond to A (if Ab > Ac, often Ba > Ca).

6. Peterson (1974).

CHAPTER NINE

1. Zimen (1976*b*).

2. See also Meyer-Holzapfel (1956), Loizos (1966), Zimen (1972) and Bekoff (1974).

3. Rabb et al. (1967).

4. Altmann (1975).

5. Murie (1944).

6. These and the following data from Alaska are from Rausch (1967).

7. Pimlott et al. (1969).

8. Peterson (1974).

9. Personal communication from Haber, 1973 and 1975.

10. See Chapter 12.

11. Mech (1975).

12. Rausch (1967).

13. Van Ballenberghe and Mech (1975).

14. Van Ballenberghe and Mech (1975).

15. Jordan et al. (1967).

16. Maynard Smith and Price (1973).

17. Mech (1978).

18. Bertram (1975).

19. Dawkins (1976).

20. Wickler and Seibt (1977).

21. Peterson (1974).

CHAPTER TEN

1. Eibl-Eibesfeldt (1975) goes into this question fully.

2. The most important publications on this matter are Mech (1966); Jordan, Shelton, and Allen (1967); Wolfe and Allen (1973); and Peterson (1974).

3. Mowat (1965).

4. Summarized by Mech (1970).

5. Bubenik (1966).

6. This and the following information about the ecology of the wolf come, unless otherwise stated, from Mech (1970).

7. Personal communications with Haber 1975.

8. Pulliainen (1965).

9. Young (1944).

10. Rutter and Pimlott (1968).

11. Kolenosky (1972).

12. Pimlott et al. (1969).

13. Mech (1966).

14. Murie (1944).

15. Peterson (1974).

16. Cowan (1947).

17. Peterson (1974).

18. Fuller (1966).

19. Dawkins (1976).

20. Dawkins (1976).

CHAPTER ELEVEN

1. Mech (1977*b* and 1978), Peterson (1974).

2. Mech (1978).

3. Burkholder (1959).

4. Zimen (1976b).

5. Mech (1966).

6. Mech (1978).

7. Mech (1966).

8. Illustrated description of the possible interaction between ecological factors, wolf behavior, and pack size or size of the wolf population:

The total effect of the various factors is summed up in the black box. A + input (a) increases and a − input (b) decreases the output (c). If + or − are in parentheses, it means that the positive or negative effect of the input quantity is restricted to a small field.

The input quantities are added (a + b = c)

The quantities entering the black field are subtracted from the other input quantity or quantities (a − b = c)

The input quantities are multiplied (a × b = c)

One input quantity is divided by the other $(a \div b = c)$

r = specific growth rate

Integration of r in the course of time. This governs the result, in this case the size of the pack or the size of the wolf population.

9. Zimen (1976b).

CHAPTER TWELVE

1. Information supplied by the headquarters of the Parco Nazionale d'Abruzzo at Pescasseroli.
2. Zimen and Boitani (1975).
3. Mech (1974).
4. Most of the findings reported here come from Zimen and Boitani (in the press). A further full account of the Abruzzi project is in preparation.
5. In 1974 as a result of 152 applications, compensation was paid for the loss of 1,392 animals: 1,263 sheep, 90 goats, 20 cows, 15 horses, and four pigs. The total sum paid out was 37,736,400 lire.
6. Leyhausen (1956 and 1965).
7. Pulliainen (1965).
8. Mendelssohn (1973).
9. Young (1944).

CHAPTER THIRTEEN

1. Sandoz (1961), Zenner (1963).
2. Gunn (1965).
3. Clark (1969).
4. Weatherby (1944).
5. Stephenson and Ahgook (1975).
6. Gerholm and Magnusson (1966).
7. Siennes (1976).
8. Gerholm and Magnusson (1966).
9. Jacoby (1974).
10. Young (1944).
11. Jacoby (1974).
12. Schaeffer (1955), p. 20.
13. Schaeffer (1955), p. 255.
14. Lorenz (1950).
15. Most of the information on this comes from Dent (1974).

16. Fengewisch (1968).
17. Varjola (1970).
18. Fengewisch (1968).
19. Haglund (1969).
20. Myrberget (1978).
21. Bjärvall (1978).
22. Fengewisch (1968).
23. This and the following information about the extermination of wolves in North America come from Young (1944).
24. Personal communication from Corbett 1977 and 1978.
25. Mech (1970).
26. Personal communication from Pulliainen 1978.
27. Michurin (1970).
28. Personal communication from Pulliainen 1978.
29. Pulliainen (1978).
30. Lorenz (1971).
31. Godenhjelm (1891).
32. Fengewisch (1968).
33. Young (1944).
34. Zimen (1974, 1975b, and 1976c).

POSTSCRIPT

1. *Grafenauer Anzeiger*, February 17, 1978.

Appendix: Tables

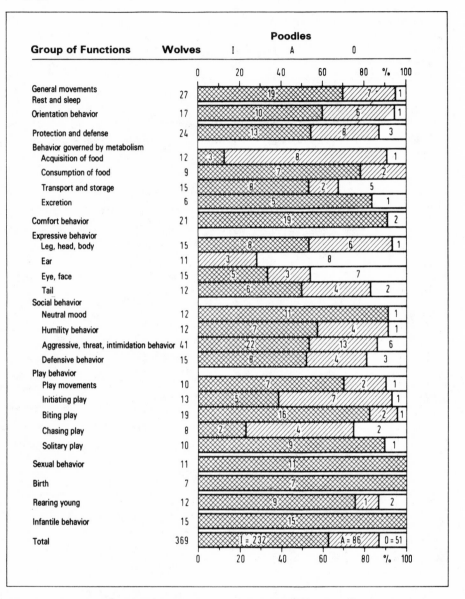

Group of Functions	Wolves	Poodles I	A	0
General movements / Rest and sleep	27	19	7	1
Orientation behavior	17	10	6	1
Protection and defense	24	13	8	3
Behavior governed by metabolism — Acquisition of food	12	3	8	1
Consumption of food	9	7		2
Transport and storage	15	8	2	5
Excretion	6	5		1
Comfort behavior	21	19		2
Expressive behavior — Leg, head, body	15	8	6	1
Ear	11	3	8	
Eye, face	15	5	3	7
Tail	12	6	4	2
Social behavior — Neutral mood	12	11		1
Humility behavior	12	7	4	1
Aggressive, threat, intimidation behavior	41	22	13	6
Defensive behavior	15	8	4	3
Play behavior — Play movements	10	7	2	1
Initiating play	13	5	7	1
Biting play	19	16	2	1
Chasing play	8	2	4	2
Solitary play	10	9		1
Sexual behavior	11	11		
Birth	7	7		
Rearing young	12	9	1	2
Infantile behavior	15	15		
Total	369	I = 232	A = 86	0 = 51

Table 1. Wolf and poodle behavior compared. The "wolves" column shows the number of times behavior belonging to each group of functions was observed. The "poodles" column shows how many times this behavior was observed in identical form (squares), in modified form (hatching), or not at all (blank).

Status of Howl Initiators

Animals no longer in pack	297
Animals integrated into pack:	
Superior adults (≥ 1.2)	10
Inferior adults (≤ 1.3)	176
Juveniles	93
Total	**576**

Table 2. More than half the howl initiators were wolves that had left the pack. Members of the pack who initiated howling were generally low-ranking adults.

	Sex	Initial	Date	Born at	Country of Origin	Father	Mother	In pack until	Notes
Anja	♀		3/31/67	Neumünster zoo	Yugoslavia			Dec. 69	Became too aggressive
Alek	♂		April 67	?	?			July 67	Died of intestinal stoppage
Grosskopf	♂							Dec. 69	
Anselm	♂		5/23/67	Rotterdam zoo	Finland			July 69	Died of overdose of Valium
Andra	♀							Dec. 69	
Alexander	♂	A						*In enclosure but left pack	
Näschen	♂	N	4/27/68	zoo at Hamburg	Finland			Feb. 76	Died of wounds
Wölfchen	♂	W						Jan. 77	Removed because scapegoat (small pack)
Mädchen	♀	M						Feb. 76	Died of wounds
Psenner	♂	P	4/10/71	zoo at Innsbruck	Russia			Jan. 77	Removed because scapegoat (small pack)
St. Oswald	♂	Q						July 74	Removed because scapegoat
Schönbrunn	♀	S	April 71	Afghanistan (North) (wild)				July 74	Removed because scapegoat
Finsterau	♀	F						Jan. 77	Removed because scapegoat (small pack)
Rachel	♀	R	April 71	Afghanistan (South) (wild)				July 74	Removed because scapegoat
Lusen	♀	L						July 74	Removed because scapegoat
Olomouc	♂	O						Jan. 77	Removed because scapegoat
Tatra	♀	T	5/31/72	zoo at Olomouc	Slovakia			* 1.1. ♀	
Brno	♀	B						Jan. 76	Escaped; was the first to be shot
1 ♀								June 72	Died of heart failure
Gelbauge	♂	GA							
Braunauge	♂	BA	4/29/73	Bavarian Forest		N	F	Jan. 76	Escaped
Gelbraunauge	♂	GBA							
1 ♀								July 74	
Grauer	♂								
Blasser	♂								
Schöne	♀		4/20/74	Bavarian Forest					
Vorsicht	♀					O	F	Jan. 76	Escaped
Scheu	♀								
1♂, 1♀								July 74	
Türk	♂		1974	Turkey (wild)				*scapegoat	
Ho	♂							*1.1. ♂	
Tschi	♂		4/21/75	Bavarian Forest		O	F	*1.2. ♂	
Minh	♀							June 75	Died of heart failure

Table 3. Particulars of individual wolves

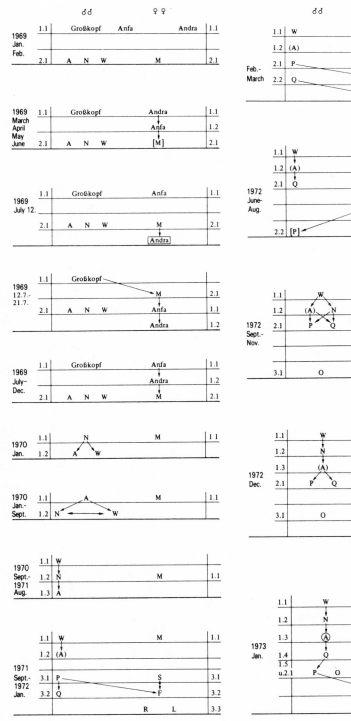
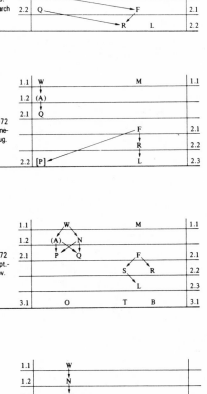
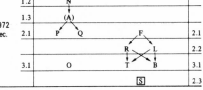
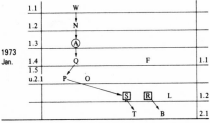

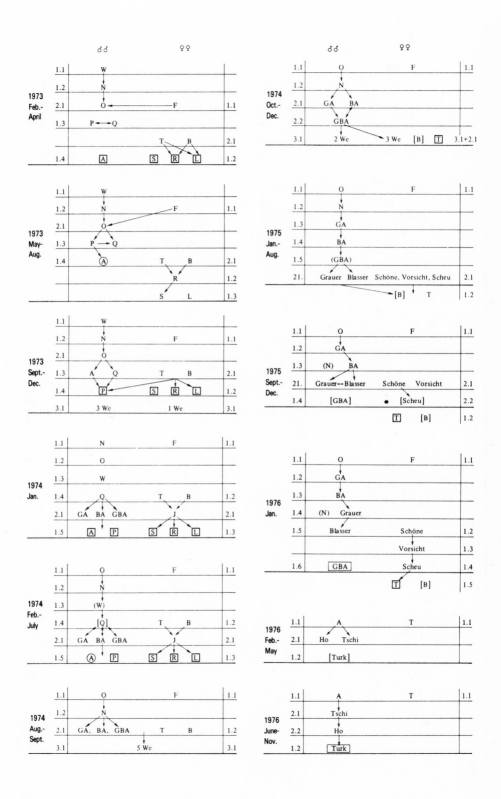

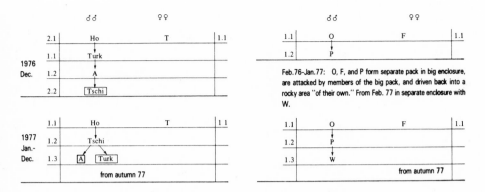

Feb.76-Jan.77: O, F, and P form separate pack in big enclosure, are attacked by members of the big pack, and driven back into a rocky area "of their own." From Feb. 77 in separate enclosure with W.

Table 4. Development of social ranking order from January 1969 to December 1977. Dominance between wolves both of the same and of opposite sex is shown either by one of them being at least two ranks higher (i.e., separated by two lines) or, in the case of animals of neighboring rank, by an arrow. (A double arrow indicates that a change of rank is taking place.) An undirected arrow indicates that all the wolves at that level are superior to those at the level immediately below.

Key to abbreviations:
Age: 1 = adult (aged one on Dec. 31)
    2 = juvenile (under one on Jan. 1, one year old on Dec. 31)
    3 = cub (under one on Dec. 31)
Rank:.1, .2, ...5 indicates the animal's position in the ranking order in its age or sex group.
Status: (X) indicates that the animal generally stays away from the pack "voluntarily."
    X indicates the wolf remains constantly "voluntarily" away from the pack.
    [Y] indicates the wolf remains generally apart because of attacks by individual members of the pack.
    Y indicates the wolf remains constantly away because of attacks by many members of the pack.

For particulars of individual wolves see Table 3.

	Joined group	
	Without cub	**With cub**
Ho	1	12
Tschi	5	13
Total	6	25

Table 5. Choice made by free-running cub between two groups separating in open country. One group consisted of the cub's twin brother and one person. The other consisted of two wolves (Alexander and Wölfchen), a dog (Flow), and two persons. The experiments were made from August 22 to 30, 1975. Age of cubs: four months.

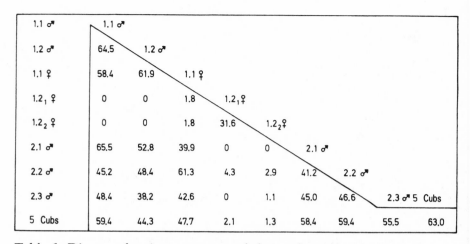

Table 6. Diagram showing percentage of observed occasions in December 1974 on which wolves lay closer than 30 meters to other wolves in the enclosure (observations totaled 32,055; average for each combination of animals, 411). Example: the 1.2 ♂ (Näschen) and the 1.1 ♀ (Finsterau) lay in 61.9 percent of all observed instances within 30 meters of each other, while the 1.2 ♂ (Näschen) and the 1.2 ♀ (Tatra) never lay within 30 meters of each other.

		M	N	A	P	Total
Wölfchen	1.1 ♂	18.0	13.1	11.3	8.9	51.3
Mädchen	1.1 ♀		2.8	1.7	2.4	24.9
Näschen	1.2 ♂			9.2	15.6	40.7
Alexander	1.3 ♂				5.7	27.9
Psenner	3.1 ♂					32.6

(between)

Table 7. Frequency of contact between four free-running adult wolves and a cub. Every form of body contact was recorded, including not only the usual social contacts such as coat smelling, muzzle contact, or play but also mere running side by side with brief body contact or joint sniffing at the same hole in the ground.

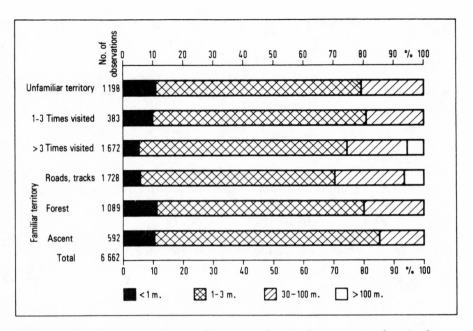

Table 8. The distance maintained between four wolves running free in the National Park in the Bavarian Forest depended on their familiarity with the country and its structure. In unknown territory, in dense forest, and on steep ascents they kept closer together, but they kept farther apart in familiar country and above all on forest roads or tracks.

Composition of Group	2 juveniles 1 person	1 juvenile L.G.	3 juveniles 1 person	L.G.	3 juveniles 2 persons	L.G.	3 juveniles 3 persons	L.G.	3 juveniles > 3 persons	L.G.
Number of individuals in each group	3	3	4	2	5	2	6	2	> 6	2
Alexander	0	8	1	9	6	6	7	4	4	2
Wölfchen	0	8	2	11	5	7	5	7	6	3
Mädchen	0	8	0	8	2	11	6	2	9	2
Total	0	24	3	28	13	24	18	13	19	7

Table 9. Separation experiments carried out with three juvenile wolves aged between 13 and 16 months at Rickling from May 16 to August 25, 1969.
L.G. = Leading Group (Anfa and the author).
When two groups each consisting of three individuals separated, all three experimental animals followed the group that included Anfa and the author. The other group was followed with increasing frequency as its size increased.

	Remain	Go on	Remain	Go on	Remain	Go on
Composition of Group	3 juveniles 1–3 persons	Leading Group	Leading Group	3 juveniles 1–3 persons	2 juveniles Leading Group	1 juvenile 1 person
No. of individuals in each group	4–6	2	2	4–6	4	2
Alexander	0	4	(1)	4	(2)	(4)
Wölfchen	0	2	0	6	(2)	(3)
Mädchen	0	8	(2)	4	(3)	(2)
Total	0	14	(3)	14	(7)	(9)

Table 10. Separation experiments made at Rickling. A party split into two, one group continuing on its way while the other remained resting. There was a distinct preference for the group that continued on its way.

Individual frequency	Initiator / Recipient									
Behavior pattern	Average frequency	1.1 ♂	1.2 ♂	1.3 ♂	1.4 ♂	1.1 ♀	1.2 ♀	1.3 ♀	Juvenile ♂	Juvenile ♀	Cub
Muzzle contact	2.64 / 2.64	1.70 / 1.70	2.32 / 2.37	2.16 / 2.19	1.86 / 1.83	3.24 / 3.24	1.57 / 1.54	.91 / .91	5.46 / 5.02	4.68 / 5.08	2.50 / 2.52
Coat sniffing	2.31	2.97 / 2.37	4.03 / 2.24	1.57 / 1.32	1.32 / 1.08	2.69 / 4.05	1.32 / 1.18	.99 / .73	3.52 / 3.17	2.63 / 2.40	2.07 / 4.57
Jostling	0.44	.28 / 1.57	.42 / .70	.14 / .15	.28 / .28	.93 / .58	.29 / .06	.17 / .09	.93 / .59	.60 / .25	.37 / .13
Active oppression	2.35	.01 / 10.14	1.88 / 4.11	.77 / 1.05	.76 / .28	1.08 / 5.63	1.84 / .11	.76 / .24	5.41 / 1.37	6.47 / .52	4.41 / .01
Aggressive threatening	1.18	1.51 / 1.77	4.76 / 1.04	.40 / 1.78	.48 / .53	1.58 / .19	.19 / .49	.16 / .32	.76 / 2.22	.47 / 1.33	1 52 / 2.14
Biting fray	0.19	.04 / .04	.07 / .07	.25 / .25	.18 / .18	.03 / .03	– / –	– / –	.76 / .76	.25 / .25	.30 / 30
Intimidating	0.61	1.50 / .12	1.51 / 1.10	.34 / 1.54	.34 / .85	1.03 / .03	.12 / .38	.01 / .14	1.08 / 1.23	.18 / .66	– / –
Surrounding, cornering	0.58	.17 / –	1.35 / .04	.12 / 1.45	.60 / 2.49	.49 / .01	.08 / .37	.02 / .55	1.67 / .64	.99 / .17	.32 / .09
Aggressive advance	0.26	.06 / .02	.64 / .09	.05 / .43	.35 / 1.02	.17 / .09	.06 / .12	.02 / .22	.56 / .48	.42 / .08	.23 / –
Sniffing	0.24	.16 / .24	.76 / .16	.09 / .50	.24 / .76	.27 / .03	.06 / .13	– / .30	.36 / .22	.27 / .07	.21 / .02
Biting	0.11	.08 / .08	.15 / .12	.01 / .04	.01 / .05	.38 / .08	.02 / .21	.02 / .21	.21 / .18	.21 / .13	– / –
Pursuing	0.22	.27 / –	.90 / .09	.40 / .74	.06 / .73	.18 / –	.01 / .26	– / .15	.20 / .19	.17 / .05	.01 / –
Hunting	0.11	.01 / –	.10 / –	.06 / .05	.05 / .07	.46 / –	.02 / .35	.03 / .43	.14 / .13	.24 / .08	– / –
Defensive threatening	1.05	– / .76	.20 / 2.01	2.29 / .39	1.85 / .64	.20 / 1.34	.94 / .13	1.51 / .06	1.14 / 2.60	.91 / 1.42	1.48 / 1 17
Keeping distance	0.27	– / .25	– / .89	.63 / .45	.85 / .04	– / .63	.55 / .03	.43 / .02	.15 / .13	.04 / 1.21	– / –
Flight	0.13	– / .01	– / .09	.04 / .04	.05 / .03	– / .63	.41 / .05	.21 / .09	.09 / .15	.21 / .19	.03 / –
Biting play	7.47	.80 / .80	2.52 / 2.52	5.80 / 5.80	3.85 / 3.85	2.01 / 2.01	2.61 / 2.61	2.37 / 2.37	16.40 / 16.40	16.36 / 16.36	21 98 / 21.98

Table 11. The frequency with which some social behavior patterns appear in the wolf pack. Figures under "average frequency" show how many times per hour per wolf different behavior patterns were observed in the enclosure. (Thus each wolf showed muzzle contact 2.64 times or intimidation behavior 0.61 times an hour.) The individual frequencies show the average number of times individual wolves showed the behavior pattern refferred to depending on age, sex, and rank. This is shown by the figure over the stroke. The figure under the stroke shows how often the behavior referred to was directed at them. The figures are based on 1,108 hours of observation between November 1971 and February 1975. The following behavior patterns were also recorded (average frequency in parentheses):

Coat biting (0.25)
Coat licking (0.30)
Genital sniffing (0.21)
Genital licking (0.21)
Anal sniffing (0.05)
Anal licking (0.03)
Standing over another animal (0.15)
Falling or lying on back (0.59)
Biting and shaking (0.02)
Pushing (0.01)
Molesting (0.01)
Jumping up at (0.06)

Pinning down with body (0.06)
Pinning down with head (0.12)
Standing over opponent (0.03)
Attack
Chasing away
Muzzle biting (0.29)
Mounting sideways (0.06)
Intimidatory pushing (0.08)
Defensive snapping (0.48)

Defensive biting (0.06)
Defensive teeth chattering (0.02)
Defensive pushing (0.08)
Defensive circling (0.05)
Initiating play (0.67)
Chasing play (1.15)
Sexual mounting (0.08)
Sexual pelvic thrusting (0.04)
Presenting (0.03)

Coat sniffing

Average frequency 2.31*

	Σ →	Recipient									
		1.1♂	1.2♂	1.3♂	1.4♂	1.1♀	1.2♀	1.3♀	Juvenile♂	Juvenile♀	Cub
		2.37	2.24	1.32	1.08	4.05	1.18	0.73	3.17	2.40	4.57
1.1♂	2.97	–	.64	.16	.10	.70	.12	.05	.55	.23	.42
1.2♂	4.03	.70	–	.22	.15	1.41	.13	.08	.49	.35	.50
1.3♂	1.57	.20	.14	.01	.08	.24	.13	.11	.26	.19	.21
1.4♂	1.32	.05	.09	.05	.09	.33	.09	.09	.11	.13	.29
1.1♀	2.69	.41	.48	.11	.19	--	.14	.03	.35	.24	.74
1.2♀	1.32	.19	.13	.12	.07	.26	.07	.01	.10	.09	.28
1.3♀	0.99	.06	.04	.05	.08	.05	.03	.10	.03	.05	.50
Juvenile♂	3.52	.35	.35	.22	.17	.56	.21	.11	.60	.48	.47
Juvenile♀	2.63	.21	.20	.19	.11	.24	.20	.08	.38	.45	.57
Cub	2.07	.20	.17	.19	.04	.26	.06	.07	.30	.19	.59

*Number of observed muzzle-to-coat contacts per hour per wolf

Table 12.

Active subjection

Average frequency 2.35

	Σ →	Recipient									
		1.1♂	1.2♂	1.3♂	1.4♂	1.1♀	1.2♀	1.3♀	Juvenile♀	Juvenile♂	Cub
		10.14	4.11	1.05	.28	5.63	.11	.24	1.37	.52	.01
1.1♂	.01	–	.01	.00	.00	.00	.00	.00	.00	.00	.00
1.2♂	1.88	1.76	–	.00	.00	.12	.00	.00	.00	.00	.00
1.3♂	.77	.40	.22	.02	.01	.00	.00	.00	.12	.00	.00
1.4♂	.83	.44	.25	.03	.01	.02	.00	.01	.07	.00	.00
1.1♀	1.08	.52	.45	.02	.02	–	.00	.00	.07	.00	.00
1.2♀	1.84	.54	.25	.19	.09	.68	.00	.00	.08	.01	.00
1.3♀	.76	.28	.16	.05	.01	.16	.02	.00	.07	.01	.00
Juvenile♂	5.41	2.99	1.21	.00	.00	1.10	.00	.00	.09	.02	.00
Juvenile♀	6.47	2.13	.92	.50	.00	2.74	.01	.00	.16	.01	.00
Cub	4.41	1.08	.64	.24	.14	.81	.08	.23	.71	.47	.01

Table 13.

Aggressive threatening

Average frequency 1.18

	Σ →	Recipient									
		1.1♂	1.2♂	1.3♂	1.4♂	1.1♀	1.2♀	1.3♀	Juvenile♂	Juvenile♀	Cub
		1.77	1.04	1.78	.53	.19	.49	.32	2.22	1.33	2.14
1.1♂	1.51	–	.67	.04	.05	.02	.03	.02	.55	.05	.08
1.2♂	4.76	1.56	–	1.41	.27	.09	.07	.04	.89	.29	.14
1.3♂	.40	.01	.05	.02	.03	.02	.04	.01	.07	.11	.04
1.4♂	.48	.01	.01	.04	.02	.03	.06	.03	.16	.10	.02
1.1♀	1.58	.11	.21	.13	.06	–	.10	.09	.29	.47	.12
1.2♀	.19	.00	.00	.01	.00	.00	.13	.01	.01	.02	.01
1.3♀	.16	.00	.00	.00	.01	.00	.01	.08	.00	.01	.05
Juvenile♂	.76	.07	.07	.08	.06	.03	.03	.04	.17	.11	.10
Juvenile♀	.47	.01	.03	.05	.03	.00	.02	.01	.07	.15	.10
Cub	1.52	.00	.00	.00	.00	.00	.00	.01	.01	.02	1.48

Table 14.

B's Behavior

Threatening as a consequence of	No. of observations	Percentage of observations	Subdom. Dom.	Snapping	Other reactions besides threatening			
					Teeth chattering	Biting	Muzzle seizing	Intimidating
Attack	7	1	100	5	—	3	—	—
Surrounding and attacking	254	37	94	153	31	30	—	—
Standing over, pinning down	8	1	100	3	—	4	—	9
Intimidating	83	12	87	55	—	4	—	—
Approaching while lying down	33	5	21	3	—	—	—	—
Approaching while eating	54	8	39	7	—	—	44	—
Threatening, spontaneous	75	11	20	3	—	—	5	19
Threatening in play	44	6	64	24	—	—	—	7
Total	688	100	—	254	31	37	49	35

Table 15. Threatening by a wolf (B) as a reaction to various kinds of behavior directed at it by another member of the pack (A). Of 688 observations of threat behavior that were evaluated, 569 (83 percent) were reactions to behavior by A, 44 (6 percent) occurred in play, and 75 (11 percent) were "spontaneous," i.e., were nonreactive (took place without discernible cause).

The fraction $\dfrac{\text{subdominant}}{\text{dominant}} \times 100$ shows how often B showed itself to be inferior in rank to A (as a

percentage of all reactions to behavior by A). Thus only dominant wolves display attack, chasing away, standing over and pinning down, while only subdominants react to these things with snapping, teeth chattering, and biting. Also only inferiors or equals in rank show jostling and active submission, while dominants react, as they mostly do when another wolf approaches, by threatening or displaying spontaneous threat behavior. In the latter cases further aggressive behavior patterns such as muzzle seizing or intimidation often follow. Altogether 401 (or 58 percent) of threats were directed by subdominants against dominants, while 287 (or 42 percent) were directed by dominants (or equals) against inferiors (or equals).

Intimidation behavior
Average frequency 0.61

		Recipient									
		1.1 ♂	1.2 ♂	1.3 ♂	1.4 ♂	1.1 ♀	1.2 ♀	1.3 ♀	Juvenile ♂	Juvenile ♀	Cub
	Σ →	.12	1.10	1.52	.85	.03	.38	.14	1.23	.66	.00
1.1 ♂	1.50	–	1.03	.22	.08	.01	.00	.00	.15	.01	.00
1.2 ♂	1.51	.03	–	1.07	.29	.00	.01	.00	.10	.01	.00
1.3 ♂	.34	.00	.02	.01	.08	.00	.00	.00	.23	.00	.00
1.4 ♂	.34	.00	.00	.01	.15	.00	.01	.00	.17	.00	.00
1.1 ♀	1.03	.00	.00	.00	.02	–	.32	.12	.13	.46	.00
1.2 ♀	.12	.00	.00	.00	.00	.00	.02	.01	.00	.09	.00
1.3 ♀	.01	..00	.00	.00	.00	.00	.00	.00	.00	.01	.00
Juvenile ♂	1.08	.09	.05	.21	.23	.02	.02	.01	.44	.01	.00
Juvenile ♀	.18	.00	.00	.00	.00	.00	.00	.00	.11	.07	.00
Cub	.00	.00	.00	..00	.00	.00	.00	.00	.00	.00	.00

Table 16.

Biting play
Average frequency 7.47

		Recipient									
		1.1 ♂	1.2 ♂	1.3 ♂	1.4 ♂	1.1 ♀	1.2 ♀	1.3 ♀	Juvenile ♂	Juvenile ♀	Cub
	Σ →	.80	2.52	5.80	3.85	2.01	2.61	2.37	16.40	16.36	21.98
1.1 ♂	.80	–	.02	.02	.00	.07	.01	.00	.29	.10	.29
1.2 ♂	2.52	.02	–	.27	.05	.09	.03	.01	.98	.75	.32
1.3 ♂	5.80	.02	.27	1.09	.56	.07	.14	.17	2.09	1.04	.35
1.4 ♂	3.85	.00	.05	.56	.07	.27	.26	.10	.94	1.52	.08
1.1 ♀	2.01	.07	.09	.07	.27	–	.04	.03	.68	.24	.52
1.2 ♀	2.61	.01	.03	.14	.26	.04	.16	.32	.24	1.02	.39
1.3 ♀	2.37	.00	.01	.17	.10	.03	.32	.36	.09	.55	.74
Juvenile ♂	16.40	.29	.98	2.09	.94	.68	.24	.09	6.73	3.58	.78
Juvenile ♀	16.36	.10	.75	1.04	1.52	.24	1.02	.55	3.58	6.62	.94
Cub	21.98	.29	.32	.35	.08	.52	.39	.74	.78	.94	17.57

Table 17

| | Period A (Normal) | | | Period B (Hungry) | | | |
	No. of observations	> 30m.	Percentage	No. of observations	> 30m.	Percentage	Difference
Ho	173	12	6.9	132	13	9.8	+ 2.9
Tschi	188	21	11.2	149	32	21.5	+ 10.3
Tatra	169	9	5.3	132	9	6.8	+ 1.5
4 cubs	299	24	8.0	414	112	27.1	+ 19.1
Alexander	117	111	94.9	133	120	90.2	− 4.7
Türk	199	192	96.5	160	148	92.5	− 4.0

Table 18. The number of occasions on which roaming members of the pack were observed to be more than 30 meters from the nearest wolf. Two periods were compared. Period A was from three days before the last feed until three days after it, i.e., conditions were normal. Period B was from the fourth to the sixth day after the last feed (i.e., the wolves were hungry). At the time of the experiment Alexander and Türk had left the pack. The increased mobility of members of the pack during the hungry period explains why they were seen more frequently near another wolf.

Country	Number[1]	Estimated area inhabited by wolves (in sq. km)	Percentage of territory inhabited by wolves	Current situation[2]	Status	Source
Norway	10			A	Protected since 1973	Haglund (1975); Myrberget (1978)
Sweden	10			A	Protected since 1965	Haglund (1975); Bjärvall (1978)
Finland	100[3]			A	Partly protected outside reindeer areas	Haglund (1975); Pulliainen (1978)
European Russia	10,000[4]	10 million	50	C	No protection, bounty for killings, state organized efforts to reduce numbers	Bibikov (1975)
Poland	200	25,000	8	B	Legal provisions, but protection totally inadequate	Suminski (1975, 1978)
Czechoslovakia	100	10,000	8	B	No protection, bounties paid[5]	Slovak Institute (1975)
Rumania	2,000	40,000	17	C	No protection, bounties paid	Rumanian Academy (1975)
Bulgaria	125	No information	No information	B	No protection	Pimlott (1975)
Yugoslavia	Not known; about 900 shootings a year	140,000	55	A	Partial protection in some republics, none in others	Bojovic and Colic (1975)
Albania	No information	No information	No information	Presumably B or C	No information	
Greece	Not known; about 700 shootings a year	70,000	70[6]	C	No protection, bounties paid	Economics Ministry (1975)
Italy	100	8,600	3	B	Protected for trial period 1972–1976 Protected since 1977	Zimen and Boitani (1975)
Spain	200	60,000	8	B	Partially protected	Garzon (1974)
Portugal	100	15,000	17	B	No protection	Garzon (1974)

[1]Very rough estimate in some cases
[2]A, practically exterminated; B, endangered; C, no immediate threat of extermination
[3]No reproducing population, but regular exchange across Soviet frontier
[4]Population may have increased (Pulliainen, 1978)
[5]Protection aimed at
[6]Greek mainland only

Table 19. Estimated number and distribution as well as status of the wolf in Europe in 1973 (from Zimen and Boitani, 1975).

Bibliography

ALTMANN, D. 1975. Beziehungen zwischen sozialer Rangordnung und Jungenaufzucht bei Canis Lupus. *Zoologische Garten* 44:235–236.

BANFIELD, A. W. F. 1954. Preliminary investigation of the barren ground caribou. Canadian Wildlife Service, *Wildlife Management Bulletin,* Series 1, No. 10b.

BEKOFF, M., ed. 1974. Social play in mammals. *American Zoologist* 14(1):266–427.

BERTRAM, B. 1975. The social system of lions. *Scientific American* 232(5):54–65.

BIBIKOV, D. I. 1975. The wolf in the USSR. In *Wolves,* ed. D. H. Pimlott, pp. 53–62, IUCN Publication Services, Supplementary Paper No. 43, Morges, Switzerland.

BJÄRVALL, A. 1978. An interview study of attitudes to the wolf in Sweden. Wolf Symposium, Edinburgh, April 1978.

BOITANI, L., and ZIMEN, E. 1978. The role of public opinion in wolf management. In *The behavior and ecology of wolves,* ed. E. Klinghammer. New York: Garland Press.

BOJOVIC, D., and COLIC, D. 1975. Wolves in Yugoslavia with special reference to the period 1945–1973. In *Wolves,* ed. D. H. Pimlott, pp. 53–62, IUCN Publication Services, Supplementary Paper No. 43, Morges, Switzerland.

BOURLIERE, F., and VERSCHUREN, J. 1960. *Introduction à l'écologie des ongules du Parc National Albert.* Bruxelles: Institut des Parcs Nationaux du Congo Belge.

BUBENIK, B. 1966. Vliv rysa a vlka na struktura populaci srnci a jelent zvere. *Mammaliologicke Zpravu: Lynx* 6:7–13.

BURKHOLDER, B. L. 1959. Movement and behavior of a wolf pack in Alaska. *Journal of Wildlife Management* 23:1–11.

CAGNOLARO, L.; ROSSO, D.; SPAGNESI, M.; and VENTURI, B. 1974. *Inchiesta sulla distribuzione del Lupo in Italia e nei Ticino e Grigioni (Svizzera).* Bologna: Laboratorio di Zoologia Applicata alla Caccia.

CALVO, E. F., and DANCETTE, V. 1977. *Die Bestie ist tot—Der zweite Weltkrieg bei den Tieren.* Dreieich: Abi Melzer Prod.

CLARK, E. 1969. *Indian legends of the Pacific Northwest.* Berkeley: University of California Press.

COWAN, J. M. 1947. The timber wolf in the Rocky Mountain national parks of Canada. *Canadian Journal of Research* 25:139–174.

CRISLER, L. 1958. *Arctic wild.* New York: Harper & Bros.

DARWIN, C. 1872. *The expression of the emotions in man and animals.* London.

DASMAN, R. F. 1964. *Wildlife biology.* New York: John Wiley & Sons.

DAWKINS, R. 1976. *The selfish gene.* Oxford: Oxford University Press.

DENT, A. 1974. *Lost beasts of Britain.* London: Harrap.

EIBL-EIBESFELDT, I. 1967. *Grundriss der vergleichenden Verhaltungs-forschungen.* München: Piper Verlag.

EIBL-EIBESFELDT, I. 1975. *Krieg und Frieden.* München: Piper Verlag.

EISFELD, D. 1966. Verhaltungsbeobachtungen an einigen Wildcaniden. *Zeitschrift wissenschaftlicher Zoologie,* 174(3/4):227–289.

EWER, R. F. 1973. *The carnivores.* London: Weidenfeld and Nicolson.

FENGEWISCH, H. 1968. *Grossraubwild in Europas Revieren.* München: BLV.

FISCHEL, W. 1956. Haushunde. *Handbuch der Zoologie,* 8:1–16.

FOX, M. 1971. *Behavior of wolves, dogs and related canids.* New York: Harper & Row.

FOX, M. W. 1972. Socio-ecological implications of individual differences in wolf litters: a developmental and evolutionary perspective. *Behaviour,* 41:298–313.

DE LA FUENTE, F. R. 1975. Protection of the wolf in Spain—notes on a public awareness campaign. In *Wolves,* ed. D. H. Pimlott, pp. 103–112, IUCN Publication Services, Supplementary Paper No. 43, Morges, Switzerland.

FULLER, W. W. 1966. The biology and management of the bison of Wood Buffalo National Park. Canadian Wildlife Service, *Wildlife Management Bulletin,* Series, No. 16.

GARZON, I. 1974. Especies en Peligro—el Lobo. *Adena,* No. 8, WWF, Spain.

362

GERHOLM, T. R., and MAGNUSSON, S. 1966. *Idé och samhälle*. Skolöverstyrelsen, Stockholm: SÖ-Förlaget.

GODENHJELM, U. 1891. *Minnen från fran Vargåren 1880–82*. Helsingfors. (Excerpts in *Jaktmarket och Fiskevatten*, No. 2, Stockholm 1972).

GOLDMANN, E. A. 1944. *The wolves of North America*, Part II. Washington, D.C.: American Wildlife Institute. (New ed. 1969, New York: Dover Publications).

GREEK MINISTRY OF NATIONAL ECONOMY 1975. The kill of wolves in Greece, 1964–1972. In *Wolves*, ed. D. H. Pimlott, pp. 81–82, IUCN Publication Services, Supplementary Paper No. 43, Morges, Switzerland.

GUNN, S. W. A. 1965. *The totem poles in Stanley Park*. Vancouver, B.C.: Whiterocks Publications.

HAGLUND, B. 1969. *De fyra stora*. Stockholm: Nordstedt.

HAGLUND, B. 1975. The wolf in Fennoscandia. In *Wolves*, ed. D. H. Pimlott, pp. 36–43, IUCN Publication Services, Supplementary Paper No. 43, Morges, Switzerland.

HAMILTON, W. D. 1964. The genetical theory of social behavior, I, II. *Journal of Theoretical Biology* 7(1):1–52.

HARRINGTON, F., and MECH, D. (in preparation). Wolf howling and its role in territory maintenance. *Behaviour*.

HERRE, W., and RÖHRS, M. 1971. Domestikation und Stammesgeschichte. In Heberer, *Die Evolution der Organismen*, Stuttgart: Fischer Verlag.

JACOBY, M. 1974. *Wargus, vargr—Verbrecher Wolf: eine sprach-und rechtsgeschichtliche Untersuchung*, Uppsala: Acta Universitatis Upsaliensis.

JORDAN, P. A.; SHELTON, P. C.; and ALLEN, D. L. 1967. Numbers, turnover and social structure of the Isle Royale wolf population. *American Zoologist* 7:233–252.

JOSLIN, P. W. B. 1967. Movements and home sites of timber wolves in Algonquin Park. *American Zoologist* 7:279–288.

KLATT, B. 1921. Studien zum Domestikationsproblem. Untersuchungen am Hirn. *Bibl. Genetica*, Vol. II, Leipzig.

KLEIMANN, D. 1967. Some aspects of social behavior in the Canidae. *American Zoologist* 7:365–372.

KOLENOSKY, G. B. 1972. Wolf predation on wintering deer in east-central Ontario. *Journal of Wildlife Management* 36(2):356–369.

LEYHAUSEN, P. 1956. Verhaltensstudien an Katzen. *Zeitschrift für Tierpsychologie*, Beiheft 2, Berlin: Paul Parey-Verlag.

363

LEYHAUSEN, P. 1965. Über die Funktion der relativen Stimmungshierarchie (dargestellt am Beispiel der phylogenetischen und ontogenetischen Entwicklung des Beutefang von Raubtieren). *Zeitschrift für Tierpsychologie* 22:412–494.

LOIZOS, C. 1966. *Play in mammals*. Symposium, Zoological Society of London, 18, pp. 1–9.

LORENZ, K. 1940. Durch Domestikation verursachte Störungen arteigenen Verhaltens. *Zeitschrift für angewandten Psychologie und Charakterkunde* 59:2–81.

LORENZ, K. 1943. Die angeborenen Formen möglicher Erfahrung. *Tierpsychologie* 5:235–409.

LORENZ, K. 1950. *So kam der Mensch auf den Hund*. Wien: Dr. G. Borotha-Schoeler Verlag.

LORENZ, K. 1963. *Das sogenannte Böse*. Wien: Dr. G. Borotha-Schoeler Verlag.

LORENZ, K. 1971. Der Sinn für Harmonie. *Kosmos* 67:187–191.

MAYNARD SMITH, J., and PRICE, G. R. 1973. The logic of animal conflict. *Nature* (London) 246:15–18.

MECH, L. D. 1966. *The wolves of Isle Royale*. Washington, D.C.: U.S. National Park Service, Fauna Series 7.

MECH, L. D. 1970. *The wolf—the ecology and behavior of an endangered species*. New York: Doubleday.

MECH, L. D. 1973. *Wolf numbers in the Superior National Forest of Minnesota*. St. Paul, Minnesota: USDA For. Serv. Res. Pap. NC97.

MECH, L. D. 1974. Current techniques in the study of elusive wilderness carnivores. *Proceedings of the Eleventh International Congress of Game Biologists* (Stockholm) pp. 315–322.

MECH, L. D. 1975. Disproportionate sex ratios in wolf cubs. *Journal of Wildlife Management* 39:737–740.

MECH, L. D. 1977a. Productivity, mortality, and population trends of wolves in northeastern Minnesota. *Journal of Mammalogy* 58(4):559–574.

MECH, L. D. 1977b. Wolf pack buffer zones as prey reservoirs. *Science* 198.

MECH, L. D. 1978. *The wolf: an introduction to its behavior, ecology and conservation*. Wolf Symposium, Edinburgh, April 1978.

MENDELSSOHN, H. 1973. A case of free pair-bond formation between female wolf and domestic dog. *Abstracts*, XIIIth International Ethological Conference, Washington, D.C.

MEYER-HOLZAPFEL, M. 1956. Das Spiel bei Saugetieren. *Handbuch der Zoologie* 8(2):1–26.

MICHURIN, L. N. 1970. The influence of wolves on population of wild reindeer in the north of Middle Siberia. *Transactions of the Ninth International Congress of Game Biologists* (Moscow).

MOWAT, F. 1965. *Never cry wolf.* New York: Dell.

MURIE, A. 1944. *The wolves of Mount McKinley.* Washington, D.C.: U.S. National Park Service, Fauna Series 5.

MYRBERGET, S. 1978. *The past and present of the wolf in Norway.* Wolf Symposium, Edinburgh, April 1978.

PETERS, R., and MECH, D. 1975. Scent-Marking in Wolves. *American Scientist* 63(6):628–637.

PETERSON, R. 1974. *Wolf ecology and prey relationship on Isle Royale.* Unpublished thesis, Purdue University, Michigan (to be published by U.S. National Park Service, Fauna Series, Washington, D.C.).

PIMLOTT, D. H. 1967. Wolf predation and ungulate populations. *American Zoologist* 7:267–278.

PIMLOTT, D. H.; SHANNON, J. A.; and KOLENOSKY, G. B. 1969. *The ecology of the timber wolf in Algonquin Park.* Ontario Department of Lands and Forests, Wildlife Research Report 87.

PULLIAINEN, E. 1965. Studies of the wolf in Finland. *Annal. Zool. Fennici* 2:215–259.

PULLIAINEN, E. 1978. *The present status of the wolf in Finland and adjacent areas.* Wolf Symposium, Edinburgh, April 1978.

RABB, G. B.; WOOLPY, J. H.; and GINSBURG, B. E. 1967. Social relationships in a group of captive wolves. *American Zoologist* 7:305–311.

RAUSCH, R. A. 1967. Some aspects of the population ecology of wolves. *American Zoologist* 7:253–265.

RUMANIAN ACADEMY, NATURAL MONUMENTS COMMITTEE 1975. Data of the situation of the wolf in Rumania. In *Wolves*, ed. D. H. Pimlott, pp. 44–52, IUCN Publication Services, Supplementary Paper No. 43, Morges, Switzerland.

RUTTER, R. J., and PIMLOTT, D. H. 1968. *The world of the wolf*, Philadelphia: J. B. Lippincott.

SANDOZ, M. 1961. Crazy Horse. *Bison Book.* University of Nebraska Press.

SCHAEFFER, R. 1955. *Deutsche Tierfabeln*, Berlin: Rütten & Loening.

SCHENKEL, R. 1947. Ausdrucksstudien an Wölfen. *Behaviour* 1:81–129.

SCHENKEL, R. 1967. Submission: its features and functions in the wolf and the dog. *American Zoologist* 7:319–329.

SCOTT, J. P., and FULLER, J. L. 1965. *Genetics and the social behavior of the dog.* Chicago: University of Chicago Press.

SIENNES, R. 1976. *The order of the wolf.* London: Hamilton.

SILVER, H., and SILVER, W. 1969. *Growth and behavior of the coyote-like canid of northern New England, with observations on canid hybrids.* Wildlife Monograph No. 17.

Slovak Institute for the Conservation of Natural Monuments. 1975. Status, distribution and problems of protecting wolves in Slovakia. In *Wolves*, ed. D. H. Pimlott, pp. 63–72, IUCN Publication Services, Supplementary Paper No. 43, Morges, Switzerland.

Stephenson, R., and Ahgook, B. 1975. The Eskimo hunter's view of wolf ecology and behavior. In *The wild canids*, ed. M. Fox. New York: Litton Publishers.

Suminski, P. 1975. The wolf in Poland. In *Wolves*, ed. D. H. Pimlott, pp. 44–52, IUCN Publication Services, Supplementary Paper No. 43, Morges, Switzerland.

Suminski, P. 1975. *The wolf in Poland*. Wolf Symposium, Edinburgh, April 1978.

Theberge, J. P., and Falls, J. B. 1967. Howling as a means of communication in timber wolves. *American Zoologist* 7:331–338.

Tinbergen, E. A., and Tinbergen, N. 1972. Early childhood autism—an ethological approach.

Trumler, E. 1971. *Mit dem Hund auf Du*. München: Piper Verlag.

Trumler, E. 1974. *Hunde ernst genommen*. München: Piper Verlag.

Van Ballenberghe, V., and Mech, L. D. 1975. Weight, growth and survival of timber wolf pups in Minnesota. *Journal of Mammalogy* 56(1):44–63.

Varjola, P. 1970. *Den stygga vargen.* Nordkalottmuseet, Oulu, Luleaa and Tromsö.

Weatherby, H. 1944. *Tales the totem tell*. Toronto: Macmillan.

Wickler, W., and Seibt, U. 1977. *Prinzip Eigennutz*. Hamburg: Hoffmann and Campe.

Wilson, E. O. 1975. *Sociobiology*. Cambridge, Mass.: Harvard University Press.

Wolfe, M. L., and Allen, D. L. 1973. Continued studies of the status, socialization and relationships of Isle Royale wolves. *Journal of Mammalogy* 54(3):611–633.

Woolpy, J. H., and Ginsburg, B. E. 1967. Wolf socialization: a study of temperament in a wild social species. *American Zoologist* 7:357–364.

Young, S. P. 1944. *The wolves of North America*, Part I. Washington, D.C.: American Wildlife Institute (new ed. 1964, New York: Dover Publications).

Zenner, F. E. 1963. *A history of domesticated animals*, New York: Harper & Row.

Zimen, E. 1972. *Wölfe und Königspudle—Vergleichende Verhaltungsbeobachtungen*, München: Piper Verlag.

Zimen, E. 1974. Der Wolf. *Die Pirsch* 8:395–403.

ZIMEN, E. 1975a. Social dynamics in the wolf pack. In *The Wild Canids*, ed. M. Fox. New York: Litton Publishers.

ZIMEN, E. 1975b. Vargen i Sverige. *Sverige Naturs Årsbok*, pp. 163–173.

ZIMEN, E. 1976a. Das Wolfsgeschehen im Bayerischen Wald. *National-park* 3(76):5–10.

ZIMEN, E. 1976b. On the regulation of pack size in wolves. *Zeitschrift für Tierpsychologie* 40:300–341.

ZIMEN, E. 1976c. Wolf reintroduction: Suitable areas and techniques. In *Reintroductions: Techniques and ethics*, ed. L. Boitani, pp. 151–161, Serie Atti e Studi No. 2. Rome: WWF.

ZIMEN, E., and BOITANI, L. 1975. Number and distribution of the wolf in Italy. *Zeitschrift für Säugetierkunde* 40:102–112.

ZIMEN, E., and BOITANI, L. 1978. Status of the wolf in Europe and possibilities of conservation and reintroduction. In *The Behavior and Ecology of Wolves*, ed. E. Klinghammer. New York: Garland Press.

SUGGESTIONS FOR FURTHER READING

Ecology of the wolf

Murie (1944)
Mech (1966, 1970, and 1977a)
Peterson (1974 or 1978)

Also in more popular form

Crisler (1958)
Mowat (1965)

Behavior of the wolf

Schenkel (1947)
Fox (1971)
Zimen (1972 and 1976)

Distribution and protection of the wolf

Young and Goldmann (1944)
Mech (1970)
Pimlott (ed.) (1975)

367

So-called wolf symposia take place at irregular intervals.

In 1966 at the University of Maryland the papers were chiefly on behavior and ecology of the wolf (published in the *American Zoologist*, vol. 7, no. 2, 1967).

In 1973 in Stockholm the papers were chiefly on the distribution and protection of the wolf in Europe (published in book form by D. H. Pimlott, ed., *Wolves*, IUCN Publication Services, Supplementary Paper No. 43, Morges, Switzerland).

In 1975 at Wilmington, North Carolina, the papers were chiefly on the distribution, protection, and the possibilities of reintroducing the wolf (published in book form by E. Klinghammer, ed., *The Behavior and Ecology of Wolves*, New York: Garland Press, 1978).

In 1978 at Edinburgh the papers were chiefly on the ecology, behavior, distribution, and protection of the wolf (to be published 1979, ed. T. Boyle and R. Soutar, University of Edinburgh, Centre of Human Ecology).

Index

Abruzzi, 22, 153–54, 191, 193, 213, 216, 226, 234, 245–46, 250–91, 294, 298, 310, 328–30
Acoustical communication, 26, 36, 68–76
Actinomycosis, 222
Adolescents (juveniles), 203–4. *See also* Rank
Africa, 214, 219, 333
Age, 54, 73, 153, 161–64, 191, 193. *See also* Ecology; Rank; Social behavior
Aggression, 32, 42ff., 51–52, 54–60ff., 147–51, 177–84, 192–93, 200ff., 236, 237, 240, 242–43ff. *See also* Hunting and killing; Play; Rank; Sex; Social behavior; specific wolves
Agonistic behavior, 177–84. *See also* Aggression
Alaska, 189–91, 193, 196, 225–26, 235, 316, 318, 341. *See also* Mount McKinley
Alek (male cub), 19, 21, 22
Alexander, 80, 81, 88–89, 90, 98ff., 107, 113, 115, 118ff., 136, 142, 145, 164, 166ff., 179, 183–84, 192, 242
Algonquin Park, 71, 72, 190, 212–13, 221, 224
Allen, D., 211
Alpha position, 50, 64, 197–202. *See also* Pack; Rank; Sex
Alps, 251, 302, 315, 316, 320
Alsatians, 284, 306–7, 316
America. *See* North America
Anal glands, 48
Andra, 19, 79, 90ff., 96, 98
Anfa, 7–17, 18, 20, 26, 29, 35, 41ff., 50, 51, 62, 71, 74, 78–79, 86ff., 98, 101–2, 112, 142, 170, 171, 328
Anger, 54. *See also* Aggression
Annoyance, 178
Anogenital region, 43, 48, 76, 132, 195
Anselm, 19, 79–80
Apennines, 251, 252. *See also* Abruzzi
"Appetence behavior," 279

Arabian peninsula, 319
Arctic, 213, 216
Arctic Ocean, 212
Asia, 214, 319
Attack, 66. *See also* Aggression; Rank
Australia, 318
Autumn, 151, 152, 164, 172, 194, 195, 240. *See also* specific places

Back (lying, rolling on), 81, 177. *See also* Submission; Wallowing
Barking, 26, 33, 69
Barrasso, Paolo, 268, 283
Basenjies, 81–82
Bavaria, 1–3, 240–42, 335. *See also* Bavarian Forest
Bavarian Forest (National Park), 1ff., 30, 46, 68, 71–72, 75, 106–25, 163–64, 166ff., 181–84ff., 192ff., 200–1, 217, 251, 264, 286, 287, 303, 315, 328, 329, 333, 335, 337–38
Beagles, 82
Bears, 214, 254, 265, 277, 279, 312, 315, 328, 336
Belly, licking, 76
Bertram, B., 201–2
Birds, 286
Birth rate, 73, 190, 238, 246ff.
Bison, 227, 293
Biting, 45, 179, 180, 186 (*see also* Aggression; Play; Rank); inhibition, 60–64, 88, 186–87; and rabies, 330–31
Bjärvall, Anders, 315
Blind, Per, 312–13
Body contact (tactile communication), 76–77, 87, 166–67, 176–77. *See also* Rank; Sex; specific parts of body
Boitani, Luigi, 211, 213, 250ff., 260, 262ff., 276, 280ff., 286ff., 328
Bonding, 50, 158–72, 238–39, 240
Bounties, 315, 317, 318, 321, 322, 334

369

Brains, 9
Brno, 118, 123, 132, 137, 140, 143, 144
Buffalo wolves, 316–17, 318

Canada, 38–40, 219–20, 233, 293, 316, 318. *See also* specific places
Cape hunting dogs, 219
Capercaillie, 310, 333
Caribou, 216, 218–19, 233, 234, 242, 244, 248
Carpathians, 2, 214, 303, 327, 335
Cats, 52, 217, 275, 279, 331
Cattle (cows), 28–29, 110, 278, 279, 309, 312, 318
Central Europe, 315–16, 320, 335
Chamois, 226, 254, 291
"Chase away," 66, 67, 180, 181
Children, 4, 42–43, 112, 300, 303, 306–7, 326–27, 328, 338; autistic, 24
Chows, 32
Christianity, 296–98
Climbing, 169–70
Coat contact, 43, 76, 87, 132, 176
Cocker spaniels, 82
Communication, 35–77. *See also* Body contact.
Corpses, eating, 300, 309, 328, 330
Coyotes, 9, 67, 214, 293–94, 341
Criminals, 300
Cub mortality, 7, .164, 194–95, 244, 248. *See also* Death rate
Cubs, 7–8ff., 18–20ff., 30ff., 42ff., 62ff., 68ff., 76, 78–90, 113–18ff., 127, 134–41ff., 147, 151ff., 162–63ff., 172, 177ff., 186–87ff., 201–2, 204, 236, 238, 240ff., 294. *See also* Birth rate; Cub mortality; specific behavior
Cuckoos, 198–99
Czechoslovakia, 1–2, 3, 117, 214, 322, 335, 337

Dachshunds, 181
Dall's sheep, 221–22
Darwin, Charles, 51–52, 306
Dawkins, R., 146, 202, 228
Death rate, 190, 235, 246ff. *See also* Cub mortality; Pack
Deception, 197–98
Deer, 86–87, 112, 209, 212, 214, 220, 224, 226, 227, 230, 243, 244, 248, 254, 261, 262, 285ff., 289, 291, 295, 315, 336; white-tailed, 218, 220, 221, 226, 229, 232, 234
Denmark, 311
Dens, 7–8, 16, 134–36
Dingoes, 318
Diphtheria, 300
Distance, 30–31, 87–88, 159–61. *See also* Spatial organization
Distribution, 319–22. *See also* Ecology
Dogs (and puppies), 8–11, 18–34, 35, 42–43, 48, 81–82, 142, 181–83, 245, 255–56, 258, 277, 279, 296, 298, 308, 314, 328, 338 (*see also* Puwos; specific breeds); caught in traps, 266ff.; expressive behavior, 51–52, 54; fable of hungry dog, 302; hybridization in Abruzzi, 283–84; and rabies, 331
Domestication (domestic animals), 9–10, 84–85, 303; game 230–31
Drugs, 21, 80

Ears, position of, 54, 55, 60, 65
Ecology, 207–31, 232–49, 323–26. *See also* Population
Eisenmann, Herr, 286
Elk, 229, 311, 313–14, 315
Energy balance, 220–21
Environment, 169–70. *See also* Ecology
Eskimos, 228–29, 293, 294
Europe, 310–19ff., 330ff.
Evolution, 146, 155ff., 306
Expressive behavior, 43, 51–68. *See also* Social behavior; specific behavior
Expulsion, 122–23, 161. *See also* Ecology; Lone wolves; Pack; Population; Rank
Eyes (*see also* Optical sense): and expressive behavior, 60, 66, 67

Falls, J.B., 71, 72
Fascism, 307
Fear, 54–60. *See also* Biting, inhibition; History; Stories; Strangers
Feces (defecation), 12–13, 48, 49, 76, 112, 113, 268; wallowing in, 51
Fighting. *See* Aggression; Rank
Finland, 216, 279, 312, 314, 322, 326–27, 335
Finsterau, 108, 114, 115, 118–21, 123ff., 131ff., 139ff., 143ff., 154, 166, 192ff., 206
Flight, 18ff., 33, 47, 69, 70
Flow, 29–30, 46, 143, 164, 192, 193
Food and feeding (eating), 11–12, 19ff., 64, 70, 79, 80, 82ff., 112, 127, 137, 138, 186, 193, 200, 213–15, 238–43ff., 294 (*see also* Cubs; Ecology; Hunting and killing; specific places); bad-smelling, 36, 50, 51; going without, 216–17; regurgitating, 20, 64, 70
Fox, Mike, 85
Foxes, 67, 68, 214, 217, 261, 266–67, 268, 275, 281, 300, 328, 331
France, 316
Friendliness (friendship), 41–43, 52, 64–65, 75, 156–57, 200ff. *See also* Bonding; Rank; Sex; Social behavior
Fuller, J.L., 22, 81ff.

Genitals. *See* Anogenital region; Sex
German shepherds. *See* Alsatians

370

371

North American (Americans), 4, 73–74, 207–13ff., 216–19, 226ff., 233ff., 281, 284, 327, 330ff. *See also* Indians; specific places
Norway, 312, 314, 322
Nose and nostrils, 60, 69

Oil, 212
Old Testament, 295
Olfactory signals, 36, 47–51
Olomouc, 118, 123, 124, 132, 133, 137ff., 143ff., 154, 165–66, 201, 206
Ontario, 220. *See also* Algonquin Park
Optical sense (sight), 35–36, 51–68
Osio, Arturo, 260
Otters, 333
Oswald, 10, 81, 115, 121–22, 124, 125, 137, 139, 142, 154, 192

Pack (pack size), 38–41, 141–45 151–54, 158–74, 170–72, 183–84, 190–91, 195, 200, 232–49. *See also* Birth rate; Death rate; Ecology; Rank; Social behavior; Spatial organization; specific places, wolves
Passive submission, 43. *See also* Submission
Paws, 37
Peters, Roger, 49, 50
Peterson, Rolf, 173, 190, 211, 212
Pheasants, 28
Pigs, 245, 258. *See also* Swine, wild
Pimlott, Doug, 71, 72, 191, 194, 212, 220, 221, 260–61
Play, 45, 62, 65–68, 70, 91, 92, 102, 118, 119, 137, 167–68, 183, 184–87, 240
Pointers, 28. *See also* Flow
Poison, 261, 280ff., 284, 286, 288, 291, 308, 311, 317, 318
Poland, 322, 335
Poodles, 8ff., 18, 21, 24–25ff., 82, 84, 92, 93, 98, 118. *See also* Puwos
Population, 232–49. *See also* Distribution; Ecology; Spatial organization
Protection of wolves, 331–36
Pruscha, Helmuth, 176
Psenner, 107, 108, 115, 119, 121–22, 124, 125, 132, 133, 136, 139, 142, 145
Pulliainen, Erki, 279, 322
Puma, 214
Puwos, 8ff., 18, 21ff., 33, 98, 194

Rabbits, 30, 214, 217, 242, 243, 318
Rabies, 330–31
Rachel, 108, 114, 119, 120, 122, 123, 134, 136, 139, 140, 142
Rank, 54ff., 66, 71, 78–105, 106–30, 146–57, 165–67. *See also* Aggression; Pack; Sex; specific behavior, wolves
Rasa, Anne, 184–85
Regurgitation, 20, 64, 70

Reindeer, 219–20, 225, 227, 303, 312, 314–15, 319, 322
Retrievers, 28
Rickling, 11–17, 18–24ff., 41–43ff., 48, 71, 74, 75, 78–98, 118, 162, 163, 166, 170–72, 181, 217
Rodents, 213, 214
Roe, 28ff., 87, 112, 212, 214, 217, 226ff., 234, 243, 254, 261, 262, 285ff., 289, 291, 295, 315, 336
Rome, 4, 252, 260, 266, 269, 270, 295–96; University of, 288
Romulus and Remus, 4, 295–96
Rumania, 320, 322
Russia (Sov. Union), 314, 320, 321–22, 327

Sachs, Hans, 302
Scandinavia, 335. *See also* specific countries
Scent marking, 48–50. *See also* Urine
Schenkel, Rudolf, 43
Schissler, Petrus Petri, 327
Schönbrunn, 108, 114, 117ff., 122, 123, 134, 140–41, 142, 164
Scotland, 254, 308
Scott, J.P., 22, 81ff.
Seibt, U., 146, 202
"Selfish" gene, 155–57, 210
Selfishness, 85
Separation, 47–48, 71–72, 159, 170–72, 172–73. *See also* Expulsion
Sex (heat; mating; sexes; sexuality), 31ff., 50, 55, 68, 69, 75ff., 90–104, 132–45, 147ff., 165, 174, 177, 178, 187–94, 195–96, 197–202, 204–6, 238. *See also* Cubs; Rank; Social behavior; specific places, wolves
Sheep, 217, 218, 221–22, 226, 234, 245, 254, 258–59, 275–80, 282, 289, 295, 309, 317, 318
Sheepdogs, 275ff.
Shelties, 81–82
Siberia, 319
Sight. *See* Optical sense
Skins, 321
Sledge, use of, 88–90
Sleeping, 30, 32, 162
Smell. *See* Olfactory signals
Smith, Maynard, 196
Snarling, 45, 68, 69, 100, 103, 179
Sniffing, 43. *See also* Olfactory signals; specific parts of body
Social behavior (socialization), 16, 18ff., 30–31, 175–206, 236–38ff. *See also* "Language"; Pack; Rank
Sound. *See* Acoustical communication
Spatial organization, 49–50, 232–35, 282–83. *See also* Distance; Ecology
Squealing, 45ff., 62, 68, 70, 79, 119, 137
Steinhöwel, Heinrich, 302
Stories, 326–30. *See also* History
Strangers, 14–15, 41–43, 48, 75, 181–83, 200, 238. *See also* Friendliness; Rank